The Theory and Creation of Music

A Comprehensive Guide to Composing Your Own Music

Author
Ryan Taylor

Publisher
Project Ado

Year of Publication
2018

© 2018 Project Ado, LLC

All rights reserved. No portion of this book or the associated audio tracks may be reproduced in any form without permission from the publisher, except as permitted by U.S. copyright law.

Request permissions at: contact@projectado.com

www.projectado.com

ISBN: 978-1-7324819-1-6

A Primer in Four Questions and Answers

What is this book about?

The aim of this book is to enable people to write their own high quality music. With this end goal in mind, the following text takes the reader on a journey through a deep understanding and experience of sound. A variety of learning approaches are employed and integrated in a way that is rare, if not unique, in the world of music education. These integrated approaches represent a new method of musical learning and, from a broader perspective, reveal a new method of learning anything.

What is this new method of learning?

At its most essential level, the method presented in this book is a synthesis of the intellectual with the creative. It incorporates and balances three synergistic aspects of learning – learning of concepts, learning by example, and learning through action. I'll argue that all of these are profoundly necessary yet rarely included in one interconnected system of musical learning as they are here. During the writing this book, this method also gave rise to a new system of presenting information. The main content of this book is categorized into colored boxes that describe what aspect of learning the box is focused on. These boxes are then connected with each other in such a way that they can be read in a variety of sequential orders. This allows for a more personalized and engaging journey through the study of music. All of this is presented in more detail in the *Introduction* on page 9.

What topics does this book address?

Within the primary subject of creating high quality, original music, many related topics are addressed. The topics of composition, improvisation, music theory, and the philosophy of how musical expression comes to be are all central to the study we are embarking on here. This book will also briefly touch upon the subjects of arranging, music production, acoustics, and music history. However, please note that this book should not be taken as a comprehensive guide on these secondary subjects.

Who is this book for?

This book is for anyone interested in creating original music through a deep understanding of his or her craft. No prior experience or knowledge is required to benefit from this book. The instruction starts from the beginning and goes into intermediate and advanced topics.

The information in this book is generally applicable to all instruments and will be useful regardless of what instrument you play or would like to learn. The information in this book is also generally applicable to all styles of music. A wide variety of styles, from classical to blues to electronic, have been included in the musical examples and often multiple sets of terminology are presented that correspond to different traditions. The focus of this text is on the fundamental ideas, experiences, and processes that are a part of all of these styles of sonic art.

What makes music sound happy? What makes it sound sad? Tense? Relaxed? Beautiful? Powerful? Scary? Nostalgic? We will seek to answer the fundamental question: What makes music sound the way it sounds? The more deeply we can answer this question, on both logical and intuitive levels, the more aptly we will be able to create the music we want to create.

-An excerpt from Chapter Two

We have artists with no scientific knowledge and scientists with no artistic knowledge and both with no spiritual sense of gravity at all, and the result is not just bad, it is ghastly.

-Robert M. Pirsig, *Zen and the Art of Motorcycle Maintenance*

Contents

- Condensed -

A Primer in Four Questions and Answers • 2
Introduction • 9

Part One – Foundations

Group One – A Theoretical Model of the Musical Experience
    Chapter One – Fundamental Aspects of Sound • 27
    Chapter Two – Fundamental Aspects of Musical Expression • 45

Group Two – An Introduction to the Musical System
    Chapter Three – The Basics of Pitch • 66
    Chapter Four – The Basics of Rhythm and Dynamics • 86

Part Two – Musical Relationships

Group Three – Intervals and Interval Structures
    Chapter Five – Intervals • 119
    Chapter Six – The Interval Structure of Chords • 137
    Chapter Seven – The Interval Structure of Scales • 174

Group Four – The Expression of Proportional Relationships
    Chapter Eight – Relationships in Time • 211
    Chapter Nine – Relationships in Pitch • 240

Part Three – Creation and Exploration

Group Five – Putting It All Together
    Chapter Ten – Musical Styles • 288
    Chapter Eleven – Arranging and Production • 310
    Chapter Twelve – Development and Structure • 334

Group Six – Advanced Harmony
    Chapter Thirteen – Additional Chord and Scale Types • 388
    Chapter Fourteen – Chromaticism • 412

Conclusion • 428

Contents
- Expanded -

A Primer in Four Questions and Answers • 2

Introduction
A New Approach to Musical Learning • 9
Embracing the Intellectual and the Creative Together • 10
Three Aspects of Learning • 10
How to Use This Book • 11
The Piano • 16
Where to Find Audio for the Examples • 17
Music Theory Doesn't Always Make Sense • 17
The Courage to Learn • 18
Quality Listening • 19
Being Your Own Teacher • 19
Pathways Through the Book • 21

Part One – Foundations
Group One – A Theoretical Model of the Musical Experience

Chapter One – Fundamental Aspects of Sound • 27
What Is Music? • 27
What Is Sound? • 28
Pitch and Frequency • 30
Loudness and Amplitude • 33
Timbre and Harmonic Composition • 34
Location • 44

Chapter Two – Fundamental Aspects of Musical Expression • 45
What Is Meaning? • 46
Seven Basic Spectra of Musical Expression • 47
The Dance of Musical Elements • 50
Three Tools of Musical Analysis • 52
Musical Centers and Gravity • 54
Four Roles in the Ensemble • 56
Five Musical Activities • 58
Three Methods of Writing Music • 60

Group Two – An Introduction to the Musical System
Chapter Three – The Basics of Pitch • 66
Pitch and Note Names • 66
A Simple Technique for Finding Notes • 69
Octaves • 70
Notation Basics • 74
Chords and Chord Voicings • 78
Scales • 82
A Simple Technique for Finding Chords • 84

Chapter Four – The Basics of Rhythm and Dynamics • 86
Beat and Tempo • 86
Dynamics • 88
Measures • 89
Note Values and Time Signatures • 90
Rests • 94
Rhythmic Positions • 97
Dots and Ties • 99
Time Signatures Expanded • 100
Pick Ups • 107
Crescendo and Diminuendo • 108
Accelerando and Ritardando • 109
Repeats and Double Bar Lines • 110

Part Two – Musical Relationships
Group Three – Intervals and Interval Structures
Chapter Five – Intervals • 119
What Are Intervals? • 119
Half Steps and Whole Steps • 119
The Numeric-Quality Interval Naming System • 122
Compound Intervals • 128
Interval Inversions • 129
The Sonance of Intervals • 129

Chapter Six – The Interval Structure of Chords • 137
Basic Chord Types • 137
Voicing Considerations • 148
Chord Progressions • 151
Voice Leading • 154
Related Series Analysis • 157

Chapter Seven – The Interval Structure of Scales • 174
- Building Scales • 174
- Key Signatures, Accidentals, and the Circle of Fifths • 178
- Scale Degrees • 184
- Solfege Syllables • 187
- Transposing • 191
- Musical Gravity in Chord Progressions • 195
- Pentatonic Scales • 199
- Improvising With Pentatonic Scales • 202

Group Four – The Expression of Proportional Relationships

Chapter Eight – Relationships in Time • 211
- Percussion Notation • 211
- Articulations • 214
- Strong and Weak Rhythmic Positions • 217
- Grooves and Drumbeats • 225
- Temporal Gravity • 229
- Tuplets and Polyrhythms • 231
- Swing Rhythms • 234
- An Analysis of Rhythmic Expression • 235

Chapter Nine – Relationships in Pitch • 240
- Two Levels of Relationships • 240
- The Character of the Scale Degrees • 241
- Melodic Analysis • 245
- Harmonic Positions and Relationships • 251
- Harmonic and Melodic Minor Scales • 256
- Cadences • 260
- Progression by Fifths • 262
- Modes • 263
- Analysis of Faure's "Pavane" • 269
- Lyrics • 276
- Writing Themes • 278

Part Three – Creation and Exploration

Group Five – Putting It All Together

Chapter Ten – Musical Styles • 288
- Introduction to Musical Styles • 288
- Classical • 291
- The Birth of Blues and Gospel • 294
- Jazz • 297
- Country • 300
- Blues, R&B, and Rock • 301
- Later R&B Styles and Jamaican Music • 305
- Electronic Music (EDM) • 306

Chapter Eleven – Arranging and Production • 310
- Principles of Arranging and Production • 310
- Applications for Each Role in the Ensemble • 312
- Harmonized Melodies • 314
- Counterpoint • 317
- Transposing Instruments • 319
- Creating and Capturing Sounds • 321
- Mixing and Mastering • 326

Chapter Twelve – Development and Structure • 334
- Structural Elements of Notation • 334
- Thematic Development • 339
- Structural Development • 344
- Possibilities in Form • 346
- Analysis of Beethoven's Fifth Symphony • 350
- Analysis of Pachelbel's Canon • 369
- Creating a Complete Composition • 380

Group Six – Advanced Harmony

Chapter Thirteen – Additional Chord and Scale Types • 388
- Ninth, Eleventh, and Thirteenth Chords • 388
- Polychords • 392
- Constant Interval Voicings • 393
- More Chord Types • 395
- More Scale Types • 405
- Chord and Scale Structure Reference Charts • 409

Chapter Fourteen – Chromaticism • 412
- Modulation • 412
- Chromatic Harmony Techniques • 415
- Melodic Chromaticism • 418
- Music Without a Scale • 419

Conclusion
- Acknowledgments • 428
- Bibliography • 431
- Track List • 433
- Glossadex • 437
- About the Author • 471

Introduction

- A New Approach to Musical Learning -

Music is conventionally taught by learning pieces of music written by others. Generally, students learn these pieces by reading sheet music. In addition, but unfortunately often as an afterthought, the subject of music theory will be introduced at some point. This may start by learning about the meaning of various symbols in the sheet music like "time signatures" or "key signatures." But it quickly progresses to studying a large variety of vocabulary terms – "whole steps," "half steps," "major triads," "minor triads," "scales," "modes," "chromaticism," "sequences" and so on. The list goes on and on. In the complexity, many students get lost.

All the while, one might ask, "What is the point of all of this?" Perhaps one might receive the answer that music theory helps us to perform with higher proficiency, to write our own music, to improvise, or to arrange music for ensembles of instruments. But these artistic pursuits are addressed weakly, if at all, in the conventional approach to teaching music theory. Furthermore, the idea of creating original music, perhaps the clearest application of music theory, is rarely approached until a student has studied performance, reading music, and various amounts of theory for many years.

The result is that many students are presented with music theory as a complicated, difficult subject that seems to have no real purpose or application. A student's inspiration to learn about music in the first place seems quite distant in a haze of technical terminology, redundant naming systems, and seemingly unnecessary complexity. Upon further examination, we find that much of this complexity exists only as the summation of centuries of traditions built up one after another, creating a system that is often inefficient and confusing for musicians in the modern era.

Encountering these stumbling blocks, students often become uninterested and distance themselves from the entire subject of music theory. Meanwhile, musical endeavors, such as performance, composition, improvisation, and arranging, suffer from a lack of understanding of what music fundamentally is and how it operates.

The issue illustrated here is one of learning in the abstract without applying the learned knowledge to an activity and, in reverse, practicing an activity without learning the abstractions that illuminate the working principles behind the activity. The solution is to pursue both the abstract and its application together and more profoundly unite the two into a single, unified understanding that enables the heightened practice of musical creation. The conveyance of this unified understanding is the purpose of this book.

- Embracing the Intellectual and the Creative Together -

As the title of this book suggests, we are dealing with essentially two facets of the musical experience – the theoretical and the creative. On the one hand, we will be understanding music with the intellect and, on the other hand, approaching music with feeling, intuition, and active creativity.

I think of the arts as those endeavors that require not just the intellect, but also felt or intuitive capacities. Musicians generally recognize that this truth applies to music on some level. However, many make the mistake of thinking that music can concern itself with only the felt and intuitive, while disregarding the intellect entirely. The truth of the matter is that the intellect cannot express nor grasp all of the beauty and profundity of music, but *this does not mean we can leave it behind altogether*. The more we can understand about the inner workings of sound, expression, and emotion, the more empowered we are to become the musical artists we want to be. I believe the most effective approach is to attempt to grasp as much of that overwhelming beauty and profundity as our intellects can handle.

At the same time, music theory tends to concern itself only with intellectualizations and not at all with anything felt, intuitive, or applicative. In this book, we will seek to embrace both the intellectual and creative sides of music with depth, fullness, and gusto. The idea here is not merely to moderate the intellectual and creative sides so that they stay in balance but to recognize the beauty and utility in both and, thus, strive to maximize our musical experience in a broader and fuller spectrum from intensely scientific to wondrously artistic.

- Three Aspects of Learning -

In learning about any subject, one will find three primary types of learning will occur. The first is the *concept learning process*. This type of learning deals with ideas, systems, labels, naming, abstractions, patterns, and principles. The second type of learning is learning by example. I refer to this kind of learning as the *expression learning process* because it deals with the expression of an idea in the physical world. This type of learning has to do with observation, listening, and imitation. The third type of learning is the *action learning process*. This is the process of learning through doing. This type of learning has to do with experimentation, creativity, and evaluation – learning from one's successes and failures.

Let's take the example of learning to swim competitively. On the conceptual level, one could study the mechanics of the optimal swimming stroke. Perhaps in this type of learning, students would learn to think of different parts of the stroke and the reasons that each part must be crafted just so to produce the best result. On the level of expression learning, one could study examples of the best swimmers. Perhaps students would watch videos of world-class swimmers or have coaches demonstrate various components of ideal swimming form in person. Students might also study how the best swimmers train – what they eat, what schedule they follow, how they think, what their attitude is, and so on. On the level of action learning, students practice the swimming form for themselves. This level of learning might involve various practice techniques, evaluating your own performance, and, more often than not, lots and lots of rote practice with dedication to implementing all of one's understanding about ideal swimming form.

Music theory, as it is often taught and understood, is something like learning to swim by reading about the mechanics of ideal swimming form and doing nothing else. In fact, music theory has gone so far in this direction that the connection to an actual activity or purpose has been all but forgotten. In truth, music theory serves as a conceptual guide to the creative musical pursuits of writing, crafting, and playing original music. This book is first and foremost a text on these creative musical pursuits. Music theory is used here as a part of a greater whole and, as such, is given much greater meaning. When music theory is studied in conjunction with its practical applications, not only do we develop the ability to shape our creativity intelligently, but the purely intellectual value of music theory is deepened as well. Just imagine how much would be lost from the study of the ideal swimming stroke if we had forgotten that the purpose behind our study was to improve our ability to swim! What would be left? Whatever is in your imagination answering that question is essentially the state that music theory is in today.

While the theorists are left in this predicament, the artists interested in creating original music are often left with the opposite problem. The study of composition, improvisation, and other creative musical endeavors lacks a solid intellectual framework to inform the practice of musical creation and infuse it with meaning. Once again, we can refer to our swimming analogy. How well do you imagine a person could learn to swim if he or she could not study any instruction on swimming form or technique?

This book presents a remedy to this situation. By using a balance of concept, expression, and action learning, this book illustrates a deeper understanding and practice of music. Each learning process plays an important role and provides a unique contribution to one's study. And as each aspect is cultivated, synergy between all three emerges.

This approach to learning can be applied to any subject. Although this book is of great value in terms of musical development, it is also a guide, by example, of how to learn anything effectively. In any pursuit, you can now bring awareness to the balance between the three aspects of learning. You may start to ask yourself the following questions:

1. Am I looking at the underlying patterns and ideas in this subject?
2. Am I studying examples of the best quality in this subject?
3. Am I learning from my own active experience in this subject?

Ensuring that you can answer yes to each of these questions will enhance your ability to learn and master any endeavor.

- How to Use This Book -

Described above is a new method of learning. And a different kind of learning requires a different kind of teacher. This book is more than ideas written on a page. It is a teacher, brought to life by the unique qualities of its students. The learning process is organic, ever changing, and ongoing. It is unique for every student and requires the engagement of the student to shape and create the optimal path forward. The format of this book – what I call *descriptive non-linear format* – reflects these natural traits inherent to the learning process.

The main content of this book is organized in boxes that contain anywhere from one to several paragraphs. I use the term "non-linear" in the name of this format because the boxes can be read and repeatedly referenced in a variety of sequential orders. The information is organized in such a way that you can chart a unique, personally directed path through the book. This level of freedom allows you to focus on learning what you are really interested in and passionate about. Through this process, you become actively involved in the learning process, not just as a student, but also as your own teacher, creating your own curriculum as you go.

To create a successful non-linear presentation, it is necessary for the learner to be informed about where different information exists in the book so that he or she can make good decisions about what to learn and in what order to take on different subjects. To fulfill this need, I have included a wealth of information embedded into each box in the form of titles, colored borders, and connections to other boxes. This is the *descriptive* aspect of this format.

Let's examine the colored boarders first. The color coding system used throughout this book reveals what aspects of learning different sections of content are focused on. Concept learning is associated with the colors blue and purple, expression learning is associated with green, and action learning with red. Each box has a colored outline that reveals what aspect of learning is present in the given box. To convey that multiple aspects of learning are present in a box, the colors blue, green, and red are mixed together in representative proportions to form new colors. Examine the diagram below to see what colors are created through the combinations of different aspects of learning.

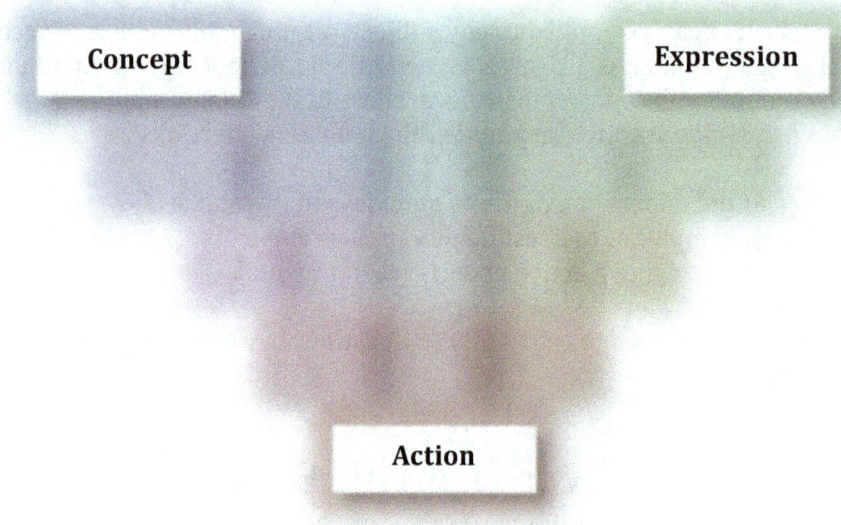

Boxes with colors closer to the concept end of the spectrum will present ideas about how music works, what makes it tick, and what underlying patterns we can utilize in our creative endeavors. Information toward the concept end of the spectrum can either be deeply philosophical or of a more utilitarian nature. In addition to fundamental principles of sound and emotion, concept boxes also present information about the workings of our modern music theory system. This information includes the naming systems, vocabulary, and notation used by the music community.

Boxes with colors closer to the expression end of the spectrum discuss the musical examples presented in the book as well as the musical or emotional expressions that are created in sound when the concepts of the given topic are applied. There are over one hundred fifty audio example tracks included with this book to aid you in your learning process. Expression boxes will call your attention to various elements in these examples and their connection to the rest of the text, acting like a listening and observational guide through the material. The expression learning thread of the book will reveal the connections between the abstract concepts of the book and the lived experience of listening to music.

The expression learning aspect of the book also goes into some deeper analyses of examples to help demonstrate how various concepts operate in real music and what they sound like. In particular, I have included three detailed analyses of well-known classical pieces: Faure's "Pavane," Beethoven's Fifth Symphony, and Pachelbel's Canon in D. Through our study of these great works, we will glean some insight into masterful examples of musical creativity.

Moving forward, we come to our last aspect of learning, which deals with action and development through the actual practice of the musical craft. Boxes with colors closer to the action end of the spectrum give you the opportunity to integrate the knowledge you are learning into your creative journey. At times, action boxes present techniques for practicing various skills and direct you on how to progressively rise to higher and higher levels of musical aptitude. Other action boxes guide you through the process of making your own original music. Each topic throughout the book is relevant to some step or aspect in the musical creation process. The action-oriented thread of this book seeks to empower your ability to apply the understanding you are developing to the creative pursuits of composition, performance, improvisation, arranging, and production (all of which we will define and discuss in more detail later on).

In addition to the aspects of learning, the colored borders surrounding each box also reveal the level, from most basic to most advanced, of the given box. More basic information is represented by bolder colors (see the example box to the left); and more advanced information is represented with lighter colors (see the example box to the right).

Basic Information	**Advanced Information**
This is an example of a more basic, expression learning box.	This is an example of a more advanced, expression learning box.

More advanced boxes are defined as boxes that require more knowledge and integrated understanding of basic information as a prerequisite. In contrast, the most basic boxes are intended to be understandable with no prior knowledge.

Sometimes, if a big break occurs in the level of the material being discussed, I'll use the following symbol to give you some extra warning that advanced material is coming up:

Advanced

Anecdotal information is represented with an outline, as shown in the example box below. Anecdotes deviate from the primary topic being presented in that section and are also generally not built upon in other sections of the book.

Anecdote Box

This is an example of an anecdote box.

Principles and big picture ideas that I want to highlight are presented in special *principle boxes*, like the example below.

Principle Box

Beauty is in the eye of the beholder.

Many boxes are connected to other boxes through a notes section that follows the main content of the box. This notes section contains the titles of related boxes and the page on which each box can be found. Connections are often used to link the reader to later sections of the text that expound upon an idea presented in the given box or early sections that explain more basic, prerequisite material that is built upon in the given box.

The titles in the notes section are colored to reflect the type and level of information present in the related box. This allows the reader to evaluate the basic description of a given box before deciding to locate and read the box in the book. In the example below, one connection has been made to a more basic box and a second connection has been made to a more advanced box. By their red color, we can infer that both focus on the action-oriented learning process.

General Connections

The main content of this box would appear here.

- *Title of Box Concerning Related Basic Information, Page 600*
- *Title of Box Concerning Related Advanced Information, Page 601*

To connect a specific word or sentence to another box, superscript numbers are used throughout the main content of the box with corresponding numbers in the notes section. In the example box below, two connections are made to the imaginary topics "A" and "B."

Connections to Specific Words or Sentences

In this box, you will need to be familiar with topic A[1] and topic B.[2]

1. *Title of Box About Topic A, Page 602*
2. *Title of Box About Topic B, Page 603*

If a connection relates to a box as a whole instead of a specific word or sentence, the symbol of four small diamonds shown in the "General Connections" box is used in place of a number.

Sometimes connections will be made to entire sections or chapters. In this case, the connections will be colored black, as sections and chapters generally involve a variety of different aspects of learning. These connections will still be shaded from dark to light to reflect the corresponding level of the section or chapter from basic to advanced.

Connections to Sections or Chapters

This box is related to the following sections.

❖ *Basic Section, Page 604*
❖ *Advanced Section, Page 605*

I will also occasionally provide additional information about a certain connection in regular, non-italicized, non-colored text.

Additional Information

The primary content of this box would appear here.

❖ Here are some thoughts about this connection. See *Section A, Page 606*

Yellow boxes are used to highlight a specific part of a diagram or selection of music notation.

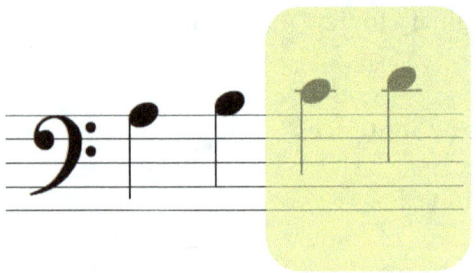

Italics are used to highlight new vocabulary terms and other important information.

Vocabulary Terms

A *system* is a group of interrelated, usually interacting or interdependent, parts.

All the vocabulary terms in the book are compiled into what I call a "glossadex" – a combination of a glossary and an index – at the end of the book (see page 437). The glossadex includes a definition for each term, the page number where the term is first presented in the book, and page numbers for any other relevant information, if needed.

In addition to the boxes, which contain the primary instructional content of the book, you will also find information outside of the boxes that provides descriptions and overviews of the surrounding material. I refer to this thread of the book as the *guide information*, as it serves to guide the learner through the experience. The guide information generally talks *about* the main content of the book rather than presenting new ideas and is sometimes used for introductions and conclusions to sections and chapters. You will also find visual summaries of each of the six groups of chapters. These are good for reviewing the information you have learned and can also be used as a way to find out what will be presented in each group ahead of time. And finally, the *Table of Contents* on page 4 and the introductory section entitled *Pathways Through the Book* on page 21 are good resources for you to draw upon as you navigate the learning process contained herein.

- The Piano -

Piano diagrams are sometimes used throughout this book to show where notes appear on the piano keyboard. This is done because the piano keyboard is a useful aid for visualizing the modern musical system. The piano is also a good tool for the composer, not only because of its clear visualization of the musical system, but also because it can play many notes at the same time and has a very large range of low to high notes. For these reasons, pursuing even a basic level of proficiency on the piano as an aid to creative and theoretical musical pursuits can be very helpful.

Keep in mind, however, the information in this book can be applied to any instrument. Even where piano diagrams appear, the underlying concepts and sounds are the focus here and these will translate to any instrument. So feel free to explore the material presented in this book on whatever instrument you are interested in or feel comfortable playing.

- Where to Find Audio for the Examples -

At no extra cost, the audio examples for this book can be accessed online at:

http://projectado.com/tcm/audio

You can find a track list for all these examples near the end of the book on page 433. Note that I have not included audio for the three in-depth analyses of classical pieces (namely Faure's "Pavane," Beethoven's Fifth Symphony, and Pachelbel's Canon in D) or for the artists I mention in Chapter Ten as examples of different musical styles. Check out websites like YouTube, SoundCloud, and the International Music Score Library Project (IMSLP) for recordings of all these examples. Recordings for these examples should be plentiful and easy to access. I recommend you find several different performances of each piece if you can. I also certainly advocate purchasing your own copy of these recordings to support all the people involved in their creation. Other than these exceptions, audio has been included for all examples that require it.

- Music Theory Doesn't Always Make Sense -

As a quick disclaimer, I want to mention that music theory doesn't always make sense. By which I mean our system of music theory, how we name musical terms and categorize them, is not necessarily the ideal solution to describing the musical world. Sometimes, it is not even very close. After all, music theory has evolved our hundreds of years, combining many separate traditions from different musical cultures and perspectives from different eras in time. The result gets a little messy and the overall system is certainly a bit disorganized and often confusing, especially at first glance. You may notice, for example, that there is an amazing number of terms and phrases that mean the exact same thing or nearly so. Certain naming systems are needlessly complex at times. I could go on in greater detail but I'll refrain.

The purpose of this book is not to update old naming systems. In fact, we need to learn these naming systems because they are what the musical community uses today and being able to speak the lingo of musicians is of great practical value. In this book, we will go through all the naming systems for notes, intervals, chords, scales, rhythms, and more. But we will also do something else at the same time. We are going to explore the deeper mechanics of why music sounds as it does. And for this, I'll present some of my own original concepts and corresponding terminology. In particular, Chapter Two introduces many of these ideas and they are built upon throughout the book. As we go along I'll indicate which terms are original and which are based on the modern music theory system.

Hopefully, by focusing on clear and comprehensive explanations, this book will help to demystify the often confusing language of music theory. If you stick with it, there is an enormous payoff. Understanding music theory will allow us to bring a little of our intellect to the creative side of music. And with that, we can open doors to new realms of artistic depth. We'll get to explore those deeper mechanics of why music sounds as it does. After this journey, we can return to the emotional and the experiential side of music with newfound appreciation and the creative ability to bring truly higher quality art into the world.

- The Courage to Learn -

Openness and curiosity are natural qualities of the learning mind, body, and spirit. But very frequently our ego gets in the way. We become convinced that we are not good enough or that others are not good enough to learn from. We become too embarrassed to try new things or too prideful to listen to new ideas. These are common experiences, but it is a choice to believe in the fearful voice of the ego. When we succumb to our fears, our experience is limited. When we rise above them, our experience is expanded, our growth intensified.

As a starting point for musical study, we must accept the basic truth that as learning and developing people, our abilities improve with practice and experience. While we may inherit different learning styles and capacities, all people go through the learning process to become skilled and knowledgeable. All of the great musicians in history had to learn to become the legends we remember. Regardless of their natural gifts, they all started as a beginner and only with intense practice of their craft did their gifts manifest into high levels of musical achievement. Notice, too, that those individuals who do rise to these high levels of expertise will generally continue their intense practice of craft in a continual effort to reach greater and greater heights. This goes to show that it is the habit of practice that produces excellence, not excellence which bestows the ability and permission to practice.

You too have the potential to achieve great musical feats through dedicated and thoughtful practice. Rejoice in this possibility and also be patient with yourself. The first pieces of music that you write will likely sound like the compositions of a beginner – of course they will! This is a wonderful place to be. It is the beginning of the process of discovery. If you notice yourself being nervous about making mistakes or discouraged about your own potential, just remember that all people, even the best, start as beginners.

Furthermore, we learn just as much, if not more, from failures as we do from successes. A scientist whose hypothesis is disproven is not a bad scientist. Just so, an artist who writes a bad song is not a bad composer, especially if something was learned along the way.

Often the people who achieve the highest level of expertise in a field are those who are the most willing to fail. This is not to say you should aim for failure, but it is to say that great achievement asks of us great patience and great persistence, even in the face of risks. Without the aid of these virtues, failures will come to define you and your future endeavors. With them, a failure today can be turned into a success tomorrow.

The courage to learn opens up a space for the emergence of uninhibited creativity. The more we buy into and act on our fears, the more our creative process will be restricted to ever narrowing limits. But with courage we can reignite our natural curiosity and innovation. With courage, we can allow ourselves to do things that may not work and honestly examine our failures, doing our best to learn from them. These assets pave the way for a joyful and passionate path of growth. Over time this path can lead to truly inspirational works of art. The influence of such art is powerful and has the ability to reach across vast time and distance, deeply touching many lives.

- Quality Listening -

This book will present you with a wide variety of music. The examples will come from different styles, perspectives, and traditions. This diversity is included to help you make wide-reaching connections between different kinds of music. You will find that there are underlying principles that influence all the musical styles. However, to discover these connecting principles you must adopt an attitude of open listening.

Many music lovers become very interested in a particular musical style. It is wonderful to find music that we appreciate and connect with, but we must not let one discovery inhibit another. You may even commit yourself to a certain style while still remaining open to learning from other styles. The best musicians appreciate not just their kind of music, but the craft of music itself.

Many of the greatest innovations in music came from the merger of two styles. But for this to happen, musicians had to be open to sounds that were previously outside of their paradigm. This requires courage, openness, and also patience.

Sounds are interpreted by our minds. When our interpretation changes, any one piece of music can literally sound and feel different. What sounds like music to our ears undoubtedly sounds like noise to the ears of others and vice versa. This means that we cannot turn our backs on a particular type of music because of one bad experience or even because of many bad experiences. True openness means being willing to change not once, but every single time you listen.

So when you listen to the examples of music in this book (or any music that you really want to study), set aside your expectations and assumptions about what good music is or is not. Make a space where you can dedicate your full attention to open, focused listening. If you commit yourself to high quality listening, you will often discover new sounds and expressions you could not connect with before. And as this happens more and more, your knowledge and curiosity will grow together.

- Being Your Own Teacher -

This book is designed to aid you in a self-directed learning process. You are always your own first and primary teacher. Everything else is a resource for you to benefit from.

This means you must make decisions about what, when, and how to learn throughout your developmental process. One of the most valuable assets a teacher can have is the ability to follow the curiosity of the student. Dive into whatever interests you and don't hold back! If you want to read everything there is to read about a particular topic, then make that your focus. Don't be scared away by material that is more advanced or difficult. Follow your passion.
In parallel to your primary pursuits, take a moment every once in a while to look where you haven't been looking. You may find that one day you are in the mood for something different. This may be an opportunity to expand your horizons or perhaps to work on a weakness. Because new information is absorbed so quickly at the beginning of a learning process, you often can develop a weakness much faster than a strength. Often by taking advantage of this momentum, you can even transform weaknesses into strengths. If you remain open to new paths of learning and search out uncharted territory, the diversity of your pursuit will bring you balance. And with balance comes synergistic power.

Diverse and balanced learning requires approaching any topic you want to learn about from multiple angles. Make sure that you have developed each aspect of learning in regard to the subject you are interested in. That said, you may find that you want to stick with one aspect of learning for a given day or music session. Perhaps one day you may feel in the mood to listen to a lot of examples. Another day you may want to advance your conceptual understanding or practice the craft of composing or improvising. This type of approach can work well. Simply make sure that you come back to the other aspects of learning in the near future so that you will have a balanced picture of the topic you are studying.

There are more blue, or concept-oriented, boxes in this book than green, or expression-oriented, boxes and there are more green boxes than red, or action-oriented, boxes. The reason for this is that conceptual learning takes place primarily through the reading of the material in the book whereas expression-oriented and action-oriented learning require you to spend time participating in the learning process in other ways. To get the most out of this book, you'll need to spend time listening to and studying the examples. You'll need to spend time practicing the activities, in some cases many times. So, when considering the balance of your approach to learning, focus not on the number of boxes you are moving through but instead on the amount of time that you are spending on each of the three aspects of learning as well as your sense of how you are progressing in each area.

You may notice that there is not a lot of repetition in this book. I've laid the material out in this way because I intend you to read the content, study the examples, and do the activities as many times as necessary to internalize the material. In this style of learning, you are the captain of your own learning voyage. Rather than me as the author guessing at how much repetition you need to learn a given topic and writing that into the content of the book, I have created a learning system that facilitates your own ability to judge how much repetition you need and to adjust your learning process accordingly. I fully expect that most people will need to read the material in this book multiple times before they truly learn it well. And the book is set up to help you do just that. If you don't remember the details of a concept from two chapters ago, there will probably be a note linking you to the section of the book where I explained that concept so that you can go and read or reread that section. If there isn't a note linking you to the needed material, you will be able to easily find it in the *Table of Contents*, *Glossadex*, or by scanning through the titles of the boxes.

If you understand something intellectually but don't yet have a good practical feel for it, spend some more time doing the activities that were presented around that topic. You also may find the summaries presented at the end of each group of chapters to be a helpful way of reviewing and internalizing the material as well as an additional way for you to reference what concepts were talked about in what chapters. This book gives you all the conceptual material, examples, and activities you need to become an excellent composer and creative musician, but I am leaving it up to you to direct and participate in your own unique learning process. This is a great responsibility but also I feel it is truly the best and most enjoyable way to learn.

- Pathways Through the Book -

Here I'll discuss how this book is organized and some possibilities in terms of studying the different topics of the book. This text is organized into three parts. The first part is called *Foundations*. The second part is entitled *Musical Relationships*, and the third part is called *Creation and Exploration*. Each of these parts break down into two "groups," as I call them, which further break down into two or three chapters of several sections each (see the *Table of Contents* on page 4 for a visual of all this). In total, there are six groups and fourteen chapters.

The first group of the book is entitled *A Theoretical Model of the Musical Experience*, which outlines my own foundational paradigm of the major processes and components that are involved in the production of musical meaning and expression. It presents the big tools and perspectives we will use throughout the book. This group is somewhat intellectual and not necessarily the most "basic" part of the book. By which I mean aspects of the model contain some deep thoughts. But this is the foundation upon which everything else is based and a good way to orient yourself to the entire journey of understanding and creating music.

The second group, entitled *An Introduction to the Musical System*, is a bit less philosophical and a bit more utilitarian in nature. It presents the basic naming schemes and concepts of the musical "system," by which I mean the collectively understood terminology and basic paradigms of the musical community. If you already are familiar with basic music terminology, you may be able to skip some of this content. If you are a total beginner, you might find it helpful to start your journey here instead of at Group One to get your bearings with some basic music-speak. Perhaps accumulate a little experience playing your instrument and experimenting with the ideas in Group Two and then go back to Group One to get the theoretical framework that will be used throughout the book and especially with the more advanced content. This may also be appealing to those who want to start with the experiential and active, rather than starting out with abstractions. For the more abstractly inclined, however, Group One may be the best starting place.

For the more intermediate or advanced student, I should mention that there are many clarifying passages in Group Two that may be helpful to solidify your understanding of the basics of pitch and rhythm, even if you have already been introduced to this material. In addition, I recommend that more experienced students give special attention to the sections entitled *Chords and Chord Voicings* (page 78) and *Time Signatures Expanded* (page 100). The activities involving chord voicings in Chapter Three are an excellent way to begin the action thread of this process for anyone. And the *Time Signatures Expanded* section in Chapter Four contains some slightly more advanced information.

Moving into the second part of the book entitled *Musical Relationships*, we start getting into the "meat" of the theory. As the name implies, here we will be exploring the many ways in which music is a *relational* art, connecting together various musical elements in complex patterns that create meaning and beauty. Part Two is a bit more linear than the rest of the book. There is a fair bit of building on previous chapters here. So it is best to mostly stick with the order of the presentation in Part Two.

Group Three, *Intervals and Interval Structures*, discusses some traditional aspects of theory relating to chords and scales. It also goes into some preliminary ways in which these concepts can be applied. We are still in some ways setting the foundation at this stage, while introducing the beginnings of deeper concepts. Students who are already familiar with basic to intermediate music theory may be able to skip some of this content. Though, as with Part One, I would emphasize that the material here may provide some additional clarity even to those who know the basics of what is being presented. In addition, the section *Related Series Analysis* (page 157) is fairly advanced and should be novel to most any student. Beginners may consider coming back to this section during a second read-through of the book. Don't worry. There is an advanced symbol at the beginning of the section so you'll be forewarned as you are reading.

Group Four, which I've called *The Expression of Proportional Relationships*, gets into some deeper theory and some corresponding deeper expression and action content. Even intermediate students will probably find most of this material novel and beneficial. In this group, we will analyze our first full-length piece of music and begin to write our own musical themes. These are deeper creative tasks that will lead us directly into creating full songs and musical compositions.

In Part Three, a transition occurs to more action-oriented and expression-oriented material. As the name says, Part Three is about creation and exploration. To recap, in Part One, we will build up foundational perspectives and experiences to orient us to the broad subjects of music and artistic expression. In Part Two, we will learn the central theory relevant to our journey and we will look at examples of that theory as well as preliminary applications of it. In Part Three, it is time to put everything together into the process of both studying and creating musical works.

The material in Part Three can be studied in a more non-linear fashion if you wish. Chapter Ten is all about musical styles and, while filled with a lot of useful information, it is not necessary to go through Chapter Ten to go on to the other topics. Chapters Eleven and Twelve essentially take us through the process of creating a finished product. Chapter Eleven talks both about how to write for different groups or ensembles of instruments and some important basics of music technology. Depending on what you are interested in doing with music exactly, you may find these topics more or less relevant to you. Though, I would argue that it is all good stuff to know. Chapter Twelve discusses the concept of thematic musical development and includes an analysis of historical musical works, namely Beethoven's Fifth Symphony and Pachelbel's Canon in D. This is followed by a presentation of how to approach writing a full-length composition or song. This chapter is really a culmination of all the threads of learning throughout the book – conceptual, expressive, and active.

From here, we move into the last group, which has a slightly different flavor. This is where I discuss some more advanced concepts about harmony. This theory could easily be incorporated into an earlier part of your journey and if you are excited to delve deeper into the topic of harmony that may be the ideal path for you.

Chapter Thirteen presents a diverse array of different types of chords and scales. This material can be treated more as a reference. After being acquainted with basic concepts about chords and scales, which is accomplished in Group Three and the prerequisite information of the earlier sections of the book, you can access Chapter Thirteen anytime to broaden your knowledge of and ability to use different musical sounds. Many different chords and scales are presented there, so it might work well for some to take this chapter on in chunks throughout your learning process.

Chapter Fourteen can be understood with a solid grasp of the material in the first and second parts of the book. It presents some more advanced musical concepts about harmony. If you feel excited to pursue these topics after getting through Part One and Part Two, go for it! Otherwise, this chapter works naturally to add some additional possibilities to your tool kit and provides a segue into more advanced realms at the end of your journey.

I highly recommend reading in multiple passes. You may find that after gaining some more experience and conceptual reference points, the theoretical model of Group One solidifies a little more in your mind. Or you may find that the more advanced topics of the text in the second half of the book, in particular, can be appreciated or applied in new ways. You may also be more inclined to read the anecdote boxes and more advanced topics, on a second pass or later reading.

To summarize, I've created a visual layout of possible paths through the book for your reference on the following page.

And on that note, without further ado, I wish you a happy and growth-filled journey into the land of the theory and creation of music! Enjoy.

Chapter One	Fundamental Aspects of Sound	*Start here*
Chapter Two	Fundamental Aspects of Musical Expression	
Chapter Three	The Basics of Pitch	*Or start here*
Chapter Four	The Basics of Rhythm and Dynamics	
Chapter Five	Intervals	*Read straight through.*
Chapter Six	The Interval Structure of Chords	
Chapter Seven	The Interval Structure of Scales	
Chapter Eight	Relationships in Time	
Chapter Nine	Relationships in Pitch	
Chapter Ten	Musical Styles	*Read anytime.*
Chapter Eleven	Arranging and Production	*Read as relevant for you.*
Chapter Twelve	Development and Structure	*Read anytime after Chapter Nine.*
Chapter Thirteen	Additional Chord and Scale Types	*Reference anytime after Chapter Seven.*
Chapter Fourteen	Chromaticism	*Read anytime after Chapter Nine.*

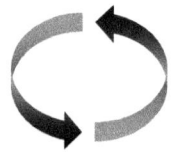 *Repeat and reference as desired.*

Part One
Foundations

Group One

A Theoretical Model of the Musical Experience

Chapter One
Fundamental Aspects of Sound

- What Is Music? -

> *Music is an expression of meaning in the domain of sound that relies heavily, though not exclusively, on the physical properties of sound and their basic perception by the sensory systems of the body.*

In contrast, language is an expression of meaning that relies more on the learned perception of sound. If one has not learned a language, the meaning of the language is largely, though not completely, lost. Music, however, is universal. People of all different backgrounds can appreciate the beauty, expression, and power of music without being taught how to do so.

Music and language form a spectrum from more reliant on innate perception of sound to more reliant on learned perception of sound. However, neither music nor language reaches a perfect extreme on this spectrum. Learned perception through culture, conditioning, and training plays a very significant role in the experience of music, just as the properties of sound and their basic perception are very influential in language.

Poetry in Relation to Music and Language

Poetry occupies an interesting middle ground between language and music. Poetry is written in the medium of language but relies heavily on the *sound* of language. Poetry uses devices such as rhyme, alliteration, onomatopoeia, meter, and form to evoke expressions of meaning. These devices all operate on the level of the sound of words rather than the learned meaning of words. Because of this combined focus on sound and the medium of language, poetry could, in fact, be aptly described as *musical writing*.

Music often incorporates sung language. The lyrics of music can be thought of as poetry. They draw some meaning from language but draw at least an equal degree of their meaning from the intuitively recognized sonic expression of the words.

- What Is Sound? -

What are the physical properties of sound mentioned in our definition of music? What is the basic perception of sound that creates the basis for musical expression? In this chapter, we will explore these questions and seek to illuminate the mystery of sound and our experience of it.

> We can think of the physical phenomenon of sound as a *continual flux of pressure or density*. Because our environment is filled with air, we often are describing the fluctuations in air pressure around us when we use the word *sound*. However, sound can travel through all different kinds of matter. The only place that sound cannot travel is in a vacuum or in the absence of matter.

> Much like the ripples on a pond, sound can be seen as waves that move over time. To get a sense of the complexity of sound, imagine staring out over a body of water and notice all of the different movements that could be happening at any given moment. There may be larger waves and smaller ripples within the waves. The wind may cause the water to move into a choppy texture or in its absence settle into stillness. Fish living beneath the surface may jump in and out of the water creating splashes. Each movement generates a cascading effect where the movement of one water molecule causes the movement of another, which then causes the movement of another. In this way, all the water becomes linked together into an intricately fluctuating whole.
>
> This image is a good analogy to what happens in the invisible three-dimensional field of air we are surrounded by in our day-to-day lives. Whenever there is movement in this field at any one point, waves are created through the whole system.
>
> For the sake of illustration, let's examine the example of a vibrating guitar string. When we say that a guitar string is *vibrating*, what we are literally saying is that the guitar string is moving very quickly back and forth over a small distance. This movement is so fast that to the human eye it appears only as a blur. But as the guitar string travels, the surrounding air is forced to move out of the path of the guitar string, somewhat like the water in front of a sailboat. The moving air will then collide with the surrounding air and form an area of high pressure or density. Like a coiled spring, the compressed air then expands and creates an area of low pressure. The air that was moved away from the guitar in this expansion will then collide with more air farther out and creates another area of high pressure. In reaction, this area too will then expand. This pattern repeats again and again, creating oscillating areas of high and low pressure that emanate from the source of the sound.

The total effect could be described as traveling waves of sound, often referred to as *sound waves*. Visualized simply, this might look something like the illustration below. Keep in mind, however, that much like traveling ripples on a pond, real sound waves occur in a complex system of countless waves and movements, all interacting and running into each other.

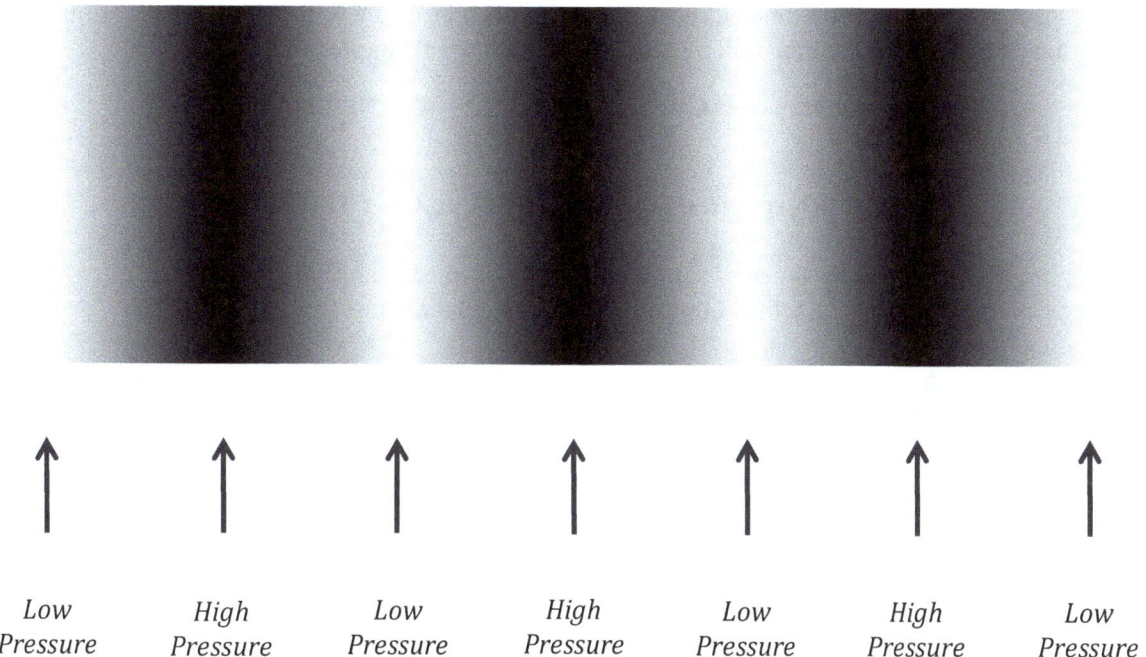

Low Pressure   *High Pressure*   *Low Pressure*   *High Pressure*   *Low Pressure*   *High Pressure*   *Low Pressure*

Human Perception of Sound

Although sound waves in our environment can be described in the simple terms of areas of high and low pressure or density, it is important to understand that humans do not experience sound directly as a one dimensional sense of pressure at the specific location of the inner ear, where sound is detected. Instead, the inner ear and brain, working together, interpret the sound of our environments with an astounding array of processes that create the multidimensional experience of hearing with which we are familiar. From the simple data of changing air pressure, the hearing mechanism of the inner ear and the interpreting faculty of the brain are so advanced that very high level information can be extrapolated – we can tell who is speaking, where a sound originated in space, and even if an object is solid or hollow. And with the evolution of thought and feeling, sound gains the capacity to carry ideas, experiences, and emotions. So what starts as a series of waves in air pressure, incredibly, can end up in our consciousness as a window into the memory, dreams, or living experience of another.

The Physical and Perceptual Studies of Sound

Throughout this chapter, we will be discussing two aspects of sound: the physical and the perceptual. On the one hand, sound waves are occurring out in the physical, external world. The study of these external sound waves and their properties is called *acoustics*. On the other hand, we have the experience of those sound waves interpreted through the perceptual systems of the human being. And this will be the area that we focus on throughout this book. However, before moving into the realm of the human experience, it is helpful to start with a basic foundation in the physical – in acoustics, which will be our topic for this first chapter of our journey.

Four Perceptual Elements of Sound Over Time

The dazzlingly complex experience of sound can be reduced to a mere four elements: *pitch*, *loudness*, *timbre*, and *location*, which continuously evolve over time.

Let us examine each of these four perceptual elements of sound in turn. For each perceptual element, we will discover that there are associated physical properties in the sound waves of the external world.

- Pitch and Frequency -

Pitch describes the perceptual spectrum of sound from low to high. When musicians say that one note is higher or lower than another, they are referring to the characteristic of pitch.[1] A *pitch* – as in "Can you play that pitch one more time?" – refers to a specific position on this spectrum from low to high.

Pitch correlates to the physical property of *frequency*. Frequency describes the speed or rate at which a sound wave is *oscillating*, or fluctuating between high and low pressure. One *oscillation* describes a cycle through a repeating pattern in a sound wave. For example, an oscillation might be the movement from ordinary or neutral pressure to low pressure to high pressure and back to ordinary or neutral. Alternatively, it could be the movement from neutral to high to low to neutral pressure. *Hertz* is a unit of measurement that describes how many times a wave goes through an oscillation in one second. Hertz is, therefore, a measure of a sound wave's frequency, which in turn correlates to the perception of a low or high pitch in a person's auditory experience.

1. *Pitch and Note Names*, page 66

The range of human hearing extends from approximately 20 to 20,000 hertz. However, by the time a person reaches adulthood, perception of the higher frequencies diminishes to a limit of somewhere around 16,000 hertz. Remember this means that, on average, we can detect sounds that go through anywhere between 20 and 16,000 to 20,000 oscillations of air pressure per second.

In other words, the vibrations we sense through our ears are happening very, very quickly. The pace of this vibration is far too fast for us to consciously register each change in air pressure individually. So instead, we simply perceive sounds as having pitch. Sounds with a low pitch represent relatively low frequency vibrations; sounds with a high pitch represent relatively high frequency vibrations.

Pulses Transforming Into Pitch

Below around 20 hertz, oscillations become slow enough to perceive each change in pressure individually. In this range of frequency, rather than perceiving a sense of pitch we will experience a series of repeating sounds. Track 1 (disc 1) plays a series of pulses that continually become faster. As the pulse reaches and then goes beyond the 20 hertz threshold, you will hear the sound progressively transform into a pitch. The pitch will start as a lower pitch and become higher and higher as the frequency of the sound increases further still.

Visualizing Pitch With Graphs

The graphs on the following page illustrate how air pressure changes over time in a relatively low frequency wave and a relatively high frequency wave. Notice how the higher frequency wave completes three full oscillations in the time it takes the low frequency wave to complete one full oscillation. This means that the high frequency wave is vibrating at a frequency that is three times higher than the low frequency wave.

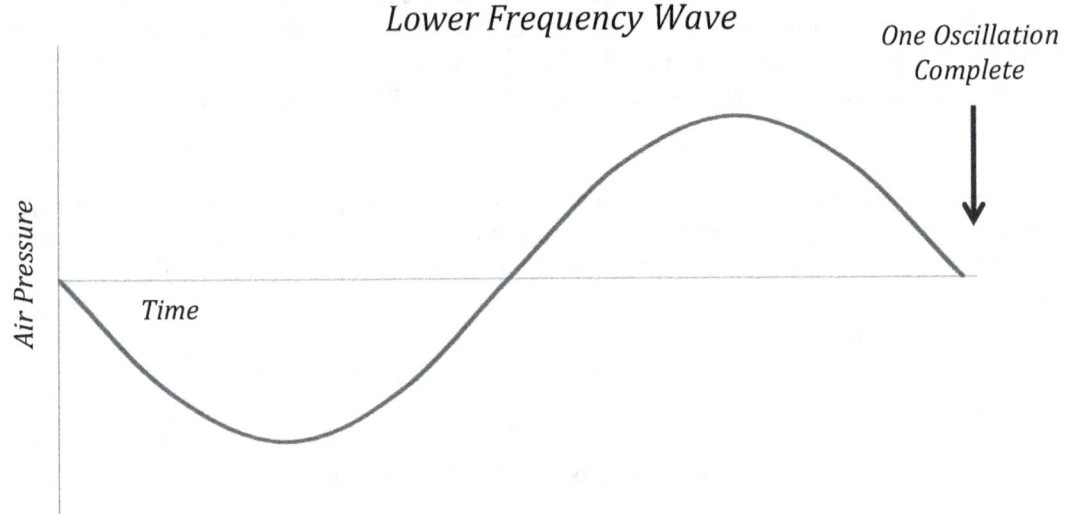

Lower Frequency Wave

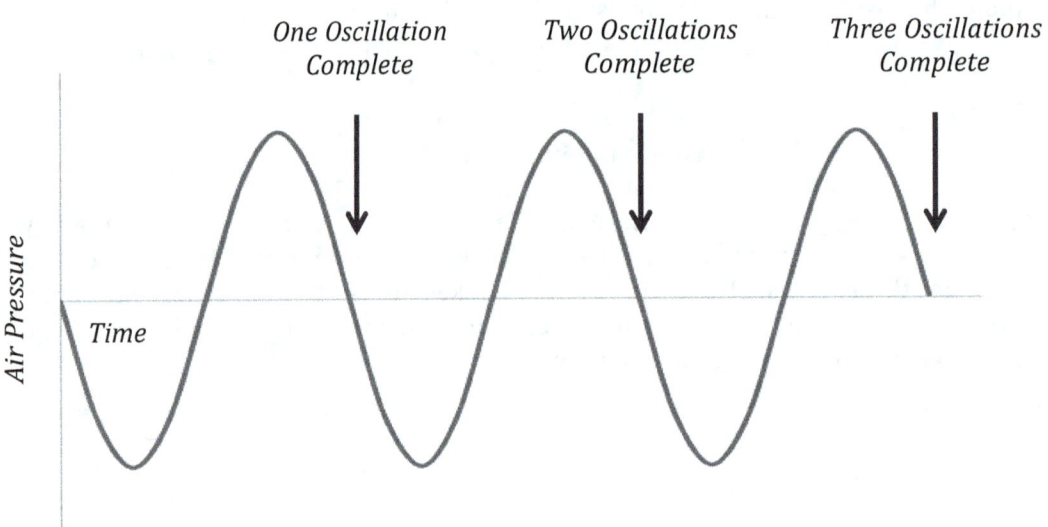

Higher Frequency Wave

The Hearing Ability of Different Animal Species

Interestingly, the hearing range of different animal species varies considerably. Dogs can hear up to 45,000 hertz. Bats go even further, hearing frequencies up to 110,000 hertz. And best of all, porpoises hear frequencies up to 150,000 hertz!

❖ See Strain, "Frequency Hearing Ranges in Dogs and Other Species" in the bibliography on page 431.

- Loudness and Amplitude -

> *Loudness* describes the perceptual spectrum of sound from soft to loud. (I'll also sometimes use the term *volume* as a synonym for loudness.) What we perceive as loudness reflects the *amplitude* of sound waves in the air. In turn, amplitude is a measure of the intensity under which air is compressed and expanded in a sound wave. Sound waves that create large differences between high pressure and low pressure in the air result in loud sounds in our perception of hearing. Conversely, quiet sounds in our perception represent sound waves that create small differences between high and low pressure.
>
> ❖ *Dynamics*, page 88

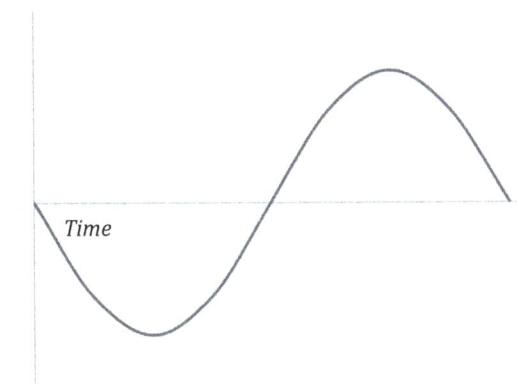

Lower Amplitude Wave   *Higher Amplitude Wave*

- Timbre and Harmonic Composition -

Timbre can be described as the quality of a sound at a given pitch and volume level. Timbre is how we can differentiate between a violin and piano playing the same note. It is also how we can differentiate the sound of one person's voice from another. The physical phenomenon that correlates to our perception of timbre is called *harmonic composition*, a full description of which is provided below.

I have found the topic of timbre and harmonic composition fascinating! However, just so you know, the following explanation of this subject is a bit more advanced than other topics examined in this chapter. If you would like to skip this section or save it for later, feel free to continue reading at the section entitled *Location* on page 44. If you choose to continue with this section, stay with me for a few pages as I introduce some necessary background information.

Advanced

Natural Frequencies

Objects tend to vibrate at certain frequencies depending on their mass and stiffness. The primary frequency an object vibrates at is called its *natural frequency*. Stiffer objects vibrate more quickly because they will travel a shorter distance in a single oscillation. Less massive objects vibrate more quickly because the distance of each oscillation is traversed more quickly.

Take the example of a vibrating string. Longer and thicker strings will vibrate more slowly because they have more mass. A string of twice the length or twice the thickness will vibrate at half the frequency. Strings that are placed under more tension become stiffer and vibrate at higher frequencies.

The diagrams below represent how a string will vibrate when placed under more tension (upper left), less tension (upper right), when the string is thicker therefore more massive (lower left), or when the string is thinner therefore less massive (lower right). The solid lines and dotted lines represent the positions that the string is oscillating or alternating between as it vibrates.

Note that I could have just as easily used a longer string for the lower left example instead of a thicker string. The key factor here is mass, which in the example of a string can be in the form of either length or thickness.

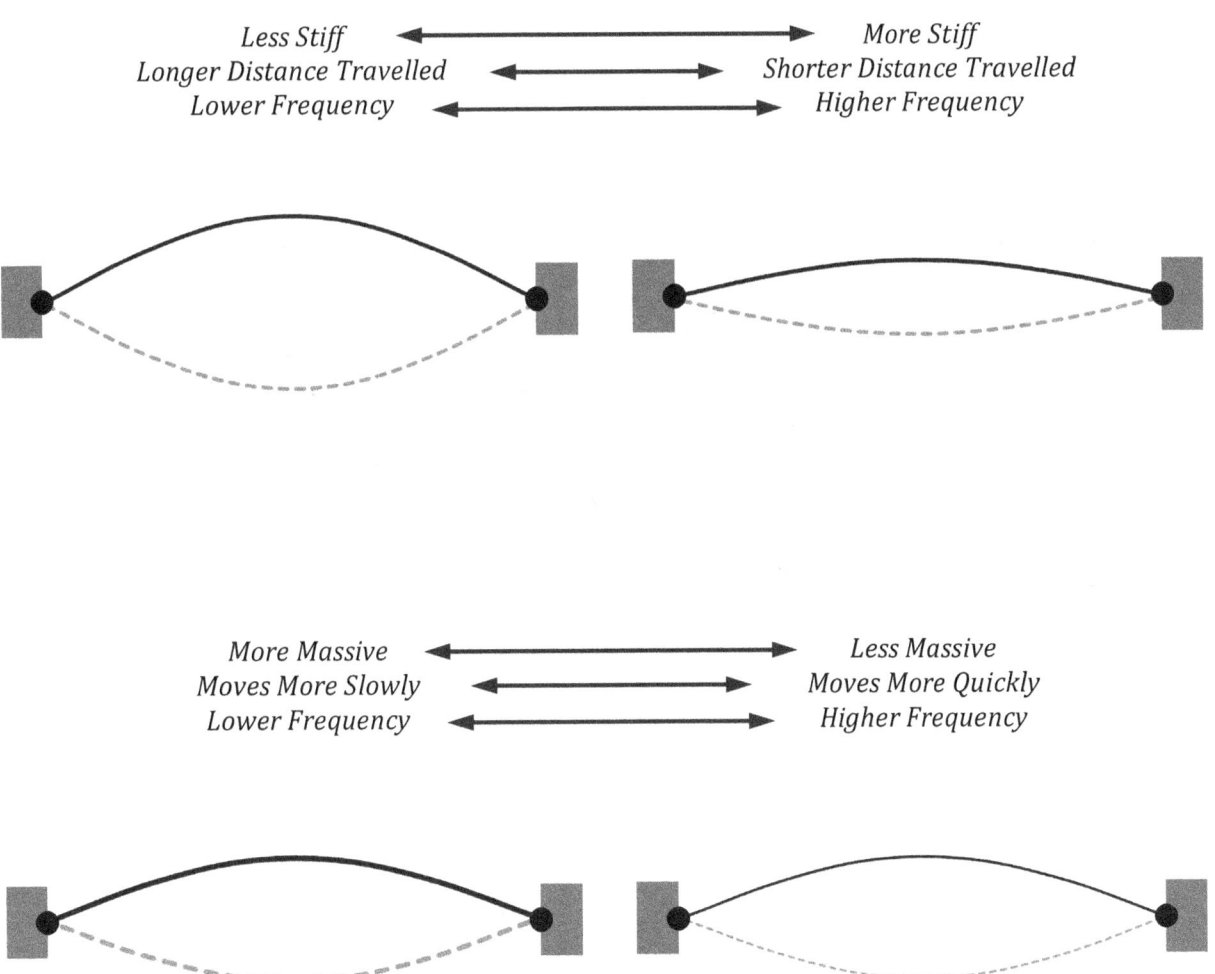

How the Sounds of Instruments Change Pitch

One of the primary ways instruments are able to produce different pitches is by changing the length of the object that is vibrating. For example, a guitarist is able to change the pitch the guitar is producing by changing the length of the string that is vibrating. Guitarists pluck strings on the guitar to create vibrations. Then by pressing a string against the fret board with a finger, guitarists can stop the vibration at the point of their finger. By stopping the vibration at a certain point, guitarists are able to change the length of the vibrating portion of the string. And when the length of the vibrating portion of the string changes, so does the mass of the vibrating object and, therefore, so does the pitch.

Every string instrument uses a variation on this mechanism to change the pitch of the sound the instrument is producing. Some instruments like the harp or the piano have a different string or set of strings for each note. Wind instruments too make use of a similar principle. By opening and closing different holes, wind instruments can change the length of a vibrating column of air inside the instrument. This results in different pitches that correspond to the length of the vibrating column of air.

Nodes and Anti-Nodes

Each end of the vibrating string below is fixed and thus cannot move. Unmoving points on a string (or other vibrating object) are called *nodes*. In contrast, the halfway point between the nodes moves the most out of all the points on the string. A point that moves the maximal amount during an oscillation compared to the other points on the string is called an *anti-node*.

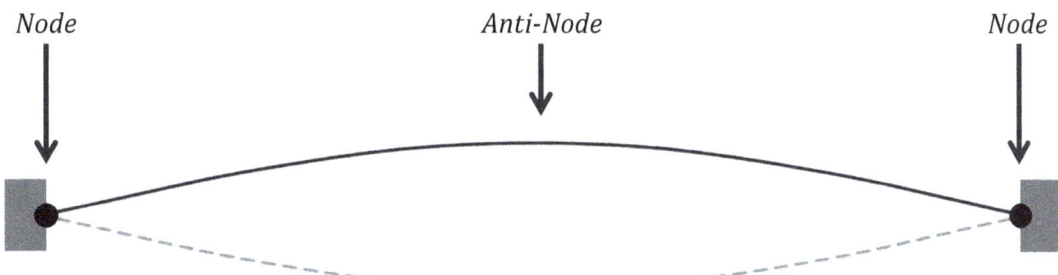

Node   *Anti-Node*   *Node*

Harmonics

The above diagram shows the traditional way we think of a vibrating string. Reality, however, is more complex. The above motion is the strongest motion that occurs in a vibrating string, but it is by no means the only motion that occurs. In fact, all of the motions shown on the following page are possible and, incredibly, exist simultaneously within a single vibrating string.

These vibrations are possible because they share the fixed nodes at the end of the string. These possibilities represent proportional relationships[1] – the motion that occurs when the string vibrates as a whole, in halves, in thirds, in quarters, in fifths, and so on. Each of these possible vibrations is called a *harmonic*.

As the harmonics progress from top to bottom, a node and a corresponding anti-node are added to the vibrational shape of the string every time the string is broken into more parts. A node occurs every time the solid lines intersect with the dotted lines. Anti-nodes occur halfway between the nodes, where a line reaches its peak high or low position.

1. We will expand on the concept of proportional relationships in Chapter Two. See *Seven Basic Spectra of Musical Expression* on page 47.

Different Waves of the Harmonic Series in a Single String

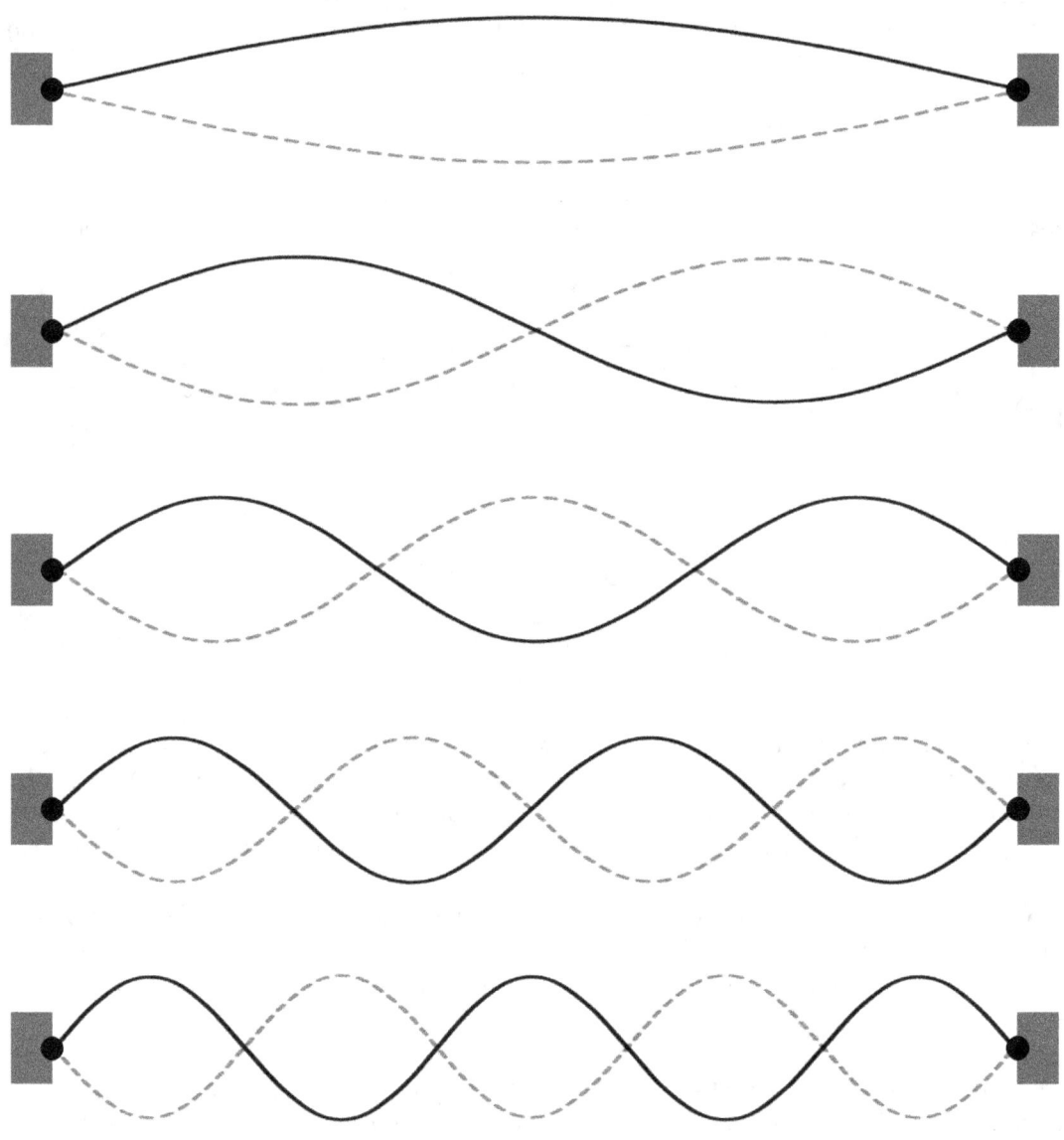

and so on...

The Harmonic Series

Each of the different movements or harmonics shown in the diagram on the previous page produce a vibration with a different frequency. As the string is divided into more and more vibrating parts, each part becomes a smaller fraction of the total length of the string. These fractional parts become shorter and shorter in distance and as a result produce higher and higher frequencies. Generally, as the frequencies become higher they also become quieter in volume.

Thus it is possible (in fact, inevitable) for a single string to produce multiple frequencies at once. Collectively, the sequence of harmonics that emanates from a single source of sound is called a *harmonic series* or an *overtone tone series*. The first or primary harmonic of a sound is called the *fundamental frequency*. In the diagram above, the fundamental frequency is being produced by the motion with only two nodes and one anti-node. This frequency is, generally, the loudest and lowest frequency present in a sound.

The frequencies of the harmonic series follow a pattern. Every harmonic represents a whole number multiple of the fundamental frequency. Using the variable "X" to describe the frequency of the fundamental frequency, the pattern is as follows:

Fundamental Frequency or First Harmonic – X
Second Harmonic – Two Times X
Third Harmonic – Three Times X
Fourth Harmonic – Four Times X
Fifth Harmonic – Five Times X
and so on…

For example, if the fundamental frequency or first harmonic of a sound is vibrating at 100 hertz, the second harmonic will vibrate at 200 hertz, the third harmonic will be 300 hertz and so on. If however, the fundamental frequency or first harmonic of a sound is vibrating at 200 hertz, the second harmonic will vibrate at 400 hertz, the third harmonic will vibrate at 600 hertz and so on, adding 200 hertz for each successive harmonic.

Connecting Timbre and Harmonic Composition

When the hearing and interpreting faculties of the brain and body detect a series of frequencies coming from a source of sound, the series is recognized, analyzed, and grouped together so that you perceive only a single *sound* out a series of related frequencies. The fundamental frequency of the series becomes the pitch of the sound you hear. The body and brain analyze the relative presence or amplitude of each of the harmonics and this becomes the basis for our perception of timbre.

We use the term *harmonic composition* to mean the physical property that describes the harmonics of a sound and their relative volume levels. In contrast, we use the term *timbre* to mean the perceptual experience of a sound's quality, which correlates to the physical property of harmonic composition.

Simple and Complex Timbres

There is practically an infinite variety of harmonic compositions, each with a distinct corresponding timbre. However, a general spectrum can be outlined from more simple to more complex.

At the simplest end of the spectrum, we have what is called a *pure sine wave*. A pure sine wave represents a single frequency without the addition of any other harmonics. This sound is essentially not ever found in nature or in acoustic (meaning non-electronic) instruments. The sound of a whistle is perhaps close but even then at least the second harmonic of a whistle is audible.

However, with the use of computers we can now hear the sound of a single frequency in isolation. Track 2 (disc 1) plays the following six frequencies in isolation one after another: 110 hertz, 220 hertz, 440 hertz, 880 hertz, 1760 hertz, and 3520 hertz.[1] Notice the unique sound of a pure sine wave. Also notice what experience of pitch corresponds to the six frequency numbers listed above.

As a sound becomes more complex, often a harmonic series arises. As the harmonic series becomes more present and begins to emphasize the higher frequency harmonics, a brighter and richer timbre emerges. In contrast, sounds that have less present harmonics, and less present high frequency harmonics in particular, are described as having a more mellow and pure sounding timbre.

1. These frequencies correspond to the following notes on the piano: A2, A3, A4, A5, A6, A7. These terms are defined in a later section of the book. See *Distinguishing Between the Many Instances of Each Note Name* on page 71 or more generally the sections *Pitch and Note Names* on page 66 and *Octaves* on page 70.

Non-Pitched Sounds

In some sounds, frequencies begin to emerge that do not follow the expected pattern of harmonics. These include frequencies that do not equal a whole number value times the fundamental frequency. These frequencies are described as *inharmonic partials*. The more inharmonic partials a sound includes, the less of a defined pitch it will seem to have. This is because the presence of inharmonic partials breaks the pattern, making it less clear what the fundamental frequency of the sound is.

When enough inharmonic partials are present in a sound, a *non-pitched sound* is created. Non-pitched sounds include timbres like cymbal crashes and drums where a single, clear pitch is not discernible. However, even in these sounds a general sense of high and low is still present. For example, we can agree that a bass drum sounds lower than a snare drum or cymbal crash. This occurs because despite the lack of a harmonic series, there is still an emphasis on a certain range of frequencies.

As even an emphasis of a particular range of frequencies is reduced or eliminated, timbres begin to sound more like noise. *White noise* is an even distribution in amplitude over all possible frequencies. This creates a sound that does not adhere to the harmonic series at all and does not emphasize one frequency over another in any way. In some sense, white noise is the most complex sound possible. Like the pure sine wave, pure white noise is not found in nature or in acoustic instruments. The sound of the wind is perhaps similar. We will hear an example of white noise at the end of track 3 (disc 1), which we will discuss shortly.

A Connection to Musical Expression (in reference to Chapter Two)

Interestingly, while more complex timbres tend to create higher energy expressions, when timbres start losing their sense of pitch, either by becoming percussive or noise-like, their expressions become much lower energy again. It would seem that we stop experiencing the complexity as competing forces or complex relationships and start to interpret the sounds as random or without significant pattern or meaning.

Advanced

The Difference Between Harmonics, Partials, and Overtones

The words *harmonics*, *partials*, and *overtones* all describe a series of frequencies that are present in a single sound. However, they all mean something slightly different. A *partial* is any frequency present in a sound. A *harmonic* is a frequency that follows the harmonic series. Harmonics are a part of a pattern that includes frequencies that are one, two, three, and so on times the value of the fundamental frequency. If a frequency does not follow this pattern, it is considered an *inharmonic partial* rather than a harmonic. Finally, an *overtone* refers to any partial that is above the fundamental frequency. Overtones do not have to follow the harmonic series and are essentially the same as partials except that they are named differently. The fundamental frequency is also the first partial and the first harmonic but it is not the first overtone. The first overtone is the second partial. The second overtone is the third partial and so on.

Other Factors That Influence Timbre

Over the course of a single sound or musical note,[1] rapid fluctuations occur in terms of frequency and amplitude. In music, the rapid fluctuation of pitch or frequency over the course of a single sound is called *vibrato*. This fluctuation is small[2] but certainly a noticeable and important characteristic of a sound. Generally, vibrato is also considered to be a part of timbre, meaning that it is a contributor to the type or quality of sound that is being perceived rather than the pitch or loudness of the sound.

Rapid fluctuations in the volume of an overall sound or even fluctuations in the volume of a single harmonic can also affect our perception of timbre. This includes the way some sounds fade in or out slowly while other sounds have more abrupt entrances and exits.[3] Some changes in volume happen so quickly that they are below our threshold of awareness. As such they are registered subconsciously as part of the timbre of a sound. Other changes in volume happen slowly enough for us to perceive them consciously but they are strongly associated with a particular instrument or source of sound. In this case, too, the changes in volume are considered to be part of timbre.

Ultimately, the difference is subjective. If a change in volume or pitch seems to be an integral characteristic of an instrument or particular source of sound, then the change falls under the category of timbre. If a change in volume or pitch is perceived independent from the instrument or source of sound, then the change falls under the category of pitch or loudness, respectively.

1. *Pitch and Note Names*, page 66
2. Often less than a half step, a term we define later on. See *Half Steps and Whole Steps* on page 119.
3. The way a sound's volume level changes from beginning to end is called an *envelope*. In the box entitled *Envelopes* on page 325, I expand on this concept in a little more detail. This explanation is presented in context of synthesizers – which are instruments that electronically produce new and original timbres – but the concept of an envelope can apply to all sounds, not just electronically produced or "synthesized" ones.

Listening to a Spectrum of Timbres

Listen to track 3 (disc 1) to hear a series of timbres that progresses from simple to complex. Keep in mind that there are many ways of becoming complex (though, interestingly, only one way of becoming simple). As the track progresses, it explores some of different possibilities that emerge in timbre as we add complexity to the harmonic composition of the sound.

We'll go through each of the sounds in order briefly (see the reference list below). The first sound is a simple sine wave, the most simple timbre. Next, is another computer-generated sound called a *triangle wave*, only this wave has been "filtered" or altered so that the upper partials of the sound are reduced in amplitude. This creates a more mellow variation of the triangle wave. Next, is the first acoustic or non-electronic timbre – a flute. Notice that many forms of complexity are present in acoustic sounds that are not in simple computer-generated waves. We can hear variation in this timbre over time in more complex ways, the sound of air flowing through the instrument, and so on. Next is a sound called an *electric piano* or *E. piano* for short. Notice the vibrato or changing pitch of this sound. Next are four acoustic (or non-electronic) timbres – a trombone, an oboe, a cello, and a piano. All of these sounds are from different *families* or categories of instruments, brass, woodwinds, strings, and keyboard instruments, respectively. Notice the different quality of brass and woodwind, the richness of the cello and low piano note, and the slow changes that occur in the piano's timbre over time. Next, is a more complex, computer-generated sound created by a *synthesizer*, but it sounds almost as if it could be acoustic. Then comes the sound of distorted or overdriven guitar (overdrive or distortion increases the higher partials of the timbre of a guitar). Next, is the shrill, loud, and high note of a trumpet. Unlike previous timbres, the trumpet sound here isn't changing much over time. However, it does have fairly prominent upper partials and the fundamental note is in a rather sensitive area of human hearing in terms of pitch – the upper-mid range. Next, is a more extravagant and clearly digital synthesizer with a lot of changes to the timbre happening over time. This is followed by a timpani, which is a percussion instrument, though still with an identifiable pitch. Next, a gong, a percussive sound, which is now starting to lose its sense of clear pitch. Then, a complex noise that seems to fluctuate randomly. And finally, pure white noise.

Track List

1. Sine Wave
2. Filtered Triangle Wave
3. Flute
4. Electric Piano
5. Trombone
6. Oboe
7. Cello
8. Piano
9. Synthesizer 1
10. Guitar With Distortion
11. Trumpet
12. Synthesizer 2
13. Timpani
14. Gong
15. Fluctuating Noise
16. White Noise

- Location -

The perceptual experiences of pitch, loudness, and timbre each have a parallel physical property: Pitch is the perceptual parallel to the physical property of frequency, loudness to the physical property of amplitude, and timbre to harmonic composition. The word *location*, however, describes both our perception and the physical phenomenon that is taking place in the world.

The methods the body and brain use to determine where a sound is coming from are complex. The brain is able to compare the differences in timing between a sound as it reaches one ear and then the other. Sound travels very quickly but not instantaneously. Amazingly, the brain can tell that a sound coming from your right arrives at your right ear before it arrives at your left ear. The brain can also determine that the sound arriving at the left ear has been altered as a result of its journey through your head!

The simple volume of a sound plays a key role in determining how far away the source of the sound is. However, there is another factor to take into account. Sound reflects off of walls and surfaces in a room. These reflections create echoes that we can hear. When this effect is very pronounced, we may consciously register the echoes. However, when the effect is less pronounced, we may simply notice a different quality of sound. Nonetheless, the brain can analyze the timing and presence of echoes to calculate the origin of a sound in a room. This all happens subconsciously, in a minuscule fraction of a second.

Putting It All Together: The Perceptual Experience of Sound

In summary, our experience of sound consists of a continually evolving dance of timbres with various pitches and volume levels scattered across our perceptual area of space. In any one moment, the experience of sound can be described with the characteristics of pitch, volume, timbre, and location. These four characteristics unfold over time like the changing colors on the screen of a movie.

In our study of music, we will be concerned with the characteristics of pitch, volume, timbre, and location as well as their relationships to each other as they develop over time.

Chapter Two
Fundamental Aspects of Musical Expression

Chapter One opened with the following: "Music is an expression of meaning in the domain of sound that relies heavily, though not exclusively, on the physical properties of sound and their basic perception by the sensory systems of the body." After reviewing this definition in contrast to language and poetry, we took on the subject of sound, its properties and its perception.

Now that we understand sound as the *medium* of music or the domain in which the art of music occurs, we can now turn our attention to the other half of our definition of music, namely music as "an expression of meaning." Can we pin down what meaning is any further than our intuitive knowledge of the word? How is it that music uses this medium or domain of sound to generate feelings, ideas, messages, and encapsulations of whole experiences?

What follows is my own model that I use to lay out the most fundamental features of music as an expresser or communicator of all varieties of experience. This model has several different components to it. So, feel free to reread and reference this chapter as necessary. It contains many important, structural concepts that we will be using throughout the rest of the book. You may find the visual summary of the first group particularly helpful as a way to solidify in your mind all the elements of this theoretical framework, which we started in Chapter One and will complete now in Chapter Two.

Buckle up. This is a big one.

- What Is Meaning? -

A fundamental source of meaning is the dichotomy of commonality and difference.

We can use the notion of a dichotomy of commonality and difference as a summary definition of meaning, at least for our purposes here. Let's take a look at how this principle plays out on both more logical and more emotional levels.

On a more logical level, consider the task of defining a word in a language. To define the word "left," for example, one must create relationships to other words. These relationships will either reveal a commonality or difference between a pair of words.

We may say that "left" refers to a quality of horizontal position or direction. This statement reveals a similarity between the word "left," and the words "horizontal," "position," and "direction." Notice that to create connections from the word "left" to other similar words, I referenced more general words that included the concept I was defining as well as other concepts. This is a common theme in many types of connections.

We could also say that "left" is the opposite of "right." This distinction reveals a difference between two words but notice that it also reveals its own kind of connectivity. The comparison of left to right creates a contrasting relationship that defines a spectrum. This contrasting form of connection also indirectly references the more general concept of horizontal direction without mentioning it specifically.

As an example that operates on an emotional level, consider the dynamics of interacting people. People often connect over shared commonality but they also connect over differences, especially complementary differences. Without any commonality, people will not be able to relate. Commonality provides a sense of belonging and a basis for connection. Difference, however, can create synergy. The strengths of some complement the weaknesses of others and in this way the whole is greater than the sum of its parts. Difference also provides the opportunity to learn from one another. People have nothing to learn from identical copies of themselves.

Throughout the book, we will continue to come back to various kinds of commonalities and differences in our examination of musical meaning. This will often come in the form of evaluating what degree of commonality or relatedness two sounds have with one another. Going forward, I invite you to keep this concept – the dichotomy of commonality and difference – in mind, as a piece of our foundational paradigm.

- Seven Basic Spectra of Musical Expression -

What Is Musical Expression?

Music is a language. I use the term *musical expression* to broadly describe what it is that music says. Musical expression is what music evokes within us. It is how music makes us feel, what it makes us think of.

On page 2, I said that "The aim of this book is to enable people to write their own high quality music." Our central approach to achieving this goal will be to develop your ability to translate the musical expression you want to create into the form of sound in the physical world where it can be shared with others.

What makes music sound happy? What makes it sound sad? Tense? Relaxed? Beautiful? Powerful? Scary? Nostalgic? We will seek to answer the fundamental question: What makes music sound the way it sounds? The more deeply we can answer this question, on both logical and intuitive levels, the more aptly we will be able to create the music we want to create.

High Energy and Low Energy Expressions

The expressive meaning of music is a product of the relationships within and between the four perceptual qualities of sound – pitch, loudness, timbre, and location. These relationships occur in any given moment of a musical piece as well as over time.

The four perceptual qualities of sound can be thought of as four spectra, each with a *lower energy* and *higher energy* polarity. Sounds of lower pitch, softer volume, more simple timbre, and more distant, more peripheral location create lower energy expressions. Sounds of higher pitch, louder volume, more complex timbre, and closer, more central location all create higher energy expressions.

Lower energy sound qualities produce expressions of release, rest, simplicity, beauty, and connectivity. *Higher energy sound qualities* produce expressions of intensity, activity, excitement, complexity, power, interest, drama, and tension.

Gradated and Graduated Spectra

Spectra fall into one of two categories: *gradated spectra* and *graduated spectra*. A gradated spectrum smoothly and continuously evolves from one end of the spectrum to the other. A graduated spectrum changes in steps that are defined by a unit of measurement.

Gradated Spectrum *Graduated Spectrum*

Proportionality

In graduated spectra, there arises the potential for proportionality. For example, the spectrum of physical length or distance can be seen as a gradated spectrum of infinitely fine positions or it can be broken up into units of measurement such as a centimeter. When a unit of measurement is assigned, it becomes possible to create proportional relationships between entities on the scale. For example, one centimeter has a proportional relationship with two centimeters. We can define this relationship as a 1:2 ratio.

Proportional relationships will be one of the most important foundational ideas for our journey throughout this book. In music, pitches and durations of time that are related to each other through simple proportional ratios like 1:2 or 2:3 feel naturally connected. This can happen, for example, between two pitches where one pitch is vibrating at a frequency twice the speed of the other or between a sound that lasts for twice the duration in time as another sound in a composition. The more parts involved in these kinds of proportional relationships the more complex and subtle we feel the connection to be. The number of total parts implied by a proportional connection can be seen in the larger of the two numbers in the given ratio of the proportional relationship. For example, a 2:5 ratio and 4:5 ratio both imply a system that includes a total of five parts.

From this perspective, we can evaluate proportional relationships on a scale from simple, involving the fewest parts, to complex, involving the most parts. Simple ratios, such as 1:2, 2:3, or 3:4, are associated with the expressions of commonality and connection. As the number of parts in a relationship increases, the connection is felt to be increasingly complex and nuanced until eventually the relationship is so complex that a sense of difference, unrelatedness, or even randomness emerges. Based on these observations then, we can see that ratios involving few parts are associated with the polarity of low energy, which expresses simplicity, connection, and commonality, while ratios involving a larger number of parts are associated with the polarity of high energy, which expresses complexity, division, and difference.

Strong or Weak Proportionality

I will refer to a relationship as having *strong proportionality* if there are a small total number of parts in the system of the relationship. I will refer to a relationship as having *weak proportionality* if there are high total number of parts in the system of the relationship.

Note that strong proportionality is associated with simplicity and the low energy polarity of expression, while weak proportionality is associated with complexity and the high energy polarity of expression.

Using Whole Integer Values

When determining the strength of a proportional relationship, ratios should be formed with whole integer values. Ratios like 1.5:2 or 1/2:2 cannot be evaluated in terms of strong or weak proportionality unless they are rewritten using only whole integer numbers – for example 3:4 or 1:4.

Defining the Seven Basic Spectra of Musical Expression

Throughout this book, we will explore seven fundamental spectra of musical expression. These will form the basis of more complex expressions that can be formed out of the relationships between the basic seven.

The first four spectra of musical expression are the four perceptual qualities of sound (pitch, loudness, timbre, and location) described on gradated spectra from low to high energy.

The fifth spectrum of musical expression is time described as a gradated spectrum. This spectrum progresses from longer durations of time on the lower energy polarity to shorter durations of time on the higher energy polarity. Time not only adds its own contribution to the mix but also represents how long each of the other spectra last. A pitch could last only briefly or for a long time. A sound could be loud just for a short time or it could sustain a high volume. Functioning in this way, time as a gradated spectrum represents *how much* of the other spectra are present. Making a high energy expression longer will make it higher energy still, while making a low energy expression longer will make it even lower energy. Long durations have a *polarizing effect*, bringing expressions toward their extremes. In contrast, short durations have just the opposite effect of bringing expressions toward moderation. The fifth spectrum, then, has a complex effect overall. It interacts with other spectra as well as contributing its own expression of low energy with long durations and high energy with short ones.

Let us now turn our attention to the graduated spectra. Traditionally speaking, musicians have employed graduated spectra in the domains of pitch and time but not in the areas of loudness, timbre, or location. For this reason, only pitch and time have been included in our seven basic spectra as graduated scales. However, there may be unexplored territory in the realms of loudness, timbre, and location as graduated spectra.

I will refer to the expressive spectra of pitch as a graduated scale as *pitch proportionality* and the expressive spectra of time as a graduated scale as *temporal proportionality*. These are the sixth and seventh spectra of our basic list. Both pitch proportionality and temporal proportionality progress from simple ratio relationships at the low energy polarity to complex ratio relationships at the high energy polarity.

The Seven Basic Spectra of Musical Expression

Spectrum Type	Spectrum Name	Low Energy Pole	High Energy Pole
Gradated	Pitch	Low	High
Gradated	Loudness	Soft	Loud
Gradated	Timbre	Simple, Mellow, Pure	Complex, Bright, Rich
Gradated	Location	Distant, Peripheral	Close, Centered
Gradated	Time	Long	Short
Graduated	Pitch Proportionality	Strong, Simple	Weak, Complex
Graduated	Temporal Proportionality	Strong, Simple	Weak, Complex

- *The Dance of Musical Elements* -

What Are Musical Elements?

I use the term *musical element* or *musical idea* to very broadly refer to any position on one of the seven spectra or any combination of positions on one or more of the seven spectra. Musical elements are the building blocks that we use as composers. Throughout the book we will explore various musical elements such as *chords*, *scales*, *intervals*, *rhythms*, *dynamics*, *melodies*, and *structures*. Each of these defines various positions on the seven spectra and as a result creates unique musical expressions. As we go through these musical elements, we will listen to and explore what combinations of positions on the seven basic spectra produce what results in our art. In this way, we will gradually develop the ability to translate our expressive inspirations into the realm of sound where they can be shared and enjoyed.

Relationships Between Musical Elements

The seven basic spectra outline some of the fundamental ways that sound expresses musical qualities. As composers and musical artists, it is our task to combine these elements just so to create the expression we desire. We use musical elements as colors to paint pictures, as words to write stories, as the movements and characters of a dance.

Music is a relational kind of art. Musical expression is derived from the meaning of connection and disconnection. Therefore, as composers we must seek to understand, not just the musical elements, but how they relate to each other to form new and more complex expressions.

Musical Compositions

Pieces of music or *musical compositions* consist of musical elements combined together and sequenced into a narrative series. In this narrative, complex system, musical elements form two basic relationships – connection and disconnection. Elements that are similar feel connected, while those that are different seem disconnected.

Stasis and Change

As our narrative of musical expression unfolds, we may choose, as musical creators, to move our music in the direction of *stasis*, which can be defined as the similarity of musical elements over time, or *change*, the dissimilarity or difference between musical elements over time.

The Spectrum of Change

Change can be considered an expressive spectrum in its own right – a kind of super-spectrum based on the relationships between the foundational seven over time. Greater change or variation creates a high energy expression, while greater adherence to stasis creates a low energy expression.

Motifs and Themes

A *motif* or *theme* is a musical element (or idea) that is repeated throughout a musical piece, often in different forms or with variations. A motif usually refers to a simpler, shorter idea, whereas a theme is generally more complex and longer but the general concept is the same.[1]

1. If you are familiar with the concept of measures, a motif might last for one measure or very often less than a single measure whereas a theme generally extends for several measures. See *Measures* on page 89.

- *Three Tools of Musical Analysis* -

If this is your first pass through the book, you might consider skipping the next two sections and continuing on with *Four Roles in the Ensemble* on page 56. You also might elect to read over the next two sections now just to familiarize yourself with the concepts they present and then head back for another reading of these sections later on.

Throughout this book, we will call upon a set of three basic tools that will help us to understand and dissect the meaning of various musical elements. These analytical tools, in no particular order, are – *common expression*, *balance*, and *context*.

Common Expression

Each musical element consists of a position or combination of positions on the seven spectra. We will continually be deepening our understanding of what positions and what combinations of positions translate into what musical expressions. One way we will accomplish this is by looking at specific examples of musical elements and then listening to and experimenting with the expressions they create. However, the number of possible musical elements is infinite or nearly so, and we cannot possibly go through all the conceivable variations of the seven spectra. So it is necessary to have a framework to extrapolate predications about the way musical elements will sound based on what we know.

One basic tool we can use for this purpose is the principle of *common expression*, which says that musical elements with similar positions on the seven spectra will create similar expressions. When we explore the expression of any one example of a musical element, there will often be similar imaginable elements that you will be able to make inferences about. To make these connections is essential for comprehending the full implications of our study here.

Balance

Some musical elements that we may not like on their own may sound wonderful in combination with other elements. If musical elements are like the ingredients of a recipe, then some elements may be comparable to flour, baking soda, or cornstarch – things that we would not consume by themselves but only in combination with other ingredients.

Most music balances higher energy elements with lower energy elements creating an overall expression that is more moderate with movements toward one side or the other throughout the piece. Occasionally composers seek to create more extreme expressions and as a result need to use more extreme elements with less counterbalancing elements to produce their intended artistic expression.

When we are putting together different elements into our musical creations, we must consider that elements that would be too energetic for our purposes by themselves may be balanced with other low energy elements to create a result that balances into the expressive area we desire. Likewise, elements that would be too low energy by themselves may be balanced with other high energy elements to produce the effect we want.

This paradigm opens up a variety of options for us as musical creators. We can combine a diverse array of both extremely high energy elements and extremely low energy elements. Or we may combine a variety of relatively moderate elements. We may use high energy elements in one of the seven spectra while balancing the overall expression with other low energy elements in the other spectra. For example, we may have highly energetic pitch proportionality with low energy temporal proportionality. We may then change which spectra are using high or low energy elements to rebalance the energy of the music, creating new and interesting expressions.

Context

Whenever we are studying the expression of a musical element, we must consider the *context* in which we are hearing that musical element. For example, we may study the musical expression of a group of pitches played together. To consider the context we must ask questions like: "What timbre are the pitches being played with?" "What volume levels are the pitches being played at?" "Were any pitches heard before or after this particular group?" All of these factors may influence the expression of the effect we are seeking to study.

For our purposes in this method of analysis, we may think of the musical context as the other musical elements and positions on the seven spectra that are heard in conjunction with the element at hand. When we listen to music, we hear the expression of all the musical elements of a piece and their interactive relationships with one another. This means that when we study a particular element we must consider what other elements or relationships might be contributing to the overall expression that we experience. Sometimes we may be able to study elements in relative isolation. However, we will also look at how elements behave in complex musical systems of several different elements. Whatever the context, we must not mistake the expression of a particular piece of music for the expression of one element in that piece.

To truly become acquainted with the expression of a musical element, one must hear the element in many different contexts to understand all the interactions and potential variations of that element. For this reason, I will offer diverse examples to provide the best opportunity to get to know the various musical elements we will be discussing. However, I encourage you to continue this process of familiarizing yourself with musical elements through your own experimentation and careful observation of the musical elements in different musical works (whether your own or the works of others).

- Musical Centers and Gravity -

Original and Derivative Centers

To have proportionality, we need to have a graduated spectrum, and a graduated spectrum has units. Whatever value represents one unit on a graduated spectrum can be called an *original center*. Values that have a strong proportional relationship with an original center may be called *derivative centers.*

For example, later in the book we will introduce the concept of a *beat*, the reoccurring pulse of a piece of music that makes us feel a sense of rhythm.[1] It is what we might tap our foot to as we listen to music. The beat is an example of an original center. The composer of a piece of music will choose how long a beat lasts, and based on that length of time many other rhythms become possible through the creation of proportional relationships to the beat. In this way, the beat becomes the unit of measurement for all lengths of time in music. Thus, the value that represents one unit on the graduated scale, in this case the value given to one beat on the spectrum of time, becomes the original center. Durations of time that have the strongest proportional relationships to the beat, perhaps the length of time of two beats or half a beat to give just a couple of examples, could then be considered derivative centers.

In music, original centers are chosen by the composer both in the realm of pitch and the realm of time. These centers then act as reference points for all the proportional relationships in the music. Based on the choice of the composer to use a set of original centers, various derivative centers are implied.

Both original and derivative centers are, by definition, positions of low energy because they create strong proportionality. Furthermore, original centers are the positions of the lowest energy possible on a given spectrum. Centers are used as positions of rest and stability in a composition. A musical center is like a metaphorical home that composers venture away from as they create more energetic expressions and return to as they create less energetic expressions. Music is always in a constant flow of moving toward or away from various centers.

1. *Beat and Tempo*, page 86

Musical Gravity

As a pitch gets closer to a center without matching it exactly, we experience, more and more intensely, a "pull" or "wanting" for the pitch to move to the center. A similar phenomenon occurs with positions in time, where we may experience a desire or expectation to hear a certain sound at a certain point in time. I use the term *musical gravity* to describe these expressions in both the realm of pitch and time. The analogue of gravity can be a helpful way of thinking about musical relationships.

Let's imagine that you are in a space ship traveling toward a planet. As you approach the planet, the force or pull of gravity that you experience increases. In the musical realm, as a pitch or position in time gets closer to a center, the subjective experience of musical gravity intensifies. We can also imagine that if we made the planet more massive, the force of gravity would also increase. In the musical realm, this is comparable to the effect of a *stronger center*, in other words, a center with a stronger proportional relationship to the original center.

The Principle of Musical Gravity

Just as physical gravity increases with proximity to a massive object, musical gravity increases with proximity to a center. Just as physical gravity increases the more massive the nearby object, musical gravity increases with the strength of the nearby center.

By creating centers in our music, we set up various pathways of motion through pitch and time. Certain pitches seem to *want* to move to others. Certain patterns of rhythm become expected and anticipated. These pathways dictate a natural manner in which our compositions might progress. As a composer, it is our choice whether we want to fulfill the expectation of following these pathways or contradict them. Both options create their own kinds of expressions that are worth exploring.

Tension and Resolution

Musical gravity describes the tendency to move from high energy expressions to low energy expressions. When a pitch or position in time lands on a center, a low energy expression is produced. When a pitch or position in time lands close to but not exactly on a center, a complex proportional relationship is created to the nearby center and as a result a high energy expression is produced.

In the musical community, the movement from high to low energy pitch proportionality is sometimes described in terms of *tension* and *resolution*. Tension represents the position of high energy, and resolution represents the movement into low energy. Tension represents the journey. Resolution represents the ending or completion of a story arc.

Listening to Expected and Unexpected Resolution

Listen to a short section of piano music that resolves in a natural and expected way, moving from high energy to low energy, on track 4 (disc 1). Notice the prolonged sense of tension that is held at the end of this section and finally released into resolution.

Listen to track 5 (disc 1) for a variation on this music where the ending moves in an unexpected direction, deviating from the natural path of resolution that we intuitively expect. This version does not finish or resolve on the original pitch center of the piece. This effect can be referred to as an *unexpected resolution*, in contrast to track 4 (disc 1), which would represent an *expected resolution*. We can feel that the unexpected resolution on track 5 (disc 1) still moves from high to low energy, but the low point is not as low as it could be. There is a remaining energy, or tension, or feeling of surprise right up to the very end. In contrast, the resolution on track 4 (disc 1) releases all the expressive energy of the music in a complete resolution to the center of pitch.

Simple and Complex Centrality

Sometimes, it is unclear or ambiguous what pitches or points in time are central or primary in their centrality. These cases of ambiguity produce a sense of complexity and contribute a great deal of the expressive depth of music. As we move forward, we will make the distinction between *simple* and *complex centrality*. Simple centrality refers to situations where the primary center is clear and other centers have strong relationships to the primary center, thus aligning the whole system toward a single center. Complex centrality describes a system where multiple centers interact, compete, or align the system toward multiple unrelated places. We will examine how these situations come to be in music and what the expressive effects are of both these dynamics.

- Four Roles in the Ensemble -

Ensembles and Parts

A musical work can either be played by a single musician or by a group of performers. A group of performers who play music together may, in general language, be called an *ensemble*. Pieces that are written for one performer only are known as *solo works*. The music that a single instrument produces within an ensemble is known as a *part*. For example, in a rock band there might be a drum part, a bass part, and a guitar part. In some cases, multiple performers may play the same part. For example, when an orchestra plays a composition, all the cellists may play the same cello part.

The Anatomy of the Composition

Each part within an ensemble serves a different function. Every player synergizes his or her efforts into the whole production. The different functions that parts may serve can be described in four distinct musical roles – the *melody*, the *harmony*, the *bass line*, and the *percussion*. All of these roles are commonly fulfilled in a single piece of music but do not have to be.

The harmony, bass line, and percussion collectively form the *accompaniment.* The melody serves as the musical foreground, while the accompaniment serves as the background. The melody is the centerpiece of the creation, but the accompaniment gives the melody context and the context is responsible for an equal share of the expressive power of music.

The melody and bass line are made up of only one pitch at a time. In contrast, the harmony very commonly uses multiple pitches at once. The percussion is characterized by the use of only non-pitched sounds. Though, many non-pitched sounds frequently occur at the same time in percussion parts.

The bass line of a piece contains the lowest pitch in the music at any given time. The pitch and rhythm[1] of the bass line establish a foundation for the rest of the composition. The harmony then creates further relationships that play out over the bass line and likewise percussion parts develop specifically the rhythmic relationships of the music. Over this tapestry, the melody sits surrounded by these contextual elements, supported by them.

Track 6 (disc 1) plays an example of a musical piece that incorporates all of the four roles described here. Listen to track 7 (disc 1) to hear the melody of this piece in isolation. Listen to track 8 (disc 1) to hear just the accompaniment. Listen to tracks 9 through 11 (disc 1) to hear the bass line, harmony, and percussion, respectively, in isolation.

1. *Rhythm*, page 86

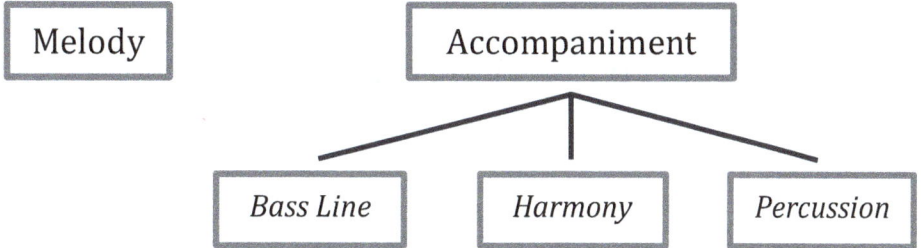

Background Melodies

Notice that the flute part in track 6 (disc 1) sounds very much like a melody. It contains only one note at a time progressing in a narrative series much as a melody normally would. You can listen to the flute part of this piece in isolation on track 12 (disc 1). However, the flute part in this composition is clearly part of the background not the foreground. It is part of the accompaniment, not the true or primary melody. We can call these kinds of melodies *background* or *secondary melodies,* in contrast to *foreground* or *primary melodies.*

Three Textures

There are three terms that describe the presence and role of melody or accompaniment parts in music – *monophonic, homophonic,* and *polyphonic.* Monophonic music or monophony comprises only a single melody with no accompaniment. Homophonic music or homophony is defined as melody with accompaniment. Finally, polyphonic music or polyphony uses multiple, simultaneous melodies. The term polyphony is also interchangeable with the term *counterpoint.* Collectively these descriptions are thought of as *musical textures.* These categories describe the general landscape of parts that are participating in a musical piece.

The Four Roles in Solo Works

Some instruments, such as the piano, guitar, and harp, are particularly well suited for playing alone because they can play both a melody and an accompaniment at the same time. The ability to play both melody and accompaniment simultaneously is somewhat rare among instruments. Many instruments can only play one note at a time. These instruments must either play melodies, bass lines, or form groups of multiple instruments to produce harmony.

- Five Musical Activities -

There are five primary activities that occur in the creation of music – *composition, performance, improvisation, arranging,* and *production.*

Composition

To *compose* means to write original music. Composition involves creating as well as editing musical ideas. Composing might also involve writing original music down as sheet music so that we can remember what we composed and share it with others. In the realm of language, composition is similar to writing a story.

Performance

To *perform* means to play music on an instrument or to sing. Performance includes playing both your own music and music written by someone else. Performance is similar to telling a story aloud to an audience.

Improvisation

To *improvise* means to create original music while simultaneously performing it. In the realm of language, improvisation is similar to conversational speaking. In a conversation, we are deciding what to say and speaking at the same time. In a similar way, improvisers are deciding what to play and playing it at the same time.

Arranging

To *arrange* music means to create parts for all the different instruments that are to play a piece of music. Often when a piece is composed, only the primary melody and a basic outline of the accompaniment are written. In the process of arranging, all the details are filled in. Arranging can happen through a formal process where every note that each musician plays is written out or it can happen in an informal, improvisational process where the performers fill in certain details for themselves as they play while sticking to the main structure of the composition. Traditionally, larger ensembles, such as jazz big bands and orchestras, use a formal arranging process whereas smaller jazz, rock, or pop groups use more of an informal arranging process.

To arrange music can also mean to take an existing piece of music and create a variation of it. In this type of arranging process, the essential features of the melody and accompaniment remain the same but the music may be changed in any number of ways. The piece might be played by a new ensemble of instruments. For example, a piece written for a rock band could be arranged for orchestra. Or, perhaps, the music may be restructured so that the first part of the piece is played second, while the second part is played first. In other cases, several pieces of music might be combined together to form something new.

Production

To produce music means to create a computer audio file or other means of reproducing a single performance of a musical piece again and again such as a tape, vinyl record, or CD. Producing includes many activities such as recording, synthesis, mixing, and mastering.[1] Production deals with creating sounds with computers and capturing sounds in our environment. Production is the last step of the creation process where a performance is solidified into a fixed form.

1. These will all be covered in Chapter Eleven. See *Creating and Capturing Sounds* on page 321 as well as *Mixing and Mastering* on page 326.

- Three Methods of Writing Music -

There are three primary ways that original, musical ideas are created – by *experimentation*, by *theoretical understanding*, and by *auditory imagination* or as we commonly refer to it by *ear*.

Experimentation

Experimentation means that we don't know the outcome before we test it. This is a critically important activity to pursue as musical creators. We must try things that are outside of our predictive powers and observe the results. Experimentation does not mean a randomly directed blunder into the unknown but rather a carefully approached and observed testing of the content outside of our comprehension. Experiments will frequently go wrong. This is expected and should not dissuade you from the pursuit, as a poor result is just as valuable to the experimenter as a good result. It is essential to focus not on the outcome of the experiment in and of itself but rather on what can be learned from the outcome.

Especially when experimentation is informed by theoretical understanding and ear training, this approach may yield some unexpectedly exciting musical ideas. An important subcategory in the approach of experimentation is synthesis. We may have two or more known effective musical elements, but how do these elements sound in combination? These types of inquiries are valuable areas to explore.

- ❖ There is, of course, a time and a place for experimentation. There are situations where we want to rely on our skills and knowledge to produce a high quality result, with confidence and assurance in the outcome. In the box *Two Creative Mindsets* on page 202, I'll introduce the distinction between an *experimenter's mindset* and a *performer's mindset*, which addresses this point in more detail.

Theoretical Understanding

Theoretical understanding can be cultivated by learning from experiments and generalizing the results of each test into patterns. This process does not have to be accomplished alone, but rather you may draw upon what humanity as a whole has learned thus far about the inner workings of the marvel we call music. When theoretical understanding develops, a composer, improviser, or musical creator of any sort has the ability to predict the expression of music based on its characteristics, in other words, the elements that comprise the content of the music. This approach relies on knowing what the expression of given musical elements are and how new expressions can be created by combining different elements together. Theoretical understanding can also give us the ability to predict the expressive effect of transforming a musical element in a particular way.

Auditory Imagination or Writing by Ear

To write music by ear means that we can mentally imagine the sound we desire to create in our work and we have the ability to translate that imagination into the musical terminology of notes and rhythms so that the music in our head can be performed in the physical world. This approach is distinctly broken into two processes. The first is the imagination of musical sounds. The second is the translation of those sounds into musical performance or notation. In either endeavor, practice will enhance skill. Imagination may be inspired intuitively, through listening to the music of others, or through the desire to create an expression and an ability to form an imagination of sound that correlates to that expression. To *train your ear* or to become skillful in *ear training*, one must go about the process of learning what musical elements sound like so that upon hearing a musical element we can recognize and name it. Thus, when we hear these elements in our imagination, we will be able to name and, thus, creatively use these sounds.

Going Forward

All of these methods will be discussed further in later sections of the book. Information will be provided to help you cultivate the skills that are relevant to each of these areas – experimentation, theoretical understanding, and auditory imagination or ear training.

Summary for Group One
A Theoretical Model of the Musical Experience

What is music?

An expression of meaning that relies heavily on the physical properties of sound and their basic interpretation.

What is sound?

The flux of air pressure or density.

What is meaning (at least for our purposes)?

A fundamental source of meaning is the duality of commonality and difference.

Seven Basic Spectra of Musical Expression

Four Perceptual Elements of Sound
1. Pitch —————— Frequency
2. Loudness —————— Amplitude
3. Timbre —— Harmonic Composition
4. Location
5. Time
6. Pitch Proportionality
7. Temporal Proportionality

Stiffer and less massive objects vibrate at higher frequencies.

Harmonic Series

Objects vibrate at whole number multiples of their natural frequency.

Perceptual Properties — Physical Properties

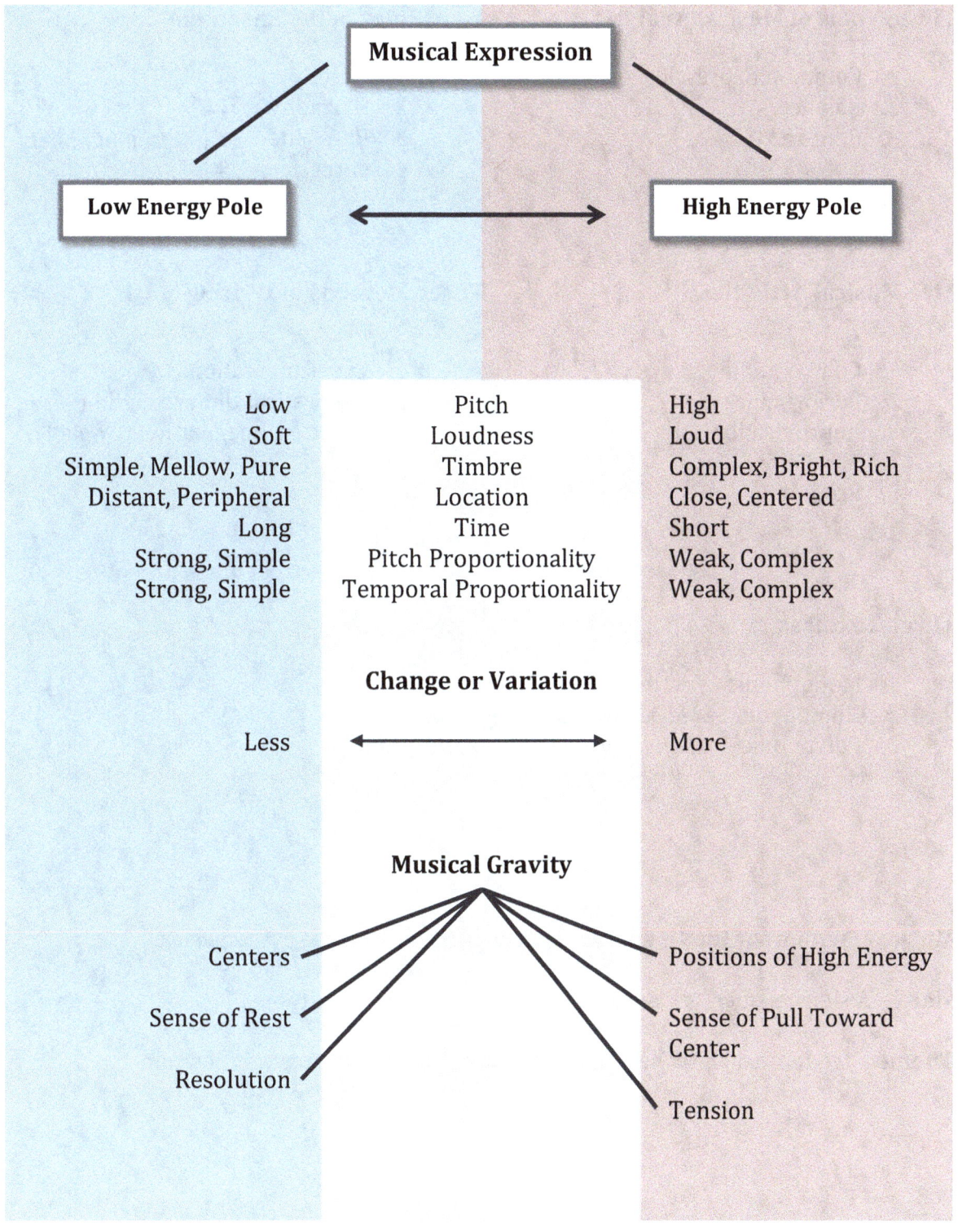

Three Tools of Musical Analysis

1. Common Expression
2. Balance
3. Context

Four Roles in the Ensemble

1. Melody
2. Harmony ⎤
3. Bass Line ⎥ *Accompaniment*
4. Percussion ⎦

Five Musical Activities

1. Composition
2. Performance
3. Improvisation
4. Arranging
5. Production

Three Methods of Writing Music

1. Experimentation
2. Theoretical Understanding
3. Auditory Imagination (by ear)

Three Textures

1. Monophonic – *Just a melody*
2. Homophonic – *Melody with accompaniment*
3. Polyphonic – *Multiple melodies at the same time*

Musical Element or Idea – Combination of positions on the seven spectra

Motif – A short element or idea used repeatedly in a composition

Theme – Moderate length element or idea used repeatedly in a composition

Group Two

An Introduction to the Musical System

Chapter Three
The Basics of Pitch

- Pitch and Note Names -

Note Names

A pitch is a position on the spectrum from to low to high sounds.[1] In this text, I'll also use the term *note* as a synonym for the term pitch. We use a repeating series of twelve *note names* to describe different pitches. The note names are easily visualized on a piano keyboard. On the keyboard, the white keys are named with the letters A through G. After G, we begin the sequence again starting at A. The notes played with the white keys of the piano are called *natural notes*.

The keys farther to the left produce lower pitches. The keys farther to the right produce higher pitches.

1. *Pitch and Frequency*, page 30

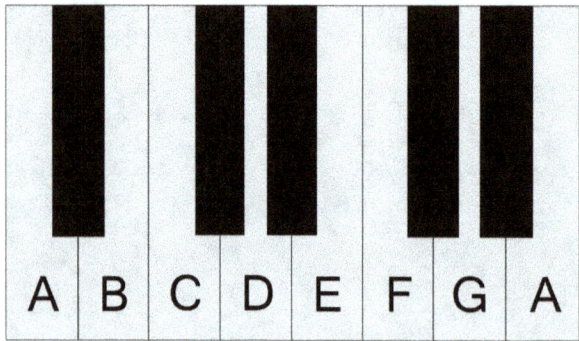

Lower ⟷ *Higher*

Flats and Sharps

The black keys are named with *sharps* (written as #) and *flats* (written as b). The term *sharp* means to be higher in pitch. *Flat* means to be lower in pitch.

Notice how in the diagram below the black key labeled A# is directly to right of the white key A. It is also labeled Bb because it is directly to the left of the white key B. All the black keys are named in this manner, with one name using a sharp and the letter directly to the left of the black key and one name using a flat and the letter directly to the right of the black key.

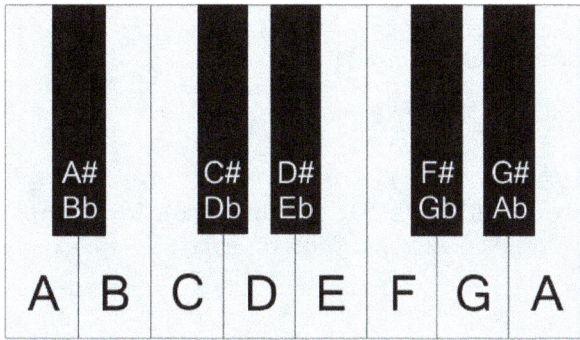

This pattern of notes repeats all the way across the piano from left to right.

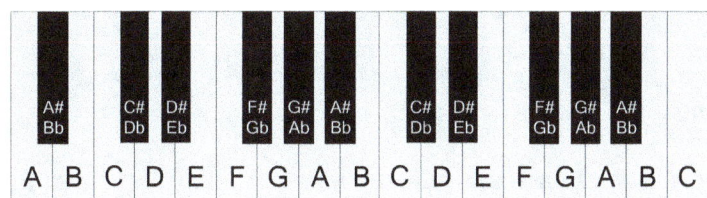

and so on...

> ### Does All Music Use the Same System of Notes?
>
> The twelve-note system described here is used ubiquitously in western music and is common to all western instruments. However, there are also other systems in different cultures and traditions around the world that use other pitches not present in Western music. Classical Indian music and Indonesian gamelan music are two great examples of this. If you are interested in hearing the differences, I recommend listening to some music from these traditions. Various types of experimental music also go outside the boundaries of pitches presented here. Often, other musical pitch systems create finer gradations of pitch than the western twelve-note system. This kind of music is therefore sometimes referred to as *microtonal* music.
>
> ❖ In Chapter Five, I will present a piece of music that ventures outside the twelve-note pitch system in the box *A Composition Outside Equal Temperament*, found on page 134. You can listen to this piece of music on track 48 (disc 1).

If this is your first pass through this material, you might consider jumping ahead now to the next section *A Simple Technique for Finding Notes* on page 69.

> ### Enharmonic Spellings
>
> One result of this naming system is that some sounds can be represented by multiple note names. For example, F# and Gb are two names that represent the same sound. Notes like these are considered *enharmonic*, which is just a fancy word meaning that the notes sound the same but are named differently. Another way that musicians sometimes talk about these situations is by saying that notes can be *spelled* differently or can have a different *spelling*. The concept of spelling refers to the sharps, flats, and letters that we use to name a sound.

> ### Getting a Bit More Advanced...
>
> Looking at the situation on a deeper level, we can actually add any number of flats or sharps to any letter A through G to produce a note name. For example, the sound of an A could also be called a *B double flat*. Believe it or not, using two flats or two sharps in this manner is not too uncommon. We could also describe the sound of a B as a *C flat* or describe the sound of an F as an *E sharp*. In every case, we simply start from the given letter of the alphabet in a note name and move one step up in pitch for every sharp and one step down in pitch for every flat. Notice that these note names break the rule about naming black keys on the piano with flats and sharps while naming white keys without them. There are reasons for using terms like B double flat or C flat that we will discuss later on.[1] I mention it now just to get you used to how the note naming system works.
>
> 1. For some examples of where these kinds of note names would be used, see *A Note on Note Naming (Scales Edition)* on page 177 or *The Whole Diminished Seventh Chord* on page 398.

You can also specify that a note has no flats or sharps by referring to it as a natural. For example, an *A natural* is an A with no flats or sharps. This, once again, may be useful later on.

All of these potential variations can be included in the concept of spelling. The spelling of a note consists of what letter is used in the name, if the note is a natural or not, and, if not, how many sharps or flats are included.

- A Simple Technique for Finding Notes -

Reference Points for Locating Notes on the Piano

Notice how the black keys are found in groups of two or three. Each of these groups can be used as a visual and tactile landmark in the musical terrain of notes. Every C is found directly to the left of a group of two black keys, and every F is found directly to the left of a group of three black keys. These are good references points to remember for locating notes on the piano.

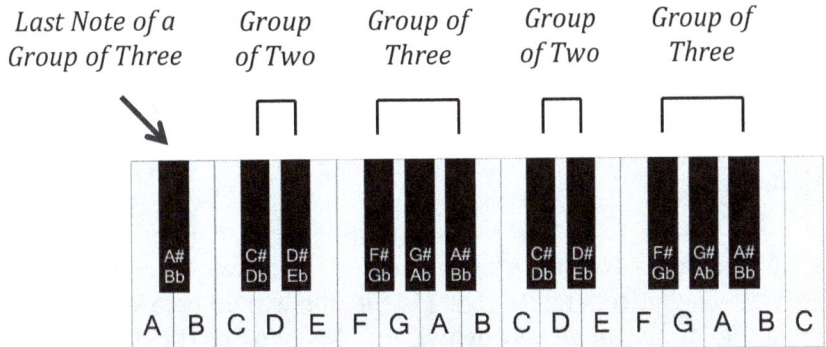

Locating Any Note With a Reference Point

Using C or F as a reference point, you can identify any note by going forward or backward in the alphabet. For example, if you want to find an E, start by locating a C. The white key to the right of C will be D. And the white key to right of D will be E. Alternatively, you can find an F as a reference point and simply go to the left one time on the white keys. This will also lead you to an E.

Practice for Speed	**Going Beyond References**
Play a few keys at random and see how quickly you can name the note you are playing.	Eventually, try to memorize where all the notes are individually. But if you are not yet familiar with this system of naming notes, reference points can help you learn in the beginning.

- Octaves -

An *octave* represents one cycle through each of the unique note names.

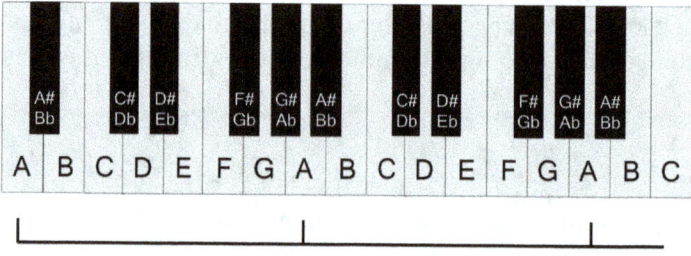

One Octave   *Two Octaves*   *and so on...*

Each octave contains thirteen notes, with the starting note of the octave being repeated one time. For example, the first octave (from left to right) in the illustration below contains two As and one of every other note. The second octave below contains two Ebs (or D#s) and one of every other note. The third octave contains two Gs and one of every other note.

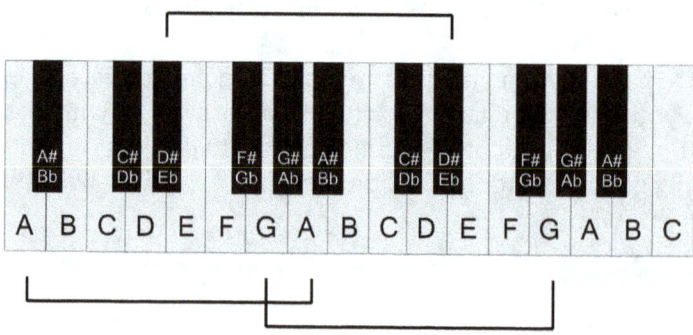

A full-sized, 88-key piano is made up of seven and a quarter octaves, starting with a low note of A and ending with a high note of C. Most notes in music are contained within this range.

Distinguishing Between the Many Instances of Each Note Name

Because of this naming system, the piano actually has between seven and eight different instances of each note. As you can imagine this can get a little confusing.

One common way to differentiate between the many instances of each note name is to reference *middle C*. Middle C is the fourth C to appear on a full-sized, 88-key piano. By establishing middle C as one particular C, you can refer to notes as being above or below middle C. For example, one could say, "I'm playing the first A above middle C."

A comprehensive naming system can be created by placing numbers after note names to indicate which octave the note falls in. For example, as the fourth C on the piano, middle C is labeled C4 in what is called *scientific pitch notation*. The C above middle C is labeled C5. All the notes between C4 and C5 are then labeled with a four. In this way we can break up the entire piano keyboard into octaves with corresponding numbers.

Notice that the first three notes on the piano, which are below the first C or C1, are labeled with a zero.

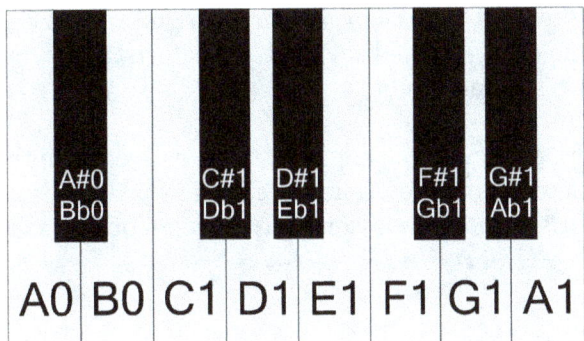

To Make Things More Confusing...

Confusingly, some systems name middle C as C3, with all the other octaves shifted accordingly. Some products that use *MIDI* technology[1] will name middle C as C3, while others name it C4. This is good to simply be aware of and check up on. The scientific notation standard (which names middle C as C4) is probably your best bet in conversational language, however.

1. *MIDI Data and MIDI Controllers*, page 324

Why C?

Middle C is the universal reference point in western music. One might wonder why the letter C is used for this special position. After all, it seems logical that A as the first letter of the alphabet would be chosen for this role.

It is perhaps helpful to know that our musical system was not designed all at once but rather has been created out of centuries of traditions and developments. When the letters of the alphabet were first assigned to pitches centuries ago, there may have been a logical reason why a certain pitch was deemed A or it may have been arbitrary. The full story isn't known. In the current musical system, C is the first note of the C major scale,[1] which contains all the natural notes, and middle C is also literally in the middle of the grand staff.[2] The scales and the notation system we now use, however, were developed gradually over time and came into their modern form well after the letters of the alphabet were associated with pitches. So it seems the letter C gained special importance over time as a byproduct of these developments.

While we are on the topic, it is also worthwhile to mention that middle C is, in fact, *not* in the center of a full-sized, 88-key piano keyboard. The center is actually between the E4 and F4 keys.

1. *Scales*, page 82
2. *The Grand Staff*, page 77

Double Meanings and Other Octave Lingo

The term octave can refer to both the range between two notes of the same note name or to the actual pair of notes with the same name. For instance, if a guitarist plays an A4 and an A5 at the same time (or one after the other), I could say that the guitarist is playing an octave. In this case, I am referring to an octave as a pair of notes.

In contrast, if I said, "There are seven and a quarter octaves are on this piano," I would be referring to an octave as a range of notes. It is also common to talk about playing notes "in" a higher or lower octave. This is another way of referring to an octave as a range of notes.

The following box and related principle box build off of the material in Chapters One and Two. Skip this content for now, if you are starting your reading of this book at Chapter Three.

The Strong Proportionality of the Octave

An octave represents a doubling in frequency, such that moving a pitch up one octave will double the frequency of the partials[1] in that note. Going the other direction, moving a pitch down one octave will halve the frequency of the partials in that note. As an example, the fundamental frequency of A4 is 440 hz. The fundamental frequency of A5 is 880 hz, and the fundamental frequency of A3 is 220 hz.

Notes that are an octave apart possess a 1:2 ratio between their fundamental frequencies. This is the lowest possible ratio that can be created between different frequencies. The only possible way to create a stronger proportionality is to make a 1:1 relationship, which would describe two instances of the same note.

The extremely strong proportionality[2] of the octave gives it a unique position in the musical system. Listen to the sound of an octave now on track 44 (disc 1). The notes C4 and C5 are played first from low to high, then from high to low, and finally at the same time. Musically speaking, we describe these variations as playing the octave in an *ascending* order, playing the octave in a *descending* order, and playing the octave *harmonically*.

Notice how the octave sounds. The effect could be described as harmonious, stable, and open.

Because of the strong proportionality of the octave, the notes in an octave are often felt to be very related. This is part of the reason that we label notes separated by an octave with the same note names.

1. Meaning any frequency that is part of a sound. See *The Difference Between Harmonics, Partials, and Overtones* on page 41.
2. See *Seven Basic Spectra of Musical Expression* on page 47 and especially *Strong or Weak Proportionality* on page 49.

Pitches labeled with the same note name share similar expressions and properties in a given musical situation.

- Notation Basics -

Written music is called music *notation*. Music is written down or notated on *staves* (plural of *staff*). Each staff contains five horizontal lines. Notes can be placed on lines or in spaces between lines. Each new line or space represents a new letter in the alphabet. Notes that are higher in pitch are written higher on the staff. For example, in the diagram below the note on the left is higher than the note on the right.

Notes are written with circles called *note heads*. Most notes are also written with a line connected to the note head called a *stem*.

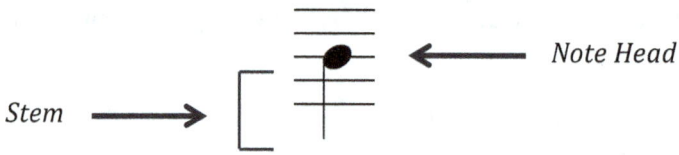

Stems Up or Down?

Notes written on the third line of the staff or higher are written with the stem below the note head (sometimes referred to as "stems down"), and those below the third line of the staff are written with the stem above the note head (sometimes referred to as "stems up").

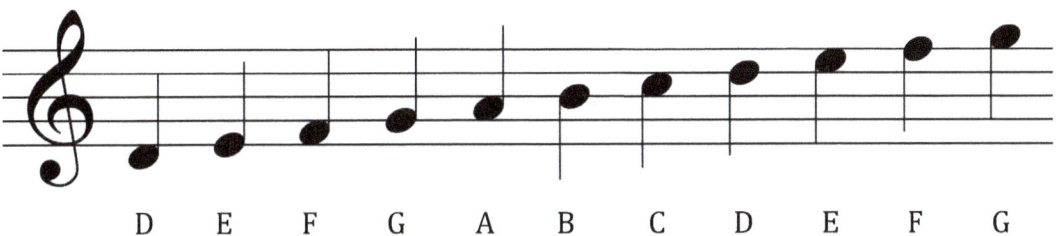

D E F G A B C D E F G

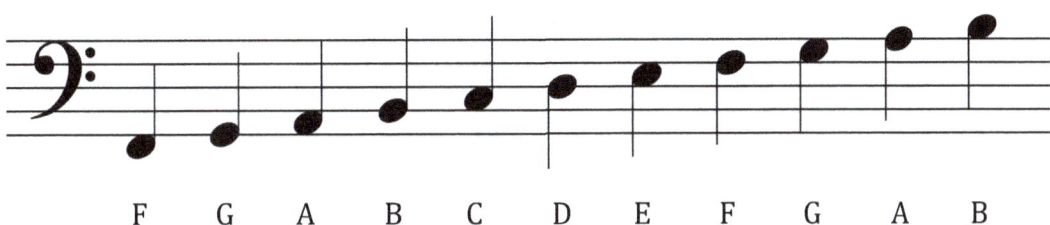

F G A B C D E F G A B

The Treble and Bass Clefs

Notice the sign at the far left hand side of the first staff above. This is called the *treble clef* or the *G clef*. Clefs tell us what range of notes our staff covers. The spiral of the treble clef circles around the second line from the bottom in the staff to indicate that the second line is a G, specifically the first G above middle C or G4.

The second staff above uses a bass clef or *F clef*. The two dots of the F clef center around the fourth line of the staff from the bottom, which represents the F below middle C or F3.

Getting Familiar With the Notes on the Staff

Play each note on the staves above and notice the following things:

1. The sound and pitch of the note
2. The name of the note
3. Where the note is located on your instrument
4. Where the note is located on the staff

Where Did the Clefs Come From?

Originally the G clef was a stylized way to write the letter G and the F clef was a way to write the letter F. I would have never guessed.

Notating Sharps and Flats

To write a sharp or flat on the staff, place the respective sharp or flat symbol directly to the left of the note you intend to describe. On the staff below, a Bb is written on the left and a F# is written on the right.

Flats are written like this. →  ← *Sharps are written like this.*

Music is read left to right, with the notes on the left being played first and the notes on the right being played last.

Groups of notes that are played at the same time may be shown with multiple note heads on one stem. For example, in the notation below the notes F, A, and C are played at the same time.

Notes that are played at the same time and are vertically adjacent on the staff are offset from one another to enhance readability by preventing the note heads from crowding into each other. An example of this situation is shown below. Although one note appears slightly to the right of the other, both notes are played at the same time.

Ledger Lines

Ledger lines are short lines that can be added above the top line of a staff or below the bottom line of a staff. These lines act as an extension of the regular five-line staff.

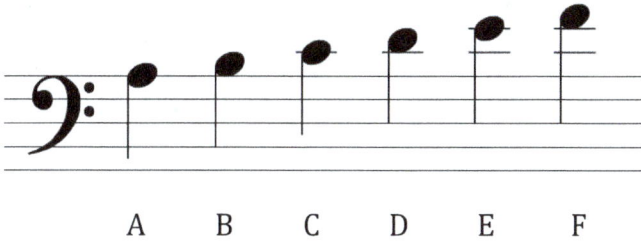

The Grand Staff

The piano and other instruments with large ranges are written on the *grand staff*, which combines two staves together, usually one with a treble clef and one with a bass clef. Beware, however, that sometimes a grand staff will use a different combination of clefs so it is important to check and make sure that you reading music notation with the correct clef in mind!

In piano music, the music written on the lower staff is generally played by the left hand, and the music written on the upper staff is generally played by the right hand.

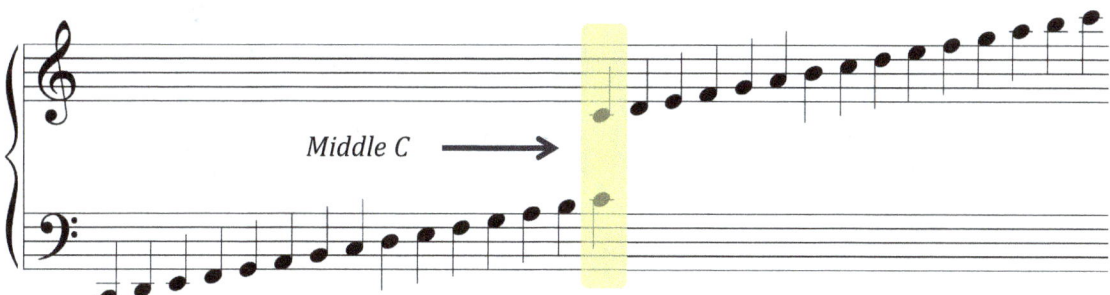

Middle C in the Middle

Middle C is literally in the middle of the grand staff. It is written with one ledger line above the staff when using bass clef or one ledger line below the staff when using treble clef.

Ledger Lines Between the Staves

It is also possible to have multiple ledger lines extend between the upper and lower staves of the grand staff. For example, to the left, an F3 is written on the upper staff and a G4 is written on the lower staff. If this notation were for a piano piece, it would indicate that the F3 should be played by the right hand while the G4 would be played by the left hand. Note that despite how the music notation appears, the first note (F3) is indeed lower than the second note (G4).

- Chords and Chord Voicings -

What Are Chords?

Chords are groups of notes that sound good together or, at least, groups of notes that produce a certain useful effect from a composer's point of view. There are many different types of chords, each with a distinctive sound. A chord can also be called a *harmony*.

The chord notated and diagrammed below is called *C major*.

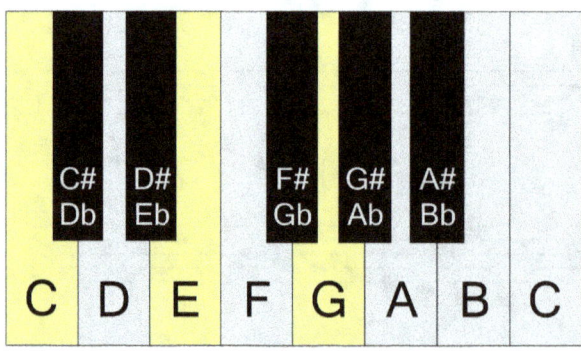

Triads

The C major chord is considered a *triad* because it has three notes. Triads are the most basic type of chord. Generally speaking, chords have at least three notes.

Listening to C Major

Listen to the sound of the C major chord on track 13 (disc 1) or alternatively play the notes of the C major chord on an instrument. Like the octave, the C major chord has a pleasant and mellow sound. You might notice that a three-note chord sounds a little fuller than an octave, which only contains two notes.

Chord Voicings

The C major chord contains the notes C, E, and G, but these notes may appear in any octave while maintaining the same basic sound of the C major chord. For example, in the chord below, I have moved the E one octave up from the original C major chord. Note that I am still playing the notes C, E, and G, but now they are in a different order.

The distribution of the notes of a chord into different octaves is called the *voicing* of the chord. Therefore, creating a variation in this manner can be described as creating a new voicing of the C major triad.

Notes with the same note names have similar musical properties.[1] This means that if one E sounds good in a C major chord, it is fair to assume all Es will sound good in a C major chord (at least to some extent). Based on this concept, we now can create a large number of variations on the original C major chord just by placing the notes of the chord in different octaves.

1. See *Common Expression* on page 52 and the principle box on page 73.

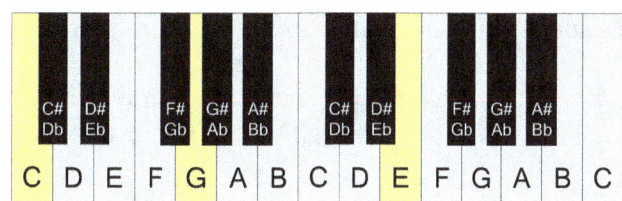

Listen to this new voicing of the C major chord on track 14 (disc 1) or play this voicing on an instrument.

Doubled Notes

Here another possibility is illustrated. In the voicing below, two different Cs have been included. This is commonly referred to as *doubling a note*, and is fair game in the world of voicings. In fact, we can include as many instances of a single note as we desire. For example, we might include three or more Cs in different octaves within a voicing of the C major chord.

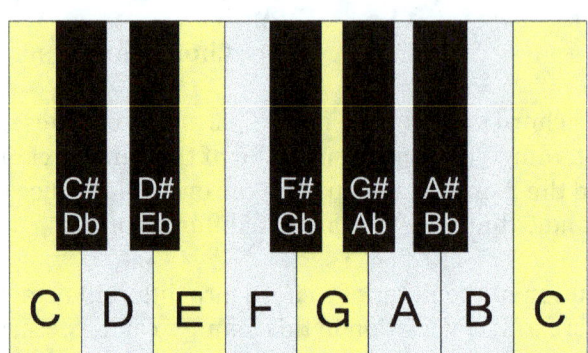

Listen to the C major chord with a doubled C as illustrated above on track 15 (disc 1) or play this voicing on an instrument.

Chord Patterns and Arpeggios

To increase the number of possible variations even further, we can consider the aspect of time. The notes of a chord can be played all at once or one after another. A chord voicing that is played in a specific way over time is called a *chord pattern*.

Arpeggios are a common type of chord pattern in which the notes of the chord are played one at a time from low to high or from high to low. For example, this is a C major arpeggio that moves from low to high.

Listen to this C major arpeggio on track 16 (disc 1) or play this arpeggio on an instrument.

Other Chord Patterns

The notation below describes another possibility. This is not an arpeggio because the notes of the C major chord are played out of order but this still is an effective sequence of notes in this chord.

Listen to this C major chord pattern on track 17 (disc 1) or play this pattern on an instrument.

Alberti Bass

This pattern – where the notes proceed from lowest to highest to middle and finally back to highest – is called an *Alberti bass.*

Sustain Pedal of a Piano

Note that on track 17 (disc 1) the *sustain pedal* of the piano is being held down. The sustain pedal is the most commonly used pedal on a piano. Most acoustic pianos have three pedals. The sustain pedal can be found on the right. Most electronic keyboards only have a sustain pedal and do not include the other two less frequently used pedals. The sustain pedal of a piano can be very useful in blending sounds together. Normally, when you release a key on the piano that note will stop sounding. However, when the sustain pedal is used, notes are allowed to continue to ring out long after each key is released. When the sustain pedal is held down over multiple notes, a smoothing out or blending effect is created.

In Conclusion

All of these variations could be the beginning of a harmony part based on the C major chord. As you can see, the possibilities are nearly infinite, and we have only talked about one chord. There exists a vast array of chords, each with a unique sound that can be transformed and shaped like we have done here with the C major chord.

Creating Chord Voicings and Patterns

Try creating some different variations of the C major chord. You can use any of the following techniques:
1. Putting notes in different octaves
2. Doubling notes
3. Playing notes at different times or in different orders
4. Using the sustain pedal to blend sounds together (if you are playing a piano)

Listen to each of your creations carefully, noticing how each change affects the sound of the chord. If you find something you like, I invite you to write it down so you can remember your discovery and come back to it.

- Scales -

What Are Scales?

Like chords, *scales* are groups of notes that sound good together or produce a certain useful effect. A scale may also be called a *key*. However, there is an important distinction between chords and scales. When a composer uses a chord in a piece of music, it is common and even expected that other notes outside of the chord will be played at the same time. This happens most frequently in the melody, but accompaniment parts can also include notes that are not in the current chord.

With scales, the assumption is that the composer will commit to being "in" a scale for an entire piece or at least for a section of a piece. This means the composer is using notes only from that scale to construct both the melody and the accompaniment. Composers might stick to this rule either absolutely or include a few exceptions.[1] So, if I say the popular song "Over the Rainbow" is in the key of Eb major, what I'm really saying is that this song only uses a certain set of notes that are related to Eb. You can think of scales as a palette of possibilities that composers draw from.

1. *Using Notes Outside of the Scale*, page 83

Diatonic and Chromatic

Once a composer has committed to being in a scale, all the notes in that scale are referred to as *diatonic* and all the notes outside of that scale are referred to as *chromatic*.

Seven Letters in a Scale

Most scales have seven notes. In every seven-note scale, you will find one of each of the seven letters used in music. Although they all contain the same letters, each scale has different flats and sharps assigned to those letters.

Compositions in C Major

All of the natural notes on the piano form a scale. It is the C major scale. For a piece to be in C major, it must use only C, D, E, F, G, A, and B (and no flats or sharps), but those notes could appear in any octave and in any order or combination.

The Tonal Center

Scales describe a set of note names, but they also describe a *tonal center*. The tonal center is the first note of the scale and it is the note that is used to name the scale. For example, the tonal center of the C major scale is the note C. The tonal center is the primary or original center of pitch in a composition or section of a composition.[1] All the other notes in a musical piece are heard in relation to the tonal center. If the pitches of a composition are like a solar system, the tonal center is like the sun. It is also the position in the scale that expresses the strongest sense of resolution.

1. *Musical Centers and Gravity*, page 54

Using Notes Outside of the Scale

In theory, a composition in a certain key uses only the notes in that key. In practice, composers frequently seek to push the boundaries and limitations of working within the framework of a scale. In some pieces, notes outside of the scale can be become just as common as the notes within the scale. In this context, scales become less of an exclusive group of notes the composer must choose from but rather a foundational set of starting points that can be moved away from or returned to at the composer's discretion to create certain musical effects.

❖ We will address this topic in detail in *Chapter Fourteen*. See page 412.

- A Simple Technique for Finding Chords -

Alternating Notes

You can learn many chords very quickly if you know one simple technique. Alternating notes in a scale will always form some type of chord. Because all the natural notes form a scale (specifically the C major scale), this means that alternating natural notes will form chords. Examine this picture of a C major chord on a piano. Notice how the chord starts on C, then skips a note, continues with E, skips a note, and finally ends with G.

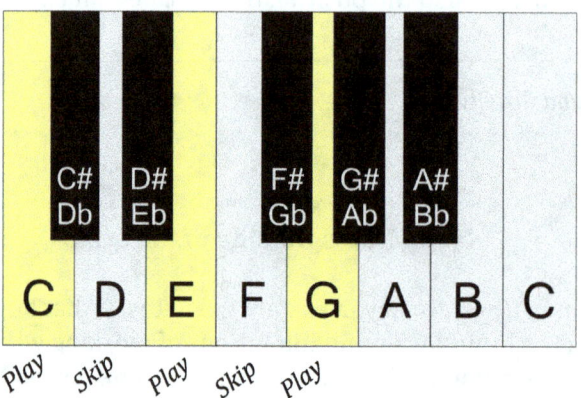

Listen to the Seven Triads of C Major

This process could be repeated starting on D to form a new chord consisting of the notes D, F, and A and again to produce a chord consisting of the notes E, G, and B. Using this alternating technique, we can construct a triad off of each of the white keys for a total of seven chords.

These are the seven triads available to us as composers in the C major scale. In other words, these are all of the three note chords that can be constructed with only natural notes.

Listen to each of these chords on track 18 (disc 1) or play them on an instrument. Notice how each chord has a different sound and flavor to it.

Creating Voicings and Patterns with the Seven Triads of C Major

If you would like, you can repeat the *Creating Chord Voicings and Patterns* activity[1] with any of the triads in C major. To find a chord on the piano:

1. Choose a white key to start on and hold it down.
2. Skip the next white key.
3. Hold down the following white key. This is the second note of your chord.
4. Skip the next white key.
5. The next key will be the third and final note of your chord.

And there you go! Now that you know the notes in your chord, you can experiment with moving these notes into different octaves and placing them in different orders to create new chord voicings and patterns.

I suggest that you do not start with the triad that begins on B (consisting of the notes B, D, and F). This is a more advanced type of chord and is more difficult to use effectively than the others. You might notice that this chord has a higher energy or more tense expression than the other chords do.

1. *Creating Chord Voicings and Patterns*, page 82

Chapter Four
The Basics of Rhythm and Dynamics

In Chapter Three, we began to examine our "musical system" or collective naming systems and basic concepts that we use as musicians to communicate with each other. We began this part of our journey in the domain of pitch. Now we will turn our attention to what happens when these pitches (with corresponding timbres and volume levels) are heard *over time*. This adds a whole different dimension to the way we perceive music – the dimension of *rhythm*. And with that added dimension comes a new domain of relationships, interactions, and expressions.

- Beat and Tempo -

Rhythm

Rhythm is the dimension of music that deals with the characteristics of time and, secondarily, though still significantly, loudness or volume. Musicians may also sometimes refer to *a rhythm* as a musical element or idea that specifies the timing and emphasis, in terms of loudness or volume, of a group of sounds.

The Beat

Music tends to align itself in time with a *beat* or *pulse*. This is what you tap your foot to when you are listening to a piece of music. This is what guides your body when you dance. Most fundamentally, the beat is a recurring increase in volume or loudness. In music, an increase in volume or loudness at a specific point in time is referred to as an *emphasis*.

Tempo

In a particular piece of music, each beat generally occurs after a consistent amount time. While there may be slight variations during the course of a composition, some amount of consistency is needed to "feel the beat."

Commonly, the beat occurs around 50 to 200 times every minute, with extreme possibilities outside of that. That is somewhere in the range of a beat once, twice, or maybe three times a second.

What we are describing here is *tempo*, the speed or frequency of the beat. Traditionally, the tempo of a piece of music or a section of music is notated with a *tempo marking* written in the Italian language. In modern times, it has also become common to write a numeric tempo marking in beats per minute (bpm).

Below is a table of common tempo markings and their corresponding descriptions in terms of beats per minute.

Tempo Markings

Italian Word	Translation	Approximate Beats Per Minute
Grave	Very slow and solemn	25-45
Largo	Very slow	40-60
Lento	Slow	45-60
Adagio	Slow, at ease	66-76
Andante	At a walking pace	76-108
Moderato	Moderate	108-120
Allegro	Fast, quick, and bright	120-168
Vivace	Fast, lively	168-176
Presto	Very fast	168-200

This is not a complete list of tempo markings, but this includes the most common terms that you may encounter.

Italian Phrases

Tempo markings are written in Italian. In fact, most phrases in music notation are written in Italian. This comes from Italy's history as a very influential musical center in the times of early classical music when the notation system we use today was being codified.

The Expression of Tempo

Time as a gradated spectrum increases in energy as lengths become shorter and decreases as the lengths become longer. Therefore, faster tempos produce higher energy expressions, and slower tempos produce lower energy expressions.

Track 19 (disc 1) and track 20 (disc 1) illustrate this difference in expression. Both tracks play exactly the same music except that track 20 is played at twice the tempo of track 19. Switch back and forth between listening to these tracks and see what expressive differences you notice.

❖ Defining the Seven Basic Spectra of Musical Expression, page 49

Notating Tempo Markings

Tempo markings are written above the staff. You can choose to use a traditional Italian tempo marking, a description in terms of beats per minute, or you may include both. To indicate a beats per minute marking, write the symbol for a note followed by an equals sign and the beats per minute of the given tempo. This is done in parentheses if also accompanied by a traditional Italian tempo marking, as shown below.

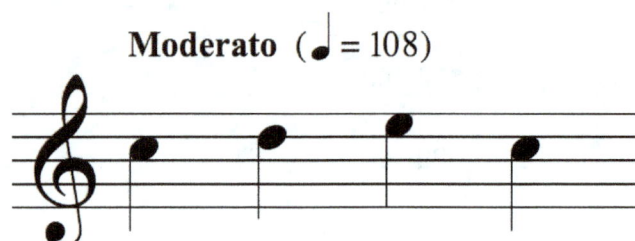

- Dynamics -

What Are Dynamics?

Dynamics deal with the volume or loudness of a section of music. In contrast to emphases, which describe an increase in volume at a specific moment in time, dynamics deal with an average volume over a period of time in a musical piece.

There are a number of symbols that indicate how loud a section of music should be played. These symbols are based on Italian words just like tempo markings. These original words, their translation in English, and their symbols are written on the following page.

Dynamic Markings

Italian Word	Translation	Symbol
Pianissimo	Very Soft	*pp*
Piano	Soft	*p*
Mezzo Piano	Moderately Soft	*mp*
Mezzo Forte	Moderately Loud	*mf*
Forte	Loud	*f*
Fortissimo	Very Loud	*ff*

Dynamic markings are written below the staff as shown below.

- Measures -

Music is broken up into *measures*. Measures are short sections of music made up of a set number of beats.

Downbeats

The first beat in a measure is called a *downbeat*. Downbeats are usually more emphasized than normal beats and they often mark important musical changes such as the presence of a new chord.

Bars

Measures can also be called *bars*. This term comes from the vertical bars or *bar lines* that indicate the end of one measure and the start of another. For example, you could say that there are four measures or bars of music on the following page.

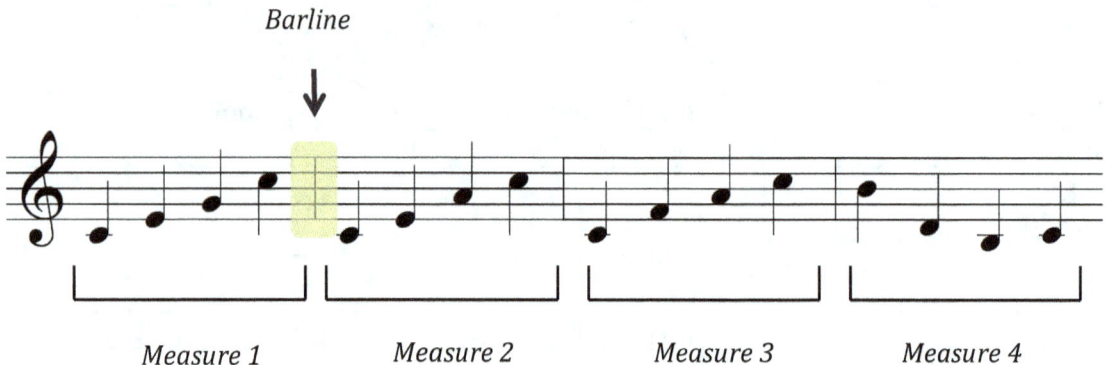

Double Barlines

A thicker *double barline* like the one at the end of the notation below indicates the end of a composition.

- Note Values and Time Signatures -

Note Values, Time Signatures, and Rhythm

Note values describe how many beats a note lasts for. *Time signatures*, which may also be called *meters*, are made up of two numbers stacked on top of one another. We will go over all the details you need to interpret these numbers in the upcoming section entitled *Time Signatures Expanded*.[1] For now, I'll just say that the top number of a time signature determines how many beats are in each measure, and the bottom number determines what note value represents one beat.

Time signatures group beats into distinctive *rhythmic patterns*. Each rhythmic pattern creates a different *feel* or *groove*. Just like you can be "in" a scale, you can be "in" a meter. It is a similar concept except that instead of a composer committing to a set of notes, the composer is committing to a certain rhythmic pattern – in other words, a pattern of when and with what level of emphasis notes are played.

1. *Time Signatures Expanded*, page 100

The most common time signature is 4/4 and as such it is sometimes referred to as *common time*. Note values are given names based on their duration in a measure of 4/4.

Below are the three most basic types of note values – the *whole note*, the *half note*, and the *quarter note*. In 4/4, a whole note will last for one whole measure or four beats. A half note will last for a half of a measure or two beats. A quarter note will last for a quarter of a measure or one beat.

Try Counting It

In 4/4, there are four beats in each measure and the quarter note represents one beat. Notice how in the notation above there are a different number of notes in each measure but each measure still has exactly four beats.

Listen to the music notated above on track 21 (disc 1). Before the notes are played a voice counts the numbers "one, two, three, four" at the tempo of the music, representing each of the four beats in a measure. This is called a *count off* and is used to set the tempo of a piece before the music starts.

Can you continue to count the numbers one through four in a cycle at the same tempo as the count off while listening to the track? If you count consistently, you should be able to hear the four beats in each measure.

3/4

3/4 is one of the most common time signatures after 4/4. In 3/4 there are three beats in each measure and, just like in 4/4, the quarter note represents one beat.

Listening to 4/4 and 3/4

Listen to a moderately slow piece played by a trio of bass, drums, and electric piano in 4/4 on track 22 (disc 1) and a very similar piece in 3/4 on track 23 (disc 1). Notice the different character and rhythmic *feel* of these two pieces.

Note Values in Time Signatures Other Than 4/4

In 4/4, all note values will represent the fraction of the measure they last for. For example, a quarter note in 4/4 lasts for a quarter of a measure. In other time signatures, however, this may not be the case. For example, in 3/4 a quarter note still lasts for one beat but there are only three beats per measure. This means that a quarter note in 3/4 actually lasts for one third of a measure.

For this reason, moving forward it may be most helpful to think about note values in terms of how many beats they last for rather than the fraction of a measure they last for.

- ❖ Note that the quarter note does not always represent one beat. See *Time Signatures Expanded* on page 100.

Notating Time Signatures

Time signatures appear at the beginning of a composition's notation and at any point when the time signature of the piece changes. Below is an example of four measures of music written in 4/4.

Eighth Notes and Sixteenth Notes

All notes faster than a quarter note are written with *flags* – lines branching off the stem of a note. Each flag doubles the speed of the note. *Eighth notes*, which are written with one flag, and *sixteenth notes*, which are written with two flags, are depicted below. In 4/4, eighth notes last for an eighth of a measure or a half of a beat and sixteenth notes last for a sixteenth of a measure or a quarter of a beat.

Theoretically, one can continue to double the speed of notes by adding flags indefinitely.

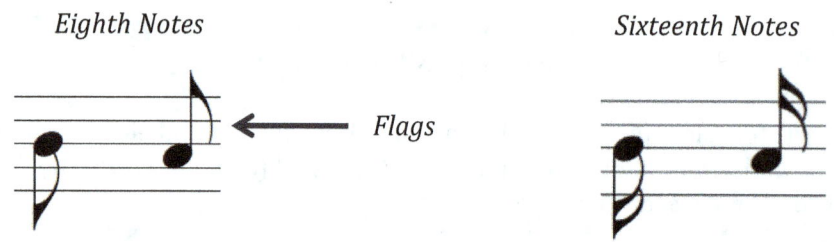

Eighth Notes   *Sixteenth Notes*

Linking Flags

When multiple notes with flags are written next to each, their flags can be linked together as shown below.

Eighth Notes

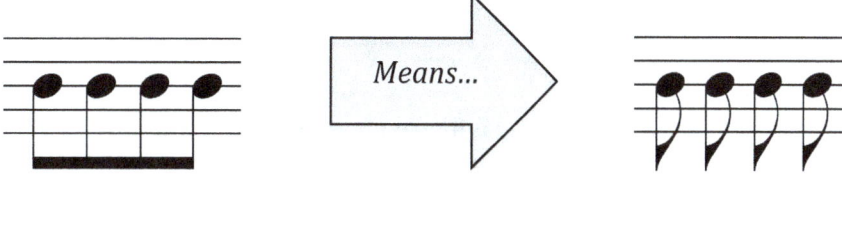

Sixteenth Notes

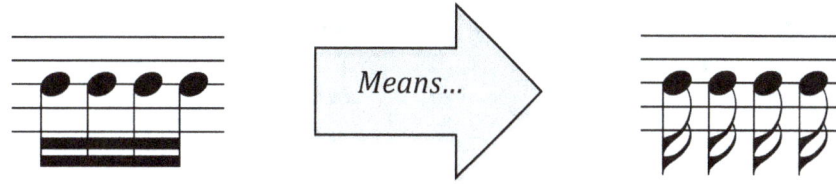

Groups

When flags are linked together in this manner, they may be used to show rhythmic groups.

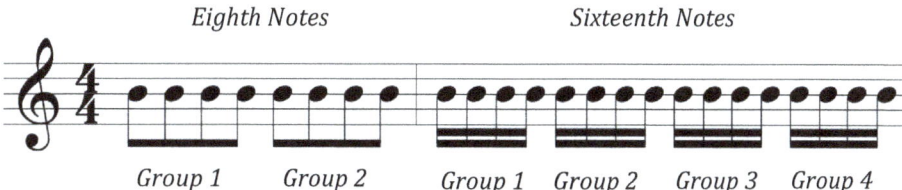

Eighth notes and sixteenth notes can be grouped together as well.

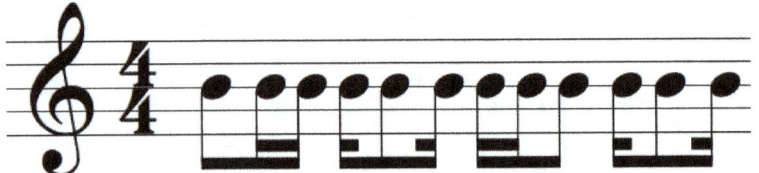

Listen to track 24 (disc 1) to hear this rhythm played on a snare drum.

Notes with one flag are eighth notes. Notes with two flags are sixteenth notes. In the diagram below the sixteenth notes are highlighted.

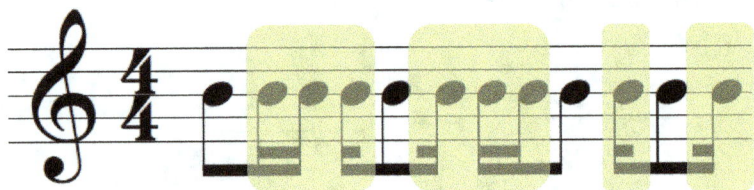

- Rests -

What Are Rests?

It is sometimes said that the silence in music is just as important as the sound. This is true. *Rests* represent periods of silence in music. There is a corresponding rest for each note value. The symbols for whole rests, half rests, quarter rests, eighth rests, and sixteenth rests are written below.

Whole Rest *Half Rest* *Quarter Rest* *Eighth Rest* *Sixteenth Rest*

An Example of Expressive Silence

Let's take this opportunity to explore what the expressive impact of *space* or *silence* is in music. Listen to track 25 (disc 1). You can follow along with the notation of the melody for this piece on the following page. Note that the measures are numbered one through fifteen to help you find any locations in the piece I reference below. Numbers like these are called *measure numbers* and commonly used in music notation.[1]

This piece exemplifies the use of musical space in an orchestral context. I'd like to mention a few moments in particular but first let's look at the general structure of the rhythms that are used in the piece. This section of music continually uses and comes back to a single rhythmic motif.[2] This rhythmic motif is rather spacious in and of itself, which produces a mild sensation of anticipation and almost a kind of reservation or holding back.

The piece begins with the rhythmic motif repeated three times, after which the fourth measure leads us into an emphasized note on the downbeat of the fifth measure. After this emphasis, the remainder of the fifth measure is left empty. We do hear, however, a gong continuing to ring out during the space. So it is not a total silence. Nevertheless, a sense of a pause and even an anticipation of the coming music is present.

At the end of measure eight, the strings break their established rhythm and then almost all of measure nine is left totally empty. This is an example of unmitigated silence through the whole ensemble. Notice the expression here. A more powerful suspense or surprise is created that extends into a more drawn out anticipation. This is only relieved when the strings reenter at the end of the ninth measure.

The very end of this section of music is also worth noting with regard to use of space. Here a building movement of energy culminates into something of a miniature climax and then pauses… once again creating anticipation. And this time when the anticipation is released, it is done with strong, emphasized sounds that bring about a sense of resolution.

These different moments illustrate some of the different ways that space can be used. A sense of reservation, a sense of holding back, a sense of building, a sense of anticipation that leads into further building, or an anticipation that is resolved are all possible musical expressions that can be created with this aspect of sound.

1. *Measure Numbers*, page 334
2. Meaning a rhythm or rhythmic idea that is repeated or used in different forms throughout a composition. See *Motifs and Themes* on page 51.

Comments on the Notation

There are a few symbols in the notation above that we haven't covered yet. If you are unfamiliar with these, don't worry – we'll discuss them later. However, for the curious, here's a short explanation now:

The dots that appear below some of the notes are staccato marks, which indicates that the given note should be played for a slightly shorter than normal duration. The arrow-like symbol you see below the last note of the notation and in a few other places is an accent, indicating that the given note should be played with an emphasis or more loudly than normal. Both of these symbols are cover in the *Articulations* section on page 214.

Additionally, there are sharp symbols in measures seven and fourteen. In measure seven, all of the notes in the measure are actually a C#. See the section *Key Signatures, Accidentals, and the Circle of Fifths* on page 178 for a complete explanation.

Expressive Silence Within Individual Parts

Track 26 (disc 1) is another good example of expressive silence, though in a much different way than track 25 (disc 1). Here the entire ensemble never stops entirely but a spacious expression is created within the rests of certain parts. The bass carries a melodic part in the beginning and then the piano takes over.

Both the bass and piano, when they are being featured as the melodic instrument, use space to create a certain relaxed expressive character as well as to separate out chunks of their melody into *phrases*, providing greater structure and intelligence to the sound. We will revisit the concept of phrases and the example piece on track 26 (disc 1) in Chapter Seven.[1]

1. See *Melodic Phrases* on page 204. See *Examples of Phrasing* and *Try Soloing With Phrases* on page 205.

- Rhythmic Positions -

What Are Rhythmic Positions?

A specific place in a measure is called a *rhythmic position*. Each rhythmic position can be referred to with a name.

Each beat of a measure is named with a number, starting with one and counting up until the last beat of the measure. In 4/4, the last beat of the measure would be beat four. After a measure ends, a new measure will begin starting back at beat one.

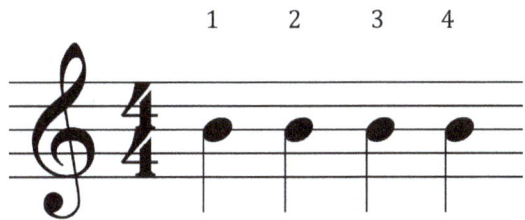

Ands

The rhythmic positions halfway between the beats are referred to as *"ands."* This comes from the way musicians might count out a measure saying "one and two and three and four and." Each "and" can be referred to by the beat that proceeded it. For example, the second eighth note below is played on the *"and" of one*.

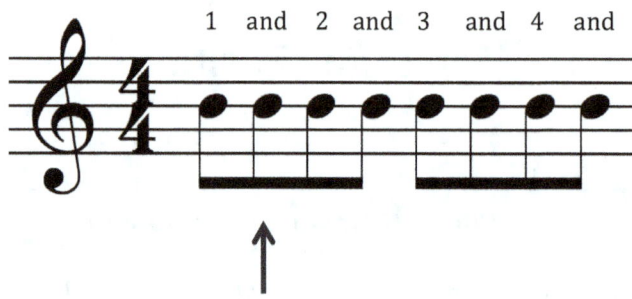

Es and As

In a similar fashion, each rhythmic position that falls halfway between a beat and an "and" is called an *"e"* or an *"a."*

Use "e" to label rhythmic positions that come after a beat but before the next "and." Use "a" to label rhythmic positions that come after an "and" but before the next beat.

Each "e" and each "a" can also be referred to by the beat that proceeded it. For example, the last sixteenth note in the notation below falls on the *"a" of four*.

- Dots and Ties -

Dotted Rhythms

In music notation, *dots* can be added immediately after any note or rest to increase the duration of that note or rest by half of the original value. Below a dot has been added to a half note. This type of note is called a *dotted half note*. In 4/4, a regular half note has a duration of two beats. The dot adds half of this original value to the duration of the note, producing a total of three beats.

Dotted rhythms have the potential to produce more complex rhythms, especially with shorter note values. For example, in 4/4, the dotted quarter note lasts for one and half beats. The dotted eighth note lasts for three quarters of a beat.

Ties

Multiple notes of the same pitch can be *tied* together to produce one sustained sound lasting for the total duration of all the tied notes. For example, below, a note that lasts for five beats has been created by tying together a whole note and a quarter note.

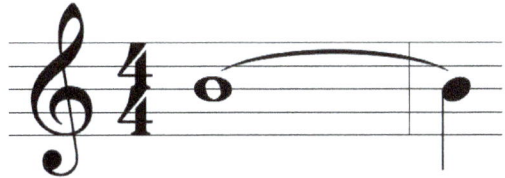

Ties are used to notate pitches that start in one measure and last into the next. Ties also may be used within a single measure to produce durations that would not otherwise be possible.

- Time Signatures Expanded -

This section contains somewhat more advanced material. If this is your first pass through the book, you may consider skipping ahead to the next section, *Pick Ups*, on page 107.

Simple, Compound, and Complex Time Signatures

There are three basic types of time signatures – *simple*, *compound*, and *complex*. In simple time signatures, beats are divided into two. In compound time signatures, beats are divided into three. Complex time signatures are time signatures that do not neatly fall into either of the other two categories. Often in complex time signatures, some beats are divided into two while other beats are divided into three. Complex time signatures can also be called *asymmetric* or *irregular* time signatures.

Interpreting Simple Time Signatures

In simple time signatures, the top number of the time signature signifies how many beats are in one measure and the bottom number signifies the note value that represents one beat. Use the following formula to interpret the bottom number of simple time signatures:

Bottom Number of a Time Signature – Simple Meter

1/(the bottom number of the time signature) notes last for one beat.

For example, in the time signature 4/4, the top number signifies that there are four beats in a measure. If we plug the bottom number, 4, into the formula above the sentence reads: "1/4 notes last for one beat," which we can then translate into "quarter notes last for one beat." In the time signature 2/2, the top number signifies that there are two beats in a measure. If we plug in the bottom number, 2, into the formula, we can ascertain that half notes represent one beat.

Why Represent the Beat With Different Note Values?

The note value that represents one beat is chosen to make the notation appear the most readable. Assigning the beat to a longer note value reduces the amount of faster note values and thus the amount of flags in the notation. Assigning the beat to a shorter note value does the opposite. Therefore, music that is rhythmically complex and fast-paced is best notated with a longer note value representing the beat.

In the example below, the two lines of notation sound exactly the same. They are played with the same rhythm and speed. However, notice that in the example using the 4/2 time signature the note values are twice the duration of the note values in the 4/4 example. This gives the notation in 4/2 example a simpler appearance, while representing the same sound.

Determining the Tempo

At the beginning of this chapter, we listened to tracks 19 (disc 1) and 20 (disc 1). Track 20 plays the same music as track 19, except at twice the tempo. Track 19 is played at 110 bpm, whereas track 20 is played at 220 bpm. Both pieces are played in 4/4.

Try tapping your foot to both tracks or otherwise keeping track of the beat. Notice how the tempo of the 220 bpm version is so fast that it may be easier to tap your foot to every other beat, in other words only on beats one and three. This raises the question: "Does the 220 bpm version really have a tempo 220 bpm or is the tempo actually 110 bpm with two beats per measure?"

The answer is ultimately subjective. It comes down to what pattern of emphasis is felt to be the primary "foot tapping" pulse of the music. This is something that the composer needs to decide, especially when it comes time to notate a piece.

Note that you may have alternatively found yourself counting the first version of this piece at 55 bpm (this would be the case if your counting aligned with the kick drum). This piece can arguably be counted this way, just as the 220 version can be counted at 110 bpm. This once again illustrates the ambiguity around what the "correct" tempo of a piece of music is.

If you are unsure about which rhythms or pulses correspond to which bpm numbers, you may find it helpful to use a metronome to hear the speed of these different pulses (55 bpm, 110 bpm, and 220 bpm) and then go back to listening to the tracks with that experience in mind.

Cut Time

Cut time is another name for 2/2. Complex or fast-paced music with a rhythmic pattern similar to the piece in track 20 (disc 1) is often notated in cut time. Cut time conveys that the beat of the music is felt to be in a pattern of two rather than a pattern of four. We could also notate this music in 2/4. However, if we did not change the representation of the beat to a half note, the tempo of the piece would need to be cut in half while the note values would need to be doubled to produce the same rhythmic feel and sound. Using cut time (while still maintaining half tempo) allows us to convey a sense of two without the added complexity of the note values that the 2/4 solution would require.

Examine the notation below to see the music in track 20 (disc 1) notated in 4/4, 2/4, and cut time. Just the melody part is used here as an example.

What Does This Symbol Mean?

This is called a key signature. We'll talk about this later (see page 178). Feel free to investigate, but key signatures only affect pitch, not rhythm, so it has no bearing on the discussion here.

Leftover Symbols From Mensural Notation

4/4 is sometimes written with a C-like shape, as shown below. It is sometimes said that this notation stands for common time, which is another name for 4/4, but in actuality it is a leftover symbol from *mensural notation*, a system used in the Medieval and Renaissance time periods. The C-like shape is actually a broken circle and signifies what was thought of as "imperfect time." In the Catholic church, groups of threes in music were thought of as perfect because they represented the holy trinity. In mensural notation, music based in threes was notated with a complete, unbroken circle.

2/2 or cut time also is sometimes notated with a symbol from this older notation system. Cut time is represented with a broken circle and a vertical line going down the middle, as shown below.

Interpreting Compound and Complex Time Signatures

In compound and complex meters, the numbers of the time signature refer to the *division of the beat* rather than the beat itself.

Whatever fraction a beat is initially broken into can be called a *division*. If a division is broken down further into smaller parts, these smaller units of time can be called *subdivisions*. In simple time signatures, the division of the beat is equal to a half of a beat. In compound time signatures, divisions are equal to a third of the beat. In complex time signatures, divisions can be equal to a half of a beat, a third of a beat, or another fraction entirely. For all time signatures, subdivisions are equal to a half of a division unless otherwise indicated and this pattern of breaking down into halves is assumed to continue indefinitely.

For compound and complex time signatures, the top number of the time signature signifies how many divisions of the beat there are in one measure. For example, the top number of 6/8, one of the most common compound time signatures, signifies that there are six divisions of a beat in each measure. This also means that there are six-thirds of a beat or two beats in each measure.

The bottom number of a compound or complex time signature signifies what note value represents a division of a beat. Use the following formula to interpret the bottom number of a compound or complex time signature:

Bottom Number of a Time Signature – Compound and Complex Meter

1/(the bottom number of the time signature) notes last for one division of the beat.

In 6/8, for example, the bottom number of the time signature signifies that the eighth note represents one third of the beat. Therefore, the dotted quarter note, which lasts for the equivalent of three eighth notes, represents one beat.

Compound time signatures are always written with a multiple of three as the top number and, most often, with an eight as the bottom number.

Alternative Names for Time Signatures

A *duple meter* is a time signature with two beats per measure. Likewise, a *triple meter* and a *quadruple meter* are time signatures with three and four beats per measure, respectively. These terms are often combined with the description of a meter as simple – dividing beats in groups of two – or compound – dividing beats into groups of three.

As a result, we have the terms *simple duple meter*, *simple triple meter*, and *simple quadruple*. These terms correspond to the 2/4, 3/4, and 4/4 time signatures, respectively. However, they may also describe other similar time signatures, specifically ones with different bottom numbers. For example, 2/2 or cut time is also an example of a simple duple meter because it contains two beats, making it a duple meter, and the beats break down into groups of twos, making it a simple meter.

We can also use the terms *compound duple meter*, *compound triple meter*, or *compound quadruple meter*. These correspond to the time signatures 6/8, 9/8, and 12/8, respectively. Note that in compound time signatures the bottom number of the time signature will usually be an eight, as in these examples.

Grouping Flagged Notes and Beat Divisions

When linked together, the flags of notes are used to show groupings of beat divisions. Generally speaking, for time signatures that have an even number of beats in each measure, flags should not be linked across the halfway point of the measure. This increases the readability of the notation.

In the following examples, a stream of eighth notes is written in both 4/4 and 6/8 time. In both cases the eighth notes are grouped to clearly outline the two halves of the measure. In 4/4, each half of the measure contains four eighth notes and a total of two beats. In 6/8, each half of the measure contains three eighth notes and a total of one beat.

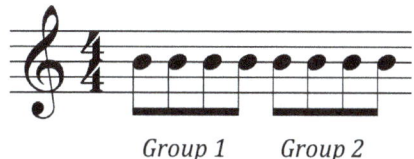

Group 1   Group 2

Group 1   Group 2

Patterns of Emphasis

These groupings are more than simply cosmetic, they represent patterns of *emphasis* in terms of volume. The first note in a grouping will tend to be slightly more emphasized than the rest of the notes.

For example, below you can examine a stream of eighth notes in 3/4 and a stream of eighth notes in 6/8. Both measures contain six eighth notes, which makes them seem similar. However, the patterns of emphasis are quite different. In 3/4, there are three beats and, thus, three emphasized eighth notes. In 6/8, there are two beats and thus only two emphasized eighth notes.

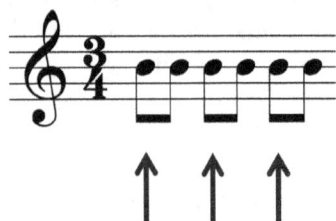 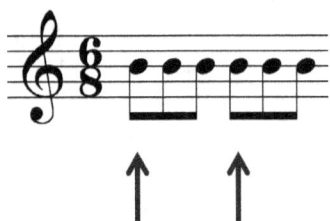

Patterns of emphasis can be a bit more complicated than the groupings in music notation let on. We will cover this topic in more depth in Chapter Eight.[1]

1. *Strong and Weak Rhythmic Positions*, page 217

Groupings of Divisions for Complex Time Signatures

A single complex time signature may represent multiple possible rhythmic patterns. 7/8, for example, might represent a group of three divisions, followed by a group of two divisions, followed by another group of two divisions. Or it may represent a group of two divisions, followed by a group of three divisions, followed by a group of two divisions. Finally, it may represent a group of two divisions, followed by a group of two divisions, followed by a group of three divisions.

Some time signatures may even express these divisions in place of the top number of the time signature as 3+2+2/8, 2+3+2/8, and 2+2+3/8, respectively. These are referred to as *additive time signatures.*

If the pattern of a complex time signature is not expressed in this way, the grouping of the divisions should be clear based on the way the flags of the notes are grouped and the way the way the music is written to emphasize certain divisions.

Listening to Complex Time Signatures

See the section *An Analysis of Rhythmic Expression* on page 235 in Chapter Eight to listen to an example composition – played on track 79 (disc 1) – that makes use of different complex time signatures.

- Pick Ups -

A *pick up*, as it is called in jazz and popular traditions, or *anacrusis*, as it is called in the classical tradition, is a partial measure used at the beginning of a piece when the music starts on a rhythmic position other than the downbeat. Traditionally, the length of the pick up measure is subtracted from the last measure of the piece. This practice may be helpful in some cases where a pick up measure is included in a repeated section.

Listen to an example of a pick up on track 27 (disc 1). Notation for the melody part is provided below. You will hear the piano play a pick up and an accompanying band enter on the first downbeat of the piece. (Note that I have not subtracted the length of the pick up measure in the last measure shown below because we can assume that this piece would continue on after only eight measures. But traditionally, the last bar of the entire composition would be two beats shorter than normal.)

- Crescendo and Diminuendo -

Crescendos (abbreviated as cresc.) and *diminuendos* (abbreviated as dim.) are used to describe changes from one volume level to another. Crescendos indicate that the music should grow louder while diminuendos indicate that the music should become quieter.

These changes in volume happen gradually over the course of the written symbol. Listen to track 28 (disc 1) to hear an orchestra playing a crescendo followed by the same music played with a diminuendo. Once again notation for the melody part is used as an example below. Notice how much the dynamics change the expression of the music (the growing volume of the crescendo compared to lessening volume of the diminuendo) even using the exact same pitches and rhythms.

Crescendo

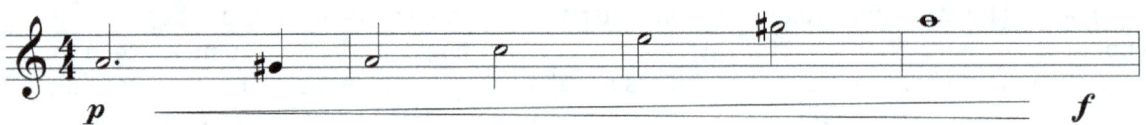

Diminuendo

Note you may not always see dynamics symbols such as *p* or *f* included in crescendos or diminuendos. Sometimes a generic arrow symbol will be used to indicate that the music should become louder or softer with the details being filled in at the performer's discretion.

- Accelerando and Ritardando -

Accelerando

The term *accelerando* describes an increase in tempo. In music notation, accelerandos are abbreviated as "accel." and are placed above the staff to indicate that the tempo is increasing. Listen to a band playing an accelerando on track 29 (disc 1). Notice that this has a quality of intensification to it like the crescendo but in a different way.

For this example, I have used the notation for the bass line part, which serves as a kind of unconventional foreground or melody in this piece in the absence of more standard melody.

Ritardando

The term *ritardando* describes a decrease in tempo. In music notation, ritardandos are abbreviated as "rit." and are placed above the staff to indicate that the tempo is slowing down. Track 30 (disc 1) plays the same music as track 29 only with a ritardando. Notice what happens to the expression in this version. What does slowing down feel like? The objective here is to get in touch with the different feelings or expressions that we can create through these different changes. If you don't have the words to describe exactly what the expression is, that's okay – as long as you know what it is internally!

Rallentando

Descreases in tempo can also be described with the word *rallentando* and are abbreviated as "rall." in music notation.

A Tempo

After an accelerando or ritardando, the phrase *a tempo* may be used to return to the original tempo. Listen to what this would sound like on track 31 (disc 1).

- Repeats and Double Bar Lines -

These final two topics for this chapter – repeats and double bar lines – are not technically part of the subject of rhythm and dynamics. But I felt that it would be appropriate to include them here to round out the presentation of the basic features of music notation. In addition, we will be using this information for later examples. We will be covering more topics about music notation throughout the book. However, after this section you should have everything you need to notate basic pitches and rhythms.

Double Bar Lines

As mentioned earlier in this chapter, a thick *double bar line* like the one shown below indicates the end of a song or composition.

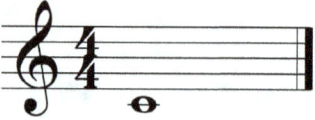

Repeat Signs

A thick double bar line accompanied by two vertically aligned dots to the left of the double bar line indicates that the performer should return to the beginning of the piece and repeat the musical material up to that point.

Forward Facing Repeat Signs

Upon reaching a repeat sign, the performer may also be instructed to return to a previous point in the composition rather going to the very beginning. To specify a starting point for a repeat other than the beginning of the piece, include a mirror image of the repeat symbol, with the dots to the right of the double bar line, at the point where the performer should return to. This mirror imaged repeat sign is called a *forward facing repeat sign*.

For example, the following notation…

…indicates that the performer should play the following.

Repeats With Multiple Endings

We may also create a repeated section of music that ends differently the second time it is played. To do this add a bracket with the number one in the top left hand corner of the bracket over the music that is to be played only the first time around and label the second ending with a bracket and a number two.

In the notation above, the performer would play the first measure, followed by the first ending, repeat back to the beginning of the piece, skip the first ending and then play the second ending resulting in the following.

Summary for Group Two
An Introduction to the Musical System

- Pitch -

Note names – Repeating set of seven letters with sharps and flats for a total of twelve different note names

Octaves – The twelve note names repeat in octaves

Scientific Pitch Notation – Numbers all the note names by octave starting with the first C on a full-sized, 88-key piano as "C1"

Middle C is the fourth C on a full-sized, 88-key piano, called C4 in scientific pitch notation.

Pitches labeled with the same note name share similar expressions and properties in a given musical situation.

Music notation is used to write music down on paper or on a computer. Music notation is written on a staff, which contains five lines with possible extending lines called ledger lines. Notes can be placed in the lines or spaces between lines. The grand staff comprises two staves, often one with a treble clef and one with a bass clef.

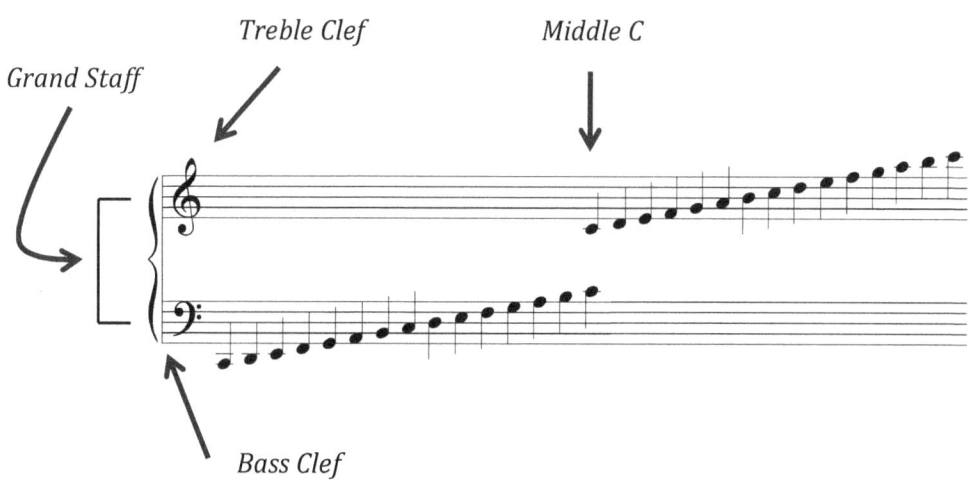

- Time (Rhythm) -

Rhythm – The subject of music dealing with the timing and emphasis of sounds

Beat – Recurring emphasis over time, the thing you might tap your foot to

Tempo – The speed of the beat, commonly ranging from 50 beats per minute (bpm) to 200 bpm, with possible extremes outside of that range

Dynamics – The spectrum from piano (soft) to forte (loud)

Measures – Groups of beats

Downbeats – First beat of the measure

Note value – Determines the length of a note from whole note to half note to quarter note to eighth note and so on

Time Signatures or **Meters** – Distinctive rhythmic pattern that repeats with each measure

Simple Meter – Beat is broken into two

Compound Meter – Beat is broken into three

Top Number of Time Signature – How many beats/divisions are in each measure

Bottom Number of Time Signature – What note value equals one beat/division

Simple Meter	Compound or Complex Meter
1/(the bottom number of the time signature) notes last for one beat.	*1/(the bottom number of the time signature) notes last for one division of the beat.*

Rests – Periods of silence broken up into whole rests, half rests, quarter rests, eighth rests, and so on

Dots – Extends note value by half the original value

Ties – Links different notes into a single, longer sound

Pick up or **Anacrusis** – A partial measure at the beginning of a piece

Rhythmic Position – A specific place or position in the rhythmic pattern of a measure

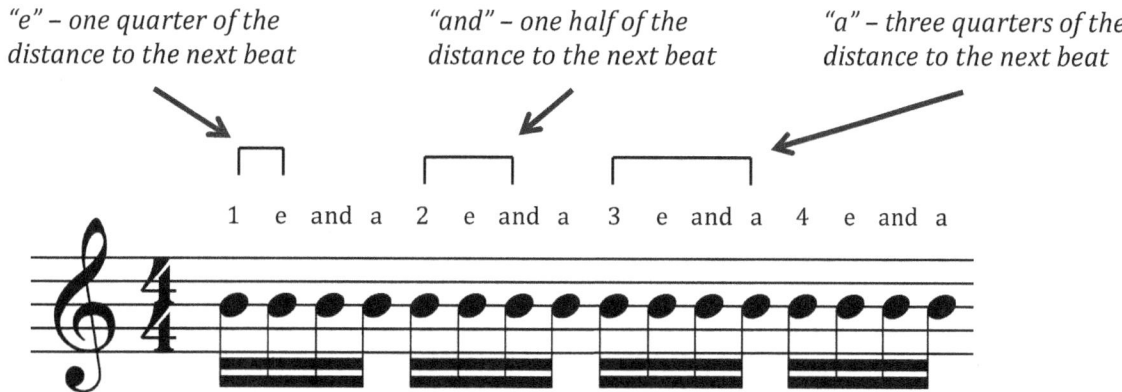

Crescendo (notated *cres.*) – Growing louder

Diminuendo (notated *dim.*) – Getting softer

Accelerando (notated *accel.*) – Speeding up

Ritardando (notated *rit.*) or **Rallentando** (notated *rall.*) – Slowing down

A Tempo – Back to previous tempo

Double Bar Line – End of composition

Repeat Sign – Go back to beginning or to the proceeding forward facing repeat sign

- Chords and Scales -

Chords – Groups of notes that sound good or are useful

Triads – Three-note chords

Voicings – Distribution of notes in a chord into different octaves

Arpeggios – Notes of a chord one at a time bottom to top or top to bottom

Chord Patterns – A sequence of notes over time within the structure of a chord

Scales – Groups of notes that sound good or are useful but unlike with chords, composers commit to staying within a scale

Diatonic – In the scale

Chromatic – Outside of the scale

Tonal Center – First note of the scale and metaphorical "home" of a composition

All seven letters in the musical system (A to G) are used once in a seven-note scale, with various flats and sharps added to the letters depending on the scale.

Part Two

Musical Relationships

Group Three

Intervals and Interval Structures

Chapter Five
Intervals

- What Are Intervals? -

Intervals are sometimes thought of as groups of two notes. They also can be seen as the distance from one note to another note, like a musical measuring tape.

In Chapter Three, I actually presented one example of an interval: the octave.[1]

1. *Octaves*, page 70

Common Expression of Intervals

Groups of notes that are separated by the same intervals (that is to say groups of notes that share the same spacing or distances between notes) create similar expressions and have similar musical properties.

❖ *Common Expression*, page 52

- Half Steps and Whole Steps -

There are a few different systems that musicians use to describe intervals. One is based on *half steps* and *whole steps*.

What Are Half Steps?

A half step is the distance from one note to the note directly above or below it.

Most commonly, half steps are found between one white key and one black key on a piano. For example, the distance between C and C# is a half step.

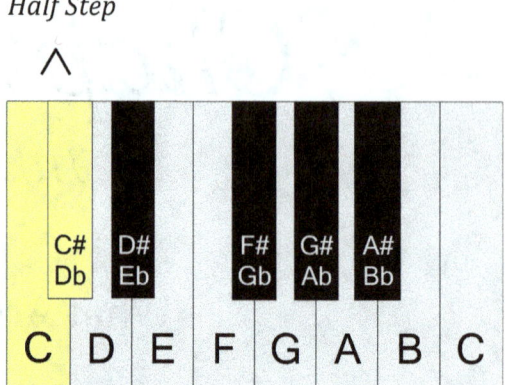

Sometimes two white keys can also form a half step – the distance between E and F is a half step and the distance between B and C is a half step.

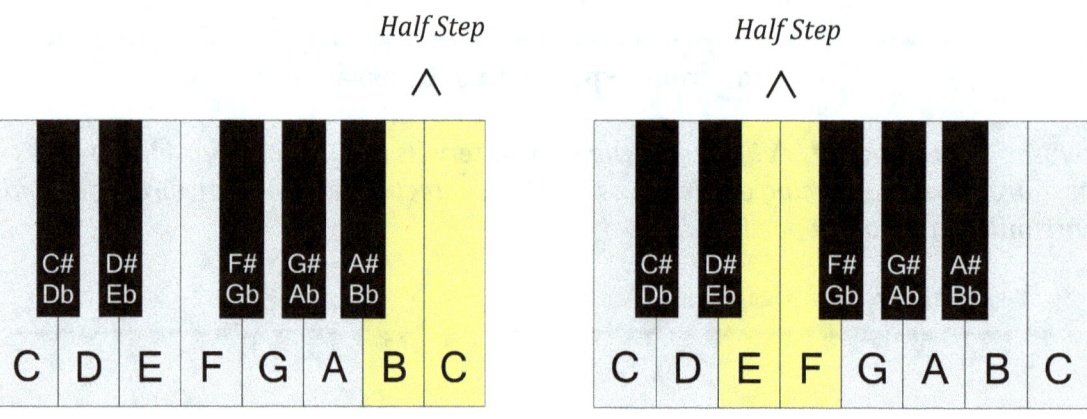

Listening to the Half Step

Try playing these examples of half steps and listen to the result. Try singing back what you hear. Alternatively, listen to track 33 (disc 1) to hear a half step played from low to high, then high to low, and then with both notes at the same time. While you listen, fix your intention on remembering the sound of a half step so you could recognize it or sing it at a later time.

What Are Whole Steps?

Whole steps are nothing more than intervals that represent the distance of two half steps. On the piano, these intervals will extend from one key to another with exactly one (white or black) key between them. Check out the diagrams below to see some examples of whole steps on the piano.

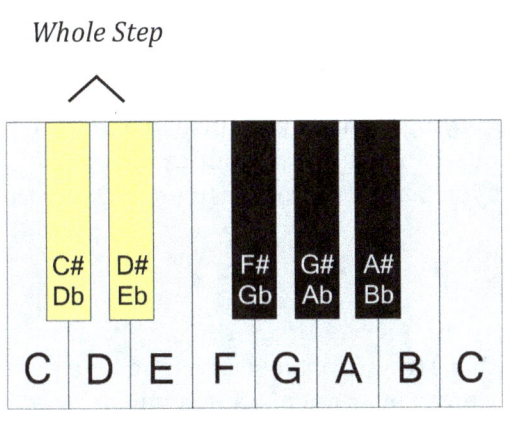

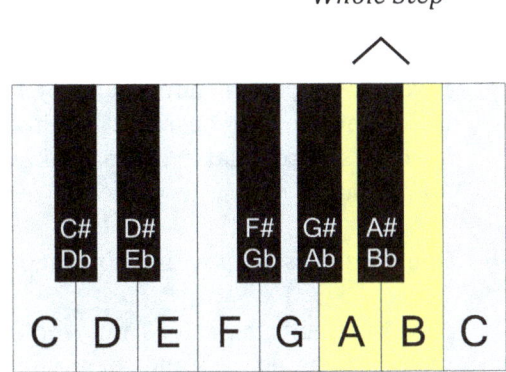

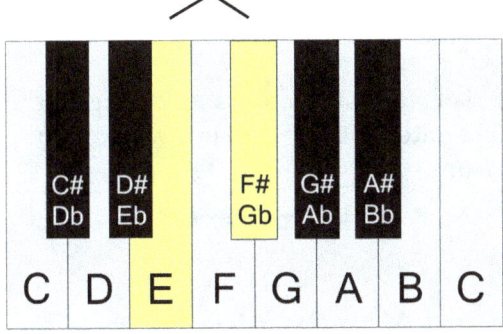

Listening to the Whole Step

Repeat the directions in *Listening to the Half Step* on the previous page with these examples of whole steps. Play track 34 (disc 1) to listen to a whole step.

Test Yourself With a Friend – Half Steps and Whole Steps

Can you differentiate between the sound of a half step and that of a whole step? Test yourself with a friend: Have a friend play a half step (such as C and C#) or a whole step (such as C and D) at random and attempt to determine which interval is being played without looking at his or her instrument so that you must rely completely on your sense of hearing.

Singing Half Steps and Whole Steps

1. On your preferred instrument, find a pair of adjacent notes (separated by a half step) in a comfortable singing range for you.

2. Play these two notes back and forth to solidify the sound of a half step in your mind. Repeat as many times as necessary.

3. Now, play a whole step using the same starting note as before. Once again, listen to the sound carefully. Continue to play the half step and whole step until you can remember them after you have stopped playing.

4. Next, try singing the notes of a half step while playing them on your instrument. Match the pitches you are hearing with the pitches you are playing. If you notice your voice become sharp or flat in comparison with what you hear from your instrument, correct your voice to match.

5. Repeat the last step with whole steps.

6. Now try singing half steps and whole steps without the aid of an instrument. If you would like to, go back and check your accuracy on an instrument after singing.

Steps and Leaps

Intervals can be broadly grouped into two categories. Half steps and whole steps make up the first group, which can be collectively referred to as *steps*. Intervals larger than a whole step make up the second group and are collectively called *leaps*.

- The Numeric-Quality Interval Naming System -

There are names for leaps or intervals larger than a whole step as well. To name these intervals, we will need to use a second interval naming system. I refer to this system as the *numeric-quality interval naming system*. The table on the following page lists the names for all the intervals up to an octave in this system. Each interval name is given with an equivalent number of half steps.

List of Intervals up to an Octave

Equivalent Number of Half Steps	Interval Name
0	Unison
1	Minor Second/Half Step
2	Major Second/Whole Step
3	Minor Third
4	Major Third
5	Perfect Fourth
6	Augmented Fourth/Diminished Fifth/Tritone
7	Perfect Fifth
8	Minor Sixth
9	Major Sixth
10	Minor Seventh
11	Major Seventh
12	Octave

Explaining the Interval Names

At first, these names may appear confusing but there is a method to the madness. The numeric name of an interval (such as second, third, fourth and so on) represents the letters in the interval and their distance from each other in the alphabet. Adjacent letters, such as A and B, are a *second* apart. However, this numeric label does not take into account the sharps and flats that may be added to the notes in the interval. For example, A and Bb are also a second apart. To differentiate between the many variations of a numeric label, such as the interval of a second, we use descriptive labels called *qualities*.

Qualities

There are five qualities: major, minor, augmented, diminished, and perfect. Qualities are used to describe intervals, chords, and scales. The terms major and augmented describe larger intervals, whereas the terms minor and diminished describe smaller ones.

Pairing Numeric Interval Names With Qualities

Any pair of note names containing letters that are adjacent in the alphabet is described as a second. A and Bb, for example, are described as a *minor second*. A and B are also a second apart but A and B are described as a *major second*. Notice that the major second is one half step larger than the minor second.

Thirds are intervals where the letters of the notes in the interval are one step further than adjacent in the alphabet. For example, A and C are a third apart. A and D are a fourth apart. The distance between any pair of two letters can be described through a continuation of the pattern outlined here. And as with the example of a second, the sharps and flats assigned to the letters of the two notes are represented with some kind of quality.

Refer to the table on the previous page to see how different qualities are paired with the numeric interval names.

The Unison

A unison is the equivalent of a zero on the musical measuring tape. A unison refers to multiple instances of the same note, in the same octave. For example, if a clarinet and an oboe both played an $A4^1$ at the same time they would form a unison.

1. *Distinguishing Between the Many Instances of Each Note Name*, page 71

The Tritone

The tritone gets its name from being equivalent to three whole steps.

Listening to the Intervals

Listen to each interval, from unison to octave, on tracks 32 through 44 (disc 1). Each interval is played ascending (low to high), then descending (high to low), and finally harmonically or with both notes being played at the same time. The unison is played using two instruments – a piano and a viola. The piano plays first, followed by the viola. Afterward, both instruments play together.

Augmented Fourth or Diminished Fifth?

The terms "augmented fourth," "diminished fifth," and "tritone" can all be used to name the same interval – the interval equivalent to six half steps. However, the terms "augmented fourth" and "diminished fifth" are used in different situations. For example, technically, A and D# form an augmented fourth. However, A and Eb (which sound identical to A and D#) form a diminished fifth. Both A and D# as well as A and Eb can be called a tritone.

The difference between the augmented fourth and the diminished fifth has to do solely with the letters in the two intervals. The logic of this can be seen by counting through the alphabet in the following way: Adjacent letters in the alphabet, such as A and B, form seconds. Therefore, A and C form a third, A and D form a fourth, A and E form a fifth and so on. These statements hold true regardless of the sharps and flats associated with the notes in the interval. Consequently, the notes A and D# must be described as some kind of a fourth and the notes A and Eb must be described as some kind of a fifth.

Using this process, you can determine what situations call for the use of an augmented fourth and what situations call for the use of a diminished fifth. Simply start on the first note of the interval and count through the alphabet to determine the numeric name of the interval. Afterward, you may assign the appropriate quality to the interval to specify the exact distance of your interval in terms of half steps.

General Numeric Interval Names

Sometimes musicians will refer to intervals by their numeric name (second, third, fourth, etc.) only. When the specificity of a quality is not needed, this can make talking about intervals faster and easier.

For example, I could say, "The diagrams below depict some examples of seconds and thirds." To be more exact, I could say that "A and C form a minor third, C and E form a major third, B and C form a minor second, and lastly C and D form a major second."

I'll define a numeric interval name without a quality as a *general numeric interval name.* An interval name that contains both a numeric name and a quality descriptor can be called a *numeric-quality interval name.* Both ways of referring to intervals are correct. Each method is helpful in different situations.

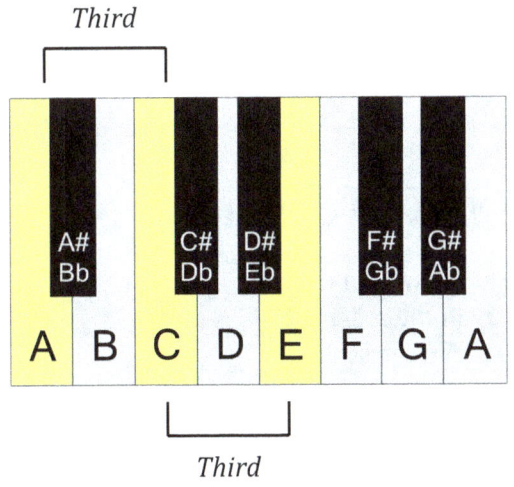

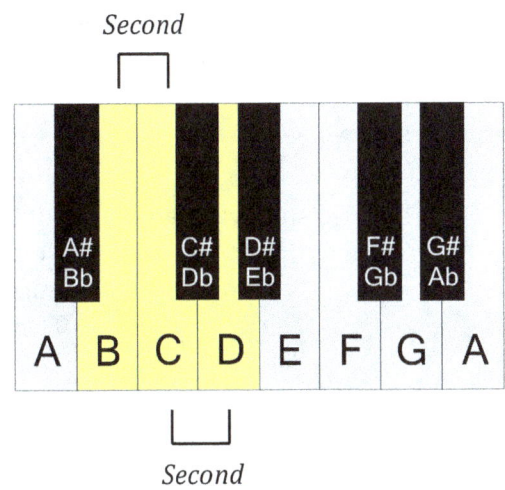

Intervals and the Repeating Musical Alphabet

Keep in mind that our musical system only uses the letters A through G. After G, the next note higher is A. Therefore, G and A are a second apart. These notes are considered adjacent in the "musical alphabet."

It is important to take into account the repeating nature of our note system when naming other intervals too. As an example, let's say you want to find the note a fifth above an F. This can be accomplished by stepping through the musical alphabet. A second above F is G. A third above F is A. Here we must remember that the musical alphabet repeats back to A after G. From this point, we can continue stepping through the alphabet. A fourth above F is B. And finally, a fifth above F is C. We have arrived at our answer.

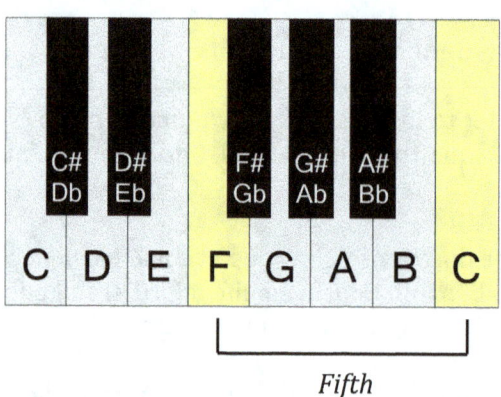

Fifth

Numeric Interval Names and Scales

Because major and minor scales have exactly one of each letter A through G, with various flats and sharps assigned to those letters, seconds not only represent notes with adjacent letters in the alphabet but also notes that are adjacent in major and minor scales. Each numeric interval name represents a distance one step greater in a major or minor scale. Seconds represent notes that are adjacent in a scale. Thirds represent notes that are one step further than adjacent in a scale. Fourths would be a step further still and so on.

Interval Names	Distance in a Major or Minor Scale
Unison	No distance
Second	Adjacent, one step away in the scale
Third	Two steps away in the scale
Fourth	Three steps away in the scale
Fifth	Four steps away in the scale
Sixth	Five steps away in the scale
Seventh	Six steps away in the scale
Octave	Seven steps away in the scale

Numeric Interval Names and the Staff

Each numeric interval name also represents a new line or space on a staff. Below is the notation for the intervals from a second to an octave starting on C. The first staff shows intervals starting on C and going up, and the second staff shows intervals starting on C and going down. Notice how each incremental change on the staff aligns itself with a new letter and thus a new interval.

Intervals Starting on C, Going Up

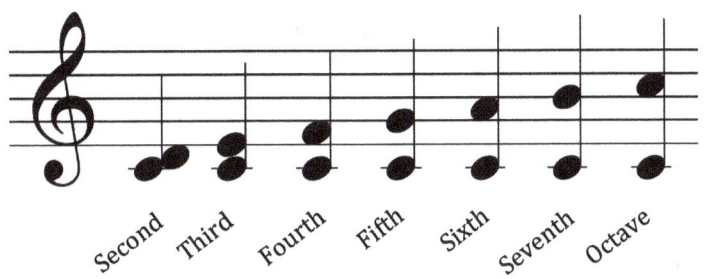

Intervals Starting on C, Going Down

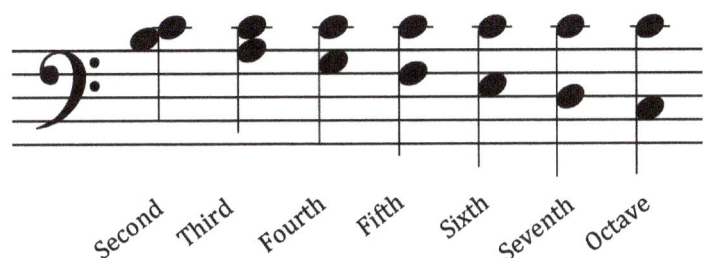

Notice the Clefs!

The first staff in the notation above is written with a treble clef; the second with a bass clef. This was done to minimize the use of ledge lines and enhance readability. Make sure to always be aware of what clef you are reading in when looking at music notation.

❖ *The Treble and Bass Clefs*, page 75

- Compound Intervals -

Compound and Simple Intervals

Compound intervals are intervals greater than an octave. In contrast, *simple intervals* include the unison and the octave and everything in between.

To create compound intervals, we simply continue to increase the number of the interval with each successive letter change and repeat the same pattern of qualities used for simple intervals. Below is an example of how this works for intervals starting on middle C.

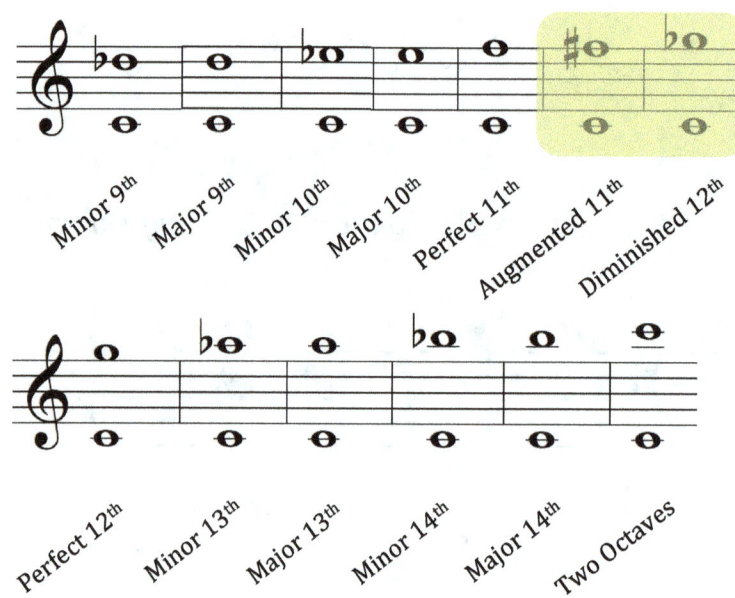

The Augmented Eleventh and the Diminished Twelfth

Note that the augmented eleventh and the diminished twelfth are two ways of describing the same sound. The relationship between the augmented eleventh and the diminished twelfth is comparable to the relationship between the augmented fourth and the diminished fifth, only with an additional octave added to each interval.

- Interval Inversions -

To *invert* an interval means to either move the top note of the interval down an octave or to move the bottom note of the interval up an octave. For example, a major third from C to E can be inverted to a minor sixth from E to C. An interval and its inverted counterpart share the same note names and are similar in their musical properties.

Interval	Corresponding Inversion
Minor Second	Major Seventh
Major Second	Minor Seventh
Minor Third	Major Sixth
Major Third	Minor Sixth
Perfect Fourth	Perfect Fifth
Tritone	Tritone
Perfect Fifth	Perfect Fourth
Minor Sixth	Major Third
Major Sixth	Minor Third
Minor Seventh	Major Second
Major Seventh	Minor Second

- The Sonance of Intervals -

In Chapter One, we discussed how the frequency of a sound wave determines the pitch that we perceive when we hear a given sound.[1] Groups of notes can be described as having strong proportionality[2] when the frequencies associated with those notes form low ratio relationships like 1:2 or 2:3. In contrast, groups of notes will have weak proportionality when their frequencies form higher ratio relationships like 8:9 or 9:16. For example, the two notes in an interval might have a frequency of 500 hz and 1000 hz, respectively. These two frequencies, and thus the two notes of the interval, have a 1:2 relationship because 1000 is twice the value of 500.

In the musical community, the pitch proportionality of a group of notes is described on a spectrum called *sonance*. On one end of this spectrum, the term *consonance* is used to refer to strong pitch proportionality (the low energy pole). On the other end of the spectrum, *dissonance* refers to weak pitch proportionality (the high energy pole).[3]

1. *Pitch and Frequency*, page 30
2. *Proportionality*, page 48, and *Strong or Weak Proportionality*, page 49
3. *Seven Basic Spectra of Musical Expression*, page 47

In addition, the term *consonant* can be used as a descriptor of sounds that are characterized by strong pitch proportionality while the term *dissonant* can be used as a descriptor of sounds that are characterized by weak pitch proportionality.

When studying proportionality in pitch, the most basic place to start is with the relationship between two notes – in other words, with intervals. Once we understand the sonance of intervals, we will move on to studying larger groups of notes, such as chords and scales.

Ordering the Intervals From Consonant to Dissonant

Below is a general order of the intervals from most consonant to most dissonant. I have grouped these intervals into four broad perceptual categories: strong consonance, moderate consonance, moderate dissonance, and strong dissonance. However, even within these broad categories the intervals generally progress from consonance to dissonance in the order shown below.

Keep in mind that the sonance of intervals is affected by a complex set of variables. The order below serves as a general guide. Further subtleties concerning the sonance of intervals are explored in the following content.

Degree of Sonance	Intervals	Tracks
Strong Consonance	Unison	Track 32 (disc 1)
	Octave	Track 44 (disc 1)
	Perfect Fifth	Track 39 (disc 1)
	Perfect Fourth	Track 37 (disc 1)
Moderate Consonance	Major Third	Track 36 (disc 1)
	Major Sixth	Track 41 (disc 1)
	Minor Third	Track 35 (disc 1)
	Minor Sixth	Track 40 (disc 1)
Moderate Dissonance	Minor Seventh	Track 42 (disc 1)
	Major Second	Track 34 (disc 1)
Strong Dissonance	Major Seventh	Track 43 (disc 1)
	Tritone	Track 38 (disc 1)
	Minor Second	Track 33 (disc 1)

Listening to the Sonance of Intervals

Track 45 (disc 1) plays the intervals listed above in order from most consonant to most dissonant. This time the intervals are played only harmonically or with both notes being played at the same time. Can you feel the progression of sonance as you listen?

Different Ways of Using the Terms Consonance and Dissonance

The terms "consonance" and "dissonance" can describe the two poles of the spectrum of pitch proportionality as a general, abstract concept, but we can also use these words to reference an actual group of notes. For example, we could say "This interval is a dissonance," or "This chord is a strong consonance."

The Application of Dissonance in Context

According to our perspective on context laid out in the *Three Tools of Musical Analysis* section,[1] the expression of any particular musical element can vary according to the surrounding musical environment. This applies very much in the realm of intervals.

In isolation, dissonant intervals may seem to produce an undesirable effect. However, in a musical context, the expression of these dissonant intervals is often transformed dramatically. What is heard as a lack of connection in isolation can become a source of complexity, energy, and excitement in an intelligently designed musical context.

Examine the short excerpt of a piano piece on the following page. This piece has a very mellow and peaceful expression but nonetheless it contains some dissonant intervals. There are two notable moments of dissonance in this excerpt that I have highlighted in the notation below. The first moment occurs when a tritone is formed between the notes of the right and left hands at the beginning of the second measure of the excerpt. The other moment occurs when a major ninth is formed in a similar fashion at the beginning of the fifth measure. When listening to these intervals in the context of the piece, however, we notice almost no sense of overt harshness or tension. Instead, the expression could perhaps be described as a gentle rising in the flow of the music.

Listen to track 46 (disc 1) to hear the excerpt of the piano piece notated below. After a short pause, the track will play the two highlighted intervals – a tritone and a major ninth – in isolation without the context of the music. Notice how dramatically the context of the music shapes the sounds of these intervals. As you listen, follow along with the notation and make sure that you recognize these two dissonant intervals as they occur in the piece.

1. *Context*, page 53

What Does This Symbol Mean?

This is called a key signature. We will discuss key signatures on page 178 in Chapter Seven. It essentially indicates that all notes in the piece on the lines or spaces of the staff that have a flat on them here at the beginning should be flat throughout the entire duration of the notation. Whether you are familiar with key signatures or not, you should be able to follow along with the notation regardless by watching the rhythms and the general increases and decreases in pitch.

Advanced

Tuning Systems and Sonance

The idea of a twelve-note musical system has been around since at least the time of Pythagoras (6th century BCE). However, exactly what frequencies those twelve notes represent has changed a lot throughout history. To *tune* a pitch means to adjust its frequency slightly. A *tuning system* standardizes what exact frequencies the note names represent. When a pitch matches the ideals prescribed by the given tuning system, we describe that pitch as being *in tune*. When it does not, we describe it as *out of tune*. Tuning systems can have a very significant impact on the sonance of intervals.

The modern standard tuning system is called *equal temperament.* In equal temperament, the frequency of pitches doubles with each octave, and each of the twelve half steps in the octave represent a change of one twelfth of a doubling. This means that the exponential increase in pitch created by the doubling frequency of each octave is evenly distributed in a smooth curve.

Earlier in history, however, tuning systems were based on a starting pitch and other pitches were tuned to create low ratio relationships with the starting pitch thus enabling the expression of consonance or strong pitch proportionality. The starting pitch then became the tonal center for music written in such systems.

Tuning systems like these, which are based on creating low ratio intervals to a tonal center, are considered to be forms of *just intonation*. Just intonation works well but, unlike the modern tuning system, once an instrument is tuned in just intonation it can only use one tonal center. To change the tonal center, the instrument must be entirely retuned.

As music evolved, people began to be interested in creating a tuning system that could use multiple tonal centers. This need led to the creation of the equal temperament system. In equal temperament, all of the twelve pitches can be used as a tonal center, with an equally consonant result in each case.

There is a disadvantage to equal temperament however. The equal temperament system *approaches* ideal, simple ratios but does not create them exactly. Examine the table below to see the ratios that a tuning system would ideally create for each interval up to an octave. In a just intonation system, these ratios could be created to a high degree of accuracy but only for one tonal center. In equal temperament, the octave is the only interval that exactly matches its low number ratio. All the other intervals end up being off by this or that amount – in some cases, by up to 15 percent of a half step. This difference is noticeable and, in fact, affects how we perceive consonance and dissonance.

When two notes come very close to forming a low ratio relationship, we do not simply perceive the expression of a much higher ratio relationship that the frequencies match exactly. The auditory processing faculties of the brain can tell that the frequencies are approaching a position of strong proportionality. The effect is an added layer of complexity, in which we seem to perceive a consonance that is out of tune (rather than perceiving a strong dissonance). Therefore, the general order of intervals from consonant to dissonant in both equal temperament and just intonation is best represented by the ratios shown below despite their tuning differences.

Nevertheless, equal temperament strays enough from the ideal ratios of just tuning that the order of the intervals from consonant to dissonant in equal temperament does not perfectly correspond to the order of the ideal ratios from lowest to highest as shown below. As you can verify with your own comparison, however, the two are roughly similar.

Intervals	Ratio
Unison	1:1
Octave	2:1
Perfect Fifth	3:2
Perfect Fourth	4:3
Major Sixth	5:3
Major Third	5:4
Minor Third	6:5
Tritone	7:5 or 7:10
Minor Sixth	8:5
Major Second	9:8
Major Seventh	15:8
Minor Seventh	16:9
Minor Second	16:15

Tritone as 5:7 or 7:10

In equal temperament, the tuning of the tritone falls between 5:7 and 7:10. To be represented exactly, it would have to be described with a much larger ratio. For our purposes, we can consider the tritone as being ambiguously either 5:7 or 7:10.

Listening to the Sonance of Intervals in Just Intonation

Track 47 (disc 1) plays the intervals listed on the previous page in a just intonation tuning system that exactly represents the ratios that appear in the table. The intervals are played harmonically.

Notice the progression from consonance to dissonance. Also pay special attention to how a just tuning system produces different qualities of sonance. Can you hear that the consonances are stronger when compared to the equal temperament version?

A Composition Outside Equal Temperament

Track 48 (disc 1) plays a piece of music that uses pitches outside of the equal temperament system. This composition was created out of sine waves and other electronically created sounds that were tuned to exact simple ratios. The pitches in this piece are not even really modified versions of our standard twelve-note system. These pitches are really just frequencies, mathematically related by simple ratios.

While listening to this composition, draw your attention to the sense of sonance. Can you discern the difference between the tuning of this piece and that of a regular equal temperament tuning? If so, what is the impact for you?

Sonance and Timbre

Another example of the principle of context[1] is the relationship between sonance and timbre. The partials or harmonics[2] of two notes in an interval interact, forming relationships. Each of these relationships can be described as a ratio and has a corresponding impact on the sonance of the interval. In different timbres, the partials of a note will be more or less emphasized in amplitude. These variations in amplitude may emphasize or deemphasize relationships between the partials of the two notes in an interval. The result is that intervals may express different levels of sonance based on their timbre.

1. *Context*, page 53
2. See *Harmonics* on page 37 and *The Difference Between Harmonics, Partials, and Overtones* on page 41.

Harmonic Beating

Our ears and brains generally separate different fundamental frequencies as pitches in our experiential sense of hearing. However, when sounds are very close together in frequency, at a certain point we are unable to distinguish the sounds as separate entities. When this happens, we hear a single pitch at an average of the indistinguishable frequencies that is oscillating in volume. This phenomenon is known as *harmonic beating* and sounds like a pulsing effect.

Harmonic beating occurs because of *interference* between two sound waves. Say, for example, that two frequencies are being produced, one at 99 hertz and another at 100 hertz. Initially, the sound waves will align well so that when one wave is condensing the air into a high pressure state, the other wave is doing the same thing and when one wave is expanding air into a low pressure state, the other wave is also at the same point in its cycle. However, every time these two waves go through an oscillation the 99 hertz wave will be a little bit more behind. Eventually, the waves will fall so far out of sync that one wave will be condensing air, while the other is expanding air. Then, the waves will gradually come back in sync to start the whole cycle again.

When the two are at a similar point in their cycles, they are said to produce *constructive interference*, which makes the overall sound of the frequencies louder. When the sound waves are at opposing points in their cycles, they are said to produce *destructive interference*, which makes the overall sound of the frequencies quieter. The alternating constructive and destructive interference creates a change in volume that oscillates at a rate equal to the difference between the two frequencies, in this case 1 hertz. The result is an experience of a pitch at a frequency of 99.5 hertz oscillating in volume at a rate of 1 hertz.

When two frequencies are very close together, the harmonic beating produced between them is slow. As the frequencies move apart, the harmonic beating increases in speed. Eventually, the individual beats are not discernable, and the effect of beating or pulsing is transformed into a roughness between the two sounds. As the frequencies continue to move farther apart, they are experienced as separate frequencies. You have actually already heard an example of this effect in track 1 (disc 1). Give it another listen now if you'd like.

If you can recognize the sound of harmonic beating, you can use the frequency of the beating as a guide for tuning an instrument. Play a note that needs to be tuned in conjunction with a version of that note that is in tune and then adjust the pitch of the first note so that the beating slows in frequency. When the beating stops altogether, you will know that the pitches are in tune with each other.

As an interesting side note, you might hear harmonic beating in dissonant intervals. Dissonant intervals often generate beating, if not between the fundamental frequencies of the two notes in the interval then between their harmonics or partials. If you would like, go back to some of the example tracks of dissonant intervals presented in this chapter (ones that were played harmonically or with both notes played at the same time) and listen for a subtle "beating" sound.

Test Yourself With a Friend (Intervals Edition)

Have a friend play an interval at random from an agreed-upon list of possibilities and then try to determine which interval you are hearing without looking.

Have your friend play the intervals either ascending (low to high), descending (high to low), or harmonically (at the same time) at random, so that you can become familiar with all of these various sounds that a single interval can create.

Focus on becoming familiar with just a few intervals at a time.

My suggestion is to start with half steps and whole steps:

- Half Steps (track 33, disc 1)
- Whole Steps (track 34, disc 1)

Once you become comfortable with half steps and whole steps, add in the perfect fourth, perfect fifth, and octave:

- Perfect Fourths (track 37, disc 1)
- Perfect Fifths (track 39, disc 1)
- Octaves (track 44, disc 1)

Next, add in the thirds and sixths:

- Minor Thirds (track 35, disc 1)
- Major Thirds (track 36, disc 1)
- Minor Sixths (track 40, disc 1)
- Major Sixths (track 41, disc 1)

And after that add in the rest of the simple intervals:

- Tritones (track 38, disc 1)
- Minor Sevenths (track 42, disc 1)
- Major Sevenths (track 43, disc 1)

And if you master all the intervals from a unison to an octave, then slowly add in the compound intervals up to two octaves.

You may find that a particular interval or group of intervals is particularly difficult for you. If this is the case, create a smaller group of possibilities that includes the intervals you have difficulty with and work with that group for a while.

Making a List of Reference Compositions for Hearing the Intervals

Sometimes associating intervals with a musical example can be useful while learning the sound of the intervals. Memorable moments in melodies often work well. For example, the first two notes of "Over the Rainbow" form an octave. If you can remember the sound at the beginning of "Over the Rainbow," you'll be able to remember the sound of an octave too!

If you'd like to, make a list of reference songs or compositions that will help you remember each interval. But you'll have to decide which pieces work best for you. Be sure to pick pieces that use the particular interval you are working with in a memorable and prominent way. You may find it helpful to make separate lists for ascending, descending, and harmonic intervals.

Chapter Six
The Interval Structure of Chords

- Basic Chord Types -

Interval Structures

I use the term *interval structure* to refer to a specific set of intervals or interval patterns. In the coming chapters, we will see how interval structures characterize both chords and scales in very important ways. In this chapter, we will focus on applying an understanding of intervals to chords and then in the next chapter we will do the same for scales.

Chord Types

A *chord type* refers to a group of chords that share a specific pattern of intervals or interval structure.

For example, *major triads* are defined by having a major third between the first and second notes and a minor third between the second and third notes. As a result, an interval of a perfect fifth forms between the first and third notes.

A *minor triad* is defined by having a minor third between the first and second notes and a major third between second and third notes. This once again results in a perfect fifth between the first and third notes.

Major triads and minor triads are both examples of chord types – groups of chords that are defined by a particular set of intervals. In the diagrams below, the interval patterns for major and minor triads are depicted using the C major triad and the C minor triad as examples.

Whenever I present a new chord type in this book, I will use some kind of C chord as an example. However, by definition, the pattern of intervals in these example chords will be the same for all the chords in the given chord type.

Major Triad
Chord Symbol: C

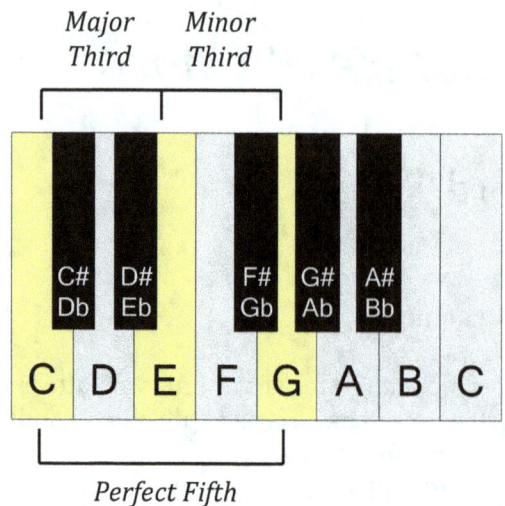

Minor Triad
Chord Symbol: Cm, Cmin, C-

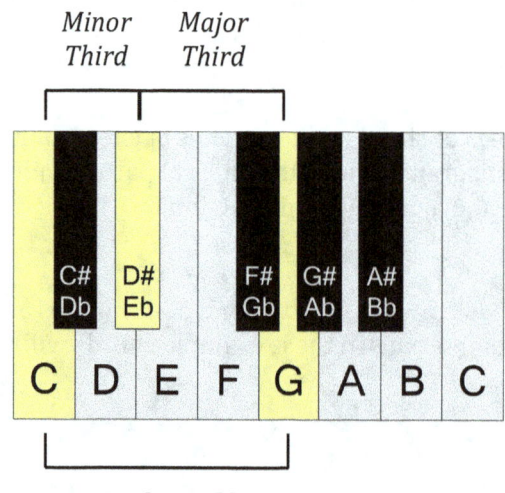

Naming Chord Tones

All notes in a given chord can be referred to as *chord tones*. Each chord tone has a special name in the context of a chord. The first note of a chord is called the *root*, the second note of a chord is called the *third*, and the third note of a chord is called the *fifth*. The names third and fifth are based on the distance the given note is from the root or first note of the chord. In any chord, the second note is a third away from the root and the third note is a fifth away from the root. However, the qualities of those intervals will change depending on the chord type.

This pattern continues with chords that contain more than three notes. All chord tones can be referred to by the numeric interval name that describes that chord tone's relationship to the root.

Original Voicings

We know from Chapter Three that chords can be put into different voicings based on the octaves in which we play the notes of a chord.[1] A single chord can have many different voicings all possessing a different interval structure. However, every chord has what I call an *original voicing*. This is the voicing where the root of the chord is the lowest note and each note is separated by a third from the adjacent notes.

Considering the possibility of different voicings, it is important to understand that naming chord tones as the root, third, or fifth refers to the position of these chord tones in a chord's original voicing. In a chord's original voicing, the root will be the first or lowest note, the third will be the second note, and the fifth will be the third note. When we change the voicing of a chord, however, both the interval structure and the order of the notes in the chords can change. Nevertheless, chord tones are always named by referring to their positions in the chord's original voicing.

1. *Chord Voicings*, page 79

Chord Symbols

Notice the *chord symbols* listed in each chord diagram. Chord symbols are abbreviated ways to write chords. Chords always include the root note of the chord and additional symbols or letters. The major triad is represented simply with the root note of the chord and no additional symbols or letters.

Often a single chord type will have multiple possible chord symbols. These are all synonymous ways of writing the same chord.

These chord symbols use C as an example root note, but they can be used with any of the twelve note names.

Listening to Major and Minor Triads

Track 49 (disc 1) plays an example of what the major triad sounds like in a piece of music. Track 50 (disc 1) plays a similar piece for the minor triad. Before the given example piece, you will hear a C major triad on track 49 (disc 1) and a C minor triad on track 50 (disc 1) in isolation. These isolated chords are intended to give you a reference point for the sound of the simple, unaltered, original voicing of the chord being presented. Keep in mind, the example pieces use different voicings and sequences of notes to create various musical expressions. Both examples start out with solo piano music and then demonstrate how the given type of chord might be used in an ensemble context. The major example uses the chords C major, F major, and G major. The minor example uses the chords C minor, F minor, and G minor.

How would you describe the expressions of the major and minor triads in these example pieces? In my mind, major triads often express happiness, brightness, harmony, pleasantness, hope, familiarity, openness, or simplicity. In contrast, minor triads often sound sad, dark, mellow, cool, melancholy, sentimental, angry, or powerful. Hopefully, these descriptions in conjunction with the example pieces of track 49 (disc 1) and 50 (disc 1) help to give you a taste of the essential flavor of major and minor triads. Keep in mind that the context in which we hear these chords is very important and will determine what aspect of the "essential flavor" is expressed in the given piece of music.

Constructing Chords With Intervals

If you know the intervals that define a chord type, it is possible to build a chord of that type starting on any note. To do so, choose the note you want to be the root of the chord and follow the interval pattern to obtain the other notes in the chord.

Let's say, for example, I want to know the notes of the G major triad. I will first find a G on my instrument, then find the note a major third above G. Remember, a major third is the same as four half steps.[1] One half step gets me to G#, two gets me to A, three gets me to A#, and four gets me to B. We now know that B is the third[2] of our chord. Now, I need to find the note a minor third above B. A minor third is the same as three half steps. One half step from B gets me to C, two gets me to C#, three gets me to D. We now know that D is the last note or fifth of our chord. So, the notes G, B, and D form the G major chord.

You can use intervals to create all of the minor triads as well. The only difference is that you will need to count to three half steps to obtain the third of your chord and then count to four steps to obtain the fifth of your chord.

If you would like to, repeat this process on one or more chords of your choosing. As you construct major and minor triads, notice the different visual appearance they create on your instrument.

1. *The Numeric-Quality Interval Naming System*, page 122
2. Meaning the second note of a chord or the note that is a third above the root in a chord's original voicing. See *Naming Chord Tones* on page 139.

You can also notice how chords constructed with the major pattern of intervals sound different than the chords constructed with the minor pattern of intervals. Over time, memorize as many chords as you can so you can recall them quickly while playing or composing.

Throughout this process, feel free to reference the table below. It is good to be familiar with the general concept of constructing chords, but you can use this table to either check the accuracy of chords that you have constructed or look up chords as a quick reference.

Major Triads

Chord Name	Root	Third	Fifth
A Major	A	C#	E
Bb Major	Bb	D	F
B Major	B	D#	F#
C Major	C	E	G
Db Major	Db	F	Ab
D Major	D	F#	A
Eb Major	Eb	G	Bb
E Major	E	G#	B
F Major	F	A	C
F#/Gb Major	F#/Gb	A#/Bb	C#/Db
G Major	G	B	D
Ab Major	Ab	C	Eb

Minor Triads

Chord Name	Root	Third	Fifth
A Minor	A	C	E
Bb Minor	Bb	Db	F
B Minor	B	D	F#
C Minor	C	Eb	G
C# Minor	C#	E	G#
D Minor	D	F	A
D#/Eb Minor	D#/Eb	F#/Gb	A#/Bb
E Minor	E	G	B
F Minor	F	Ab	C
F# Minor	F#	A	C#
G Minor	G	Bb	D
G# Minor	G#	B	D#

Experimenting With Voicings and Patterns of the Triads

Choose a chord from the two tables on the previous page and try experimenting with different voicings of that chord. Experiment with playing the notes in different orders as well. Do this with as many as chords as you would like.

A Note on Note Naming (Triad Edition)

Notice that in the tables above I have chosen to write each chord with either flats *or* sharps, not both. For example, I have written the Ab major chord as Ab, C, and Eb. I did not write Ab, C, and D#. It's often easier to think in terms of sharps *or* flats in a given musical situation, rather than using both at the same time.

In theory, I could also have chosen to describe the Ab chord as a G# chord with all sharps, giving me the notes G#, B#, and D#. However, I choose not to do this because B# can be a confusing term. This sharp note is not a black key at all on the piano. Remember that the white keys B and C have no black key between them. B#, literally meaning one half step higher than B, is the same as C. As mentioned in Chapter One,[1] unusual spellings or ways of naming notes like this do come up in music theory. Sometimes, the correct way to name a note requires an unusual spelling like B#. However, I avoid such terms when I have the choice.

"So why not write our chord as G#, C, and D# then?" you might ask. G#, C, D# is technically an incorrect way to describe a G# major triad. The notes C and D# use letters that are adjacent in the alphabet. This means that they are a second apart. Likewise, G# to C should form a fourth. Chords are traditionally supposed to have thirds between all of their notes in their original voicings. Exactly one letter of the alphabet should be skipped between each note. This is really more of a tradition than a functional distinction, but I have kept to it nonetheless.

Using this line of thinking, I've written the names of each chord above using only sharps or flats for each chord, not both, and also maintaining thirds between the notes of the chords.

1. See *Enharmonic Spellings* and *Getting a Bit More Advanced...* on page 68.

Diminished and Augmented Triads

The next page illustrates the interval patterns for two more chord types – the *diminished triad* and the *augmented triad*. These triads are more dissonant[1] than their major and minor counterparts and as such can be somewhat more difficult to use.

1. *The Sonance of Intervals*, page 129

The diminished triad is defined by having a minor third between the first and second notes as well as the second and third notes. This creates an interval of a diminished fifth between the first and third notes of the chord. The augmented triad is defined by having a major third between the first and second notes as well as the second and third notes. This creates an interval of eight half steps between the first note and the third note. This interval should technically be called an *augmented fifth*[1] but the sound is identical to a minor sixth.

The diagrams below use the C diminished triad and the C augmented triad as examples, but the same interval pattern applies to all diminished triads and augmented triads, respectively.

1. *Why an Augmented Fifth? (Diminished and Augmented Intervals)*, page 144

Diminished Triad
Symbol: Cdim, C°

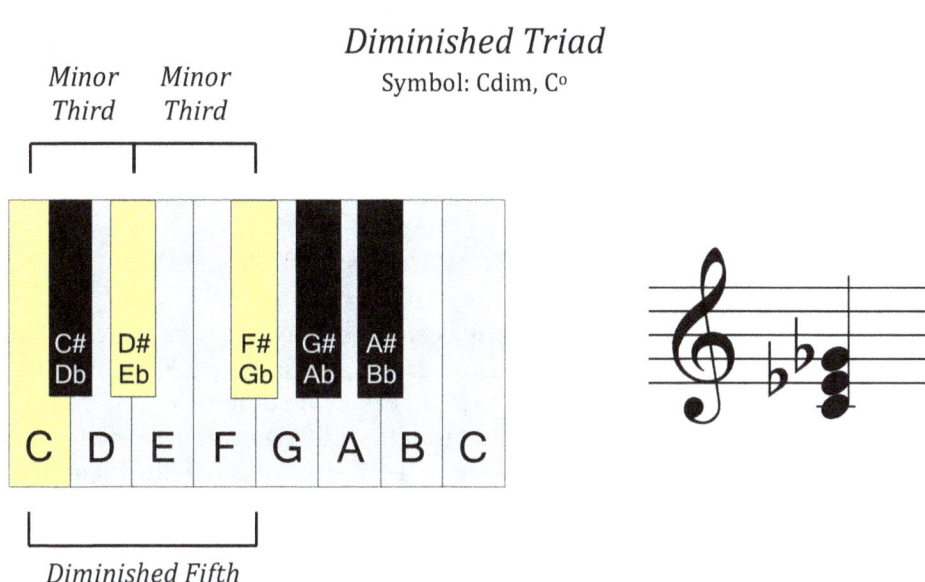

Augmented Triad
Symbol: Caug, C+

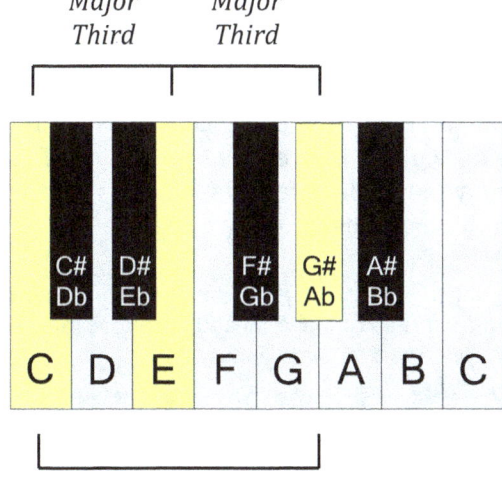

Why an Augmented Fifth? (Diminished and Augmented Intervals)

The notes of a C augmented triad are C, E, and G#. Technically, the third note of the chord must be called G# not Ab because chords are traditionally built in thirds. Based on the alphabetic names of the notes, E and G# are a third apart whereas E and Ab are a fourth apart. Consequently, C and G# must be described as a fifth, not a sixth. But what quality can we assign to a fifth to produce an interval equivalent to eight half steps?

Any perfect or major interval can be extended by one half step by using the augmented quality. Likewise, any perfect or minor interval can be reduced by one half step by using the diminished quality. In the example of the augmented triad, the perfect fifth can be extended by a half step by changing the quality to augmented, thus giving us an augmented fifth between the first and third notes of the chord.

With the exception of the augmented fourth and the diminished fifth, augmented and diminished intervals are rare. But in certain situations where the letters of the notes must preserve certain numeric interval names, it is necessary to use these labels. Well, necessary if you want to use the technically correct terminology, that is. After all, there are many technically incorrect ways to describe these things that get the point across well enough.

Listening to Diminished and Augmented Triads

Listen to a diminished triad and a corresponding example piece on track 51 (disc 1). The example is a short piano excerpt that moves from a C major triad to an F major triad to B diminished triad and then back to a C major triad. Because the diminished chord is a relatively dissonant sound, it is often used in motion from one harmony to another, as it does in this example, rather than as a resting place. See the notation on the following page if you need to follow along to make sure you are hearing what part of the example plays the diminished triad.

Track 52 (disc 1) plays an augmented chord and a short orchestral example of how it might be used. In this example, there is no movement of harmony – just a single C augmented chord. You'll hear how choosing not to resolve[1] this dissonant harmony creates a lot of tension. But in this case, the tension is intentional and creates a particular musical effect that we might desire.

As you listen to these example pieces, notice the expressions of the two chords and particularly the differences between them. The diminished and augmented triads are both more dissonant sounds so they can be a little difficult to differentiate. Take note of your own personal impressions of these chords now and you will be able to use that as reference in the future for recognizing or composing with these chords.

1. The term "resolve" means to allow the music to move from a position of higher energy to a position of lower energy. See *Tension and Resolution* on page 55 and, for more information, jump ahead to *Musical Gravity in Chord Progressions* on page 195.

Diminished Triad Example

> ### Seventh Chords
>
> Triads are three-note chords. *Seventh chords* are four-note chords. Seventh chords get their name from the interval of a seventh that is formed between the bottom and top notes. Below are the interval patterns for the three most common seventh chords – the *major seventh chord*, the *minor seventh chord*, and the *dominant seventh chord*.
>
> In these examples, C is used as the root note, but these patterns can be used on any note to create other chords of the same type.

Major Seventh Chord
Chord Symbol: Cmaj7, Cma7, CM7, C△7

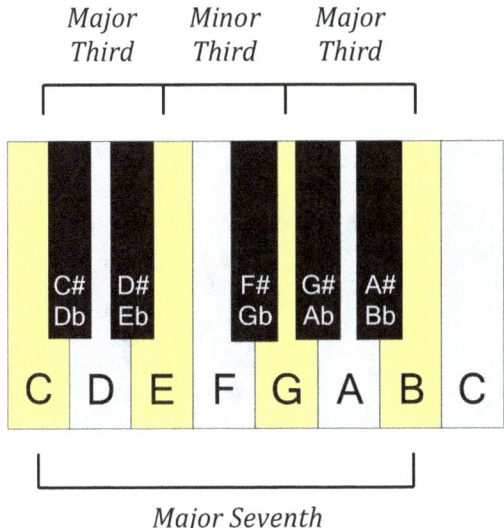

Minor Seventh Chord
Chord Symbol: Cmin7, Cmi7, Cm7, C-7

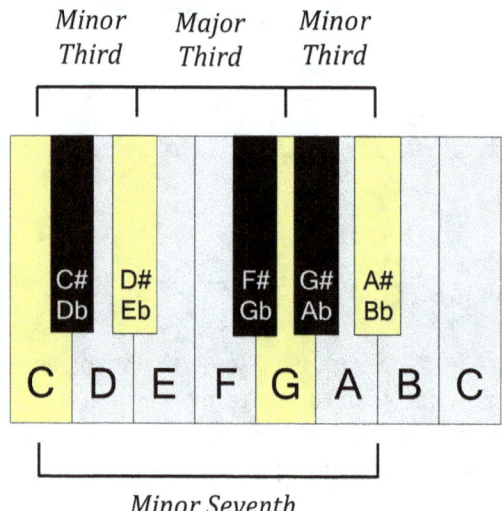

Dominant Seventh Chord
Chord Symbol: C7

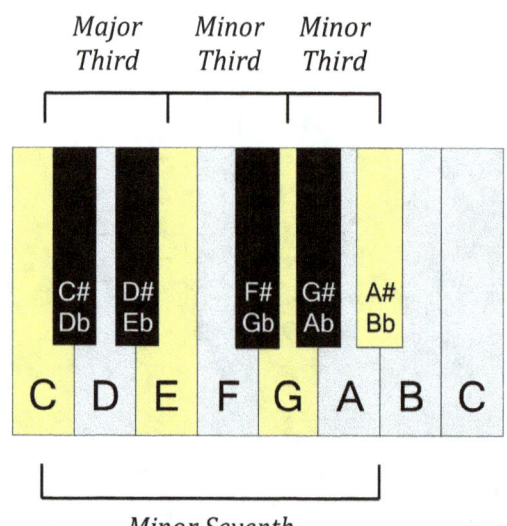

Abbreviated Names

The C major seventh chord and the C minor seventh chord can be referred to as C major seven and C minor seven, respectively. The C dominant seventh chord can also be referred to as C seven. These variations can also be used with all the other possible root notes.

Exploring the Expression of Seventh Chords

You may notice that these seventh chords have a few dissonant intervals. Each chord creates a relatively dissonant seventh interval, between the root and the top note of the chord. In the case of the major seventh chord, the seventh interval is major. In the case of the minor seventh chord and the dominant seventh chord, the seventh is minor. In the dominant seventh chord, there is also a dissonant tritone interval between the third of the chord and the seventh of the chord.

I like to think of the major seventh as having a wondrous quality. The chord retains the basic major quality of a major triad but with an added element of complexity. There is a subtle feeling of mystery to the sound. In different contexts, the major seventh may sound magical, sentimental, beautiful, or awe inspiring.

The minor seventh has a similar expression to the minor triad but it is more subdued and more subtle. Where the minor triad has a relatively direct sad or dark quality to it, the minor seventh sounds cool and mellow.

The dominant seventh chord is energized by the presence of a dissonant tritone but retains an essentially major quality to it. The expression of the dominant seventh chord is bright and even fun sometimes. The dominant seventh chord is a basic building block for the sound of the blues.

You can listen to an example of a major seventh chord being used in a few different musical contexts on track 53 (disc 1). This track starts off with solo jazz piano and progresses into a sampling of a couple ensemble flavors that are possible with the major seventh chord. Track 54 (disc 1) plays a similar example for the minor seventh chord. This track shows two sides of the minor seventh chord. The first half of the track is mellow, played by just a solo piano. The second half becomes more energetic and adds an accompanying drum part. The second half of this track is an example of how the minor seventh chord, which often creates more of a cool and mellow expression, can sound in conjunction with more energetic rhythms and dynamics. Finally, track 55 (disc 1) plays a blues piece to exemplify one possible use of the dominant seventh chord. As with the early examples, the chord being presented will be played in isolation before the example piece on each track. Note that the dominant seventh chord is also a frequently used chord that resolves to a harmonic center, much like the example of the diminished triad on track 51. This use of the dominant seventh chord is discussed more in Chapter Nine.[1]

1. See *Musical Gravity in Chord Progressions* on page 195 and, for more information, see *Chapter Nine* on page 240.

- Voicing Considerations -

Highest and Lowest Notes

The highest and lowest notes of a voicing[1] are often the most clearly audible and have a strong influence on the sound of a chord.

The lowest note of the chord tends to be heard as the *harmonic center* of the chord, a harmonic center simply being the center of a harmony or chord. We talked about centers in Chapter Two as being positions of low expressive energy. We also compared the feeling of a center to a metaphorical home that can be ventured away from or returned to in a composition. Another analogy we talked about is that centers are like planets or stars that exert a gravitational pull on nearby objects.[2]

The lowest note of a chord voicing tends to take on the expressive qualities of a center – the feeling of home, weight, stability, foundation, and so on. By choosing a different note to be the lowest note of a chord voicing and thereby assigning the role of center to a different note, we can change the expression of the voicing.

It is possible to hear a note other than the lowest note as the primary center of a chord. However, the lowest note will always produce a certain pull of centrality. The upper notes of a voicing tend to be heard in relation to the lowest note.

The highest note of a voicing is also influential but in a different way. The highest note stands out prominently; it is easily heard. It seems to rest on top of the other notes of the chord, which often fulfill a more supportive role. The highest note of a chord can become the center of focus and can easily be used as the note of a melody.

1. *Chord Voicings*, page 79
2. *Musical Centers and Gravity*, page 54

Inversions

Inversions specify which note of a voicing is the lowest in pitch. In a triad, *root position* refers to the position where the root of the chord is the lowest note. *First inversion* refers to the position where the third of the chord is the lowest note, and *second inversion* refers to the position where the fifth of the chord is the lowest note. In a seventh chord, the terms are the same with the addition of the *third inversion*, which refers to the position where the seventh of the chord is the lowest note.

Listen to each inversion of the C major chord on track 56 (disc 1) and to each inversion of the C7 chord on track 57 (disc 1).

C Major Triad Inversions

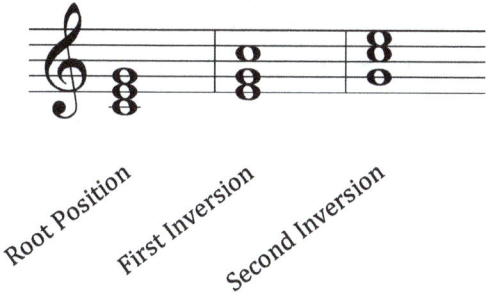

C7 Inversions

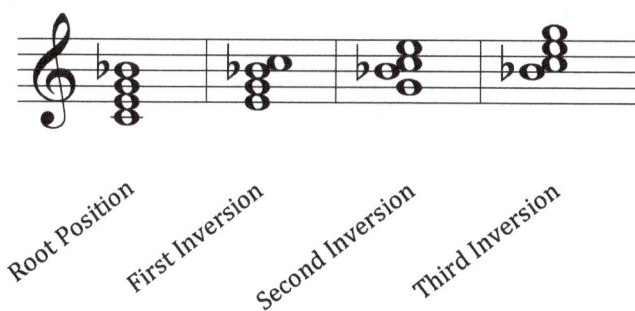

Muddiness

Groups of notes played together begin to sound *muddy* if they are both low in pitch and placed close together in terms of pitch. For example, listen to the muddy, unclear sound of a C2 and an E2 played together on track 58 (disc 1).

Generally, this kind of muddy sound is avoided. However, it is possible that you may find that a muddy sound works in particular places in your music. Simply be aware that chord voicings and intervals may begin to take on this muddy quality if they are placed too low and contain too many small intervals.

Because of this muddiness effect, it is generally best to maintain larger intervals between the lower notes of your voicings, while higher notes can be treated more flexibly, with large or small intervals as desired.

Also keep in mind that muddiness may become more intense with richer, more complex timbres. More simple timbres may allow the use of lower and smaller intervals without producing an overly muddy sound.

Interval Relationships

It is important to consider the interval relationships you are creating when choosing a particular voicing. By moving notes into different octaves it is possible to invert intervals or to add octaves of space into your intervals. Some intervals are more consonant when inverted, while others are less consonant. Some intervals may sound more consonant with the addition of octaves, while others do not.

Open or Close

You will also want to consider how big the interval relationships are in your voicing. Does your interval occupy the territory of five octaves with just a few notes or does it fit all within a single octave? Voicings that use the notes of the chord in the smallest possible space, in terms of pitch, are called *close voicings*. Another way to think about this is that a close voicing will not "skip" any notes of the chord as it proceeds from the lowest note of the voicing to the highest. In contrast, an *open voicing* refers to a voicing that is spread out and does skip some notes of the chord, playing only chosen chord tones in each octave.

I think openness is a good descriptor of the expression of a voicing where the notes are spread out across the spectrum of pitch. In comparison, close voicings sound denser, if you will.

Emphasis of Notes and Intervals

By adding repetitions of pitches with the same note name in different octaves, we can emphasize certain aspects of a chord's character. The same is true of intervals. By doubling notes or rearranging notes in different octaves, it is possible to create multiple instances of a given interval. Especially with larger chords, voicings can be constructed based on the repetition of a specific interval.[1]

1. *Constant Interval Voicings*, page 393

Constructing and Experimenting With Chords

In this chapter, we have studied the most common types of chords and their corresponding interval patterns. Using these interval patterns, we can construct each of the chord types we have studied on any of the twelve notes. For an example of how to do this, refer to the box entitled *Constructing Chords With Intervals* on page 140.

Try using this technique to construct some diminished or augmented triads. Try constructing some major, minor, or dominant seventh chords as well. Once you have constructed a chord, try experimenting with different voicings, sequences, and arpeggios to get a sense of the chord's possible expressive variations.

You can also use this opportunity to experiment with some of the characteristics of chord voicings we have discussed in this section: lowest and highest notes, muddiness, interval relationships, open and close voicings, and, finally, emphasis of particular notes or intervals.

- Chord Progressions -

What Are Chord Progressions?

Chord progressions are sequences of chords. Often, pieces of music or songs will repeat a single chord progression many times. Some pieces are more diverse harmonically and others are more repetitive. Each option creates a different effect. Variety can be interesting, but creating a repeating chord progression can add a component of stability and cohesion.

Chords Diatonic to Major and Minor Scales

When writing a chord progression, chords are generally chosen from a set of possibilities that are determined by a scale. The major and minor scales each contain seven notes. Each of these seven notes can be used as the root note of a triad or seventh chord. Therefore, in any major or minor key there are seven diatonic[1] triads and seven diatonic seventh chords. Each of these diatonic chords will have a designated chord type based on the interval pattern of the given scale type.

The following page shows the triads in the C major scale and the C minor scale. Underneath the triads are the seventh chords in the C major scale and the C minor scale. In scales with different tonal centers,[2] the notes of the diatonic chords will change but the intervals and, thus, the chord types will remain the same within a given type of scale. In other words, all major scales follow the pattern of chord types for diatonic triads and seventh chords shown on the next page. And likewise, all minor scales follow the pattern of chord types for diatonic triads and seventh chords shown on the next page.

1. Diatonic means to be in a scale. See *Diatonic and Chromatic* on page 82.
2. A tonal center is the first note of a scale. See *The Tonal Center* on page 83.

Triads Diatonic to the Major Scale

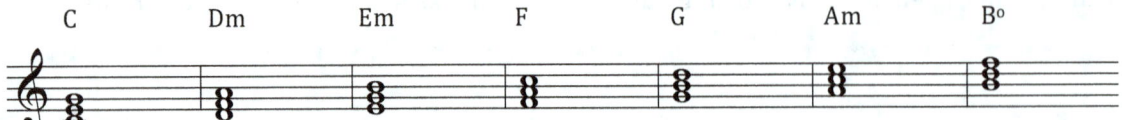

Triads Diatonic to the Minor Scale

Seventh Chords Diatonic to the Major Scale

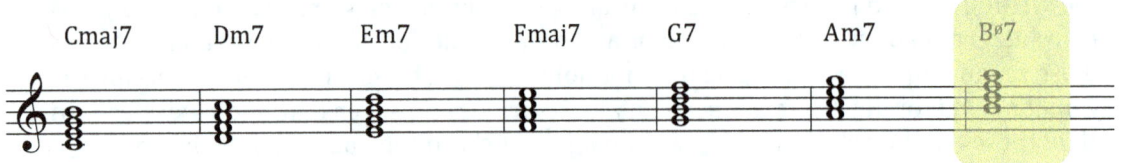

Seventh Chords Diatonic to the Minor Scale

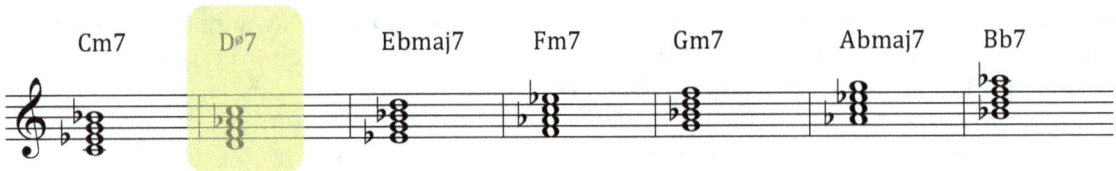

The Highlighted Chords

The highlighted chords above are called *half-diminished seventh chords*. This is a more advanced type of chord that we haven't covered yet. See Chapter Thirteen for a description of this chord.

❖ *More Seventh Chords*, page 396

Describing Chords With Roman Numerals

In the context of a scale, chords can be described with Roman numerals that represent which note of the scale the chord starts on. For example, the C major triad is considered the *I chord* in the key of C major because the root note of the C major triad is the first note of the scale. The D minor triad is called the *II chord* in the scale of C major because the root note of the D minor triad is the second note of the scale. This pattern repeats for all seven triads and all seven seventh chords in a scale.

We can even replace the letter indicating the root note in a chord symbol with a Roman numeral to indicate both the position of the chord in a scale and the type of chord being played in that position. For example, IVmin or IV- represents a minor triad built on the fourth degree of a scale and V7 represents a dominant seventh chord built on the fifth degree of a scale.

I-IV-V-I Progression in C Major

Using Roman numeral names, we can describe the chord progression below as a I-IV-V-I progression in the C major scale. These Roman numerals represent the position of the root note of each chord in the scale.

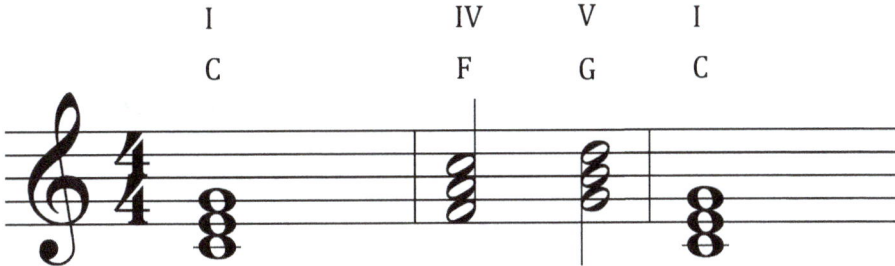

Try playing this chord progression on an instrument or listen to the progression on track 59 (disc 1).

Harmonic Rhythm

The rhythm in which a chord progression changes is called the *harmonic rhythm*. Notice how the F and G chords only last for half a measure but both C chords last for one whole measure.

Chords commonly last for half a measure, a full measure, or two measures. Of course, chords can last for durations outside of this range as well.

- Voice Leading -

To *voice lead* a chord progression means to create voicings for a chord progression that minimize the amount of movement between notes from chord to chord. In other words, voice leading is the process of creating the smallest intervals between the notes of one chord and the notes of the next. This makes your chord progression easier to play in many cases, and it also makes the chord progression sound smooth and easy on the ears.

Below is a voice-led version of the I-IV-V-I progression in C major that we discussed in the previous section.

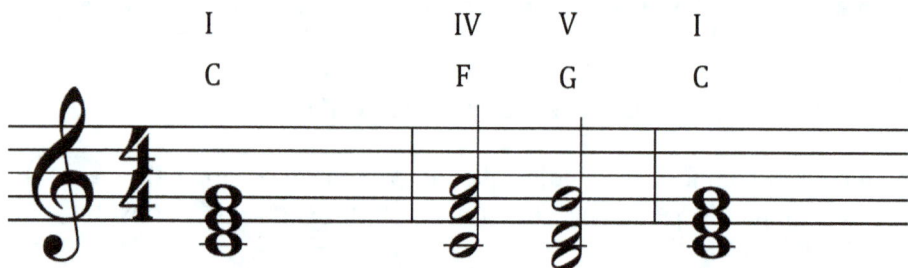

Listening to the Voice-Led Chord Progression

Listen to track 60 (disc 1) to hear this voice-led progression. Listen to track 59 (disc 1) to hear the original for comparison. Notice how this version has less movement and sounds smoother.

Comparing the Two Chord Progressions

Let's examine the effect of this voice-leading process in more detail by comparing the intervals in the two versions of the chord progression. When we are dealing with voice leading, we are not concerned about the intervals between notes that are being heard or *sounding* at the same time. We are concerned with the movement from chord to chord. We will be looking at the intervals between each of the bottom notes of the chords, each of the middle notes of the chords, and each of the top notes of the chords.

We will group the intervals between the notes into three categories according to size – *common tones*, steps, and leaps. Common tones are notes that are shared between two chords. Steps include both half steps and whole steps, and leaps include all intervals larger than a whole step.

We will represent common tones with blue arrows, steps with green arrows, and leaps with red arrows.

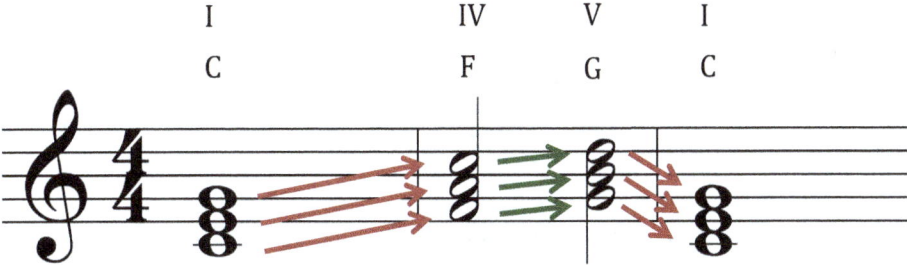

Our original chord progression contains six leaps and three steps.

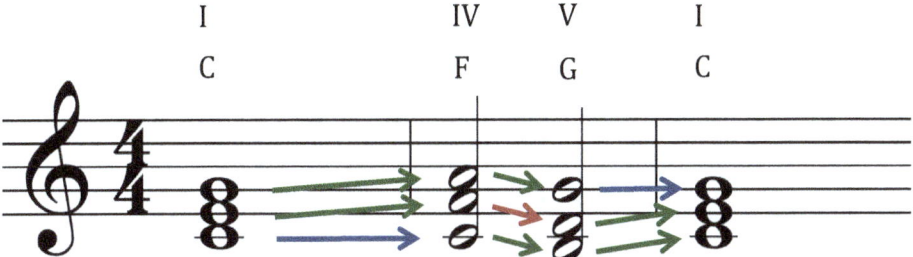

The new version of our chord progression has significantly less movement with one leap, six steps, and two common tones.

Conjunct and Disjunct

We could say that the voice-led version of the chord progression is more *conjunct*, meaning that there are smaller intervals between the notes that change in the chord progression and fewer notes that change at all. In contrast, we could say that the original chord progression is more *disjunct*, meaning that there are larger intervals between the notes that change in the chord progression and more notes that change overall.

Conjunct music tends to sound smoother and creates a listenable flow. Disjunct music can create energy and interest or can become jarring or confusing if the leaps become too extreme.

Generally, harmony parts are likely to be voice led in the manner described here. However, within a single chord, patterns of notes often create significantly larger intervals. Composers can do this without creating a jarring effect because the notes of a single chord are connected together as a single harmony. However, when a chord changes and a large interval leap occurs at the same time, the listener may experience a disconnect.

Melodies also can be described as more conjunct or disjunct. Melodies commonly use leaps here or there but are often written in a conjunct manner. Conjunct melodies are thought of as more singable and can create lyrical, smooth expressions.

Writing Chord Progressions

Try writing some chord progressions!

1. Choose a scale to write in.

2. Choose a chord to start your progression that falls in the scale you are writing in.

3. Create a voicing or pattern out of your first chord. At this point, you can choose to create a rhythm for your chord pattern or you can choose to write a sequence of voicings *out of time*, meaning that you are not adhering to any strict rhythm. If your chord pattern does have a rhythm, decide what time signature and tempo you will be writing in.

4. Now experiment with other chords in the same scale that could follow your first chord. Voice lead your second chord so that the intervals between the two voicings are relatively small. If you have established a rhythm for your first chord, continue it with your second chord or perhaps create a variation, but ensure that your progression sounds cohesive and connected.

5. Continue to add chords in this way a few more times. To start with, see if you can create a progression that lasts for four measures. See if you can create the progression so it can be repeated. This means that the last chord will need to be voice led so that it creates small interval relationships with the first chord (if you intend to create a conjunct expression). As you gain experience, try creating longer and more complex progressions.

Sustain Pedal and Chord Progressions

If you are playing your sequence of chords on a piano and you are using the sustain pedal, you'll probably want to make sure to lift up the sustain pedal immediately after switching chords and then quickly put it back down for the next chord. If you do not do this, the sustain pedal will mix the sounds of your chords together and this could result in an unintentionally murky or unclear sound.

Advanced

- Related Series Analysis -

Delving Deeper Into the Mechanisms Behind Harmonic Expression

With a pair of notes, the expressions of consonance and dissonance are produced as a result of the proportional relationship between the two notes. In groups of three notes, the expressive range of possibilities increases enormously in complexity and even more so in groups of four notes. The more notes there are in a chord, the more relationships are created between all the constituent notes of the chord and the result is a more subtle, nuanced, and complex expressive character.

Try the following experiment. Listen to and feel the expression of various pairs of two notes. Experiment with several intervals, taking in the range of expression that is produced by all the different intervals. Now start experimenting with groups of three notes. You may use triads, voicings of triads, or other groups of three notes, even random groups. Try a number of different things. How is this experience different? Repeat the process again with seventh chords, voicings of seventh chords, and other four-note groups. Do you hear a progression of increasing complexity in the sound and feeling that is produced? What new avenues of expression are opened up with the addition of a third or fourth note in the chord? If you would like, continue this process with five, six, or seven-note chords and notice the results in terms of the complexity of expression.[1]

1. See information about larger chords in the section *Ninth, Eleventh, and Thirteenth Chords* on page 388.

How are these more complex expressions being produced? What makes the major triad happy and bright while the minor triad is sad and dark? The augmented triad seems especially filled with tension, perhaps more than we might expect from a group of notes that contains the interval relationships of two major thirds and one minor sixth – reasonably consonant intervals overall. And what of the still more sophisticated expressions of the seventh chords?

What follows is a system for analyzing groups of notes, with accompanying original terminology (not necessarily common in the musical community). After covering this system, we will then apply it here and throughout the book to answer these and other more complex questions.

Sonance of Groups of Three or More Notes

In the last chapter, we examined the sonance of intervals or pairs of two notes. Now that we are moving into the larger interval structures of triads and seventh chords, the question arises: "How do we determine the sonance of groups of three or more notes?"

For intervals, we looked at the frequencies related to both notes in the interval and created a proportional ratio that described the relationship between the two frequencies. From this point, we said that an interval was consonant if it could be described by a low ratio and it was dissonant if it was described by a high ratio. A ratio is low if it implies a small number of parts in the overall system it describes. It is high when it implies a large number of parts. In turn, we can equate the total number of parts in the system to *the larger number in the given ratio*. For example, a 3:5 ratio describes a system with five total parts and an 8:9 ratio describes a system with nine total parts. Systems with fewer parts can be described as simple, and systems with more parts can be described as complex.

For larger groups of notes, this process remains essentially the same. We could, for example, describe a group of three notes with the ratio 3:4:5. To describe the complexity of the group, we equate the total number of parts in the system to the *largest number in the given ratio*. In this example, the complexity of the system is represented by the number five because five total parts are needed to create the relationships described by the given ratio, in this case the ratio 3:4:5.

- ❖ *Proportionality*, page 48
- ❖ *Strong or Weak Proportionality*, page 49
- ❖ *The Sonance of Intervals*, page 129

Note Groups and Subgroups

I call any group of notes, including but not limited to intervals, chords, and scales, a *note group*. In groups of three or more notes, subsets of the notes in the group can function independently creating their own expression within the larger group. I call these *subgroups*, indicating that they are groups of notes contained within larger groups of notes.

Subgroup Relationships

Consider a note group that can be represented by the proportion 4:5:6. Here, the total complexity of the group can be represented by the number six. But going deeper, let's look at the relationships that are generated between all of the pairs of notes that exist within this system of three notes. In any three-note group, there will be three, unique subgroups, each of which will be a pair of two notes. A subgroup exists between the first note of the system and the second, between the second note of the system and the third, and finally between the first note and the third. In this case, the ratios that represent the subgroups are 4:5, 5:6, and 4:6, which can be simplified to 2:3.

The simplified ratio of 2:3 tells us that within the system of six parts, there is a subgroup that can be described with only three parts. Hearing this group, we may perceive a stronger consonance present between these two notes but in the context of a larger, more complex system.

Multiple Levels of Relationships

In a pair of notes, the only relationship in the system is the relationship between the two notes. In a group of three notes, there is the relationship between all three notes, as well as the three relationships between each subgroup of two notes. In a group of four notes, there is one relationship between all four notes, four relationships between subgroups of three notes, and six relationships between subgroups of two notes. In a group of four notes, we can describe three different levels of relationships happening within the system. There are the relationships between four notes, between three notes, and between two notes.

In any group of notes, relationships form in subgroups of any possible number of notes within the subgroup, from two notes all the way up to the total number of notes in the group.

Relationships Between Subgroups

The process of breaking down a group of notes into subgroups reveals all the relationships between the notes in the group. To deepen our analysis further still, we can consider that subgroups themselves can have relationships to one another and to other individual notes. We can evaluate these relationships by describing the proportions of both subgroups (or a subgroup and an individual note) together in a larger group and comparing the complexity of this overall group to the complexity of the isolated subgroups.

For example, consider a group of notes that can be represented by the proportional values two, four, five, and six. Within this group, we can make a subgroup out of the numbers two, four, and six. Isolated into a subgroup, these numbers can be simplified to the values, one, two, and three. This subgroup has a complexity represented by the number three. By introducing the last note back into the group, we must rename these numbers two, four, and six to describe the proportions of the group with whole integer values. Consequently, the overall complexity of the group goes from three to six. This jump in complexity implies that there is a certain kind of strain to the relationship between this particular subgroup and the individual note represented by the number five.

The Overtone Series

As you can see, even relatively small groups of notes, can generate a large number of relationships. As we increase the total number of notes, the number of relationships increases exponentially. These relationships theoretically contain all the information we need to explain the complex expressions of all possible note groups. However, we now are facing the practical obstacle of keeping track of all these relationships and being able to use them in musical settings like performing, improvising, or composing. This challenge is obviously a considerable one any way you tackle the problem. However, I would like to offer you a paradigm of analysis based on the overtone series,[1] which may make things a little easier.

The overtone series is a very special pattern in that it represents all possible proportional relationships progressing from the strongest to the weakest. The ratio from the fundamental to the second harmonic is 2:1. The ratio from the fundamental to the third harmonic is 3:1 and so on. Ratios between two and a number higher than two can be found in the overtone series in the intervals from the second harmonic to each higher harmonic. We can then find ratios between three and a number higher than three by starting at the third harmonic and forming ratios with each higher harmonic. Proceeding in this fashion, we can produce a pattern of all possible proportional relationships, starting with the strongest relationships, which use the lowest numbers, and proceeding to progressively weaker relationships, making use of higher numbers.

Due to its special proportional properties, the overtone series becomes a very useful tool for us as composers when translated into musical notes. Below is the overtone series for the note C2. The overtone series for any other note can be produced by using the same intervals as the notation below while using the desired fundamental pitch as the first note of the series.[2]

1. The overtone series can also be called a harmonic series. For information on the overtone series, see *Timbre and Harmonic Composition* on page 34. Especially relevant to this topic are the boxes entitled *Harmonics* on page 37 and *The Harmonic Series* on page 39.
2. This process can be described as *transposing* the harmonic series. The transposing process is discussed in more detail in the section entitled *Transposing* on page 191.

Inaccuracies in Tuning

In the equal temperament tuning system,[1] the overtone series can be approximated but it cannot be played exactly with the available frequencies. Some parts of the series can be approximated quite well while others deviate significantly. In the notation above, each note is labeled with a value that indicates how far off the note is in equal temperament from its mathematical ideal. The values are given in a unit called *cents*, which represent a hundredth of a half step. Positive values indicate that the note in equal temperament is sharp in comparison to its ideal, while negative values indicate that the note in equal temperament is flat in comparison to its ideal. Notes that have been left blank are exactly accurate.

1. *Tuning Systems and Sonance*, page 132

The Exponential Increase of Musical Pitches

The overtone series progresses linearly in frequency. That is to say, the increase in frequency from one note to the next is the same at every step of the series. Considering this, it is interesting to note that the increase, in terms of musical intervals, from one note to the next is reduced as we continue up through the overtone series. The reason for this is that the notes of the musical system progress exponentially, rather than linearly, in frequency. Every octave doubles in frequency. This means that the distance in frequency between each octave, and thus each note, is greater and greater as one progresses to higher and higher pitches.

Related Series and Related Fundamentals

In the last chapter, we saw that after the unison, the most consonant interval is the octave, followed by the perfect fifth, perfect fourth, and the major third and sixth.[1] Notice that in the overtone series above, between the first and second harmonics is an interval of an octave. The perfect fifth forms between the second and third harmonics, and the perfect fourth forms between the third and fourth harmonics. The major third forms between the fourth and fifth harmonics, while the major sixth forms between the third and fifth harmonics. The order these intervals appear in the overtone series corresponds with their level of sonance. And the numbers of the harmonics where we find each interval correspond with the ratio that defines the interval. For example, the major sixth interval is defined by a 3:5 ratio and the third and fifth harmonics of the overtone series form a major sixth interval.

Seeing this connection, we can relate any interval or group of notes to a particular overtone series where the ratio that defines the note group corresponds with the numbered positions where we find the given note group in the overtone series. I call an overtone series that matches this description a *related series*, and I call the fundamental note of such a series a *related fundamental*.

1. *Ordering the Intervals From Consonant to Dissonant*, page 130

For example, a note group whose proportions are represented by the numbers two, three, and five will have notes at the second, third, and fifth harmonics of the group's related series. Therefore because the positions in the related series correspond to the ratio that describes the group, we may assess the sonance of a note group by looking at its position in the corresponding related series. In ratios, the highest number in the group represents the total complexity of the group and, thus, its sonance. In a similar way, the highest numbered harmonic in the related series of a note group represents the complexity of the group.

Considering Tuning Inaccuracies for Ratios

Generally speaking, we will want to associate note groups with the harmonic numbers that appear *first* in the series and, thus, use the *lowest* possible ratio numbers. However, sometimes tuning inaccuracies may create exceptions to this rule. For example, we said in Chapter Five that the interval of a minor seventh is defined by a 9:16 ratio. We do indeed find a minor seventh between the ninth and sixteenth harmonics of the overtone series. However, we also find a minor seventh several times earlier in the overtone series. The earliest instance is between the fourth and seventh harmonics. But if you consult the notation above, you will find that the minor seventh between the ninth and sixteenth harmonics is significantly more accurate than all the previous instances of the interval. So I've chosen to, in this case, use the 9:16 ratio to get a somewhat more accurate representation of the minor seventh interval.

Similar thinking can be applied to finding any interval in the overtone series. See the notation on page 160 for guidance on what tuning issues might be relevant.

Finding the Related Fundamental of a Group

To find the related fundamental of a note group, you will need to find the overtone series in which the note group appears in the lowest possible positions (tuning inaccuracies aside, as mentioned in the previous box). The fundamental note of this series will be your related fundamental.

To help get you started, I have provided a list of the related fundamentals for all the simple intervals.[1] These relationships are a solid starting point. However, my recommendation is to eventually become familiar with the overtone series starting on each of the twelve notes as well. With this information, you'll be able to recognize larger groups of notes and place them in the appropriate related series.

1. Meaning intervals less than an octave. See *Compound Intervals* on page 128.

Intervals	Ratio of Interval	Position of Related Fundamental (Interval Below Higher Note)	Position of Related Fundamental (Interval Below Lower Note)
Unison	1:1	Unison	Unison
Octave	2:1	Octave	Unison
Perfect Fifth	3:2	Octave and a Perfect Fifth	Octave
Perfect Fourth	4:3	Two Octaves	Octave and a Perfect Fifth
Major Sixth	5:3	Two Octaves and a Major Third	Octave and a Perfect Fifth
Major Third	5:4	Two Octaves and a Major Third	Two Octaves
Minor Third	6:5	Two Octaves and a Perfect Fifth	Two Octaves and a Major Third
Tritone	7:5	Two Octaves and a Minor Seventh	Two Octaves and a Major Third
Tritone*	10:7	Three Octaves and a Major Third	Two Octaves and a Minor Seventh
Minor Sixth	8:5	Three Octaves	Two Octaves and a Major Third
Major Second	9:8	Three Octaves and a Major Second	Three Octaves
Major Seventh	15:8	Three Octaves and a Major Seventh	Three Octaves
Minor Seventh	16:9	Four Octaves	Three Octaves and a Major Second
Minor Second	16:15	Four Octaves	Three Octaves and a Major Seventh

Wondering why the tritone is listed with two different ratios? See page 133.

Related Series Analysis

We can use the knowledge we have laid out so far in this section about the sonance of note groups, systems of subgroups within a larger note group, and the concept of a related series to construct an analysis paradigm that we can apply to any harmony or group of notes. I call this paradigm *related series analysis*.

Related series analysis is essentially a two-step process. First, we will need to find the related fundamental of the subgroups in the given harmony. In the beginning, you may need to do this exhaustively, perhaps going through every possible interval, every possible three-note combination, every possible four-note combination, and so on in the given harmony. As you gain experience, you may be able to expedite the process by intuiting which subgroups are most relevant to your understanding and focusing attention only on these.

The second step is to compare the related fundamentals with one another and to the *sounding notes* of the harmony. I use the term sounding notes to mean the notes of the harmony that are actually being played and heard. This is in contrast to *implied notes*, which are notes that may be relevant to various relationships in a note group but are not actually being played.

To make comparisons between related fundamentals or from related fundamentals to sounding notes in the harmony or note group, we will look at the sonance of the intervals that are created in the given comparison or relationship, with consonant intervals representing a strong sense of connection and the low energy pole of the expressive spectrum and dissonant intervals representing the opposite, disconnection and the high energy pole of the expressive spectrum. Evaluating the sonance of these interval relationships is another way to think about and represent the proportional ratio relationships we looked at earlier in this section. Subgroups whose related fundamentals form consonant relationships can be combined into a larger group, which contains all the subgroups, while increasing the proportional complexity of the overall group, in comparison with the original subgroups, by only a small amount. In contrast, combining subgroups whose related fundamentals form dissonant relationships will result in a significantly higher complexity for the overall group than for the individual subgroups.

The end result of these properties is experienced on a spectrum I describe as moving from simple to complex centrality.[1] Simple centrality means that the felt sense of a center is clear and unambiguous. Simple centrality is created when the related fundamentals of the subgroups in a harmony form consonant relationships. On the other end of the spectrum, complex centrality means that the sense of a center is ambiguous or perhaps seems to pull in different directions toward multiple competing centers. Situations like this arise when the related fundamentals of subgroups have dissonant relationships.

Taking all of this together, we can begin to make some very interesting conclusions by analyzing the relationships between related fundamentals and between subgroups. We may uncover implications of simple or complex centrality and, furthermore, if the centrality is complex we can discover what note or notes are most responsible for the complexity. We can discover which notes are competing with one another or aligning toward different centers. This information gives us a very rich picture of what is happening in the relationships of a harmony.

1. *Simple and Complex Centrality*, page 56

We can then take this picture and begin to understand how and why the particular expression of a note group is arising as it is.

Why Use the Overtone Series Instead of Numeric Ratios?

Everything that can be discovered with the related series paradigm can also be thought of in terms of numeric ratios. But the use of the overtone series helps us to translate this information into musical terms. The overtone series can be thought of as interval structure and shifted[1] to start on different notes depending on our needs. This makes working with the overtone series very convenient from the musician's point of view, while maintaining the same results that thinking in numeric ratios would produce.

1. In technical terms, we would say that the overtone series can be *transposed* to start on different notes. See *Transposing* on page 191.

Inversions and Changing the Octaves of Notes

The note name of the related fundamental of an interval will stay the same regardless of the octaves the notes of the interval are placed in. We may even invert[1] an interval and the note name of the related fundamental will remain the same. Changing the octaves of the notes in an interval can sometimes change the octave the related fundamental is placed in but not the note name of the related fundamental. This means that one can meaningfully talk about the note name of the related fundamental without considering the voicing of the corresponding note group.

1. *Interval Inversions*, page 129

Analysis of Basic Chord Types

With our newly codified system of analysis, let us examine the basic chord types we have learned so far – the major triad, the minor triad, the diminished triad, the augmented triad, the major seventh, the minor seventh, and the dominant seventh. These analyses will provide an example of how you can apply the related series paradigm to more deeply understand the expression of any group of notes.

Major Triad

The proportions of the major triad in its original voicing are represented by the ratio 4:5:6. But when considering the major triad in all its voicings, we can see that a particular voicing of the major triad is created with the first six notes of the overtone series.

And only the first five harmonics are needed to create a full major triad with a root, third, and fifth represented somewhere in the voicing. The related fundamentals of the intervals in a major triad are all the root note of the chord. Two of the related fundamentals fall two octaves below the sounding root of the chord, while the third related fundamental falls one octave below the sounding root of the chord. This means that the related fundamentals have strong relationships to each other and to the notes of the chord. These characteristics represent a model of strong proportionality, simplicity, and connection in a three-note group. And indeed the experience of the sound is generally heard as strong, stable, harmonious, and even uplifting in the right context.

The Minor Triad

The minor triad is a fundamental contrast to the major triad. The intervals of the major and minor triads are the same only placed in a different order. This makes them both somewhat consonant in a similar way. However, when we analyze these chords in terms of their related fundamentals, the two triads tell a very different story. In contrast to the major triad, the related fundamentals of the minor triad all possess different note names. The related fundamental of the root and third is a note two octaves and major third below the root. The related fundamental of the third and the fifth is a note two octaves below the third. The related fundamental of the root and fifth is a note one octave below the root. Collectively, the related fundamentals of a minor triad form a major triad with a root note a major third below the root note of the sounding chord. Using the C minor triad as an example, the related fundamentals are written in the lower staff of the notation below. The pair of sounding notes associated with each related fundamental is shown with connecting lines overlaid on the notation. Notice how in this example, the related fundamentals form a voicing of the Ab major triad, which is the major triad built on the note a major third below the root of the sounding chord, in this case C minor.

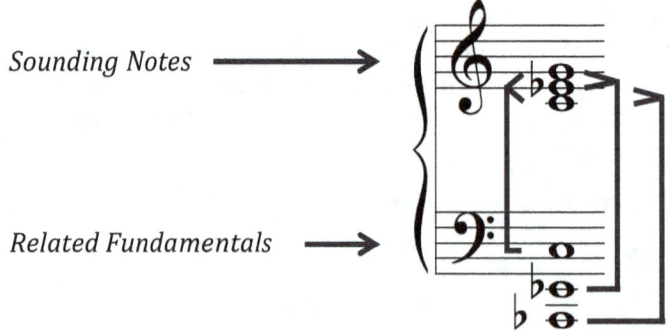

The minor triad is an example of complex centrality. In the example above, all the related fundamentals of the chord seem to point to Ab as the center and yet the root of the chord is C. On the level of the sounding notes, the perfect fifth between the root and fifth of the chord is a very strong consonance and strongly implies that C is the center. The interval between these competing centers, Ab and C, is a major third, a moderate consonance. So they are still somewhat related, yet different enough to generate the effect of complex centrality. Notice the interval of a major seventh that forms between the sounding fifth of the chord and unheard, yet central, Ab of the related fundamentals. This is a fairly strong dissonance and stands out as the most dissonant interval that is created between any of the notes of the chord or related fundamentals.

Another key factor in this chord is the alignment of *all* the related fundamentals toward one center that conflicts with the, somewhat weaker, alignment of the sounding notes. The result is a conflict between heard and unheard forces where the two camps are clearly divided against one another: one camp associated with the overt, sounding center and another camp associated with the subtle, implied center.

We can see this conflict represented in a different perspective by looking at the numbers needed to describe the proportional relationships of all three notes of a minor triad. The intervals involved are represented by the ratios 5(root):6(third), 4(third):5(fifth), and 2(root):3(fifth). These are the same ratios involved in the major triad so far. However, to relate all the notes of the chord together we must use the proportions 10(root):12(third):15(fifth). We can then simplify 10:12 to get 5:6, 12:15 to get 4:5, and 10:15 to get 2:3. The original voicing of a major triad can be represented by the proportions 4:5:6, with a collective complexity of six parts. In contrast, the minor triad is significantly more complex with fifteen parts needed to describe the relationship of the three-note group. From this perspective, we can see that on the level of two-note relationships, the minor triad is quite strong proportionally. But on the level of three-note relationships, it is relatively weak. The major triad, however, is strong on both levels.

Expressively, the minor triad seems to capture the characteristics we are describing here. The sound is consonant and yet includes a subtle form of conflict, sadness, or tension under the surface. The complex centrality, or in another perspective the complexity of the three-note group, is the property that makes the minor triad sound "minor" rather than just sounding dissonant or unrelated on the overt level. The more nuanced expression of the minor quality, associated with sadness and darkness, comes from the combination of overt consonance and subtle dissonance.

The Diminished Triad

The diminished triad can be described with the ratio 5:6:7. This correlates to the diminished chord's position in the overtone series as the fifth, sixth, and seventh notes of the series. However, there are some tuning inaccuracies to take into account. The tritone, which appears between the root and fifth of a diminished triad, can be represented with either a 5:7 or 7:10 ratio but does not create either ratio very accurately. The top two notes of the diminished triad form a minor third, which is described with the ratio 5:6. And yet the top two numbers in our three-note ratio form a 6:7 ratio, not a 5:6 ratio.

This too is a rounding inaccuracy created by the approximations used in the equal temperament system. All of that is to say, the diminished triad approximates the 5:6:7 relationship but doesn't match it terribly accurately.

The ratio itself is only moderately complex, with a total of seven parts. But notice that on the level of two-note relationships, the diminished triad is considerably more dissonant than the major or minor triad. In comparison, the diminished triad replaces the perfect fifth relationship in a major or minor triad with a tritone relationship and at the same time replaces the major third relationship in a major or minor triad with a minor third relationship. In both cases, and especially with the addition of the tritone interval, the dissonance of the chord is considerably heightened. Furthermore, notice that not only does the diminished triad gain a tritone in this comparison, it also loses the perfect fifth, which is the most consonant interval in the major and minor triads.

The centrality of the diminished chord is relatively simple though unusual in that it seems to imply that the center is a major third below the root of the chord – the same unheard note that is implied in the minor triad. Though unlike the minor triad, it creates this implication fairly unambiguously. In the minor triad, the sounding notes imply the root as the center while the related fundamentals imply a center a major third below the root. In the diminished chord however, both the sounding notes and the related fundamentals imply the unheard note a major third below the root as the center. The primary factor that is responsible for this difference is the relationship between the root and fifth. The minor triad has a perfect fifth between the root and fifth, creating a strong implication that the root is the center, whereas the diminished triad has a tritone between the root and fifth, which instead implies the note a major third below the root as the center, in congruence with the other intervals of the chord.

Overall, the diminished triad sounds somewhat dissonant and when used in context has the potential for energetic, dramatic, fun, and bright expressions. It gains a sense of expressive energy from the dissonance of its interval relationships but also maintains a fairly clear center, which can give the impression of sounding more "major" than "minor," though with quite a bit more dissonance than a basic major triad. In equal temperament, tuning inaccuracies make the diminished triad sound even more dissonant than it would otherwise. The end result is that diminished triads are generally heard as unstable harmonies, used mostly to create energy passing from one place of centrality to another.

The Augmented Triad

The intervals of the augmented triad can be represented by the ratios 4:5, 4:5, and 5:8. However, if we try to describe these notes exactly in a three-note ratio group we end up creating a very large ratio, with more than 600 total parts. It may be possible to create a more approximate, lower ratio description but anyway you interpret it, the three-note relationship of the augmented triad is very complex, indeed much more complex than its two-note subgroups.

The augmented triad is also completely ambiguous in terms of its center. The notes of an augmented triad divide an octave into the three equal parts of four half steps each. The interesting result of this configuration is that all of the close[1] inversions[2] of the augmented triad have the same interval structure, with major thirds between all the adjacent chord tones. This means that a first inversion C augmented triad is indistinguishable from a root position E augmented triad, and a second inversion C augmented triad is indistinguishable from a root position Ab augmented triad.

Because the interval structure of the augmented triad is the same in all of its inversions, no inversion seems more stable or primary than any other inversion. The result is the centrality of the augmented triad is ambiguous, in fact perfectly ambiguous.

The augmented triad has fairly consonant interval relationships between sounding notes, and this creates a degree of stability, despite the extreme complexity present on the level of three-note relationships. That said, the augmented fifth interval[3] does stand out as a somewhat more dissonant interval relationship and, as a result, contributes significantly to the distinctiveness and character of the chord. Expressively, we perceive a kind of dissonance from the augmented triad because of its complexity on the level of three-note relationships, and yet we experience a floating, uncertain, or even magical quality because of the ambiguous centrality.

1. Meaning to put all of the notes of the chord as close together as possible or in the same octave when voicing the chord, see *Open or Close* on page 150.
2. *Inversions*, page 148
3. The augmented fifth is equivalent, in terms of sound, to the minor sixth. See *Why an Augmented Fifth? (Diminished and Augmented Intervals)* on page 144 for more information.

The Major Seventh Chord

The notes of a major seventh chord are represented by the ratio 8:10:12:15 and these relationships can be achieved reasonably well, though not perfectly, in equal temperament. On the level of three-note relationships, there exists both a major triad in the first three notes of the chord and a minor triad in the last three notes of the chord as subgroups. In some sense, the major seventh is the decisive fulfillment of the ambiguity presented by the minor triad. In the minor triad, a conflict for centrality emerges between the root of the chord and an unheard but implied related fundamental a major third below the root of the chord. A major seventh chord is formed by adding a sounding note a major third below the root of a minor triad. By moving this note from the realm of the implied to the realm of sound, the centrality of the chord shifts so that it clearly establishes the root of the major seventh as the center. The major triad contained within the first three notes of the major seventh chord clearly points to the root as the center. The addition of the fourth note creates an interval of a major seventh with the root, which has an unthreatening related fundamental with the same note name as the major triad of the first three notes, simply placed an octave lower.

As a result, the major seventh chord has fairly simple centrality but with a whole group complexity equivalent to that of a minor triad, at fifteen total parts. The simple centrality accounts for the more major expression of this chord.

But the major seventh chord represents considerably more whole group complexity than the major triad and this, too, can be heard in the expression of the chord. The major seventh seems to be positive, warm, and without conflict but with a degree of intricacy and nuance. It loses some of the directness and simplicity of the major triad.

On the level of two-note relationships, most of the intervals contained in a major seventh chord are fairly consonant. However, the major seventh formed by the root and seventh of the chord creates a dissonance. This is a distinctive feature in the chord and stands out among its relatively more consonant interval companions. The interval of a major seventh can be inverted into a minor second in some voicings of the major seventh chord. This will increase the dissonance of this relationship even more. However, as you study larger chords you may begin to notice the larger a chord becomes, the less any one dissonance fills our awareness. In many voicings, the major seventh or minor second interval in a four-note chord can feel considerably more consonant than it might without the context of the other notes of the chord.

The Minor Seventh

We can think of the minor seventh chord as representing the ratio 10:12:15:18. This way of labeling the ratios is fairly accurate, though describing the minor seventh interval between the root and the seventh of the chord as a 10:18 ratio introduces a small degree of inaccuracy. Like the major seventh chord, the minor seventh contains both a minor triad and a major triad as subgroups within the chord. However, in the minor seventh chord, the minor triad is created in the first three notes of the chord and the major triad is created in the last three notes of the chord, whereas in the major seventh chord it is the other way around. The upper three notes of the minor seventh chord create a strong sense of centrality around the third of the chord. Add this to the conflict in the minor triad between the root and the implied related fundamental on the note a major third below the root and we are looking at a three-way ambiguity in the centrality of the minor seventh chord.

Interestingly, spreading out the centrality conflict among three notes reduces some of the prominent, duality-creating ambiguity of the minor triad and replaces it with a more nuanced, complex, smooth sounding expression. While the minor triad seems to be direct about its conflict, the minor seventh seems to express a conflict that is itself somewhat more complex and ambiguous.

Like the major seventh chord, the intervals contained in the minor seventh are largely consonant with the exception of the interval between the root and the seventh of the chord. This dissonant interval seems to be somewhat less prominent than the major seventh interval in the major seventh chord. Partly, this is because when the minor seventh is inverted it forms a major second, which is somewhat more consonant than the minor second interval that can occur in the major seventh chord. You should still be cognizant of the possibility of forming a major second when voicing a minor seventh chord, but the situation is not as extreme as it is for the major seventh chord.

The Dominant Seventh Chord

The dominant seventh chord can be represented by the ratio 4:5:6:7. The dominant seventh chord contains a major triad and a diminished triad in its subgroups. We can think of the dominant seventh chord as a diminished triad that adds its implied center a major third below the root as a sounding note. All the same tuning issues that emerge for the diminished triad are relevant to the dominant seventh chord. And like the diminished triad, the dominant seventh chord sounds a bit more dissonant than we might be led to believe by its total complexity of seven parts, because of tuning inaccuracies. We can consider that the interval between the root and the seventh of the chord is a minor seventh, which would normally be described in terms of a 9:16 ratio. So perhaps it is better to think of the total complexity of a dominant seventh chord as something approximately equivalent to a sixteen-part system, so between the major seventh chord (fifteen parts) and the minor seventh chord (eighteen parts) in complexity.

Notice that the related fundamentals of the major triad subgroup and the diminished triad subgroup are the same. The dominant seventh establishes the root as the center quite clearly. That said, on the level of two-note relationships, we find that the dominant seventh chord contains two dissonances. The major and minor seventh chord only create dissonant intervals between the root and the seventh of the chord. In the dominant seventh chord, not only do the root and seventh form a minor seventh interval, but the third and seventh also form a tritone. The tritone, in particular, seems to stand out as a distinctive feature of this chord.

Overall, the dominant seventh chord produces clear, simple centrality energized by some more dissonant interval relationships on the overt level. The expression of the dominant seventh chord sounds rather bright and positive, like a major triad, because of its clear center. However, the dissonant relationships add a higher energy expression to the total effect of the sound, much like the diminished triad.

Do Your Own Related Series Analysis

Perform your own related series analysis on a note group of your choice with the following steps:

1. Evaluate the note group in terms of the intervals between the sounding notes. How many consonances are there? How many dissonances? How strong are they in each case?

2. Find the related fundamental of the note group as well as all the subgroups you see as relevant, perhaps going through all the subgroups exhaustively.

3. Look at the relationships of the related fundamentals to each other and to the sounding notes of the chord. Are the relationships consonant or dissonant?

4. What center or competing centers seem to be created in this note group considering the presence of both the related fundamentals and the sounding notes? Is the centrality simple overall or complex?

5. If the centrality is complex, how many competing forces are there? Is it a simple conflict like the minor triad, a more complex conflict like the minor seventh, or a situation of total ambiguity like the augmented triad?

6. Now look at the information you have collected and ask yourself: What are the most important features or characteristics of this note group? What things stand out? What is unusual? What defines this particular set of notes and relationships? Create a summary of your conclusions.

7. Ask yourself what expressions you would expect to see based on these characteristics and compare your answer to the experience of listening to the note group. Continue to analyze and investigate with the aim of improving your predictive powers and capacity for understanding.

Create Your Own Harmony With Related Series Analysis

Using related series analysis, we can better understand why different expressions are arising from a group of notes. In turn, this also means that if we want to create a specific expression while composing, improvising, or otherwise creating our own original music, we can use this understanding to choose notes that will produce our desired expression.

Though related series analysis as a general framework can be applied to all kinds of different expressions, for this activity let's focus in on just two kinds of expressions. First, let's consider the sonance emerging from the relationships between sounding notes. And second, let's consider centrality, ranging from simple centrality, with a clear, singular center, to complex centrality, with an ambiguous center or multiple competing centers.

In this activity, try selecting a specific expression using these characteristics. Then, see if you can choose a collection of notes that when played together seems to produce the expression you were striving to create.

Follow along with these steps:

1. Specify what expression you are attempting to create. How consonant or dissonant? How simple or complex?

2. Select the center or centers in your harmony. You can choose any note or notes you want for this. The idea is just to experiment. You'll probably want to select one or two notes the first time you go through this exercise and then progressively graduate to using three or more centers.

3. Consider the related series for each center. To construct your harmony, you'll need to pick notes from each series. Doing so will ensure that the harmony will contain some implication that your selected notes will indeed feel like centers. You can experiment with choosing notes that are lower in the given related series or higher but, keep in mind that choosing notes that are lower in the series will create a stronger implication of centrality.

4. At this point, you will also want to consider how the sounding notes you are choosing for your harmony are interacting with each other. You will want to make sure that the intervals between these notes are creating the desired level of sonance.

5. Once you have your harmony, you can test the result by playing each of the intended centers below your harmony as a bass note. Alternate between playing the harmony by itself and with each of the centers as a bass note. As you listen, focus on hearing the centers in the harmony even when it is being played without an accompanying bass note. This test will help you to get in touch with how and to what degree each of the centers are actually producing the expression of centrality. If the centrality of your harmony is complex, you can also notice what expression arises out of the competing dynamics between the multiple implied centers.

6. Repeat as many times as desired, sharpening your ability to create different expressions of centrality and sonance.

Chapter Seven
The Interval Structure of Scales

- Building Scales -

Building Major and Minor Scales

In the last chapter, we saw how each type of chord is defined by a pattern of intervals. Using these patterns we were able to construct chords of a given type on any note. Scales function in much the same way. Each type of scale or *scale type* is also defined by a pattern of intervals.

Below are the patterns of intervals that define two scale types: the *major scale* and the *minor scale* (also known as the *natural minor scale*). In the following diagrams, the C major scale and C minor scale are used as examples, but keep in mind that the sequence of intervals for major scales shown below will apply to all major scales, starting on any note, and the sequence of intervals for minor scales will, likewise, apply to all minor scales. Take a moment to look over the sequences of intervals for these two types of scales.

Major Scale

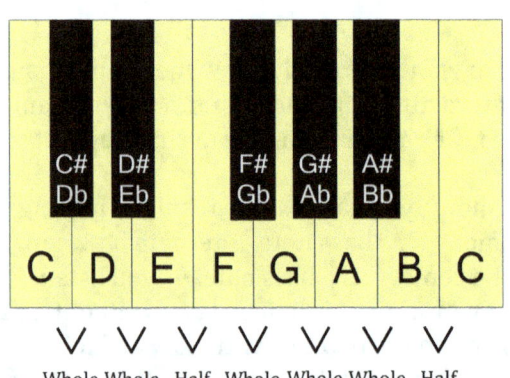

Minor Scale

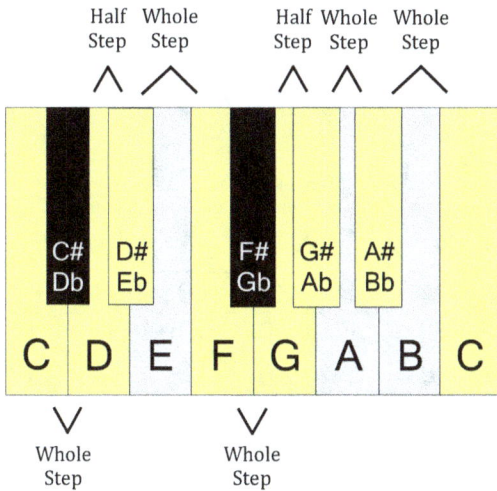

Exploring the Character of Major and Minor Scales

Listen to track 17 (disc 2) for an example of a piano improvisation in a major key and track 22 (disc 2) for a similar piece in a minor key. These pieces explore some of the possible expressions of the major and minor scales. In addition, consider revisiting tracks 49 (disc 1) and 53 (disc 1) for examples of pieces in a major scale as well as tracks 50 (disc 1) and 54 (disc 1) for examples of pieces in a minor scale.

The difference in expression between the major and minor scale is similar to the difference between the major and minor chords. For now, I'll let the examples speak for themselves and allow you to come up with your own observations.

- ❖ Note that tracks 17 (disc 2) and 22 (disc 2) are part of a group of seven improvisations presented on page 269. Feel free to listen to tracks 17 (disc 2) through 23 (disc 2) to hear the whole group. Jump ahead to the section entitled *Modes* on page 263 for further explanation about these pieces of music and more advanced discussion about the differences between the major and minor scale.

> We can construct each of the major and minor scales by following their interval patterns. See the table below for the result of this process.

Major Scales

	Whole Step	Whole Step	Half Step	Whole Step	Whole Step	Whole Step	Half Step
A Major Scale	A	B	C#	D	E	F#	G#	A
Bb Major Scale	Bb	C	D	Eb	F	G	A	Bb
B Major Scale	B	C#	D#	E	F#	G#	A#	B
C Major Scale	C	D	E	F	G	A	B	C
Db Major Scale	Db	Eb	F	Gb	Ab	Bb	C	Db
D Major Scale	D	E	F#	G	A	B	C#	D
Eb Major Scale	Eb	F	G	Ab	Bb	C	D	Eb
E Major Scale	E	F#	G#	A	B	C#	D#	E
F Major Scale	F	G	A	Bb	C	D	E	F
F# Major Scale	F#	G#	A#	B	C#	D#	E#	F#
Gb Major Scale	Gb	Ab	Bb	Cb	Db	Eb	F	Gb
G Major Scale	G	A	B	C	D	E	F#	G
Ab Major Scale	Ab	Bb	C	Db	Eb	F	G	Ab

Minor Scales

	Whole Step	Half Step	Whole Step	Whole Step	Half Step	Whole Step	Whole Step
A Minor Scale	A	B	C	D	E	F	G	A
Bb Minor Scale	Bb	C	Db	Eb	F	Gb	Ab	Bb
B Minor Scale	B	C#	D	E	F#	G	A	B
C Minor Scale	C	D	Eb	F	G	Ab	Bb	C
C# Minor Scale	C#	D#	E	F#	G#	A	B	C#
D Minor Scale	D	E	F	G	A	Bb	C	D
D# Minor Scale	D#	E#	F#	G#	A#	B	C#	D#
Eb Minor Scale	Eb	F	Gb	Ab	Bb	Cb	Db	Eb
E Minor Scale	E	F#	G	A	B	C	D	E
F Minor Scale	F	G	Ab	Bb	C	Db	Eb	F
F# Minor Scale	F#	G#	A	B	C#	D	E	F#
G Minor Scale	G	A	Bb	C	D	Eb	F	G
G# Minor Scale	G#	A#	B	C#	D#	E	F#	G#

A Note on Note Naming (Scales Edition)

Similar to the tables of major and minor triads presented in Chapter 5,[1] each scale in the tables on the previous page has been described with either sharps or flats, not both. Recall that, for chords, any note of a chord is a third away from the next highest or lowest note in the original voicing. In the last chapter we had to take this into account when naming the notes in a chord. For scales, each adjacent pair of notes in the scale is separated by a second. This means that as you play a scale from low to high, each note will use the next letter of the musical alphabet. No letters will be skipped or repeated.

Most of the time, it's not a problem to maintain seconds between the notes of a scale, but there is one major scale and one minor scale where an issue arises.

For the major scales, we are forced to use either E# in the F# major scale or alternatively Cb in the Gb major scale. These can be somewhat confusing terms. E# and F are enharmonic terms or different names for an equivalent sound. Cb and B are likewise enharmonic or equivalent. Despite the possible confusion, musicians will use terms like "Cb" at times to maintain seconds between each of the notes of the scale and thereby ensure that the seven notes of the scale use each letter of the musical alphabet once.

In the case of the Gb major scale, Cb is preceded by the note Bb and proceeded by the note Db. Therefore, the sound of Cb in this scale must be described using the letter C to maintain a second between each of the notes. If we used a B instead, the letter B would be repeated and the letter C would be skipped.

Using sharps to describe this scale leaves us with the same issue on a different note. The F# scale, uses the note E#. This note is preceded by D# and proceeded by F#. Therefore, it must be described with the letter E.

A parallel situation arises with the D# or Eb minor scale. Here we are forced to use an E# in the D# minor scale or alternatively a Cb in the Eb minor scale.

1. *A Note on Note Naming (Triad Edition)*, page 142

The A Minor Scale Consists of All the Natural Notes Too?

You may have noticed that some of the scales above share the same notes. For example, the C major scale and the A minor scale both include all the natural notes and no sharps or flats. Aren't these the same scale?

Keep in mind that a scale defines a tonal center in addition to a set of notes. So despite C major and A minor sharing the same notes, pieces written in these keys will sound different as a result of their tonal centers.

This idea is expanded upon further in Chapter 9 on page 240 and especially in the section entitled *Modes* on page 263.

- Key Signatures, Accidentals, and the Circle of Fifths -

What Are Key Signatures?

Just as there are time signatures to indicate what meter music is being played in, there are *key signatures* to indicate what scale music is being played in. A key signature consists of a set of either flats or sharps but not both.

Let's look at the D major scale as an example.

This scale contains two sharps, one on F and the other on C. Knowing this we could create a key signature for the D major scale by placing a sharp on F and C immediately to the right of our clef.

This key signature means that all of the following Fs and Cs in any octave will be sharp on this staff.

We could rewrite our D major scale with a key signature in the following way.

In a notated piece of music, the key signature comes before the time signature. Unlike time signatures, key signatures are generally repeated at the beginning of each line of music.

What Are Accidentals?

Sharps and flats that are not in the key signature are called *accidentals.* Most often accidentals are used when a composer is generally staying in a scale but there is an exception with one or more notes.

For example, the highlighted sharp below is an accidental. Normally, in the D major scale Gs are natural. However, this accidental raises this note by one half step to G#.

Flats can also be used as accidentals. Normally, in D major we use E naturals, but in this example an exception to the key signature is made with an Eb.

Natural Signs

There is also a third type of accidental – the *natural sign*. The natural sign negates the effect of the key signature. So any note that is sharp or flat because of the key signature can be changed to a natural note by using a natural sign.

For example, the second note below would be played as a C natural, not a C#, despite the key signature.

Accidentals Last for the Rest of the Measure

Accidentals remain in effect for the remainder of the measure in which they appear. This can be a confusing concept and it is easy to forget while reading music. So, be careful!

As an example, the accidental in front of the second note in the notation below not only affects the second note but also the fourth note of the measure. However, starting with the next measure the effect of the sharp sign goes away.

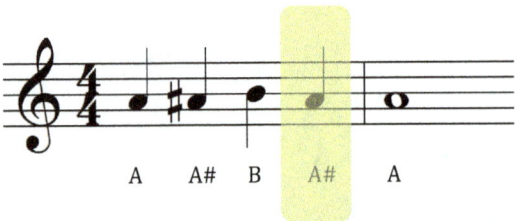

A   A#   B   A#   A

The Circle of Fifths

Starting on any note, you can move through all twelve notes by moving up or down by perfect fifths. This concept is called the *circle of fifths*.

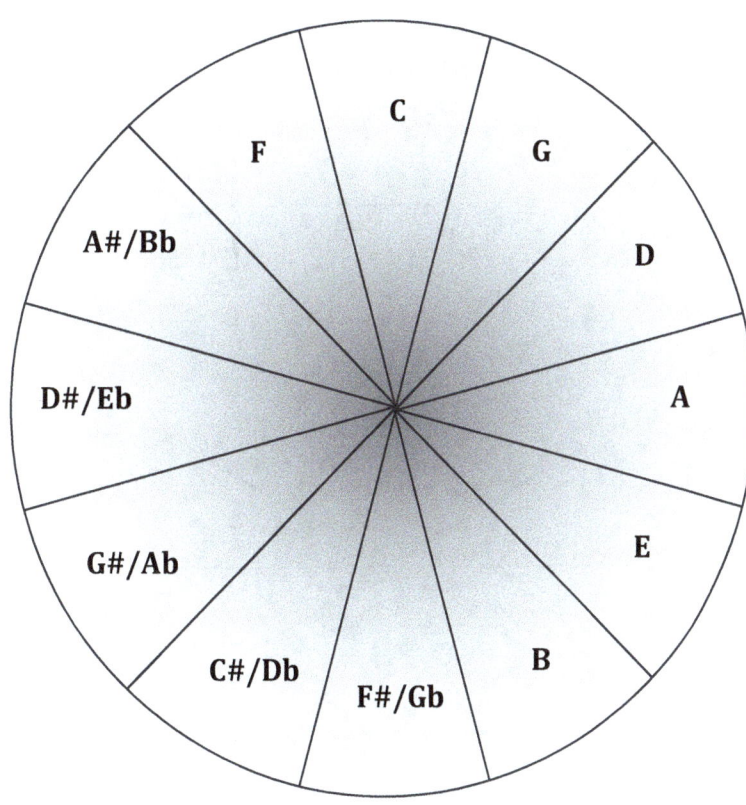

Key Signatures for the Major Scales

Below are all the key signatures for the major scales laid out in the circle of fifths. Notice that along the left hand side of the circle each scale gains another flat. Along the right hand side of the circle each scale gains another sharp.

Note that the scale at the bottom of the circle can be written as either F# major or Gb major. Both possible key signatures are written out.

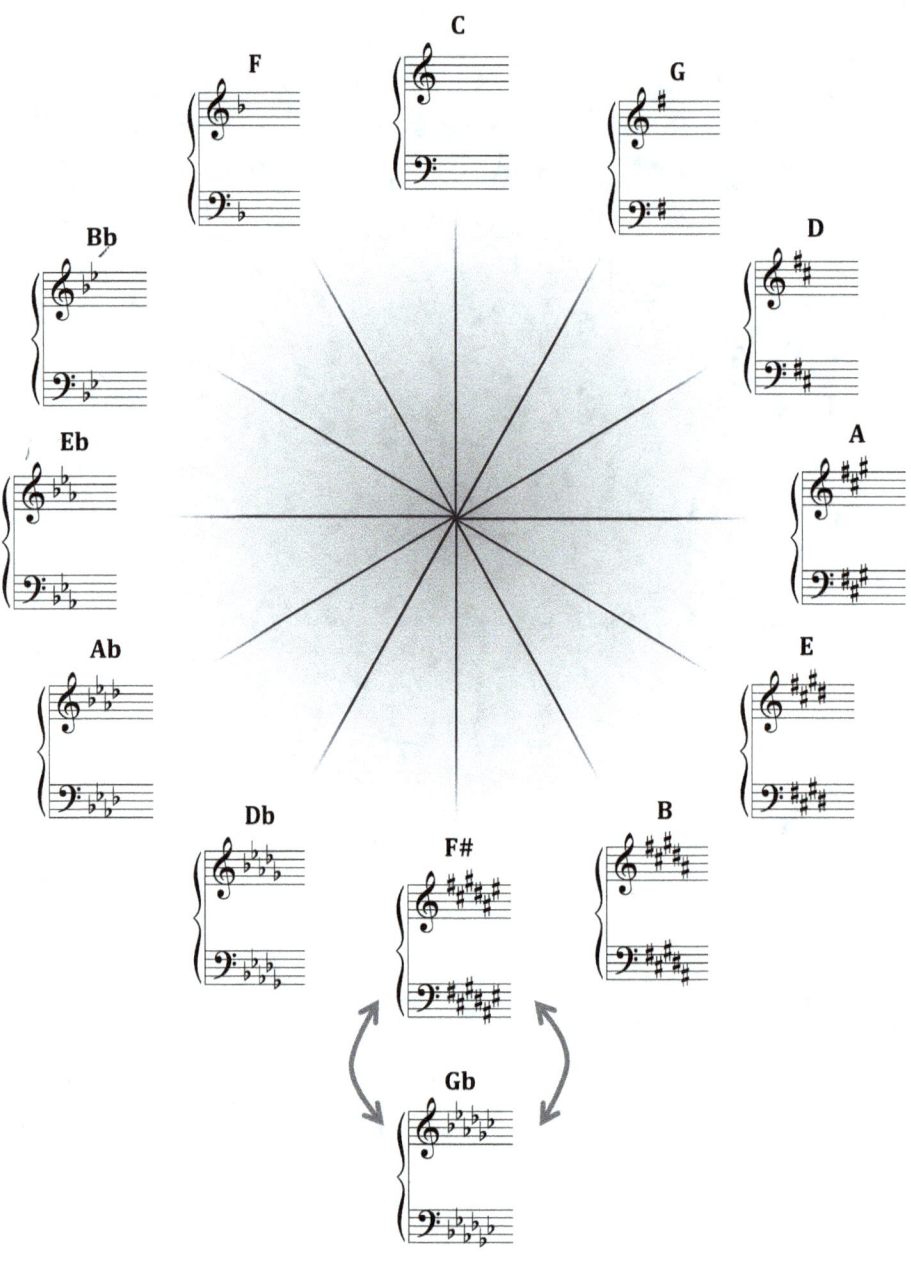

Key Signatures for the Minor Scales

Below are all the key signatures for the minor scales. Note that the scale at the bottom of this circle of fifths can be written as D# minor or Eb minor.

❖ Scales that are close to one another on the circle of fifths sound related. See the section entitled *Modulation* on page 412 for more information about this concept.

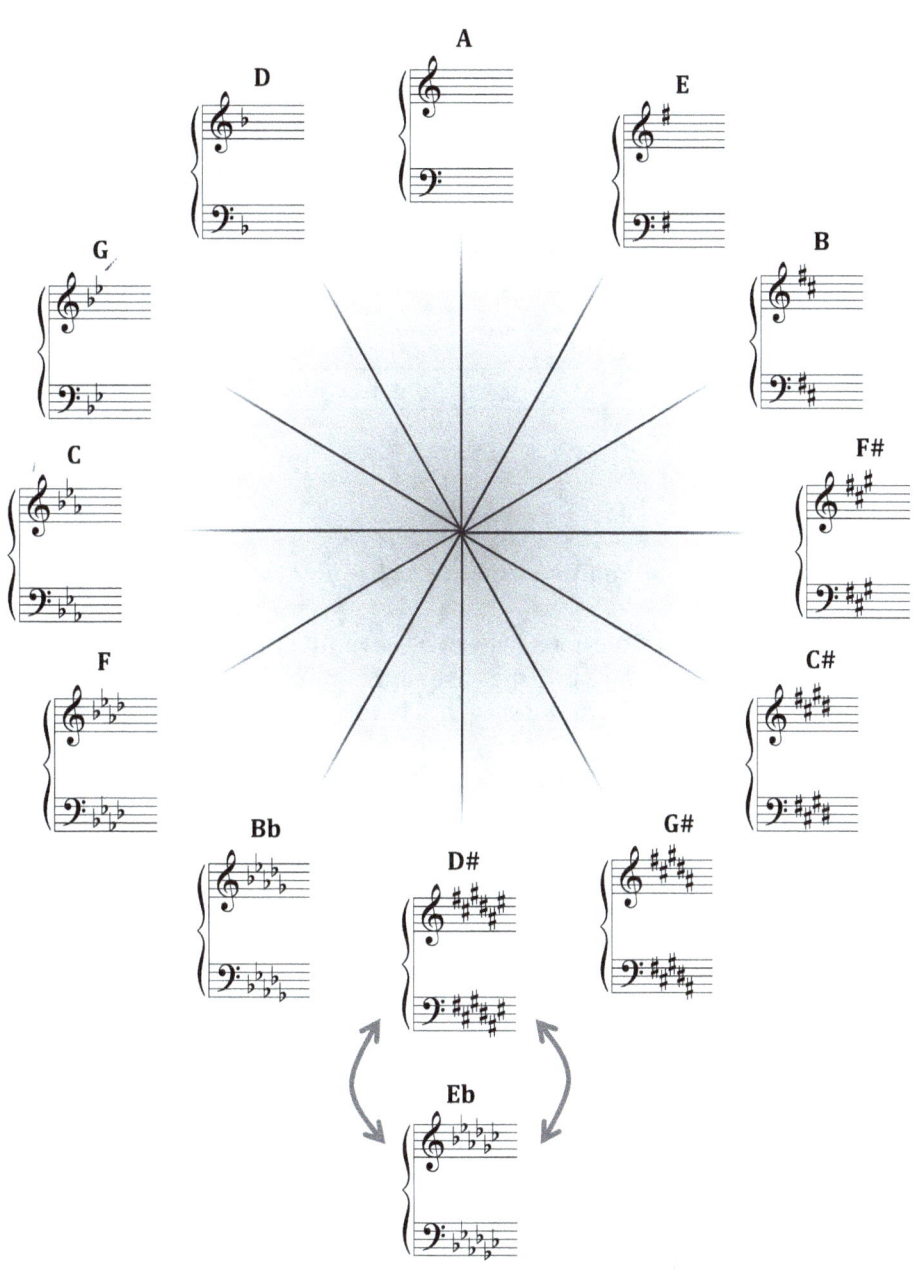

- Scale Degrees -

In the last chapter, we named each note in a chord relative to its position in the chord. There is a similar system that applies to scales. Each note in a scale has a name based on its relative position in the scale. These names are called *scale degrees*.

Scale Degrees

First Note of the Scale	Tonic
Second Note of the Scale	Supertonic
Third Note of the Scale	Mediant
Fourth Note of the Scale	Subdominant
Fifth Note of the Scale	Dominant
Sixth Note of the Scale	Submediant
Seventh Note of the Scale	Leading Tone or Subtonic

Leading Tone or Subtonic?

The term *leading tone* is used in situations where the seventh note of the scale is a half step away from the tonic note of the scale, as is the case for major scales. The term *subtonic* is used in situations where the seventh note of the scale is a whole step away from the tonic note of the scale, as is the case for minor scales.

Using the C major scale as an example, I have labeled each degree of this scale using the above method.

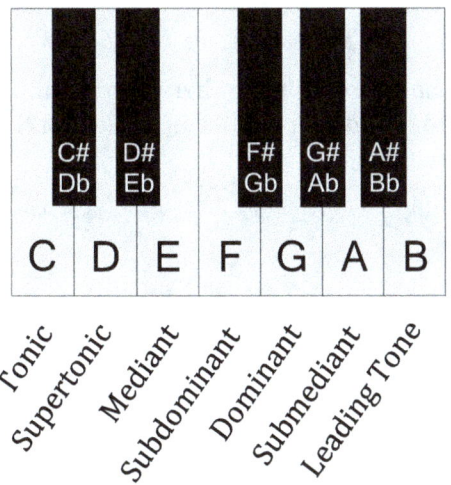

Meaning of the Scale Degree Names

At first glance, the names of the scale degrees may seem quite long-winded and arbitrary. However, there is a certain logic to the terminology.

In the term *supertonic*, the prefix "super" is meant to imply that this note is above the tonic. Whereas, in the term "subtonic," the prefix "sub" is used to indicate that this is the note below the tonic.

The terms *subdominant* and *submediant* are perhaps a little less intuitive. If the dominant is the note a fifth above the tonic the *sub*dominant is the note a fifth *below* the tonic. As it turns out the note a fifth below the tonic also appears a fourth above the tonic in a different octave, hence its definition as the fourth note of a scale. Following a similar line of thinking, if the mediant is the note a third above the tonic, the submediant is the note a third below the tonic. Because this note also appears a sixth above the tonic, we think of it as the sixth scale degree or the sixth note in a scale.

The name *leading tone* was given to the seventh degree of a scale because often this note has a tendency to *lead* the listener's ear to the tonic. In other words, it creates a sense of musical gravity.[1]

1. *Musical Centers and Gravity*, page 54

Naming Chords With Scale Degrees

Scale degree names can be used to describe not only individual notes, but chords as well. You can refer to chords by using the name of the scale degree that represents the root note of the chord. This allows you to name a chord relative to its position in a scale. For example, in the key of C major, the C major chord is the tonic chord. In the same scale, the F major chord would be the subdominant chord.

Alternatively, you can refer to scale degrees by number when naming chords. For example, you could say the C major triad is the *one chord* or *I chord* in the key of C major or call the F major chord the *four chord* or *IV chord* in C major.

- Solfege Syllables -

The *movable-Do system*, which uses *solfege syllables*, is another way to name notes relative to their position in a scale. Solfege syllables are easy to sing, unlike the scale degree names we looked at in the last section, and also provide the advantage of being able to name chromatic[1] notes relative to the scale.

In the movable-Do system, the syllable "Do" always represents the first note of the scale. From this reference point, the other syllables can be defined by their distance from Do. The table below lists all the solfege syllables, the number of half steps each syllable is from Do, and finally how these syllables relate to the major scale.

1. Meaning outside of the scale, see the box entitled *Diatonic and Chromatic* on page 82.

Syllable	Half Steps from Do	Relationship to the Major Scale
Do	0	First Note of the Scale
Di	1	First Note of a Major Scale Raised One Half Step
Ra	1	Second Note of a Major Scale Lowered One Half Step
Re	2	Second Note of a Major Scale
Ri	3	Second Note of a Major Scale Raised One Half Step
Me	3	Third Note of a Major Scale Lowered One Half Step
Mi	4	Third Note of a Major Scale
Fa	5	Fourth Note of a Major Scale
Fi	6	Fourth Note of a Major Scale Raised One Half Step
Se	6	Fifth Note of a Major Scale Lowered One Half Step
So/Sol	7	Fifth Note of a Major Scale
Si	8	Fifth Note of a Major Scale Raised One Half Step
Le	8	Sixth Note of a Major Scale Lowered One Half Step
La	9	Sixth Note of a Major Scale
Li	10	Sixth Note of a Major Scale Raised One Half Step
Te	10	Seventh Note of a Major Scale Lowered One Half Step
Ti	11	Seventh Note of a Major Scale

I have shaded the table to group together the syllables that start with the same letter. The first letter of each syllable corresponds to a scale degree. Examine this relationship on the following page.

Position in Scale	Solfege Syllables That Begin With the Letter...	Scale Degree Name
First Note of Scale	D	Tonic
Second Note of Scale	R	Supertonic
Third Note of Scale	M	Mediant
Fourth Note of Scale	F	Subdominant
Fifth Note of Scale	S	Dominant
Sixth Note of Scale	L	Submediant
Seventh Note of Scale	T	Leading Tone or Subtonic

Singing Major and Minor Scales With Solfege

Choose a major or minor scale and play it on your instrument. Now sing the corresponding solfege syllables as you play the scale, matching the pitch of your voice to the sound of your instrument.

Taken from the table above, the solfege syllables that correspond to the notes of a major scale are:
1) Do
2) Re
3) Mi
4) Fa
5) So/Sol
6) La
7) Ti

The solfege syllables that correspond to the notes of a minor scale are:
1) Do
2) Re
3) Me
4) Fa
5) So/Sol
6) Le
7) Te

The Fixed-Do System

The movable-Do system is variation on the *fixed-Do system*. In fixed-Do, the syllable Do represents the note C and the other syllables represent notes in reference to C. For example, Re represents D, Mi represents E, and so on.

In the movable-Do system, however, Do represents the first note of the scale rather than any one note. Do could represent any of the twelve notes depending on the scale you are in. For example, if you are in an F major scale, Do now represents F, Re represents G, Mi represents A, and so on.

During the course of this book, I will use only the movable-Do system.

Note Naming (Solfege Edition)

You may notice that several of the solfege syllables are different names for the same notes or sounds. For example, Di and Ra both represent the same sound in a given scale. Both of these syllables are defined as being one half step higher than Do. However, you will know which syllable to use in a given situation based on letters in the notes you are representing. Each starting letter of the solfege syllables corresponds to a letter that is used in the notes of a particular scale. For example, in a C major scale the following rules would apply:

For a C Major Scale

Position in Scale	Solfege Syllables That Begin With the Letter…	…Represent Note Names That Use the Letter…
First Note of the Scale	D	C
Second Note of the Scale	R	D
Third Note of the Scale	M	E
Fourth Note of the Scale	F	F
Fifth Note of the Scale	S	G
Sixth Note of the Scale	L	A
Seventh Note of the Scale	T	B

So in C major, Di would represents C#. C# is a half step away from Do, which in this case is C. C# also uses the letter C, which is a requirement if we are going to represent this note with a solfege syllable that begins with the letter D.

Ra, however, would represent the note Db. Db is also a half step away from Do as well and sounds identical to C#. However, Db uses the letter D and therefore must be represented by a solfege syllable that begins with the letter R.

This logic can be applied to any scale. As an example, below is a table showing the relationship between notes in a D major scale and the starting letters of solfege syllables.

For a D Major Scale

Position in Scale	Solfege Syllables That Begin With the Letter…	…Represent Notes That Use the Letter…
First Note of the Scale	D	D
Second Note of the Scale	R	E
Third Note of the Scale	M	F
Fourth Note of the Scale	F	G
Fifth Note of the Scale	S	A
Sixth Note of the Scale	L	B
Seventh Note of the Scale	T	C

You can create a table like this for any scale by substituting the letters used in the notes of your scale from first to last in the far right hand column of the table.

- Transposing -

What Is Transposition?

Track 61 (disc 1) plays an excerpt from the song "Twinkle Twinkle Little Star" first in its original key of C major, then in the key of D major, and finally in the key of C minor. Listen to this track now or try playing the notation below on an instrument.

Moving music into different keys in this manner is called *transposing* music. Transposing is accomplished by using the same scale degrees in a different key.

Accompanying the notation for track 61 (disc 1) below, are three layers of description – first the note names of the pitches being played, beneath that the solfege syllables associated with each note, and beneath that the scale degree names associated with each note.

Original Version in C Major

Transposed Version in D Major

Transposed Version in C Minor

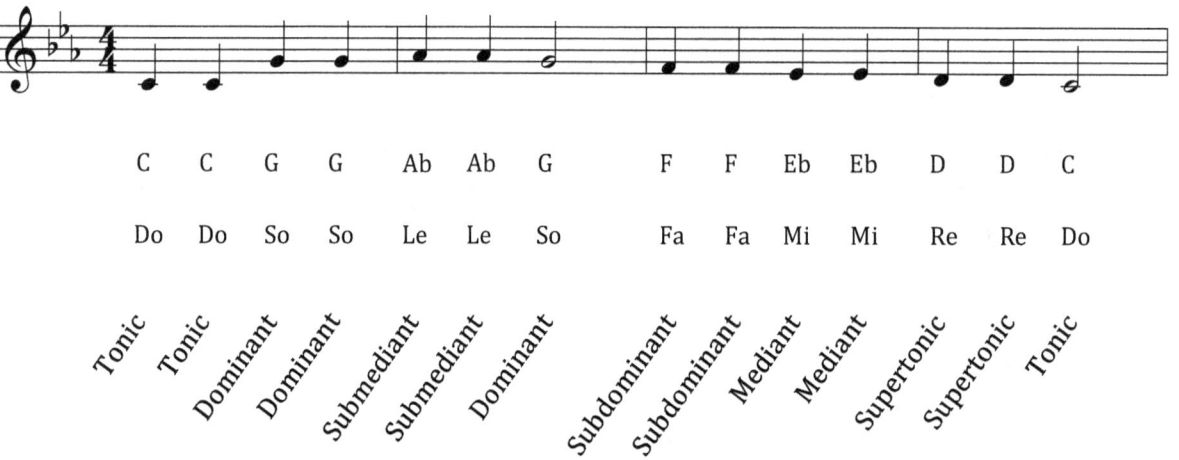

Scale Degrees, Solfege, and Intervals in Transposition

Each example above uses different notes but the scale degrees remain the same because we are using the same relative positions in the given scale each time. "Twinkle Twinkle Little Star" starts on the first note of the scale, repeats that note, then moves to the fifth note of the scale, and so on. This is true in each version above.

You may notice that the solfege syllables are the same between the version in C major and the version in D major, but they actually change for the version in C minor. When we transpose from one *type* of scale to a different *type* of scale, such as from a major scale to a minor scale or from a minor scale to a major scale, we will change the intervals between the notes. However, the general numeric intervals[1] remain the same. For example, in both the C major and D major versions of "Twinkle Twinkle Little Star" the interval between the fourth and fifth notes of the song is a major second. For the minor version, this interval is still a second but now it is a minor second rather than a major second.

In terms of solfege, we can describe this situation as maintaining the first letter of each solfege syllable while changing the endings of some syllables. For example, the fifth note in the major versions is described with the syllable La, while in the minor version this note is described with the syllable Le. Both syllables start with the letter "L" but the specific syllable changes depending on the type of scale.

Note that the intervals change when transposing from one *type* of scale (such as the major scale type or minor scale type) to a different type of scale. However, transposing from one scale to a scale of the same type as the original (as in transposing from one major scale to another major scale or transposing from one minor scale to another minor scale) results in maintaining the exact same intervals in both number and quality as well as the exact same solfege syllables.

This all makes a good deal of sense if we consider that scale types are patterns of intervals or interval structures. When we change this pattern or structure of intervals as the template for a piece of music, as we are doing when we transpose from one scale type to another, we will change the intervals between the notes in the piece as a result. When transposing from scale to scale within a scale type, however, this template interval structure is staying the same and, thus, the intervals between the notes in the music will also be the same. However, the actual pitches used will differ. For example, between the version of "Twinkle Twinkle Little Star" in C major and the version in D major, the intervals remain exactly the same. The only difference is that the pitches in the D major version are all one whole step higher than the original. For the version in C minor, both the pitches and intervals change.

1. *General Numeric Interval Names*, page 125

The Expression of Changing Scale Types

Expressively, we can hear the effects of changing the intervals between the major and minor versions of this song quite prominently. The versions of "Twinkle Twinkle Little Star" in C major and D major sound almost the same. The only difference is that the version in D major sounds a bit higher. However, the version in C minor has a distinctly different character to it. This is the case because the version in C minor has slightly different intervals (taking into account both number and quality) than the other two versions and, thus, produces a different expression in the dimension of pitch proportionality.

Interestingly, the version in C minor shares more notes with the original song than the version in D major. Nevertheless, it is this version that sounds most altered. This demonstrates how the relationships between the pitches can be more impactful than the specific pitches themselves. As we said in Chapter Two, "Music is a relational kind of art."

Happy Birthday

The song "Happy Birthday" is a commonplace demonstration of the importance of intervals and relativity in music. Do you think "Happy Birthday" is sung in the same key at every party? Actually, it is not at all. Usually, someone just starts singing and that becomes the first note of the song. But after this first note is established, people will (at least strive to) stick to the intervals that define the song. Despite the fact that we are using a different set of notes every time, we still recognize "Happy Birthday" because the intervals between the notes are staying the same.

Try Transposing!

Try transposing the example excerpt of "Twinkle Twinkle Little Star" notated above to another key. Find the notes in your scale that correspond the scale degrees used in "Twinkle Twinkle Little Star." You can refer to the notation on pages 191 and 192 to see what scale degree is used in each note of the song. And you can refer to the tables on page 176 to see what notes are in the scale you have chosen.

- Musical Gravity in Chord Progressions -

In the last chapter, we talked about the notion of chord progressions or sequences of chords played one after another. If you tried the activity at the end of the section entitled *Writing Chord Progressions*,[1] you probably discovered that some chords lead naturally into others and conversely some chords sound more disjointed and awkward when played in sequence. Each chord forms a relationship with the chord in front and behind it in a progression, and each relationship creates its own unique expression.

The tendency for some chords to lead naturally into others is a form of musical gravity.[2] We will get into a deeper explanation of musical gravity in harmonies and in melodies in Chapter Nine,[3] but for now let's explore a few basics.

1. *Writing Chord Progressions*, page 156
2. *Musical Centers and Gravity*, page 54
3. *Chapter Nine*, page 240

Strong and Weak Resolutions

In Chapter Two, we discussed the concepts of tension and resolution,[1] which correspond to our descriptions of high and low energy musical expressions, respectively. A resolution, however, is not just the position of low energy, it is the movement from higher energy to lower energy. At this point, we will introduce the distinction between a *strong resolution*, which moves from a position of relatively extreme high energy to a position of relatively extreme low energy, and a *weak resolution*, which moves from a position of relatively moderate high energy to a position of relatively moderate low energy.

In practice, a strong resolution sounds more final and more clearly complete. Strong resolutions might often be used to end a large section of music or an entire piece. In contrast, a weak resolution sounds more ambiguous and seems to suggest the possibility or even create the expectation that the music will continue on to reach a stronger resolution. Weak resolutions are often used to end smaller sections of music but could also be used to create an ending that has an expression that is itself unresolved, tense, or unsettling. Both strong and weak resolutions can be equally useful in different situations.

1. *Tension and Resolution*, page 55

The V to I Resolution

There are two important and related resolutions – the V to I resolution and the V7 to I resolution, in a major key. In other words, the progression from the fifth triad of a major scale to the first triad of a major scale and the progression from the fifth seventh chord of a major scale to the first triad of a major scale. These two resolutions are the strongest resolutions available in a major scale, and for that reason they are well-known and commonly used.

Listening to Strong and Weak Resolutions

You can listen to a V to I resolution on track 7 (disc 2) and a V7 to I resolution on track 9 (disc 2). Tracks 4 (disc 1) and 5 (disc 1) represent a stronger and weaker resolution, respectively. You could also listen to the end of track 6 (disc 1) as an additional example of a strong resolution, specifically at the end of the guitar part. The endings of the piano pieces on track 46 (disc 1) and track 17 (disc 2) are additional examples of weaker resolutions.

Why Are These Progressions Strong Resolutions?

Once again, we will discuss all of this in more detail in Chapter Nine but because these concepts are so critical to understand, we will go through an introductory pass of this topic now. Musical gravity, in the domain of pitch, is determined by the proximity of notes to centers in pitch, which could be either a tonal center of a scale or notes that are part of a chord. The closer an approaching note comes to a center, the stronger the sense is that the note wants to move to the approached center. And the smallest possible interval in our musical system is a half step. This means that being a half step away from a center will generate the strongest expression of musical gravity.

So, in our V to I progression the third of the V chord, the note B in the example below, is only a half step away from the tonal center of the scale, the note C in the example below. This *half step relationship* is largely responsible for the sense of gravity that is produced by the V chord and the strength of the resolution that is felt when the progression resolves to the I chord.

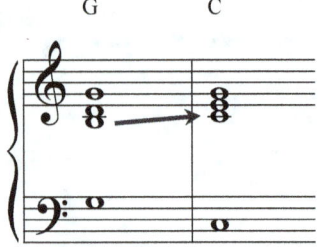

Musical gravity, in the domain of pitch, is determined by the proximity of notes to centers in pitch, which could be either a tonal center of a scale or notes that are part of a chord.

In the V7 to I progression, not only does the third of the V chord create the same half step relationship as before, but the added note of the seventh, the note F in the example below, creates another half step relationship with the third of the I chord, the note E in the example below. This strengthens both the sense of gravity and the sense resolution even further.

Common Tone Relationships

Common tones[1] between chords or *common tone relationships* can also increase the sense of gravity between chords. The reason for this is that the more similar two chords are, without matching each other exactly, the greater the expression of musical gravity will be between those chords. Half step and common tone relationships are indicators, in terms of intervals, of this broader principle.

And if we examine the two resolutions above, we will find that both have one common tone relationship. The note G is the root of the V chord or V7 chord and then becomes the fifth of the I chord. This characteristic also contributes to the strong resolving power of these two progressions.

1. Common tones are shared notes between chords. See the box *Comparing the Two Chord Progressions* on page 154 for my original presentation of this term.

The more similar two chords are, without matching each other exactly, the greater the expression of musical gravity will be between those chords.

Analyzing Gravitational Relationships

Using the information we have just covered, I invite you to do a simple analysis of a chord progression, in terms of its half steps and common tones as well as the sense of gravity that you feel when you listen to the progression. You can use a chord progression that you wrote with the *Writing Chord Progressions* activity, another progression you have written, or a chord progression from a composition you know. To do this activity properly, you'll probably want to have specific voicings for all the chords in your progression.

To begin your analysis, you will first want to establish what key your chord progression is in and what the corresponding tonal center is. Then, make a note, perhaps directly on a copy of the notation for your chord progression, of each half step and common tone relationship in the progression. If you do this comprehensively, you should have a description of a half step relationship, common tone relationship, or a blank space if neither apply between each adjacent pair of chord tones in the progression.[1]

Listening to the progression, you will probably notice that the sense of gravity and resolution increases with more half steps and common tones. You'll find this is especially true when landing on or resolving to the tonic chord or I chord. However, more subtly you will also find that there are gravitational relationships between the other chords in the scale. Listen for this and see what you can discover.

As you are listening and analyzing, see if you can observe not just the sense of gravity but any other musical expressions that might be produced in a specific sequence of chords. You might find, for example, that the combination of major and minor expressions with the gravitational expressions we are looking at in this section produce some fascinatingly complex sounds, just with these two elements alone.

When considering musical gravity, expressions that concern various types of desire and movement are particularly relevant. Listen for different variations on the themes of wanting, straining, reaching, longing, anticipating, releasing, moving, settling down, or gathering energy.

Musical gravity is a complex subject, and there is the possibility that you may find a sequence of chords that, surprisingly, has little sense of gravity to it but still contains many half step and common tone relationships. If you discover a situation like this, make a note of it and hold that thought. We will come back to more advanced relationships like these in later chapters. However, the information in this section describes many, many relationships in harmony as well as melodies. And so, you'll probably find it helpful to spend some time getting acquainted with these foundational principles.

1. Starting on page 154, there is a section entitled *Voice Leading*, which goes through the process of analyzing the intervals between the notes in a chord progression as they move over time. This kind of analysis is similar to what we are doing in this activity. If you think it would be helpful, turn back to this section for an example of how to evaluate a chord progression in terms of common tones and steps. Note that, for this activity, we are concerned specifically with half steps, whereas, in the *Voice Leading* section, we talked about "steps" in terms of the more general category that includes half steps and whole steps.

- Pentatonic Scales -

What Are Pentatonic Scales?

Not all scales have seven notes. For example, *pentatonic scales* are scales that contain five notes. Pentatonic scales tend to have a plainer, more basic sound to them than their seven-note counterparts. But they also sound very solid and strong. Pentatonic scales can be great for writing melodies, in particular.

A *major pentatonic scale* can be created by finding the first, second, third, fifth, and sixth scale degrees of an ordinary major scale. For example, take a look at the notes of a regular seven-note F major scale below.

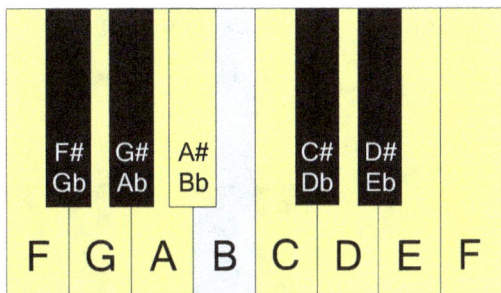

By finding the first, second, third, fifth, and sixth scale degrees…

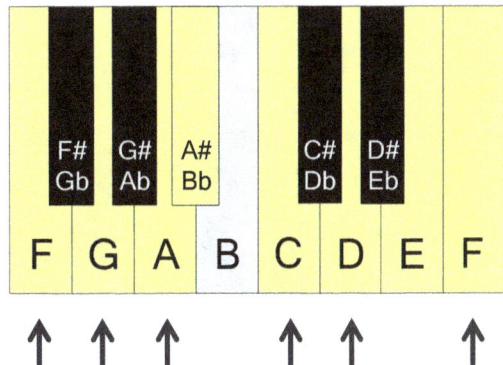

...we can easily create an F major pentatonic scale.

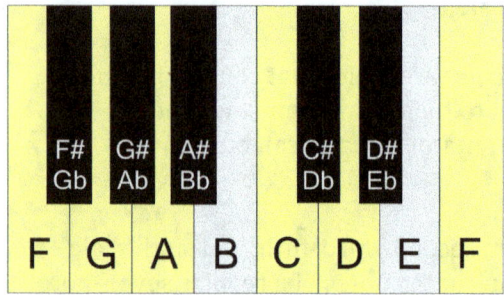
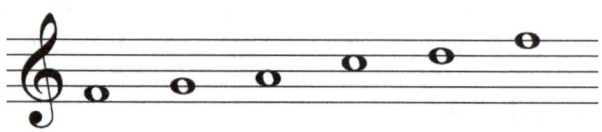

A *minor pentatonic scale* can be created by locating the first, third, fourth, fifth and seventh degrees of a minor scale. For example, we could examine the notes of an E minor scale.

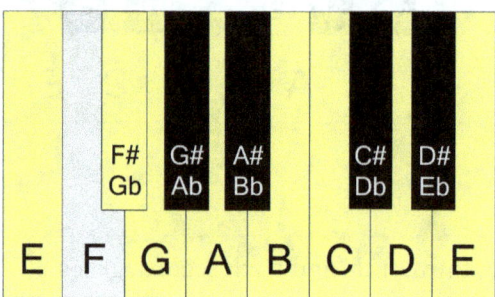

Locate the first, third, fourth, fifth, and seventh degrees...

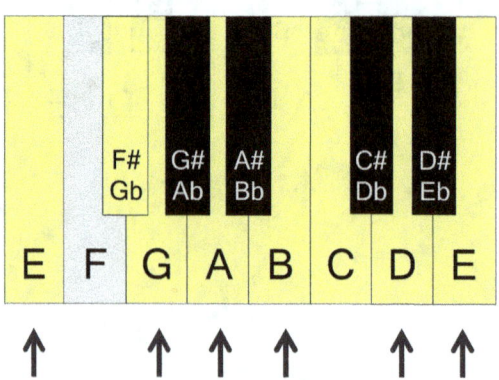

... and create an E minor pentatonic scale.

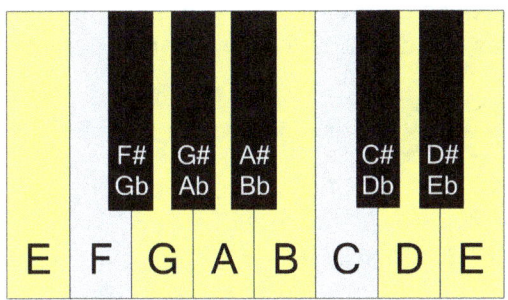
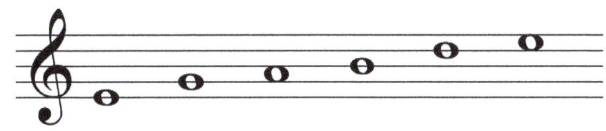

Interval Patterns for Pentatonic Scales

You can also think about pentatonic scales in terms of intervals, just as we analyzed traditional seven-note major and minor scales. All major pentatonic scales are built on the same set of intervals, and likewise all minor pentatonic scales are built on the same set of intervals. Examine the table below to see these two patterns of intervals.

	Major Pentatonic Scale	**Minor Pentatonic Scale**
Between the 1st and 2nd notes of the scale there is a...	Major Second	Minor Third
Between the 2nd and 3rd notes of the scale there is a...	Major Second	Major Second
Between the 3rd and 4th notes of the scale there is a...	Minor Third	Major Second
Between the 4th and 5th notes of the scale there is a...	Major Second	Minor Third
Between the 5th note of the scale and the 1st note of the scale one octave higher there is a...	Minor Third	Major Second

You can construct a major or minor pentatonic scale on any note by following the given sequence of intervals shown above.

Breaking the Rules

You may notice that pentatonic scales do not follow all the traditional rules. For example, pentatonic scales do not have one of every letter A through G. Pentatonic scales also do not have a second between each note. These conventions apply to the basic, seven-note major and minor scales. When we move beyond basic major and minor scales, the traditional conventions may not apply.

- Improvising With Pentatonic Scales -

Improvisation

Improvisation is the art form of creating music spontaneously, without planning what will be played before it is played. Spontaneous musical ideas are sometimes the best art that one can create. Improvisation is also a great technique for coming up with ideas and inspirations that can then be used as the basis of a composition.

Two Creative Mindsets

There are two mindsets we can approach improvisation with, and we will find moving forward that these mindsets can be applied to any creative endeavor – composing, performing, or even something else entirely. These two mindsets are that of the *performer* and that of the *experimenter*. When we approach improvisation as a performer, we are seeking to create the highest quality art we possibly can. As an experimenter, we are seeking to explore the realm of musical sounds and grow in our comprehension of the possibilities and underlying mechanics of music. In the experimenter's mindset, the end result is not important in and of itself. What is important is developing our understanding of how what you do on an instrument produces a certain expression.

In general, the performer is going to take a lot fewer risks than the experimenter. In a performance, we want some level of guarantee that the performance will be a good one. With experimentation, this is not important. We are simply learning from our mistakes and successes equally. To take on the performer's mindset, it is important to focus intensely on the task at hand. Take some small risks but mostly focus on high quality execution using what you already know will work. In contrast, the experimenter can take risks if that aids in the learning process because we aren't placing any value on the potential downside. It's okay for you to hear some unpleasant sounds as you are developing your musical skills in an educational context. And this applies to experienced musicians just as much as it does to amateurs.

When you are starting out with improvisation, I recommend primarily taking the experimenter's approach. Just see what happens if you do a certain thing on your instrument. Listen to the result and take note of the experience. By doing this repeatedly, your understanding will grow. With time, you will become increasingly able to predict how things will sound before you play them.

As you become a more experienced improviser and you begin to feel comfortable using improvisation as a performance approach, begin to alternate your methods. When a situation calls for it, use improvisation as a performance. Practice this as a skill in non-performance situations as well. Then at other times, allow yourself to experiment. Expand your horizons. Do some things on your instrument that may not work and listen to what happens. Continue to seek out new musical territory.

Listening to Solos in Pentatonic Scales

Solos are melodic parts that are played by a single, featured performer. Solos are often improvised over a predetermined chord progression.

It is very common to use the major or minor pentatonic scales for *soloing* (improvising a solo) and writing melodies. The reason is simple. The pentatonic scales produce many consonant intervals between the notes of the scale, more so than even the traditional seven-note major and minor scales. In some cases, we might want our music to have more dissonance than the pentatonic scales are capable of providing. In other cases, the pentatonic scales could be just right. Regardless, the pentatonic scales are an ideal foundation to become acquainted with for any improviser or composer.

Listen to track 62 (disc 1) and track 63 (disc 1) for an example of a solo in a major pentatonic scale and minor pentatonic scale, respectively.

Improvising a Solo

Try improvising a solo! Treat this activity with an experimenter's mindset. Your solo doesn't need to be good. The idea is to try it and learn from the experience. Take note of what results you get from various combinations or sequences of notes and rhythms.

It just so happens that both the Gb major pentatonic scale and the Eb minor pentatonic scale contain all of the black keys on a piano and none of the white keys. On a piano, this makes these scales particularly easy to remember and to start out improvising in. Track 64 (disc 1) and 65 (disc 1) play an accompaniment in the Gb major pentatonic scale and in the Eb minor pentatonic scale, respectively. You can use these accompaniments to solo over. Play one of the accompaniments on a speaker system or in headphones and then improvise along with the track. The accompaniment in Gb major pentatonic only uses a Gb major triad and likewise the accompaniment in Eb minor pentatonic only uses an Eb minor triad. Both accompaniments are in 4/4 and at 92 bpm.

If you would like, go through the following steps to become comfortable with the process of improvising over one of these tracks:

1. Find the root note of your scale. This note will be the tonal center for the music you are creating. Try playing this note on every beat of the accompaniment track. If you have trouble determining how fast the beat is, set a metronome to 92 bpm and then go back to the track and see if you feel a pulse at that speed. Now try playing this note as a half note. Play one half note on beat one and one half note on beat three. Finally, try playing this note as a whole note starting on beat one.

2. Play each note of the scale up and down slowly, perhaps as a whole note or half note. Pay attention to the sound of each note. You should be able to hear that each of the three chord tones in your track sound particularly consonant and aligned with the harmony of the accompaniment as you play them. However, all of the notes in these scales should sound relatively consonant. Notice, in particular, how the tonal center of the scale has a strong sense of gravity and centrality to it.

3. Now begin to experiment. Use a fragment of the pentatonic scale and play the notes in an ascending or descending direction. Try skipping a note in the scale and listen to the effect. What other intervals could you play that would fit in the scale? When in doubt, go back to creating conjunct melodies that go from one note of the scale to another adjacent note in the scale in either the ascending or descending direction.

Melodic Phrases

A *phrase* is a short section of a melody. Musical phrases in improvisation are like sentences in language. Each phrase conveys a small yet encapsulated expression. Phrases are created by two things: space and resolutions.

To notice a phrase as a separate entity, there will need to be some pauses between each of your musical ideas. These pauses could be in the form of a rest or a held note. Without space, your ideas may become overly monotonous or difficult to follow.

Additionally, when a phrase ends, the listener expects a sense of resolution. The end of a phrase is signified by the return to a harmonic center. We can do this by playing a chord tone at the end of our phrases. In the Gb major track, the chord tones are Gb, Bb, and Db. In the Eb minor track, they are Eb, Gb, and Bb.

Examples of Phrasing

Listen to the use of phrasing in tracks 26 (disc 1), 62 (disc 1), and 63 (disc 1). Track 26 is an example of a piece of music that uses a lot of space in its melodic phrases. Track 62 is more average, and track 63 is a little busier but nothing too crazy. These pieces of music all go in different directions in terms of their phrasing, creating different musical expressions on a spectrum from spaciousness to busyness. But all of these pieces use phrasing in one way or another. They all have identifiable phrases and distinct points of resolution. Listen to how these compositions create their own unique sense of phrasing.

Try Soloing With Phrases

If you would like, try improvising over the Gb major or Eb minor accompaniment track and this time focus on creating phrases. Think of making distinct sentences or statements. Experiment with making longer phrases and shorter ones. Remember to end phrases on a chord tone. The strongest resolutions will end on the tonal center. Listen to how this compares to resolving to the other chord tones. You can also experiment with making your resolutions stronger by ending on a downbeat.

Summary for Group Three
Intervals and Interval Structures

> *Groups of notes that are separated by the same intervals (that is to say groups of notes that share the same spacing or distances between notes) create similar expressions and have similar musical properties.*

> *Music is a relativistic kind of art. The intervals between pitches create more of the expression of the music than the actual notes themselves.*

Half Step – Distance between adjacent notes

Whole Step – Distance of one further than adjacent notes

General Numeric Interval Names – Describe distance between letters in different notes

Interval of a Second – Two adjacent letters, also two adjacent positions in a scale or on a staff

Five Qualities – Major, Minor, Augmented, Diminished, Perfect

We can add qualities to numeric interval names to specify an exact number of half steps.

Sonance – A spectrum from consonance (strong pitch proportionality, low expressive energy) to dissonance (weak pitch proportionality, high expressive energy)

Dissonant intervals can be off-putting out of context but surprisingly pleasing in context if used intelligently.

Tuning System – Specifies the exact frequencies that each note represents

- Interval Structures for Chords -

(shows number of half steps between the adjacent notes in each chord type)
Major Triad: 4, 3
Minor Triad: 3, 4
Diminished Triad: 3, 3
Augmented Triad: 4, 4
Major Seventh: 4, 3, 4
Minor Seventh: 3, 4, 3
Dominant Seventh: 4, 3, 3

- Interval Structure of Scales -

("H" represents a half step between adjacent notes in the scale; "W" represents a whole step.)

Major Scale: WWHWWWH
Minor Scale: WHWWHWW

- Naming Notes Relative to Their Positions in Chords and Scales -

Root – First note of a chord
Third – Second note of a chord
Fifth – Third note of a chord
Seventh – Fourth note of a chord

Position in the Scale	Scale Degree Name	Solfege (Major Scale)	Solfege (Minor Scale)
First Note of the Scale	Tonic	Do	Do
Second Note of the Scale	Supertonic	Re	Re
Third Note of the Scale	Mediant	Mi	Me
Fourth Note of the Scale	Subdominant	Fa	Fa
Fifth Note of the Scale	Dominant	So	So
Sixth Note of the Scale	Submediant	La	Le
Seventh Note of the Scale	Leading Tone or Subtonic	Ti	Te

Voicing Considerations
1. Highest and lowest notes
2. Muddiness
3. Close or open
4. Emphasized notes or intervals

Chord Progressions – Sequences of chords

Each chord can be assigned a Roman numeral to represent the position of the root note in the scale.

Voice Leading – Creating the minimum amount of movement between chords

- Related Series Analysis -

Find the related fundamental of a group of notes by finding the overtone series where the group of notes appears first. The fundamental of this overtone series is the related fundamental.

Consider how interval relationships between related fundamentals or between a related fundamental and a sounding note of the chord could affect the expression of the chord.

As an example, minor chords sound dark and sad as a result of their complex centrality. The root of the chord competes with the related fundamental a major third below the root for the title of "Center of the Chord."

- Resolutions -

Strong Resolution – Final and complete sounding, transitions from very high expressive energy to very low expressive energy

Weak Resolution – Incomplete sounding, transitions from moderately high expressive energy to moderately low expressive energy

V to I and V7 to I resolutions are important strong resolutions.

The more similar two chords are, without matching each other exactly, the greater the expression of musical gravity will be between those chords.

Musical gravity, in the domain of pitch, is determined by the proximity of notes to centers in pitch, which could be either a tonal center of a scale or notes that are part of a chord.

- Miscellaneous -

Transpose – Move music from one scale to another

Experimenter's Mindset – Focus on the learning process, good and bad results are equally welcome

Performer's Mindset – Focus on creating the highest quality art possible

Phrases are like the sentences of a melody.

Group Four

The Expression of Proportional Relationships

In the last group of chapters, we covered a lot of aspects of the theory system that musicians use to name and think about musical elements like intervals, chords, and scales. Now in Group Four, we are going to turn our attention more toward the musical expressions that are created through the structures we have studied so far and some deeper perspectives, why-questions, and creative applications. The cornerstone of our study will continue to be, even more so than before perhaps, the musical relationships that are formed between musical elements and especially the proportional relationships that give rise to expressions like musical gravity and centrality.

This group is divided into two chapters. The first is devoted to rhythm and how proportional relationships play out over the spectrum of time to generate different musical expressions. The second chapter is concerned with the topic of relationships in the spectrum of pitch. This will include both melodic and harmonic applications.

This group in many ways is really the essential creative use of intellectual theory that this book is all about. In the next two chapters, we will finish up Part Two, ending with a section on how to write musical themes. We will then transition into Part Three, where we will be focusing on exploring diverse applications, creative pursuits, and other subject matters related to the core material of Part One and Part Two.

Chapter Eight
Relationships in Time

- Percussion Notation -

Percussion notation is used for writing non-pitched sounds.[1] Percussion notation is indicated by a *percussion clef* or *neutral clef*, as shown below.

1. *Non-Pitched Sounds*, page 40

Percussion notation is also written with special note heads. Below is the percussion notation for whole, half, quarter, eighth, and sixteenth notes.

| Whole Note | Half Note | Quarter Note | Eighth Note | Sixteenth Note |

Percussion notation may be written on a standard five-line staff or it may be written on a one-line staff.

Notating Parts for Drum Set

There are multiple methods of notating parts for a drum set. What follows is a description of one particular system. Be aware that you may encounter different variations on the system described below. However, the general idea is usually similar.

Drum notation is written with *divisi notation*, literally meaning "divided notation." Divisi notation puts two musical parts on one staff. One musical part is written with the stems going up and the other part is written with the stems going down. In drum notation, anything that the drummer controls with his or her feet is written with the stems going down, and anything that the drummer controls with his or her hands is written with the stems going up. Parts for a drum set are written on a five-line staff. Each drum and cymbal on the drum set is represented with a different line or space. All of the cymbals on the drum set are written with percussion notation. The actual drums, however, are written with standard note heads. Usually, when percussion notation is used for the drum set, the note heads of quarter notes and faster note values are written with an "X" as in the notation below. This is simply a slightly different style of percussion notation.

Below are the positions on the staff that represent the standard pieces of a drum set – the kick drum (or bass drum), snare drum, hi-hat, ride cymbal, crash cymbal, low-tom (or floor tom), mid-tom, and high-tom. Please note that some drum sets may include other drums and cymbals as well. This is only the most common, basic setup.

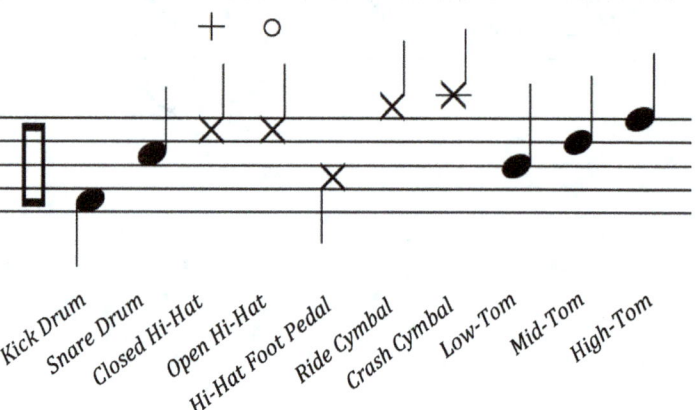

Three Directions for the Hi-Hat

You'll notice that I have indicated different notations for closed hi-hat, open hi-hat, and hi-hat foot pedal. The hi-hat consists of two cymbals pressed against one another. The hi-hat cymbals can be "opened," meaning moved away from each other in the vertical direction, or "closed," meaning brought together, with a foot pedal. In notation, the drummer is directed to strike the hi-hat cymbals with notes in the space just below the top line of the staff. A plus symbol can be added on top of the note to indicate that the drummer should strike the hi-hat in the closed position while a circle symbol can be added on top of the note to indicate that the drummer should strike the hi-hat in the open position. Both of these notes are written with stems up because the action is being controlled primarily by the drummer's arms and hands. Notes in the second space from the bottom, however, indicate that the drummer should bring the hi-hat cymbals together forcefully with the foot pedal to create a different kind of sound. In this direction, the drummer does not strike the hi-hat with a stick at all. Instead, all the sound comes from the feet and, therefore, we write these notes with the stems down.

Using Percussion Notation for Chord Progressions

We can also use percussion notation to describe a specific rhythm for a chord progression without specifying the exact voicings of the chords. For example, the notation below indicates that the performer should play a C major seven, then an A minor seven, then an F major seven in the rhythm half note, dotted quarter note, eighth note, with any voicings that the performer wishes to use.

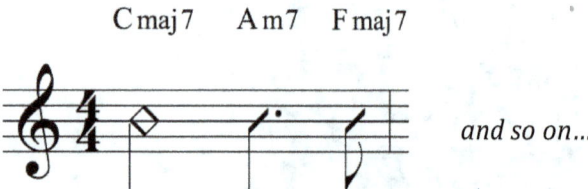

and so on...

- Articulations -

Articulations allow musicians to write down some of the finer details about the volume and length of notes. Although subtle, articulations can be very important to the musical expression of a piece of music.

Legato and Staccato

The term *legato* refers to the style of playing where notes overlap just slightly. In contrast, the term *staccato* describes the style of playing where small gaps, like short rests, are left between notes.

Slurs

The instruction to play legato is written with a *slur*. Listen to track 66 (disc 1) to hear this G major arpeggio played legato.

Staccato Markings

Here the same G major arpeggio is played staccato. The instruction to play staccato is written with small dots that are placed above or below the note head of the note the staccato instruction affects. Listen to this version of the G major arpeggio on track 67 (disc 1).

Accents

Articulations that increase the volume of a specific note are called *accents*. Standard accents are written with a small caret symbol that appears above the emphasized note.

Marcato

The symbol below is called a *marcato* and represents a stronger, more extreme accent.

Sforzando

A *sforzando* is another type of accent, which is indicated in music notation by the abbreviation *sfz* or *sf*. A sforzando is even stronger than the marcato.

sfz

Tenuto

The *tenuto* is a multipurpose articulation that can indicate any of the following directions:

1. The note should be played slightly longer than what would be expected from the rhythm of the note alone.

2. The note should be played with a slight accent or emphasis in volume.

3. The note should be played legato so that it overlaps slightly with the next note, just like a slur.

To be clear, the first direction above does not create any overlapping between notes, as the third direction does. Instead, the note marked with the tenuto symbol "pushes back" the following notes, so to speak. This version of the tenuto symbol is comparable to slowing the tempo of the piece while playing the given note.

"How can we tell which direction is meant in a given situation?" you ask. Sometimes, the context will make it clear. For example, if you see a note marked with a tenuto surrounded by notes marked staccato, there is a good chance the legato direction is the intended meaning of the tenuto.

If the context does not make the situation clear, you can listen to a few recordings of the given piece and see how other performers are interpreting the symbol.

Tenuto symbols can be written above or below the affected note.

- Strong and Weak Rhythmic Positions -

Temporal Proportionality

Every rhythmic position[1] can be evaluated in terms of its *temporal proportionality*. Temporal proportionality describes the relationship between a rhythmic position and the measure that contains the rhythmic position. This relationship can be described as a ratio, just as we can describe the proportionality of pitches with ratios. In the musical community, temporal proportionality is described in terms of *strong* and *weak rhythmic positions*. Strong rhythmic positions are positions that form simple ratios with the measure. Weak rhythmic positions are positions that form complex ratios with the measure.

In a measure of 4/4, beat three can be described with a 1:2 ratio because beat three represents the position that is halfway through the measure. Beat two can be described with the ratio 1:4 because beat two lands one quarter into the measure. Beat four, then, can be described with a 3:4 ratio because its position is three fourths into the measure.

Interestingly, following this line of thinking, beat one or the downbeat of the measure would be described with either the ratio 0:1 or 1:1. The reason for this is that beat one occurs both zero units of time through a measure (in other words, at the very beginning of the measure) as well as one full measure away from the beginning of the measure. In either case, the complexity of the downbeat can be thought of as containing one part, similar to the interval of a unison.

Continuing on, each of the "and" positions are described with a ratio where the larger number is eight. From earlier to later arrival in the measure, these ratios would be 1:8 for the "and" of 1, 3:8 for the "and" of two, 5:8 for the "and" of three, and finally 7:8 for the "and" of four. A similar process can be repeated for the "e" positions and "a" positions, which represent ratios where the larger number is 16.

Using this information, we can arrive at five broad categories of rhythmic positions in terms of temporal proportionality. From strongest to weakest proportionality, we have rhythmic positions that are created when the measure is undivided, divided into two parts, four parts, eight parts, and finally sixteen parts. Theoretically, this pattern of division could continue indefinitely. See the diagram on the following page to see where these rhythmic positions fall visually in a measure of 4/4.

1. Meaning a specific position within a measure. See *Rhythmic Positions* on page 97.

No Division
Beat 1

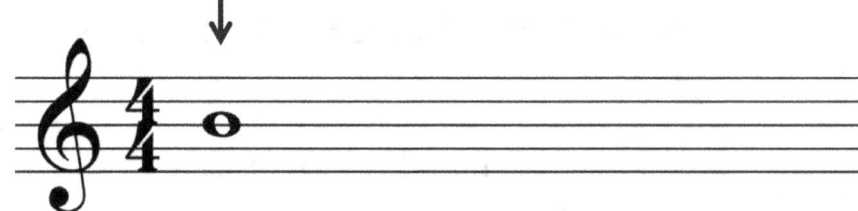

Divided in Halves
Beat 3

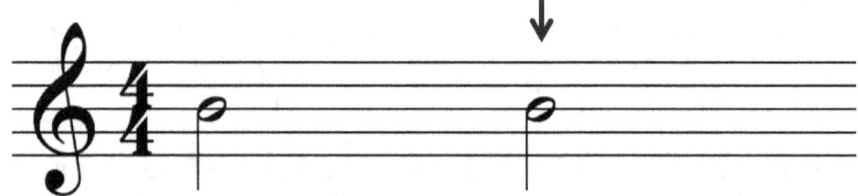

Divided in Quarters
Beats 2 and 4

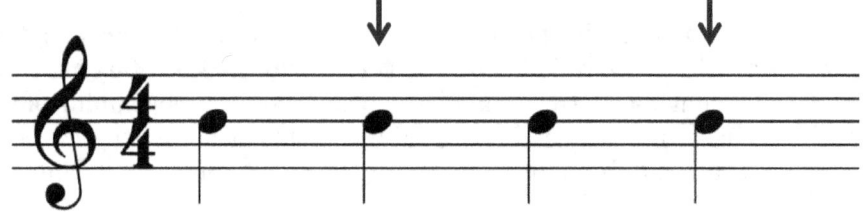

Divided in Eighths
The "ands"

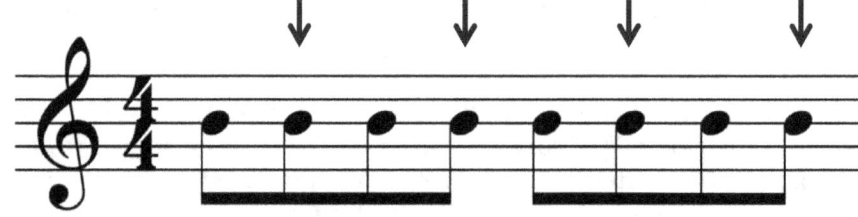

Divided in Sixteenths
The "e" and "a" positions

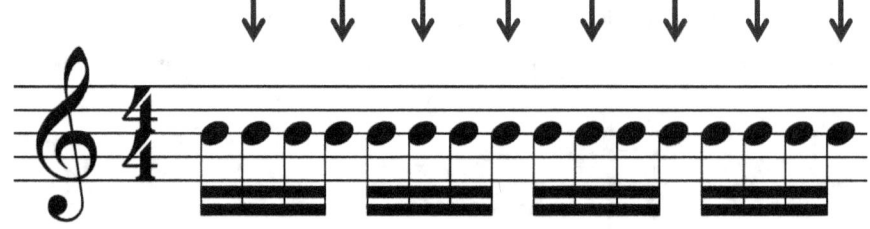

The Complete Order of Rhythmic Positions in 4/4 From Strongest to Weakest

Within the five broad categories of temporal proportionality shown above, we can further differentiate levels of strong and weak proportionality within each category. Beat two and beat four both represent ratios where the larger number is four. However, beat two is still a stronger rhythmic position than beat four. The reason for this is that the division of the measure into halves creates a stronger first half and a weaker second half. Thus, beat two, falling within the stronger half of the measure, is a relatively stronger position than beat four, which falls within the weaker half. Taken all together then, the four beats of the measure can be ordered from strongest to weakest as beat one, beat three, beat two, and then beat four.

Continuing this line of thinking to the division of the measure into eight parts, we can evaluate the strength of each "and" relative to one another. The strength of the "ands" is determined by the strength of the quarters of the measure each "and" falls halfway through. The "and" of one is the strongest because it falls within the strongest quarter of the measure. The "and" of three is next followed by the "and" of two, and finally the "and" of four as the weakest. The pattern illustrated here places the "ands" in the order of the beats they are preceded by in order from strongest to weakest. Beat one as the strongest beat, has the strongest following "and." Beat four, as the weakest beat, has the weakest following "and."

On the level of a sixteen-part measure, the "e" positions and "a" positions can be ranked from strongest to weakest by following the order of the strongest to weakest eighths of the measure that the given "e" or "a" falls within. The positions following the beats by a sixteenth of a measure are labeled with an "e" while the positions following the "ands" by a sixteenth of a measure are labeled with an "a." Because the beats are stronger positions than the "ands," the "e" positions, which follow the beats, are stronger than the "a" positions, which follow the "ands." The "e" positions go in order from the "e" following the first beat, to the third beat, to the second, and finally to the fourth. Next, the "a" positions progress in a similar pattern from the "a" following the first beat, to the third, to the second, to the fourth in order of the strength of the beats.

See the table on the following page for a visual representation of this pattern.

Undivided Measure	Beat 1															
Measure Divided into Two Parts								Beat 3								
Measure Divided into Four Parts					Beat 2							Beat 4				
Measure Divided into Eight Parts			and of 1				and of 2				and of 3				and of 4	
Measure Divided into Sixteen Parts	e of 1			a of 1		e of 2			a of 2		e of 3			a of 3		e of 4			a of 4

Strong Proportionality ⟶ Weak Proportionality

Proportionality in Groups of Three

In rhythmic groups of three, the first rhythmic position in the group will be strong, and the second and third positions will be equally weak. Below is the order of rhythmic positions from strong to weak in a measure of 3/4. In 3/4, the beats divide the measure into three, then all the following divisions break down into twos.

Because beat two and three possess an equal level of strength in this meter, the "and" of two and the "and" of three also become equally ranked on our list, as do the "e" and "a" positions of two and three.

Undivided Measure	Beat 1											
Measure Divided into Three Parts					Beat 2				Beat 3			
Measure Divided into Six Parts			and of 1				and of 2				and of 3	
Measure Divided into Twelve Parts	e of 1			a of 1		e of 2		a of 1		e of 3		a of 1

Strong Proportionality ⟶ **Weak Proportionality**

Proportionality of Other Meters

Using the information we have covered so far, you can derive the proportionality of rhythmic positions in other meters. Meters, generally, combine groups and subgroups of either twos or threes. You can, therefore, combine elements from the 4/4 pattern and the 3/4 pattern to describe other more complex meters. To do so, follow these steps:

1. Determine what the different levels of division are in the given meter. Generally, the measure will break down into either halves or thirds. Then, the subsequent parts will break down again into either halves or thirds and will continue to break down into either halves or thirds as we add more divisions. Repeat the process of determining how each level of division breaks down for as many levels as necessary. When you are finished describing this pattern of division, you should have equivalent of the diagram on page 218 for your meter.

2. Starting with the third level of division, order the rhythmic positions within each level according to the strength of the positions on the higher levels that they follow. We start on the third level of division because it takes at least two higher levels to make a meaningful distinction in this manner. Repeat this step as necessary taking into account the changes that this step produces in previous levels. Allow there to be ties when parts break down into thirds or higher fractions should that ever occur.

The TPLC Group

Low energy rhythmic positions are commonly balanced[1] with greater volume and variation, while high energy rhythmic positions are commonly balanced with lower volume and less variation. New musical elements like chords, new sections of music, and other important changes or transitions frequently occur on strong rhythmic positions. This means that there is an increase in variation and thus greater expressive energy on the spectrum of change[2] at the moment of these strong rhythmic positions. Likewise, it is also the norm to emphasize, in volume, the strong rhythmic positions. This too adds expressive energy to the strong rhythmic positions.

Interestingly, strong rhythmic positions are represented by low ratio relationships in the spectrum of time and this, in and of itself, is a low energy expression. This means that the tendencies we have outlined form a common balancing act that happens between strong rhythmic positions (low energy), high variation (high energy), and high volume (high energy); or in reverse, weak rhythmic positions (high energy), low variation (low energy), and low volume (low energy).

1. We originally introduced the concept of balance back in Chapter Two. See *Balance* on page 52. You may want to refresh yourself on this concept at this point, as balance will be a central piece of our discussions in the coming chapters.
2. See *Stasis and Change* and the principle box entitled *The Spectrum of Change* on page 51.

Temporal proportionality, loudness, and the spectrum of change are so commonly linked together in this specific way that I felt it would be useful to give this collection of attributes a name. I call it the *TPLC group*, which stands for temporal proportionality, loudness, change group.

The loudness and change aspects of the TPLC group tend to outweigh the temporal proportionality aspect. This means that as the loudness and change become higher energy while the temporal proportionality becomes lower energy, the overall effect is one of mild increase in expressive energy. And in reverse, when the loudness and change spectra become lower energy and the temporal proportionality spectrum increases in energy, the total system experiences a slight decline in energy.

In summary, the TPLC group organizes itself into a high energy polarity and low energy polarity. The high energy polarity consists of more volume and change with strong temporal proportionality, while the low energy polarity consists of less volume and change with weak temporal proportionality.

Low Energy Pole	High Energy Pole
Weak Rhythmic Positions (High Energy)	Strong Rhythmic Positions (Low Energy)
Low Volume/Loudness (Low Energy)	High Volume/Loudness (High Energy)
Low Variation/Change (Low Energy)	High Variation/Change (High Energy)

As we move forward, we will come to see that the TPLC group as a whole often balances with pitch proportionality. This arrangement works very nicely in the sense that both temporal and pitch proportionality align together, creating a clear expression of centrality on strong rhythmic positions, while the other elements of loudness and change help to balance the system, which prevents the expression from becoming too extreme at any one time.

While the patterns described here do work well and are very common, please note that these are only generalizations about common approaches. It is always possible to do things differently. The general framework of the seven spectra can allow you to explore these possibilities in a very free and unrestricted way. It is nevertheless useful to understand the norms and standard approaches, whether you choose to abide by them or not in your own creative enterprises.

Listening to Temporal Proportionality Balanced With Loudness

Listen to track 68 (disc 1) to hear an electronic sound playing an A3 as a continuous stream of sixteenth notes in a measure of 4/4. The stronger the proportionality of the rhythmic position, the louder the note is played. The weaker the proportionality, the quieter the note is played. This rhythmic pattern represents the sequence of rhythmic positions down to the sixteenth note matched with the expected, relative volume level according to the tendencies of the TPLC group.

In a real musical context, the rhythmic positions will rarely follow this exact, expected pattern of emphasis. Rather, composers will play with the listener's expectations, using some rhythmic positions at the expected volume levels at times and surprising the listener at other times. Strong rhythmic positions could be combined with quiet volume levels to produce a low energy expression. Likewise, weak rhythmic positions can be combined with loud volume levels to produce high energy expressions.

Temporal Proportionality and Pitch

In Chapter Six, we discussed how lower pitched notes have a sense of centrality within a chord voicing.[1] In a similar way, lower pitched sounds are heard as being more weighty and central in a rhythmic pattern. As such, lower sounds are often used to anchor strong rhythmic positions, while higher sounds are used to articulate more complex rhythms using weaker rhythmic positions. This can be reversed, however, for a higher energy or more unexpected effect. We'll be discussing more specific examples of this concept further in coming sections of this chapter.

1. *Highest and Lowest Notes*, page 148

Listening to Melodic Phrases Starting on Different Rhythmic Positions

Listen to the melody notated on the following page on track 69 (disc 1). The same melodic phrase is played by a vibraphone over an accompaniment eight times starting on different rhythmic positions. First, the phrase is played starting on the downbeat. Then, the entire phrase is shifted over one half of a beat so that the phrase starts on the "and" of one. Then, the phrase is shifted so it begins on beat two. The phrase continues to move by one half of a beat until it has been played on each of the beats and each of the "ands."

Notice the different character of the rhythmic positions as they are brought out by this shifting melody. You can get a sense of the expression of each rhythmic position by listening to the entrance of the phrase as it moves through the measure. You may also listen to how the character of the entire phrase changes with the starting point.

Notice what effect is produced when the phrase starts on a strong position and what effect is produced when the phrase starts on a weak position. What expressive characteristics do you notice changing in these variations?

Improvising Melodic Phrases on Each Rhythmic Position

Play track 70 (disc 1) to hear just the accompaniment in the example above. In this activity, I invite you to play this track and improvise a melody over it. This track is in the Eb major scale. Take a moment to find the notes of this scale. The harmony of the track stays on an Eb major chord the whole time.

Practice intentionally starting the phrases of your melody on different positions. Begin with each of the beats. Then, progress to the "ands." Once you become comfortable with these, move on to the "e" and "a" positions.

You may find it helpful to the count the rhythmic positions on the measure prior to playing on your instrument. When practicing the "ands" or the "e" and "a" positions, it may be helpful to count the smaller subdivisions as well as the beats (i.e. "1 and 2 and 3 and 4 and" or "1, e, and, a, 2, e, and, a, 3, e, and, a, 4, e, and, a"). Try the exercise with and without counting. See which is easier for you. I recommend, generally, starting with counting to get a feel for a given rhythmic position and then progressing to being able to start the phrase without counting as you develop a more intuitive feel for the position.

As you practice this exercise, notice how the entrance of your phrase on different positions changes the expression of what you are playing.

- Grooves and Drumbeats -

What Is a Groove?

A *groove* refers to the accompaniment of a piece of music – especially the percussion part and bass line and, perhaps, aspects of the harmony parts. Particular grooves are often associated with certain styles of music and help to define different styles in a significant way.

Syncopation

Syncopation occurs when weak rhythmic positions are emphasized in terms of volume or musical importance. Syncopation can be created by:

1. Playing notes on weak rhythmic positions more loudly

2. Including more notes on weak rhythmic positions and fewer notes on strong rhythmic positions

3. Placing new chords or other important musical events on weak rhythmic positions

4. Beginning melodic phrases on weak rhythmic positions

5. Any other event that emphasizes a weak rhythmic position in volume or importance

The Different Levels of Syncopation

Syncopation most commonly refers to the emphasis of the "ands." This is syncopation on the level of the eight-part division. However, we can also meaningfully discuss sixteenth note syncopation, which involves the emphasis of the "e" and "a" positions and the syncopation on the level of the four-part division, which involves the emphasis of beats two and four. Beats two and four are collectively referred to as the *backbeat*. It is common to clap along to music on beats two and four. It is also common for the snare drum of a drum set to play the backbeat. You can hear the drums in tracks 6 (disc 1) and 22 (disc 1) doing just that.

As for syncopation on the level of the eight-part division and the sixteen-part division, you can hear examples of those on tracks 71 (disc 1) and 72 (disc 1), respectively. Track 71 plays a drumbeat commonly used in the styles of *electronic house music* and *disco*. This drumbeat features an open hi-hat on each "and" of the measure, creating a strong sense of consistent eighth note syncopation. Track 72 plays a *funk* groove. One of the defining characteristics of the style of funk is sixteenth note syncopation. You can hear sixteenth note syncopation in all the parts of this groove but I think it is easiest to hear in the guitar part.

If you would like, listen to all these examples and see if you can get a feel for how syncopation sounds and how it *feels* on different levels of division. You'll find, I think, that the syncopations based on more divisions of the measure sound more complex and expressively energetic.

Clapping Syncopations

As an exercise, you can try clapping along to the backbeat in tracks 6 (disc 1) and 22 (disc 1). Then, try clapping on the "ands" in track 71 (disc 1). And finally, for a real challenge, try clapping on the "e" and "a" positions while listening to track 72 (disc 1).

To start out, you may want to target a specific rhythmic position to clap on like just beat two, just the "and" of one, or just the "e" of one. Then, work up to clapping on more rhythmic positions until you can hit all the syncopated rhythmic positions in the pattern you are working with.

The Basic Drum Beat

Although there really isn't *one* basic drumbeat, many drumbeats are based on something similar to the foundational template shown below and to the left, which is often varied to include more high energy elements and more complex rhythmic positions. But in writing our own drumbeats and understanding those of others, we can think of the drumbeat below and to the left along with a couple of basic variations as a starting place.

This rhythmic foundation includes, perhaps most importantly, the backbeat on the snare. We have the freedom to change a lot in the cymbals and kick drum if we just stick to that backbeat on the snare drum. Next, we will add in a kick on the downbeat. In the basic drum beat below, I've also included a kick on beat three. We could create some simple variations of this beat by taking out the kick on beat three or adding in kicks on two and four so that the kick is played on each beat. The latter of these variations is known as a *four-on-the-floor beat* and is common in some electronic music styles.

In the structure we have created thus far, the kick drum on the downbeat provides a nice low-pitched sound on the strongest rhythmic positions, either just the downbeat, the downbeat and beat three, or all of the beats. The low pitch of the kick gives this sound extra weight and is, therefore, useful for anchoring the strong rhythmic positions. The snare drum provides a simple type of syncopation, based on the four-part division of the measure.

Now we will add a relatively high-pitched and relatively fast hi-hat on all the eighth notes. A variation of this is to put eighth notes on the ride cymbal instead of the hi-hat. We also might want either the hi-hat or ride to do quarter notes or sixteenths instead of eighth notes.

These are just a few of the more basic ways we can create different drumbeats. However, more commonly than not, some more complex syncopations will be added to these relatively low expressive energy ideas. We might, perhaps, write in some kick drums on the "ands," or we might write some more interesting rhythms for the snare drum that still include a strong emphasis on the backbeat.

As a visual reference, I've notated out one version of our "basic drum beat" below to the left. On the right, I've notated measures 31 and 32 from the drum part in track 6 (disc 1) as an example of a slightly more complex drum beat that retains the same essential structure.

Writing Your Own Drumbeat

Try creating your own drumbeat. You can do this either with a real drum set or with a *DAW computer program*.[1] Use the template above and start experimenting with it. Take things out. Add things in. Pay special attention to what rhythmic positions you are using and how strong or weak they are. Also make sure to be cognizant of the emphasis or volume levels you are using with each sound. High energy rhythmic positions will sound even higher with louder volume levels. In reverse, the effect of high energy rhythmic positions will be mitigated or brought closer to moderate levels with lower volume levels.

1. *Creating and Capturing Sounds*, page 321

- *Temporal Gravity* -

Approach and Arrival

Music often is felt to lead up to or *approach* strong rhythmic positions. In the weaker rhythmic areas that precede stronger ones, there is a sense of energy, approach, and anticipation. Upon the entrance of the stronger rhythmic area, there is a sense of arrival, stability, completion, and release.

What we are describing here are the expressions of *temporal gravity* – the sense of musical gravity that plays out over time or rhythmically. We can think of temporal gravity as creating two basic expressions – *approach* and *arrival*. The expression of approach occurs in areas of weaker rhythmic positions and feels as if musical gravity is in the process of pulling us into a place of stronger rhythmic stability. The expression of arrival occurs in areas of stronger rhythmic positions and feels like we are currently in that place of strong rhythmic stability. We have *arrived*.

Approaches sometimes may become more rhythmically active or expressively energetic in general. At other times, however, approaches may be less active, using periods of silence to create a sense of anticipation. Often, approaches combine both by creating activity and then following that up with a rest to increase the sense of anticipation.

Music frequently approaches the downbeat of a group of measures or the first measure in a new section of music. One typically finds the expression of an approach during ending material of these sections and the expression of an arrival upon the entrance of a new section.

Measures are most commonly grouped in multiples of four and eight. This means that we will often see approaches on the fourth, eighth, sixteenth, and so on measures of a piece or section. Likewise, we will see arrival expressions on the fifth, ninth, seventeenth, and so on measures.

The Drum Fill

In contemporary music, the drum set often contributes prominently to the sense of approach and arrival expressions. Drummers are sometimes said to "outline the sections" of a piece. One of the primary ways that this is accomplished is through *drum fills*. Drum fills are short sections of a drum set part. They are characteristically more complex and energetic than the ordinary "beat" or rhythmic pattern of the composition. Though, they can also make use of rests to create anticipation. Drum fills frequently make use of the toms, the crash cymbal, and any other additional cymbals or drums the performer may have on his or her kit. The function of a drum fill is always to set up the coming section of music and to emphasize the movement from high energy into stability.

You can listen to some examples of drum fills on track 6 (disc 1). There is a small drum fill leading into bar 17 of this track. This fill leads into the section where the background flute melody enters. There is a somewhat bigger, more pronounced fill leading into bar 25, which is the beginning of the section where the background string melody enters. And finally, we have a drum fill at the end of the piece leading into bar 41. As an example, I have provided the notation for the final drum fill below.

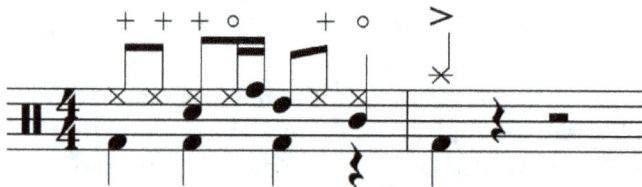

Temporal Gravity in Grooves: Micro-Approaches

Listen to a soul[1] ballad groove on track 73 (disc 1). The notation for the drums and bass line of the groove are shown below. In this groove, the bass part uses *micro-approaches* within each measure. For the first three measures of the groove, the bass part plays on the "and" of two followed by beat three and on the "and" of four followed by beat one. The kick drum also joins the bass on the "and" of two leading into beat three providing further emphasis on this rhythm. The "and" of two is a very weak rhythmic position. The movement of the "and" of two into the strong rhythmic position of beat three provides a sense of approach and arrival on a small scale. The same applies even more intensely, to the "and" of four, the weakest "and" of the measure, leading into beat one, the strongest rhythmic position. As the bass part pulses in pairs of two notes at a time, can you hear how the first note seems to lead into and then land on the second note, which is placed on a position of rhythmic strength and stability?

On a larger scale, notice how the second half of the fourth measure leads the listener back to the beginning of the four-measure group. A melodic line is played by the bass, guitar, and electric piano, which provides a sense of activity that resolves on the downbeat of the first measure.

1. For information on soul music, see *Soul, Funk, and Disco* on page 305.

Playing Behind or Ahead of the Beat

Playing behind the beat refers to playing slightly later than the rhythmic positions that have been established by the other musicians in an ensemble. *Playing ahead* or *in front of the beat* refers to playing slightly earlier than the established rhythm. These two possibilities can produce wonderful musical effects when used with intention and expressiveness.

Playing behind or ahead of the beat is similar to speeding up (accelerando) or slowing down (ritardando). The difference, however, is that with an accelerando or ritardando we will continually change the tempo more and more over the course of the accelerando or ritardando. Whereas, if a musician is playing ahead of the beat, the tempo can remain constant, but the rhythmic positions will be slightly offset in comparison to the rest of the groove or the rest of the musicians in the ensemble.

On track 74 (disc 1), a vibraphone plays a phrase six times, each with a different variation in timing over the same accompaniment heard in track 64 (disc 1). First, the phrase is played right on the beat, as expected. Then, the phrase is played slightly behind the beat, more dramatically behind the beat, slightly ahead of the beat, and more dramatically ahead of the beat in that order. Finally, the phrase is played once more right on the beat for the sake of comparison. What variations in musical expression do you sense between these different rhythmic effects?

The expressive results of using these kinds of rhythmic subtleties are somewhat complex. On the one hand, moving away from the expected rhythmic pattern in either direction introduces complexity and deviates from our expectations. In this regard, both playing behind and in front of the beat increases expressive energy. On the other hand, playing behind the beat also creates a certain kind of low energy expression, similar to how longer periods of time are associated with the low energy polarity in our seven spectra. In track 74 (disc 1), for example, playing behind the beat lengthens the time, slightly, between the earlier rhythmic positions we hear in the groove and the arrival of the soloist's notes. In contrast, playing ahead of the beat has the opposite effect, one of higher energy and shorter time between previous rhythmic positions and arrival. This means that by playing behind or ahead of the beat you will be doing at least two things at once, introducing energy by deviating from expectations while also creating a low or high energy expression based on how delayed or rushed the music feels.

- Tuplets and Polyrhythms -

Tuplets allow us to describe any fraction of a beat as a note value that we haven't been able to describe already with note values, dots, and ties. Tuplets apply to groups of notes and generally are notated with a bracket and a number, which are placed above or below the notes in the tuplet. If the group of notes in a tuplet are all eighth notes or faster, which are already grouped together by their flags, then a bracket is not necessary.

Below, to the left, is the most common type of tuplet, the eighth note *triplet*. For this tuplet, a bracket is not necessary because the eighth notes in the example are already linked. Below, to the right, is another common type of tuplet, the quarter note triplet. This example requires a bracket because the notes are not linked together with flags.

The Duration of Tuplets

Tuplets assign a duration to the note value that represents a division of a beat (half a beat in simple meter, one third of a beat in compound meter) based on the following formula:

The note value that represents a division of the beat lasts for 1/(the number above each group) of a beat.

For example, in the case of the eighth note triplet in 4/4, the division of a beat is represented by the eighth note and following the formula above we will find that eighth notes in the triplet have a value of one third of a beat. From this point we can use other note values in a tuplet based on the value of a division of a beat. For example, the quarter note triplet is twice the length of the eighth note triplet, giving us a value of two thirds of a beat for quarter notes under a triplet sign.

Listening to Triplets

On track 75 (disc 1), you can listen to a few examples of triplets being played on a vibraphone. The accompaniment is in 4/4 (and, in fact, we've used this accompaniment before on track 64 [disc 1]).

For this example, you will first hear eighth note triplets, followed by quarter note triplets. Then you will hear a descending phrase in regular (non-triplet) eighth notes. This will give you a sense of contrast, helping you to hear the difference between triplet rhythms and rhythms based on multiples of two. Next, you will hear a similar descending phrase that uses eighth note triplets.

And finally, you will hear another similar descending phrase played with quarter triplets. See if you can tap your foot or clap on the beats of this track. This may help you to internalize the rhythms you are hearing more effectively.

Clapping the Rhythms of Two, Three, and Four

This exercise is great for increasing your experiential understanding of rhythm and your performance ability. Start by tapping your foot to a beat. In the beginning, use a tempo on the slower side. You may try tapping your foot to a metronome, and I recommend at least trying this out, as it is a good experience to check your sense of "where the beat is landing" against a metronome.

Now, try clapping twice for every foot tap. Then, keeping the same tempo with your foot, try clapping three times for each foot tap and then, finally, four times. Once you have a feel for each of these individually, try going back and forth between them in different orders. Focus on keeping the tempo of the beat consistent, while you go from one rhythm to another, especially if you are not using a metronome. This exercise trains you to be able to switch between eighths notes, triplet eighth notes, and sixteenth notes. If you can master the rhythms based on these divisions, you will be comfortable in a great deal of musical territory.

Polyrhythms

A *polyrhythm* occurs when a unit of time is divided in two or more ways where the divisors are not even multiples of each other. Generally, polyrhythms are played with multiple parts, each using a different divisor. Polyrhythms can also occur with just one instrument, like between the two hands of a piano part or in two different drums in a drum set part. Polyrhythms can either be notated with tuplets or with multiple staves using different time signatures.

A *hemiola* is a common type of polyrhythm in which a unit of time is divided into two and divided into three. The triplet patterns on track 75 (disc 1) are examples of hemiolas.

Polyrhythms can be described as a ratio of one division of a unit of time to another division of the same unit of time. We can describe a hemiola as a 3:2 ratio or a 2:3 ratio.

Track 76 (disc 1) plays a few more examples of polyrhythms. The polyrhythms are played on two drums. In order, this track plays a 3:2 polyrhythm, followed by a 4:3 polyrhythm, followed by a 4:5 polyrhythm, for two measures each.

- Swing Rhythms -

Swing rhythm is a common musical element in jazz, blues, and many other musical styles. Swing rhythms move the position of all the "ands" of a measure from the halfway point between beats to the point two-thirds way through the beats. A stream of eighth notes in swing rhythm is equivalent to an alternating quarter note and eighth note under a triplet sign or, alternatively, an alternating quarter note and eighth note in a 12/8 meter as shown below. All three staves below play the same rhythm. You can listen to this rhythm on track 77 (disc 1).

Swing rhythm may be indicated on notation with the word "swing" or by writing ♫ = ♩♪ or both. To differentiate, the term *straight eighths* can be used to refer to regular (non-swing) eighth notes.

Swing Rhythms vs. Swing the Style

A style of big band jazz music popular in the 1930s and 1940s is often referred to as *swing music*.[1] Be careful not to confuse the style of swing with the rhythmic pattern shown above, which is used in a variety of styles.

1. We'll discuss swing music in Chapter Ten. See *Swing and Big Band Jazz* on page 298.

Listen to a Swing Groove

Listen to the music on track 78 (disc 1) to hear a groove characteristic of the swing style. You can listen to this groove to get a feel for both the style of swing and the rhythmic pattern of swing eighth notes. The hi-hat part in this groove is a very distinctive feature of swing music.

Can you hear how this groove almost seems to *bounce*? Here, the swing rhythms seem to provide a sense of energy and lightness to the music. By dividing the beat into three parts, rather than two, swing rhythms are somewhat more complex than straight eight note rhythms and, thus, as a generality, more energetic. Because swing rhythms place the "ands" closer to the beats they approach, swing rhythms can seem to produce a stronger feeling of temporal gravity, like the "ands" are *leading into* the beats more strongly than in straight rhythms.

- An Analysis of Rhythmic Expression -

In this section, we will talk about the composition played on track 79 (disc 1). This piece demonstrates a diverse range of rhythmic expressions. Take a moment to listen to this track once now, and, after you listen to it, we will go through an in-depth analysis of the rhythms in the track.

Measures 1 Through 16

This piece has a tempo of 76 bpm and it starts in 4/4 but goes through several time signatures. The first sixteen bars progressively build up the rhythmic complexity. The measure is broken up in two parts, then four, then eight, then sixteen, and finally thirty-two parts. This gives you a chance to hear what each of these levels of division sound like. Can you identify each time a rhythmic position is used that breaks up the measure into a greater degree of complexity?

In the first twelve bars, the lower pitched drums are placed on stronger rhythmic positions, and higher pitched drum sounds are placed on weaker rhythmic positions. However, starting on bar thirteen, a low, emphasized drum starts playing on beats two and four, in other words, on the backbeat. This change deviates from the expectation of putting lower sounds on stronger rhythmic positions and higher sounds on weaker ones.[1] Because this drum part is fairly loud, it also deviates from the expectation of using quieter volume levels on weaker rhythmic positions.[2] The result is a somewhat higher energy expression, with a fun, swinging feeling (figuratively, not the actual swing rhythm discussed on page 234). Up to this point, new expressions have been created by adding more divisions to each measure and, thus, adding new forms of possible rhythmic complexity, but now we have an example of creating a new expression just by using a more unexpected, higher energy emphasis of the same rhythmic positions we were hearing before.

There are several micro-approaches in the first sixteen bars. For example, a higher pitched drum plays on the "e" and the "a" of beat four leading into the downbeat of the ninth bar. I've notated out the rhythm of the drum part in bar eight and nine below, using the top four lines of the staff to represent the four drums that we hear, going from the lowest pitched drum on the second to lowest line of the staff to highest pitched drum on the top line of the staff.

1. *Temporal Proportionality and Pitch*, page 224
2. *The TPLC Group*, page 222

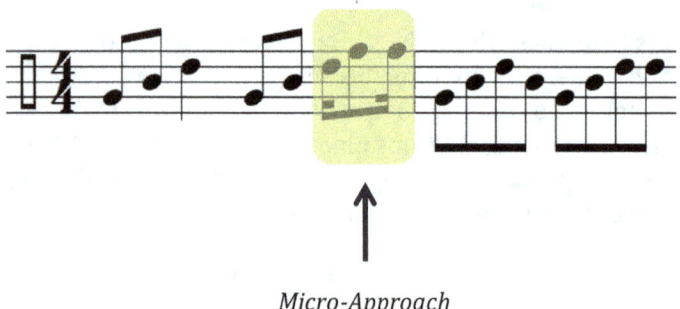

Micro-Approach

This rhythm begins to repeat and is heard, in a similar form anticipating the emphasized low drum that plays on the backbeat starting in bar thirteen.

Leading into bar thirteen, there is an approach that features more activity in the higher pitched drums and creates a sense of gravity by having the mid and low drums rest, pulling us into the downbeat of measure thirteen. The effect is emphasized and completed by the addition of the low drum on the backbeat, which adds more rhythmic energy and excitement when the tension of the rhythmic gravity is released.

Measures 17 Through 32

Now, let's discuss the next eight measures, from bar seventeen to bar thirty-two. This section is signaled by the introduction of a plucked or *pizzicato* string part as well as a change to the 3/4 time signature. The rhythm up to this point has been based on multiples of two.

What expressive characteristics do you notice with the entrance of this first grouping of three? Groups of three have their own distinct feel in comparison to groups of two. Groups of three can have a certain "bounce-y" quality to them. This is especially true of swing rhythms or other rhythms that resemble swing. In more of a classical context, the 3/4 meter is associated with the waltz and indeed groups of three have a particular flavor of dance-like quality to them. Groups of three feel less straightforward to me, in comparison to divisions based in multiples of two. There is a propensity for playful, indirect, or rhythmically flowing expressions, but, of course, these are only very general tendencies that are heavily context dependent.

Similar to the last section, as the music progresses the rhythmic complexity increases. The strings start out playing quarter notes on each beat of the 3/4 measures. Then, the strings add a part that divides each beat into three. We could describe this rhythm as eighth note triplets in 3/4 or as eighth notes in a bar of 9/8. Finally, the strings add a part that divide each beat into six parts. This can be described as sixteenth note triplets in 3/4 or as sixteenth notes in 9/8.

This is all fairly similar to the increase in complexity that we heard in the first section only with a foundation in three rather than two. However, halfway through this section, the low drum part that emphasized the backbeat in the previous section comes back. This creates a polyrhythm because most of the music is based in three but the rhythm of the low drum part is based in four.

Together, these rhythms generate more complexity and a sense of a longer cycle because it takes four measures for the downbeat of the 3/4 measures and the downbeat of the 4/4 measures associated with the low drum part to align. This feels something like creating a super-measure of twelve beats.

The 5/4 Section and the Electric Piano Solo

Starting with bar thirty-three, we hear a new kind of division – the division of the measure into five parts. The music will stay in a 5/4 time signature for the middle section of the piece, which features an electric piano solo.

Throughout this section, the bass provides structure to the groove by using micro-approaches. These often come in the form of short approaches that emphasize beat five but the bass part occasionally uses slightly longer approaches as well.

The electric piano solo takes advantage of some fast rhythmic divisions, including sixteenth and even thirty-second notes. There is, in fact, syncopation on both the sixteenth note and thirty-second note levels of division.[1] These rhythms create some very nuanced and complex expressions. In the beginning of the solo, the phrases of the solo generally start on weak rhythmic positions, either "ands" or rhythmic positions associated with sixteen or thirty-two part divisions of the measure. However, the phrases commonly end on stronger rhythmic positions, often downbeats. This creates the interesting effect of generating a sense of syncopation with the introduction of new phrases, while providing complete resolutions with the stronger rhythmic positions at the end of the phrases. A notable exception is the second phrase of the solo, which ends on the "and" of five, creating a falling away effect.

Toward the middle of the solo, the electric piano pauses for a moment and a high drum plays a *quintuplet* (a tuplet that breaks the beat into five parts). You can recognize this moment by the fact that the drum plays a fast continuous stream of hits six times in a row, starting on beat four playing each rhythmic position of the quintuplet and then ending on beat five. This is a good example of a larger, more complex tuplet, and an interesting case of using a division of five within the larger division of five – the quintuplet divides the beat into five divisions and the 5/4 meter divides the measure into five beats.

Shortly after the quintuplet, the whole ensemble plays a syncopation together. We might call this kind of unified and emphasized rhythm a *hit*. This is an important musical element because it emphasizes the syncopation in a more dramatic way by adding instruments and by making the syncopation the sole focus of our attention. In this case, the hit is also emphasized by a crash cymbal. This is a common technique used by composers and arrangers and you'll likely recognize the feel of it.

1. *The Different Levels of Syncopation*, page 226

Moving toward the end of the solo, the rhythms simplify in preparation for a resolution. Phrases start entering on strong rhythmic positions, unlike the music we have heard up to this point. The electric piano then begins a steady rise in pitch that builds up a sense of tension. These changes taken together tell us that something new is about to happen. The sense of gravity is pretty heavy here and the electric piano pauses before the next downbeat, increasing the tension even more. But rather than fulfilling our expectations of an emphasized downbeat, the electric piano rests on the downbeat, instead coming in just after it with a fast, falling phrase that leads into the end of the solo. This unexpected move creates interest in the piece, while still allowing us to experience a small sense of resolution through the decrease in pitch in the final moments of the solo. The ending to the piano solo creates a somewhat weaker resolution[1] because of the high energy expressions produced by the fast rhythmic movement as well as the note selection in the last notes of the solo. This works well in this case because the weaker resolution helps produce the sense of a transition from one section to another rather than a complete ending.

1. *Strong and Weak Resolutions*, page 195

Ending

While the piano solo is coming to close, the groove changes to a 7/4 time signature and three new timbres are added, a distinctive hi-hat sound, a synthesizer playing a chord pattern, and an electric guitar. Notice how the bass uses a familiar sixteenth-note rhythm on "e" and "a" to create a micro-approach to each downbeat.

Micro-Approach

The guitar phrases in this section provide a clear articulation of the beginning of each measure, by starting on and emphasizing the downbeat. The music changes into a 13/8 time signature briefly for two measures (this happens on the third phrase you'll hear in the guitar part), before returning to 4/4 (this happens with the new bass part that enters as the guitar part rises to its last note). Notice how the time signatures of 7/4 and 13/8 create complexity but also a sense of a longer cycle between downbeats, somewhat like the polyrhythms we heard earlier.

The next section is a small climax that features more polyrhythms between rhythms based in two and rhythms based in three, much like the earlier section that featured pizzicato strings. There is even more activity this time and a sense of almost chaotic activity. The higher drum parts include an expanded micro-approach that adds some additional interest and energy to the section. The music then begins to simplify in rhythm and reduce in the number of instruments that are playing. The complexity of the rhythm mimics the beginning of the piece, only in reverse, reducing the division in each measure from thirty-two to sixteen to eight to four to two and finally to one part per measure in the last moment of the composition.

Improvising a Rhythm

Hopefully, going through this piece has served as a good introductory tour through many of the possible rhythmic expressions that we can produce through different divisions of the measure. Of course, these are only a handful of interesting ideas out of a nearly infinite set of possibilities.

I invite you to do some of your own exploring of the possibilities of rhythm. One great way to do this is to focus on only the rhythmic aspect of music while playing music and reduce your attention on the aspect of pitch. Try picking a single note on your instrument and improvising a rhythm. You might also try clapping or playing a percussion instrument for this improvisation. You can play along to track 64 (disc 1), 65 (disc 1), 70 (disc 1), or one of the other accompaniment tracks in this book. For your reference, track 64 (disc 1) is in Gb major, track 65 (disc 1) is in Eb minor, and track 70 (disc 1) is in Eb major. Alternatively, try improvising your rhythm to a metronome.

By playing only one note or using a non-pitched sound for your improvisation, you'll be able to dedicate all your attention to just the rhythm of what you are playing. Really listen to what expressions you are able to produce in this way, while you explore the territory of rhythmic possibilities. You might pay particular attention to what happens when you play behind, on, or ahead of the beat. You might also notice the unique sound of different levels of divisions – divisions of two, three, four, five, and so on. You might also experiment with micro-approaches or the use of silence. Although eliminating pitch is in one sense very constraining, there is an incredible amount to experiment with here.

As a potential follow on, you might try slowly adding back in one or two other notes to your improvisation. See how this affects the range of possibilities you have at your disposal. After this, you might even want to try an improvisation with no restriction on what notes you can use and see if you can incorporate some of what you have learned in the previous activities into your playing.

Chapter Nine
Relationships in Pitch

- Two Levels of Relationships -

There are two primary levels of relationships in pitch – the relationship of pitches to the tonal center and the relationship of pitches to the chord tones or, in other words, the harmony. Both tonal centers and chord tones can be considered musical centers – positions of strong pitch proportionality, resolution, and low energy expressions.[1] I'll describe these musical centers, which exist and form relationships in the domain of pitch, as *pitch centers*.

As we will see in this chapter, the tonal center and the harmony can interact with each other, and both can also form relationships with the notes of the melody.

There are a few key differences between the relationships to the tonal center and the relationships to the harmony. Of these two levels of interactions, the relationships to the tonal center are more foundational and longer lasting throughout a musical piece. The tonal center will remain constant as long as a composer remains in a given scale. The chords of a musical composition, however, will likely change every measure or so. This means that the chord tones exert a more quickly fluctuating influence on the expression of the music, while the relationship to the tonal center remains a relatively stable or even constant aspect of the composition.

We must also keep in mind that we will not always be hearing the tonal center as the listener, though it may be in our memory or it may be implied by the music we are hearing in various ways. There will usually be a sounding[2] chord, however, assuming that the given piece of music has a harmony part. And so the relationship between the melody and the harmony is very important and heard very prominently as sounding interval relationships. In comparison, the relationships of the melody and harmony to the tonal center may not be heard directly and so are bit more subtle.

Overall, it would be hard to say that one of these levels of relationships is more primary or important than the other. To summarize, we can think of the relationships to the tonal center as being longer lasting and more subtle, while the relationships to the chords are shorter lived but more direct and prominent.

1. See *Musical Centers and Gravity* on page 54. For information about high and low energy expressions, see *Seven Basic Spectra of Musical Expression* on page 47.
2. "Sounding" meaning currently being played and heard. See the box entitled *Related Series Analysis* (paragraph three, to be exact) on page 164.

> **Resolving to the Root, Third, or Fifth of a Chord**
>
> In terms of chord tones, musical gravity is usually only generated in relation to the root, third, or fifth of a chord. Other chord tones generally lack the pitch proportionality to the root of the chord necessary to become a strong gravitational center. However, this is not an absolute rule. In some circumstances, it may be possible to create a sense of resolution to other chord tones.

In the following sections, we will examine various types of relationships that exist in the domain of pitch. First, we will look at each individual note's relationship to the tonal center and the musical expression that relationship creates. Next, we will consider the melody's relationship to the harmony. In the process, we will go through a paradigm of melodic analysis and look at an example to see how different expressions are created through the relationship between melody and harmony. From there, we will begin examining musical relationships and expressions of gravity in the context of chord progressions. We will look at the relationship between chords and the tonal center as well as the relationships between one chord and the next over time.

In the second half of the chapter, we will get into several other topics about pitch relationships, including new concepts about chord progressions and scales. We will finish this chapter and Part Two with an analysis of the melody in Faure's "Pavane" and an introduction into the creation of themes or musical ideas like melodies and chord progressions that can develop into full-length pieces of music. This will mark an exciting turning point in our journey, where we will take all of the theory and conceptual information that we have studied thus far and apply it to the artistic pursuit of musical creativity.

- The Character of the Scale Degrees -

> **Differentiation**
>
> The first variable we will consider about scale degrees[1] is the differing and common notes between the major and minor scale. If one compares a major scale to a minor scale built on the same tonal center, one will see that the same notes are present in the first, second, fourth, and fifth degrees of the two scales. The third, sixth, and seventh degrees of the minor scale, however, are all one half step lower than the corresponding degrees in the major scale. We can say that the third, sixth, and seventh scale degrees *differentiate* the major scale from the minor scale.
>
> 1. *Scale Degrees*, page 184

Therefore, it is the third, sixth, and seventh scale degrees that create the expression of the major scale as distinct from the minor scale and likewise the expression of the minor scale as distinct from the major scale. In a minor key, the use of the third, sixth, and seventh scale degrees evoke the classically ascribed expressions of the minor quality – sadness, darkness, mellowness, and so on. In a major key, these same scale degrees will evoke the contrasting expressions of happiness, brightness, openness, and so on.

We can also apply this concept to chords. A major and minor triad built on the same root will share the same fifth but will differ when it comes to the third. This means that the third of a triad will evoke a sense of major or minor quality whereas the root and fifth will create a relatively neutral expression, in this regard.

So that we can easily reference this concept, I'll call any note that significantly characterizes a given chord or scale in the manner we are describing here a *differentiating note*.

To put this all in terms of solfege syllables,[1] we could say that the major and minor scale share the notes Do, Re, Fa, and So. In the major scale, the differentiating notes are Mi, La, and Ti; and, in the minor scale, the differentiating notes are Me, Le, and Te.

1. *Solfege Syllables*, page 187

Gravitational Positions

We can divide the degrees of a scale into three categories based on their relationships to various pitch centers and their resultant properties in the realm of musical gravity. I call these categories *gravitational positions*. Moving from low expressive energy to high expressive energy, these are: pitch centers, notes with only whole step relationships (or larger) to the pitch centers, and notes with half step relationships to pitch centers. We can make these distinctions in relation to the tonal center of the scale or to the sounding[1] chord tones. In the context of the tonal center, the pitch centers are the root, third, and fifth of the tonic chord. These notes are equivalent to the solfege positions Do, Mi (for major scales) or Me (for minor scales), and So, respectively. In the context of the chord tones, the centers are the root, third, and fifth of whatever the sounding chord happens to be. Among these centers, the root of the chord is the strongest, followed by the fifth of the chord, followed by the third.

The notes with half step relationships to pitch centers are significant because, in our twelve note musical system, they are the closest possible distance (in terms of pitch) to a center. According to the principle of gravity, the closer a pitch gets to a center the stronger the expression of musical gravity will become.[2] This means that notes with half step relationships to pitch centers will generate the strongest sense of musical gravity out of all possible relationships in our musical system.

1. Meaning chord tones that are currently being played and heard in a piece of music. See *Related Series Analysis* (specifically paragraph three) on page 164.
2. The *Principle of Musical Gravity* is introduced on page 55 in the section entitled *Musical Centers and Gravity*. In the section *Musical Gravity in Chord Progressions* on page 195, we expand on these ideas and discuss, in particular, the basics of how musical gravity functions in the realm of pitch and the significance of half step relationships for musical gravity.

Notes in this type of gravitational position form weak proportional relationships with the pitch centers of the music, and our imaginative ear naturally hears a progression from these weak positions to the stronger positions they are next to. When a composer allows this progression to happen, a sense of resolution is created in the expression of the music. Therefore, half step relationships are useful in creating a sense of strong resolution when that is desired.

The notes with only whole step relationships to centers may also contribute to resolutions but they have a significantly weaker pull or sense of gravity. If the pitch centers are like planets and the notes with half step relationships to the centers are like orbiting moons, the notes with whole step relationships are much like asteroids floating aimlessly in the space only weakly affected by the pull of larger, distant bodies.

Taking a more detailed view, we can also consider that notes with half step or whole step relationships to centers will become more energetic the stronger the center they approach. For example, we could say that in relation to the tonic chord[1] of a major scale, Ti will be more energetic than Fa because Ti approaches Do, the root of the chord, whereas Fa approaches Mi, the third of the chord. Considering that the root is a stronger position than the third, it follows according this rule that Ti, the note approaching the stronger center, will be more energetic than Fa, the note approaching the weaker center.

1. The tonic chord is the chord built off of the first degree of a scale. See *Scale Degrees* on page 184 and especially *Naming Chords With Scale Degrees* on page 186.

Gravitational Positions for the Major Scale

Scale Degree	Solfege Name	Gravitational Position
Tonic	Do	Gravitational center
Supertonic	Re	Only whole step relationships
Mediant	Mi	Gravitational center
Subdominant	Fa	Half step relationship to Mi
Dominant	So	Gravitational center
Submediant	La	Only whole step relationships
Leading Tone	Ti	Half step relationship to Do

Gravitational Positions for the Minor Scale

Scale Degree	Solfege Name	Gravitational Position
Tonic	Do	Gravitational center
Supertonic	Re	Half step relationship to Me
Mediant	Me	Gravitational center
Subdominant	Fa	Only whole step relationships
Dominant	So	Gravitational center
Submediant	Le	Half step relationship to So
Subtonic	Te	Only whole step relationships

Listening to the Expression of the Scale Degrees

Track 80 (disc 1) plays an accompaniment in C major, and track 81 (disc 1) plays an accompaniment in C minor. Both tracks stay on their tonic chords for the entire duration. To get a feel for the expression of each scale degree in the major scale, try playing each note of the C major scale along with track 80, listening carefully to how the note you are playing sounds with the accompaniment. Do the same with the minor scale and the accompaniment on track 81.

Notice the different expressions of the chord tones, notes with whole step relationships to the chord tones, and notes with half step relationships to the chord tones. For the major accompaniment, the chord tones are C, E, and G; the notes with whole step relationships are D and A; and the notes with half step relationships are F and B. For the minor accompaniment, the chord tones are C, Eb, and G; the notes with whole step relationships are F and Bb; and the notes with half step relationships are D and Ab.

Analysis of Half Step Relationships in Major and Minor Scales

The major and minor scales each have two half step relationships. The positions and characteristics of these relationships create much of the expressive framework of these scales.

The major scale possesses a half step relationship from Fa to Mi and a half step relationship from Ti to Do. The Ti to Do relationship is particularly significant because it creates a half step relationship to the tonal center, the strongest possible resolution. The Fa to Mi relationship can create resolutions that evoke the major expression of the scale because Mi is one of the differentiating notes in a major scale.

The ascending direction of the Ti to Do resolution also creates a subtly different expression than the descending direction of the Fa to Mi resolution. The descending pitch of the Fa to Mi resolution is a subtly less energetic movement than the upward motion of the Ti to Do resolution.

Listen to an example of a Ti to Do resolution on track 82 (disc 1) and listen to an example of a Fa to Mi resolution on track 83 (disc 1). Can you hear the different characteristics mentioned? What else do you notice?

The minor scale possesses a half step relationship from Re to Me and a half step relationship from Le to So. Notice that there is no half step relationship to the tonal center in the minor scale.[1] Of the two, the resolution to So is somewhat stronger than the resolution to Me because So has a stronger proportional relationship to the tonal center. Both relationships have one differentiating note that evokes a minor expression (Me in the Re to Me relationship and Le in the Le to So relationship).

1. Technically speaking, there is no half step relationship in the *natural minor scale*, which is the type of minor scale we have been studying up to this point. However, in the upcoming section *Harmonic and Melodic Minor Scales* found on page 256, we will introduce some different versions of the minor scale, which do include a half step resolution to the tonal center.

Similar to the major scale, there is one ascending half step resolution and one descending half step resolution in the minor scale. However, in the minor scale the stronger resolution is the descending resolution whereas in the major scale the stronger resolution is the ascending resolution.

Listen to an example of the Re to Me resolution on track 84 (disc 1) and listen to an example of the Le to So resolution on track 85 (disc 1).

Improvising With Gravitational Relationships

Using the accompaniments on tracks 80 (disc 1) and 81 (disc 1), try the following experiments to explore the gravitational relationships of the major and minor scale, respectively. Recall that track 80 (disc 1) is in C major and track 81 (disc 1) is in C minor.

1. Improvise a melody on your instrument and end each phrase of your melody with a half step resolution in the scale you are playing in. For example, you might end a phrase with a Ti pitch – B in the context of track 80 – followed by a Do pitch – C in the context of track 80. Try both the half step resolutions in the scale (Ti to Do and Fa to Mi for the major scale, Re to Me and Le to So for the minor scale) and notice the different character of each.

2. Try creating resolutions that move by a whole step. Notice that these resolutions are not as strong. The gravitational pull is more moderate as is the expression of the resolution.

3. Try adding in other variables on the seven expressive spectra and notice the results. What happens at louder volume levels? What happens with longer lasting notes?

If you are playing an instrument that is able to play harmony and melody at the same time, try creating your own accompaniment for this experiment. Choose any major or minor scale and find the tonic triad of that scale. Play this chord in a voicing and pattern of your creation. It can be as simple as the original voicing of the triad played continuously as half notes or whole notes in 4/4. You may even disregard the rhythmic aspect entirely, playing in an unstructured free-form rhythm, to focus on the sound of the pitches. Once you have decided on your accompanying harmony part, proceed to experiment with improvising a melody and listening to the sound of the gravitational relationships.

- Melodic Analysis -

In this section, I will present my own model of analyzing and understanding melodies based on some of the most important aspects of the seven expressive spectra for melodic writing. In the process, we will review many of the important topics we have covered about musical relationships in both pitch and rhythm. Afterwards, we will look at a simple example of melodic analysis, focused on the relationship between the melody and the sounding chord tones.

A Model of Melodic Analysis

I feel that the following paradigm is helpful in focusing our attention on the most important and most commonly influential musical elements in the context of melodic writing. However, this model is not as foundational or comprehensive as the seven spectra. As such, the original basic seven spectra should not be forgotten.[1] I invite you to use both models as needed.

Like the seven spectra, this model also includes seven characteristics, which can increase or decrease in expressive energy. The first of these is the pitch proportionality of the melodic notes in relation to the chords that are heard in the harmony part of the music. The second is the pitch proportionality of the melodic notes in relation to the tonal center. Both of these can be evaluated in the three categories discussed earlier – pitch centers, notes with whole step relationships to pitch centers, and notes with half step relationships to pitch centers. We can then further differentiate between the root as the strongest center, the fifth as the second strongest, and the third as the weakest center of the three. And along with that, we can differentiate between notes that approach the stronger centers as being more energetic than the notes that approach weaker centers. Also recall at this point that relationships to the chord tones serve as shorter-lived expressions, whereas the relationships to the tonal center determine the long-term position of a note in relationship to the big-picture arc of the piece.

The third characteristic in our model is the quality, perhaps most prominently the major or minor quality, that is produced by notes that differentiate the scale that is being used from other possibilities.[2] When considering this characteristic, we will group notes into two basic categories – neutral notes, which do not reveal or imply anything about the type of scale that is being used, and differentiating notes, which imply a major quality, minor quality, or some other particular type of scale. This category essentially takes into account what harmonies and scales are being implied by the melody and associates the expressions of those harmonies and scales with the notes of the melody that create the given implications.

So far we have covered the musical elements of pitch proportionality and scale degree characteristics. Now add to this, the concept of the TPLC group[3] and we have, arguably, the primary block of analysis within this model. This is what we could roughly call the *proportionality block*, as it centers on the musical elements that rely on proportions in pitch and time. As a norm, we will tend to see the TPLC group balance the pitch proportionality relationships of the melody as the two move in opposing directions. This means that stronger rhythmic positions will tend to be accompanied by stronger pitch proportionality but counterbalanced by an increase of energy from louder volumes and greater change or variation.

1. *Seven Basic Spectra of Musical Expression*, page 47
2. When discussing this concept of *quality-expressions*, if you will, the most common distinction will be between the expression of the major quality and the expression of the minor quality. However, as we move through the book we will be introducing more and more types of scales and chords that will further diversify the possibilities here. For example, later in this chapter we will discuss *Harmonic and Melodic Minor Scales* (page 256) and *Modes* (page 263). These will introduce new possible quality-expressions and new corresponding differentiating notes. A similar concept can be applied to the new chord and scale types presented in *Chapter Thirteen* (page 388).
3. *The TPLC Group*, page 222

Along the same lines, weaker and, therefore, more energetic temporal and pitch proportionality will tend to be balanced by the lower energy expressions of quiet volumes and less variation.

It is worth noting here that pitch proportionality and temporal proportionality tend to move in alignment rather than balancing by moving in opposite directions, as a norm or expectation. In other words, strong rhythmic positions are likely to have notes of strong pitch proportionality on them and the reverse for weak rhythmic positions. This is interesting because in isolation, without considering the spectra of volume and change, we might think it would be likely for these two types of proportionality to balance each other.

Assuming that volume and change will balance temporal proportionality as described in the tendency of the TPLC group, we can come to a few important conclusions:

Placing a note of weak pitch proportionality and, thus, high energy on a strong rhythmic position will amplify the energy of the already high energy note.

In reverse, placing a high energy note on a weak rhythmic position will mitigate the heightened energy of the note.

In conjunction with what I deemed the proportionality block, which comprises the relationship to the harmony, the relationship to the tonal center, the differentiating qualities of the scale, and the TPLC group, we can consider the gradated spectra of pitch, loudness, and time. These form the second block of the analysis model, which we can call the *gradated block*.

Loudness is included in the TPLC group but more in terms emphasis or the short-term loudness of individual rhythmic positions. The loudness we are concerned with in the gradated block is the more general loudness of sections of music described by the dynamic levels from piano to forte as well as the fluctuations of that more general loudness described with crescendos and diminuendos.

Another term for the gradated spectrum of pitch in a melodic context is *contour*. Contour refers to the general shape of a melody as it rises and falls in pitch. The rising portions of a contour create an increase in expressive energy, while the falling ones create a decrease in expressive energy.

The gradated spectra tend to play a secondary, though significant role, helping to shape crucial subtleties of expression. Pitch proportionality and the TPLC group tend to provide the essential feeling and concept of a melody but the gradated spectra create an articulation of that essential construct that serves a vital function. It is as if the gradated spectra paint a picture or form a shape out of the raw material and color of the expression of proportionality.

The Seven Characteristics for Melodic Analysis

Proportionality Block
1. Gravitational Relationship to the Harmony
2. Gravitational Relationship to the Tonal Center
3. Differentiating Qualities of the Scale
4. TPLC Group (Temporal Proportionality, Loudness, Change Group)

Gradated Block
5. Contour (Pitch as a Gradated Spectrum)
6. Loudness as a Gradated Spectrum
7. Time as a Gradated Spectrum

An Example of Relationships to Chord Tones

Take a moment to listen to this music on track 86 (disc 1) now. Overlaid on top of the notation for this piece, I have highlighted all of the chord tones in the melody – specifically all of the notes that are either the root, third, or fifth of the sounding chord.

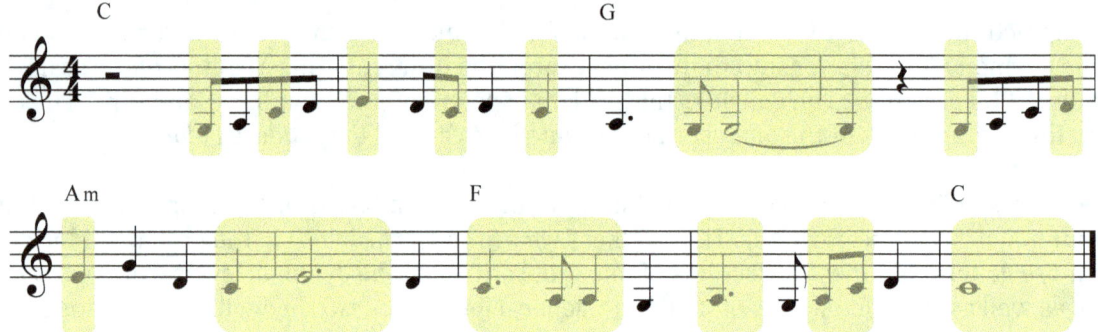

Lead Sheets and Scores

Above I've provided the notation for this piece in a format called a *lead sheet*. A lead sheet is made up of the melody of a piece of music with chord symbols above the staff that represent the harmony of the music. Lead sheets can be very useful because they provide the basic essence of a composition with a small amount of notation. Lead sheets are in contrast to *scores*, which contain all of the parts for a piece of music, with each instrument or part having its own staff. See page 352 for an example of a score. Lead sheets also come in handy for quickly learning new pieces and creating your own arrangements of other composers' work. But note that a lead sheet does not specify musical elements like chord voicings, rhythms in the harmony parts, or percussion parts. If you want to capture these kinds of musical elements in your notation, you'll need a score.

Note that in a lead sheet, chord symbols can be placed on any rhythmic position by vertically aligning to the chord symbol with the intended position on the notation, and each chord is assumed to be present and sounding until the notation reaches a new chord symbol. If you want to indicate that no harmony should be present in a section of your music, you may write "N.C." for "no chord" in place of a chord symbol.

Context

To orient ourselves, let's notice that this piece is in the key of C major. The melody fits into the C major pentatonic scale. The chord progression is C, G, Am, F, and then C, which represent the I, V, VI, IV, and I chords of the scale, respectively.

Analysis of Melodic Relationships to Chord Tones

To begin with, you can see visually from the highlighted areas in the notation that chord tones are used quite commonly in this melody and that contributes to its consonant, stable sound. In addition, most of the notes outside of the chord fall into the category of being a whole step away from the nearest chord tone. The only exception to this is the C on the fourth beat of the fourth measure, which is a half step away from B, the third of the sounding chord. This higher energy note is mitigated by its position on relatively weak rhythmic position, beat four, and its relatively short duration of an eighth note.

We'll find that most measures use a chord tone on the downbeat. This follows the expectation that strong pitch proportionality will be accompanied by strong temporal proportionality and that weak pitch proportionality will, likewise, be accompanied by weak temporal proportionality. The exceptions to this are the first measure, which rests on the downbeat, and the third measure, which actually holds an A3 for one and half beats over a G major chord. This is an interesting moment to listen to and it does result in a slightly higher energy expression at this point. However, this note resolves down to a G with only a short pause on the A, thereby releasing the tension. Along similar lines, in most measures a chord tone is sounding in the melody on beat three. The exceptions being measures two and five, which contain a note with a whole step relationships to the nearest gravitational center on beat three.

Overall, this melody seems to follow our expectations pretty closely and the expressive result matches that. The sound is strong, stable, and pleasant. As such, becoming familiar with this example will help you to learn what the expected path of a composer looks, feels, and sounds like. From there you can make more informed decisions about when to follow or deviate from your listener's expectations.

I'd like to mention one more moment in this melody, before leaving this analysis. The moment is measure five of the melody and what I'd like to call your attention to is the redistribution of expressive energy in this bar. The melody rises up in pitch creating a higher energy expression. The G4 on beat two of this measure is the highest note of this melody and we feel a sense of rising and expansion here.

The energy also increases here because measure five features a non-chord tone on both beats two and three. However, at the same time the rhythmic complexity decreases at this point. Previously, the first four measures of the melody have been based in eighth note rhythms or, in other words, rhythms that make use an eight-part division of the measure. Now, in both measures five and six, we hear only quarter note rhythms. The expression of this sounds like a simplifying and slowing over an expansion of energy. The combined effect creates some gravity and a mini-climatic moment that begins to resolve in measures seven and eight with the F major chord and fully resolves with the return to the tonal center in the melody and the tonic chord in the harmony on the ninth bar.

Improvising Over a Chord Progression

Track 87 (disc 1) plays just the accompaniment of track 86 (disc 1) but repeats it several times with small variations. Try improvising a solo over this track. All the accompaniments we have played over so far in this book have stayed on one chord. This accompaniment goes through a four-chord progression: C, G, Am, F.

This adds an extra element of complexity to the task of soloing. Now, if you want to create a resolution, you'll need to consider which chord is being played in the accompaniment and resolve to one of the chord tones that is currently sounding. Additionally, you will only be able to create a full and complete resolution to the tonic chord. If another chord is sounding, you can only create a partial resolution. In other words, you will be able to create a resolution in the relationship between your melody and the sounding chord but the sounding chord will still hold tension in its relationship to the tonal center until the harmony moves to the tonic chord.

As you play, focus on creating phrases and ending them with resolutions. Practice resolving to the different chords and tracking which chord the accompaniment is playing with your ear. Notice the different expressions of resolving to each chord.

Sing While You Play

One very helpful strategy for improving your improvisation skills is to sing what you are improvising while soloing on your instrument. The voice is a natural expresser of emotions and ideas. Even if you are not a singer or can't reproduce your solo very accurately, merely tuning into what feels natural to sing can be a very useful connection to enhance our creativity. This activity is also great for training your ear because you'll have to capture the pitches you want to improvise in your auditory imagination as part of the process of singing.

A good variation on this activity is to sing a phrase you want to improvise *first* and then play it on your instrument. This is a bit more challenging and can really take your ear training to the next level. This also may work well for a musician playing any kind of wind or brass instrument where singing and playing at the same time is not possible.

Solo With Your Eyes Closed

One more strategy for improvisation I'll mention is to try improvising with your eyes closed. The sensory input of sight can be an awful lot of information for your brain to process. By removing attention from your sense of sight, more processing power is left over for you to focus on sound.

- Harmonic Positions and Relationships -

In much the same way that individual notes take on different expressions depending on the position they occupy within a scale, chords also create different expressions depending on where they are placed in the context of a scale. For example, an F major triad used as a dominant or V chord will create a different expression than an F major triad used as a tonic or I chord.

Each of the seven scale degrees in major and minor scales define a position within a scale where a chord may be constructed. When the scale degrees are used in this context, we may refer to them as *harmonic positions*. For a given scale type, each harmonic position defines a chord type that will diatonically fit into the scale at that particular position. For example, a major triad is the only type of triad that can be built on the first degree of a major scale while only using notes in the given scale. The minor triad is the only type of triad that can be built on the second degree of a major scale. We could continue this process for every degree of the scale. Note that we could also create a specific type of seventh chord built on each scale degree. In addition, all of the chord tones associated with a harmonic position create relationships to the tonal center and the tonic chord (which uses the tonal center as its root). The summation of these relationships and the chord type created at each scale degree produces a unique expression at each harmonic position.

Analysis of Harmonic Positions

On the following page are two tables that describe the properties of each harmonic position within a major and minor scale. The type of triad and the type of seventh chord that can be constructed, within the scale, on that degree are listed on the left hand columns. To the right, you will find all of the half step relationships, described with solfege syllables, created from a chord tone associated with that harmonic position to a chord tone associated with the tonic chord. The second solfege syllable in each pair will always represent the pitch center in the relationship. The first syllable represents the note that is approaching the center by a half step.

There are certainly other properties to explore beyond what is listed in these tables. However, understanding the chord types and half step relationships that are produced at each scale degree to the tonic will give us a useful summary of the characteristics of each harmonic position.

Characteristics of the Harmonic Positions in the Major Scale

Scale Degree	Diatonic Triad	Diatonic Seventh Chord	Half Step Relationships
Tonic	Major	Major	None
Supertonic	Minor	Minor	Fa-Mi
Mediant	Minor	Minor	Ti-Do
Subdominant	Major	Major	Fa-Mi
Dominant	Major	Dominant	Ti-Do, Fa-Mi*
Submediant	Minor	Minor	None
Leading Tone	Diminished	Half-Diminished	Ti-Do, Fa-Mi

Characteristics of the Harmonic Positions in the Minor Scale

Scale Degree	Diatonic Triad	Diatonic Seventh Chord	Half Step Relationships
Tonic	Minor	Minor	None
Supertonic	Diminished	Half-Diminished	Le-So
Mediant	Major	Major	Re-Me*
Subdominant	Minor	Minor	Le-So
Dominant	Minor	Minor	Re-Me
Submediant	Major	Major	Le-So
Subtonic	Major	Dominant	Re-Me, Le-So*

*Only applies to the seventh chord built on the given scale degree.

The Quality of Chords in Relation to the Scale

Major chords produce an expression similar to that of major scales, and, likewise, minor chords create expressions similar to minor scales. It is worth noting then, that the harmonic positions of the tonic chord (first degree), subdominant chord (fourth degree), and dominant (fifth degree) chord have the same quality as the scale they belong to. In major scales, these chords will be major; and in minor scales, these chords will be minor.

As a result, the tonic, subdominant, and dominant chords become reflective of the primary expression of the scale they belong to. However, the supertonic (second degree), mediant (third degree), and submediant (sixth degree) chords in the major scale and the mediant (third degree), submediant (fourth degree), and subtonic (seventh degree) chords in the minor scale possess different qualities than those of their scale. The effect of these chords then becomes one of contrast. They represent a movement away from the overall quality of the scale.

Both the major and minor scale contain one harmonic position of a diminished quality, the leading tone (seventh degree) for the major scale and the supertonic (second degree) for the minor scale. These positions are higher energy, more dissonant, and less stable.

❖ *Scale Degrees*, page 184

Musical Gravity Between Chords

When a chord becomes similar to a central chord, the expression of musical gravity is created. The more similar the approaching chord is to the central chord, the stronger the pull is to the central chord. The stronger the proportionality of the central chord to the tonal center, the stronger the pull is to the central chord.

Relationships Between Chords

In the harmonic realm, the strongest gravity is created when two chords share many of the same notes and yet have a few notes that are different and yet close together in pitch. It is important to realize that this kind of a relationship represents a greater degree of similarity and, thus, gravity than a relationship where the notes of one chord are all in close proximity to the notes of the other chord without matching their pitch exactly.

Let's take a look at some examples. Below is the notation for two resolutions. You can listen to these two resolutions, played one after another, on track 1 (disc 2). The first moves from a G# minor triad to a C major triad and the second goes from a G augmented triad to a C major triad. These resolutions are exactly the same except that the note G# in the first resolution is substituted for a G natural in the second. In the first resolution, G# creates a half step relationship to the G of the second chord. In the second resolution, this half step relationship is eliminated and replaced by a common note relationship between a G in both chords. The overall result is that the first resolution contains three half step relationships between the notes of the two chords, and the second resolution contains two half step relationships and one common tone relationship.

The second resolution is stronger because there is more similarity between the chords. Keep in mind, that *stronger* does not mean *better*. It simply means that expressive energy is moving more dramatically. If you listen to these resolutions, I think that you will be able to hear how the second resolution sounds more complete, more final.

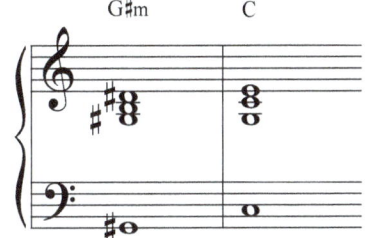 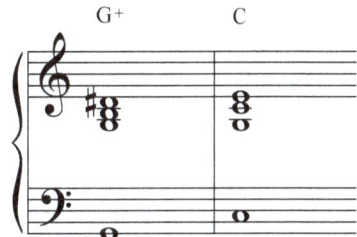

Let's look at one more example. The two resolutions below are written with a chord pattern, moving one note at a time in the right hand. Similar to the last example, the first resolution contains three half step relationships, and the second contains two half step relationships and one common tone relationship. Listen to these resolutions played one after another on track 2 (disc 2).

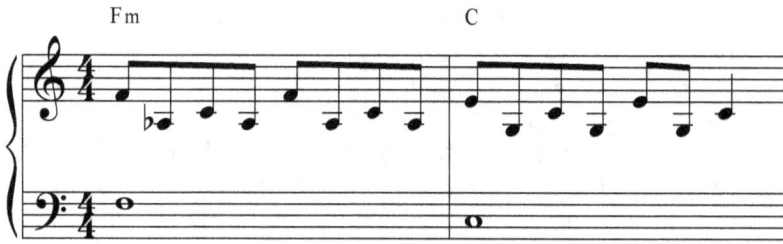

The Mysterious III to I Progression in Major

Below is a III to I chord progression in C major. Notice that this progression forms two common tone relationships and one half step relationship. Based on what we know so far, this should be an ideal combination of relationships for generating musical gravity between triads, lots of commonality with one note that differs by the smallest amount possible, a half step. However, if you listen to this progression on track 3 (disc 2) or play it yourself on an instrument, you will hear that the expression of this progression does not quite live up to this prediction. In fact, the sense of gravity is fairly weak. Stick with me for the short bit of theory below to discover the answer to this puzzling mystery.

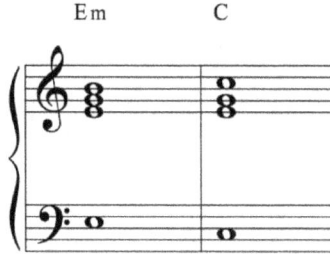

The following material uses related series analysis, a concept introduced in an advanced section at the end of Chapter Six (see page 157). If you want to proceed, you'll need to be familiar with related series analysis. Otherwise, feel free to skip ahead to the next section *Harmonic and Melodic Minor Scales* on page 256.

Relationships Between Roots and Relationships Between Related Fundamentals

The root of a chord is, at least to a degree, the pitch center of that chord. And so the movement from root to root creates an important contribution to a chord progression's musical expression. However, recall from Chapter Six that chords may have related fundamentals that differ from the root of the chord. These related fundamentals will also serve to shape the centrality of a chord – that is to say which note is felt to be the center of the chord.

It is related fundamental analysis that will reveal the cause for the mysterious lack of gravity in the III to I progression discussed above. You might remember from Chapter Six that the related fundamentals of a minor triad create an implication that the note a major third below the root is the center. This related fundamental note of a minor triad built on the third degree of a major scale ends up implying a center on the root of the tonic chord (which we can also call the tonal center of the scale). The result of this is that there is essentially no perceived movement in the center of the harmony going from the minor triad built on the third degree of the major scale and the major triad built on the first degree. Both chords imply the same note as the center. In the case of the example above, this would be the note C.

We hear this progression not as one chord being similar to another, as is necessary for musical gravity to occur, but instead as playing two parts or two aspects of the same basic harmonic structure. Considering this, we can add another principle to our understanding of musical gravity.

> *To produce an expression of musical gravity, the listener must perceive a movement from one center in pitch to another.*

We can think of musical gravity as a tension between a high sense of similarity combined with a clear sense of difference. On the one hand, the more similar the pitches between two chords, the stronger the sense of gravity; but on the other hand, without a difference in harmonic centers we will produce the expression of stasis rather than movement (or even potential movement).

The Broader Principle of Relationships Between Harmonic Centers

The example of the III to I progression in a major key is good example of how the relationships between harmonic centers – which we can define as both sounding roots as well as related fundamentals – affect the expression of our music. But how can we apply this kind of thinking to our understanding of harmony and chord progressions in general rather than just this one specific example?

We can think of the relationships between chords in terms of the sonance of the intervals between the harmonic centers of the chords. Consonant interval relationships between harmonic centers will create a greater sense of connection and similarity whereas dissonant interval relationships will create a greater sense of disconnection and unrelatedness, feeling as though the harmony is leaping from one place to another. Using this perspective, we can create a spectrum from connection to disconnection in any chord progression.

Let's apply this understanding to one more example. In Chapter Seven,[1] I said that V to I or V7 to I resolutions are some of the strongest resolutions we can create in a major scale. In these progressions, the harmonic center moves down a perfect fifth. This *harmonic movement*, if you will, represents a highly consonant relationship between the centers of the two chords. After all, the perfect fifth is the most consonant interval after the unison and octave. And while the harmonic centers are very related, we still get a sense of movement – a motion down a fifth – rather than a feeling of stasis, which comes with common tone or unison relationships between harmonic centers.

The way the centers move in these V to I progressions is ideal for creating the sense of musical gravity. Upon reaching a V or V7 chord in a major scale, the listener feels that harmonic centrality is close – it is very related to what is happening now – and yet movement is required to reach the final destination.

1. *Musical Gravity in Chord Progressions*, page 195

- Harmonic and Melodic Minor Scales -

The Harmonic Minor Scale

The leading tone to tonic or Ti to Do resolution in the major scale is quite significant because the resolution to the tonal center is the resolution to the most central position in the scale, and the half step resolution to the tonal center uses the closest possible approaching position to the tonal center in our musical system. This makes the half step resolution to the tonal center, from either above or below, the strongest possible resolution.

The minor scale does not have the ability to resolve to the tonal center by a half step, and this limits its expressive capacity. In response to this, composers began substituting Te for Ti as the seventh degree of the minor scale to recreate the possibility of the half step resolution to Do or the tonal center of the scale.

This collection of notes was found to be very useful for creating chord progressions in the minor scale. The movement from the V chord to the I chord, which creates a Ti to Do resolution in the movement of the chord tones (see second staff below), once again expressed the strength of resolution that is present in the major key but now with the emotional quality of a minor ending. Because of its usefulness in creating chord progressions, this scale was named the *harmonic minor scale*.

Harmonic Minor Scale

Do   Re   Me   Fa   So   Le   Ti   Do

Half Step Relationship of V to I Progression in Harmonic Minor

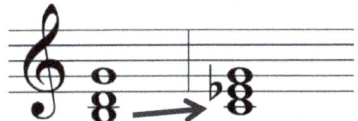

The drawback of the harmonic minor scale is that it creates a leap of an augmented second (equivalent to a minor third or three half steps)[1] between the sixth and seventh degrees of the scale. This can make melodies in the harmonic minor scale sound less smooth and fluid as they pass over this section of the scale. However, the result is not always undesirable. An example of a melody composed in the harmonic minor scale is notated on the following page. Listen to this notation on track 4 (disc 2).

1. See *Why an Augmented Fifth? (Augmented and Diminished Intervals)* on page 144.

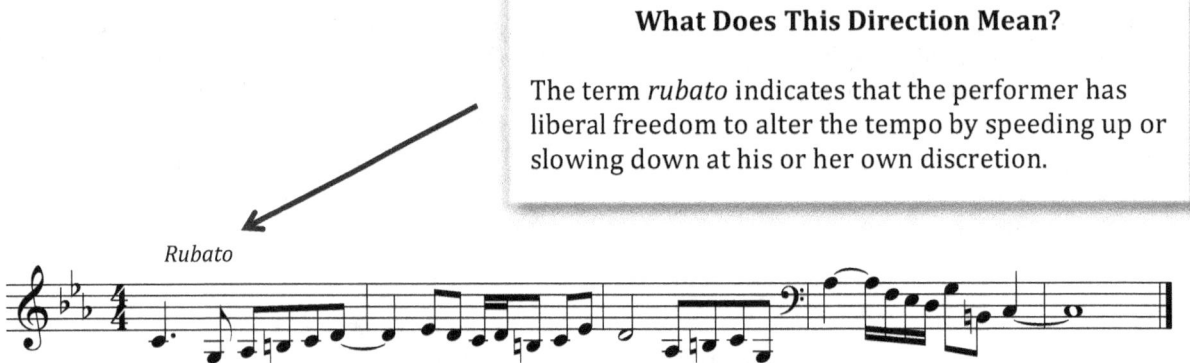

What Does This Direction Mean?

The term *rubato* indicates that the performer has liberal freedom to alter the tempo by speeding up or slowing down at his or her own discretion.

The Melodic Minor Scale

Despite the potential for creating melodies in the harmonic minor scale, the need still arose for a minor scale that could "smooth out" the relatively large gap of an augmented second. Composers discovered that by substituting Le for La as the sixth degree of the minor scale in addition to substituting Te for Ti, the potentially awkward leap of an augmented second could be changed into a whole step. Because of its usefulness in melodic writing, this scale was deemed the *melodic minor scale*.

However, there was an issue with the melodic minor scale, as well. In changing Le to La, the scale lost the half step relationship between the fifth and sixth degrees. This is also a source of important expressiveness in the minor scale and composers didn't want to sacrifice this either. The solution that was collectively arrived at was to use La and Ti in situations where the tonal center or Do is the intended pitch center, but use Le and Te in situations where the So is the intended pitch center. Another way to think about this is that La and Ti are used when the music is moving in an ascending direction and Le and Te are used when the music is moving in a descending direction because the Ti to Do resolution moves upward whereas the Le to So resolution moves downward. This was built into the structure of the melodic minor scale and, thus, it is usually notated in both an ascending direction, using La and Ti, and a descending direction, using Le and Te, as shown below.

Melodic Minor Scale

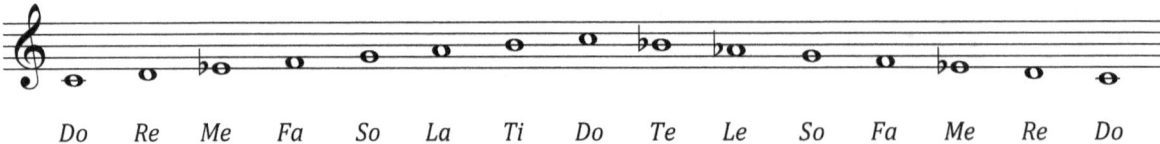

Do   Re   Me   Fa   So   La   Ti   Do   Te   Le   So   Fa   Me   Re   Do

Below is an example of a melody composed in the melodic minor scale. Listen to this notation on track 5 (disc 2).

Jazz Melodic Minor

As an alternative option, you can also use La and Ti in a minor scale for both ascending and descending directions or, in other words, for both music using both Do or So as the pitch center. The scale created in this manner is known as the *jazz melodic minor scale*. As the name implies it is more commonly used in jazz than in classical music. Listen to track 6 (disc 2) for an example of a melody in jazz melodic minor.

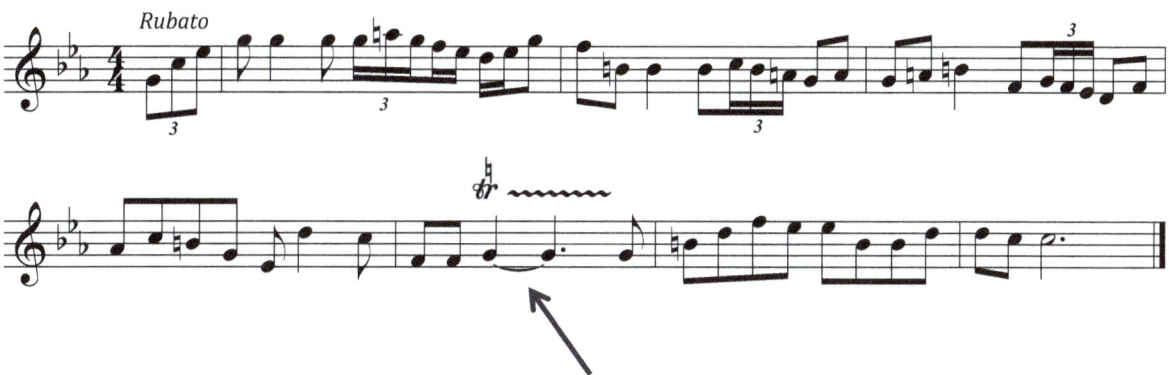

What Does This Symbol Mean?

This is a called a *trill*. A trill indicates that the performer should alternate rapidly between the written note and the note a second or a step above it in the scale. The alternating notes do not have to adhere to a specific note value and are often simply played as quickly as possible. Accidentals, like sharps, flats, and natural signs, can be added above the trill notation to modify the upper or unwritten note of the trill. For example, in this case the natural sign above the trill indicates that the alternating notes are G and A.

Differentiating the Natural Minor Scale

One can call the standard minor scale, including the Le and Te positions as the as the sixth and seventh degrees of the scale, the *natural minor scale* as a way of distinguishing it from the melodic and harmonic minor scales.

Key Signatures for Harmonic and Melodic Minor Scales

It is common practice to use the key signature associated with the natural minor scale starting on the tonal center of your composition, even if you are using a different variety of minor scale. In fact, the only commonly used key signatures are the key signatures for the major and natural minor scales. If you are using any other scale, use the key signature for the major or natural minor scale on the same tonal center and use accidentals to achieve all the notes you want from there.

- Cadences -

What Is a Cadence?

A *cadence* is a sequence of two chords that is used at the end of a progression to create or set up a resolution. Below are descriptions of the primary types of cadences and listening examples for each.

The Authentic Cadence

The *authentic cadence* represents the progression of V to I. This cadence progresses from a major V chord to a minor I chord in the minor scale. This is commonly considered to be a very strong resolution because of its half step motion from the leading tone to the tonic or from Ti to Do. We can even consider the V to I motion or the authentic cadence as the primary and strongest resolution in major scales and harmonic or melodic minor scales.

The Perfect and Imperfect Authentic Cadence

A *perfect authentic cadence* is created when the chords in the cadence are both in root position and the voicing of the tonic chord also uses the tonal center as the top note of its voicing. This means that the tonic chord will use the tonal center as both its top and bottom note. If the cadence does not meet these conditions, the progression is termed an *imperfect authentic cadence*.

Using the tonal center as both the lowest and highest notes of the tonic chord's voicing highlights the centrality and resolution of this chord. The reason for this is that the lowest and highest note of a voicing are especially impactful to a listener and are the most clearly audible.[1]

Listen to a perfect authentic cadence on track 7 (disc 2) and an imperfect authentic cadence on track 8 (disc 2).

1. *Lowest and Highest Notes*, page 148

The Dominant Seventh Chord to the Tonic

The authentic cadence commonly uses a dominant seventh chord as the first chord in the sequence. In the major scale, a dominant seventh chord creates an additional half step resolution from Fa to Mi. This makes the resolution even stronger.

Listen to a dominant seventh chord progressing to the tonic on track 9 (disc 2).

The Plagal Cadence

The *plagal cadence* describes the harmonic movement from IV to I. This cadence is also known as the *amen cadence* because of its common usage in hymns. The plagal cadence is considered to create a strong resolution but not quite as strong as the authentic cadence. The plagal cadence creates the half step resolution of Fa to Mi, whereas the authentic cadence creates a half step resolution to the tonal center.

Listen to a plagal cadence on track 10 (disc 2).

The Half Cadence

The *half cadence* describes any cadence that ends on the dominant chord or the V chord. Because the dominant chord is so commonly used to resolve, this cadence is either used to create the expression of withholding resolution or it is used to set up a new section of music that will begin on the tonic chord.

Listen to a half cadence on track 11 (disc 2).

The Deceptive Cadence

The *deceptive cadence* progresses from the dominant chord to any other chord except for the tonic. The expression of this cadence is one of surprise and unexpected movement. Listen to track 12 (disc 2) to hear a deceptive cadence that moves from the V chord to the II chord in a major key.

- Progression by Fifths -

It is common for chord progressions to move along the circle of fifths such that the root of each chord is separated by a fifth from the next chord in the progression. The perfect fifth interval is highly consonant and the effect of creating harmonic movement by perfect fifths can often be quite pleasing.

In addition, progressing by descending fifths will eventually create a resolution from the dominant chord to the tonic chord – in other words, an authentic cadence. This movement will create a strong sense of resolution and will also have the effect of setting up a pattern as the chords move through the cycle of fifths.

Moving by ascending fifths, the progression will eventually create a resolution from the subdominant chord to the tonic or a plagal cadence. This also can be an effective technique.

Progression by Fifths for Major Scales

In the major scale, the circle of fifths can be used as the basis for a chord progression across the following range while staying diatonic to the scale:

III – VI – II – V – I

Progression by Fifths for Minor Scales

If we base our chords off of the harmonic minor scale, the circle of fifths can be used to create the diatonic progression:

II – V – I

These progressions as well as sections of these progressions are very common in music of many styles. The II-V-I progression is particularly common in both the major and minor scales.

Listening to Progression by Fifths

Listen to track 13 (disc 2) to hear a II-V-I progression in a major scale. Each of the chords in this progression is a triad. Listen to track 14 (disc 2) to hear a II-V-I progression in a major scale using seventh chords. Listen to track 15 (disc 2) to hear a II-V-I progression in a harmonic minor scale using triads. And finally listen to track 16 (disc 2) to hear a II-V-I progression in a harmonic minor scale using seventh chords.

- Modes -

What Are Modes?

Before there were scales as we know them today, there were *modes*. Modes were created in medieval times and were based on the scales of the ancient Greek musical system. There are seven modes: *Ionian, Dorian, Phrygian, Lydian, Mixolydian, Aeolian*, and *Locrian*. The Ionian mode is the equivalent of the major scale, and the Aeolian mode is the equivalent of the natural minor scale. The seven modes are all defined by one set of intervals with each mode starting at a different position in the sequence. In the diagram below, the interval pattern for each mode can be found by starting at the name of the desired mode and following the sequence of intervals around the circle once in a clockwise direction.

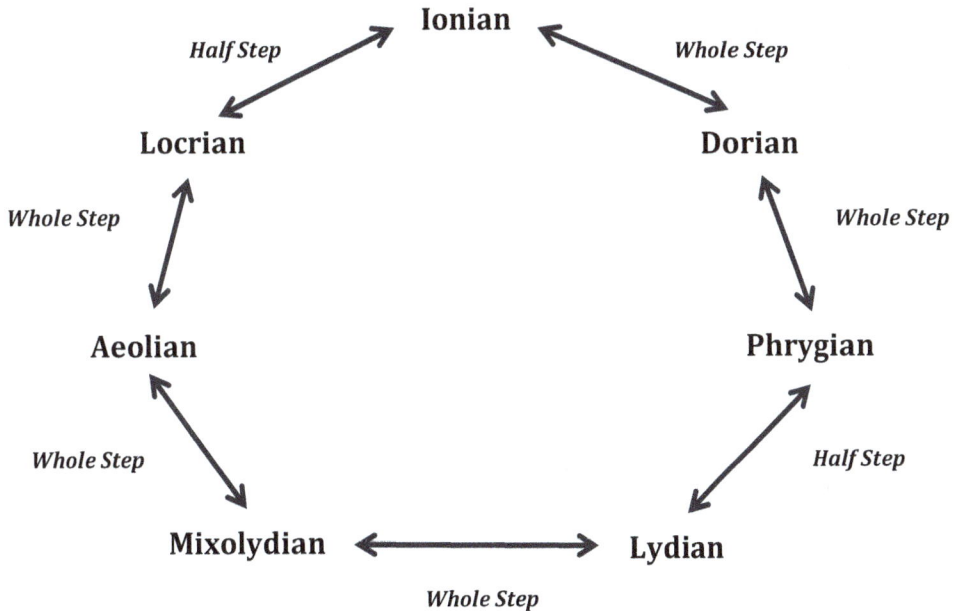

Seven Modes for One Set of Notes

For any major scale or Ionian mode, there are six other modes that contain the same notes but use a different tonal center. There are seven notes in the scale and, therefore, seven total possible tonal centers. Each of these possibilities represents a different mode of that group of notes. As an example, consider the C major scale or C Ionian. If we use this same group of notes but make D the tonal center, and thus the first note of the scale or tonic note, we create the D Dorian mode. If we use E as the tonal center, the mode becomes E Phyrgian. We could repeat this process, until every note in the group has been used as the tonal center.

While each of these modes uses the same set of notes, they, in fact, create totally different musical expressions because of the way those notes are used musically. By choosing a different note to be the tonal center, we change the focus of the composition. We change the resolutions as well as the half step relationships and pitch centers. We also assign new roles to each scale degree. The quality of the tonic chord will change from mode to mode. In the major scale, the dominant chord forms half step relationships to the tonic chord, but in other modes this may not be the case. It may be that another chord is set up better for creating resolutions. In Phrygian, for instance, the supertonic or II chord has two half step relationships to the tonic chord and is, therefore, commonly used for resolutions to the tonal center. All of these factors reorient the pitch proportionality of the music around a different center and, as a result, create an entirely different contextual harmonic and melodic landscape, each with a unique musical expression.

Relative Minor Scales and Relative Major Scales

If each set of seven notes has seven modes and if two of those are equivalent to the major and minor scale, it follows that every major scale shares the exact same notes with one other minor scale, the only difference being which of the notes in the scale is designated as the tonal center. One example of this is C major and A minor, both of which contain all seven natural notes and no sharps and flats. To describe this special connection, we can say that the A minor scale is the *relative minor* of C major and that C major is the *relative major* of A minor. Every major scale has a relative minor scale starting on its sixth degree, and every minor scale has a relative major starting on its third degree.

To reiterate, using these new terms, relative majors and minors will share the same notes but will have different musical expressions because they possess a different tonal center and corresponding system of relationships in pitch.

The Characteristics of the Modes

To explore the expression and characteristics of each mode, we will first examine the quality of the tonic chord and the location of the half step relationships in each mode.

The quality of the tonic chord will define much of the general flavor of a mode. It defines the expression of the resolved position – the expression of the metaphorical "home" or "center" of the piece. The Ionian, Lydian, and Mixolydian modes all have a major tonic triad. These are considered to be the *major modes*. The Dorian, Phrygian, and Aeolian modes all have a minor tonic triad. These are considered the *minor modes.*

The Locrian mode is the only mode that has a diminished tonic chord and so it is in a category to itself. The Locrian mode is particularly difficult to use because its primary center of resolution is a fairly dissonant chord. This means that no sense of strong resolution is really possible in Locrian. Locrian is rarely used; and when it is, the sound is generally filled with tension and dissonance.

The location of the half steps will define what resolutions are possible and, thus, how pitches will tend to move in the mode. These half step relationships will also define what chord tones strong resolutions resolve to. In some modes, strong resolutions may be possible to the root of the tonic chord, in others to the third of the tonic chord, while still in others to the fifth of the tonic chord. In some modes, the strong resolutions may move in an ascending direction; while in other modes, they may move in a descending direction. These possibilities all become important elements of a mode's expression as a piece of music goes through cycles of using these resolution patterns to alternate between higher and lower energy expressions.

Mode	Quality of Tonic Chord	Half Step Relationships
Ionian	Major	Fa-Mi (Descending), Ti-Do (Ascending)
Dorian	Minor	Re-Me (Ascending)
Phrygian	Minor	Ra-Do (Descending), Le-So (Descending)
Lydian	Major	Fi-So (Ascending), Ti-Do (Ascending)
Mixolydian	Major	Fa-Mi (Descending)
Aeolian	Minor	Re-Me (Ascending), Le-So (Descending)
Locrian	Diminished	Ra-Do (Descending), Fa-Se (Ascending)

Comparison to the Major and Minor Scales

Another way to view the modes is by comparing them to the major and minor scales. The Lydian and Mixolydian modes are only one note different than the Ionian mode or the major scale. Likewise, the Dorian and Phrygian modes are only one note different than the Aeolian or minor scale. Because people are most used to hearing the major and minor scales, the other modes sometimes sound as if they were major or minor scales with an alteration at one specific scale degree. In the purest sense, the modes are all equal, independent entities, not variations off of the major and minor scales. Nevertheless, as a result of the most common practices in Western music, musicians and listeners alike often engage in comparisons to the major and minor scales. From a musician's standpoint, if one knows the major and minor scales already, these comparisons may allow faster learning of the modes.

Dorian is the same as the natural minor scale except that it replaces Le in the minor scale with La. Phrygian is the same as the natural minor scale except that it replaces Re in the minor scale with Ra. Lydian and Mixolydian are the same as the major scale except that Lydian replaces the major scale's Fa with Fi and Mixolydian replaces the major scale's Ti with Te. These changes will stand out to an ear that is used to hearing the major and minor scales. As a result, the following scale degrees of these modes become differentiating notes[1] that strongly evoke the unique expression of the given mode.

1. *Differentiation*, page 241
❖ *Solfege Syllables*, page 187

Mode	Differentiating Degree
Dorian	La
Phrygian	Ra
Lydian	Fi
Mixolydian	Le

Harmonic Characteristics of the Modes

To go a bit deeper into the character of the modes, we can examine their harmonic properties. On this level, it is helpful to know what half relationships are available from each chord in the scale to the tonic chord of that scale. Indeed, it is even helpful to think about the half step relationships that are possible between every pair of chords in a mode, not just to the tonic chord. However, the relationships to the tonic chord are especially important, as these relationships outline the mechanisms for creating complete resolution to the tonal center.

To get you started in understanding the harmonic territory of each of the modes, I have created the following tables, which list the half step relationships from each chord in each mode to the tonic chord of the given mode. I have also included the chord types for each harmonic position as a triad and seventh chord.

Harmonic Characteristics of the Modes

Ionian (Major Scale)

Scale Degree	Diatonic Triad	Diatonic Seventh Chord	Half Step Relationships
Tonic	Major	Major	None
Supertonic	Minor	Minor	Fa-Mi
Mediant	Minor	Minor	Ti-Do
Subdominant	Major	Major	Fa-Mi
Dominant	Major	Dominant	Ti-Do, Fa-Mi*
Submediant	Minor	Minor	None
Leading Tone	Diminished	Half-Diminished	Ti-Do, Fa-Mi

Dorian

Scale Degree	Diatonic Triad	Diatonic Seventh Chord	Half Step Relationships
Tonic	Minor	Minor	None
Supertonic	Minor	Minor	Re-Me
Mediant	Major	Major	Re-Me*
Subdominant	Major	Dominant	None
Dominant	Minor	Minor	Re-Me
Submediant	Diminished	Half-Diminished	None
Subtonic	Major	Major	Re-Me

Phrygian

Scale Degree	Diatonic Triad	Diatonic Seventh Chord	Half Step Relationships
Tonic	Minor	Minor	None
Supertonic	Major	Major	Ra-Do, Le-So
Mediant	Major	Dominant	Ra-Do*
Subdominant	Minor	Minor	Le-So
Dominant	Diminished	Half-Diminished	Ra-Do
Submediant	Major	Major	Le-So
Subtonic	Minor	Minor	Ra-Do, Le-So*

Lydian

Scale Degree	Diatonic Triad	Diatonic Seventh Chord	Half Step Relationships
Tonic	Major	Major	None
Supertonic	Major	Dominant	Fi-So
Mediant	Minor	Minor	Ti-Do
Subdominant	Diminished	Half-Diminished	Fi-So
Dominant	Major	Major	Ti-Do, Fi-So*
Submediant	Minor	Minor	None
Leading Tone	Minor	Minor	Ti-Do, Fi-So

Mixolydian

Scale Degree	Diatonic Triad	Diatonic Seventh Chord	Half Step Relationships
Tonic	Major	Dominant	None
Supertonic	Minor	Minor	Fa-Mi
Mediant	Diminished	Half-Diminished	None
Subdominant	Major	Major	Fa-Mi
Dominant	Minor	Minor	Fa-Mi*
Submediant	Minor	Minor	None
Subtonic	Major	Major	Fa-Mi

Aeolian (Minor Scale)

Scale Degree	Diatonic Triad	Diatonic Seventh Chord	Half Step Relationships
Tonic	Minor	Minor	None
Supertonic	Diminished	Half-Diminished	Re-Me, Le-So
Mediant	Major	Major	Re-Me*
Subdominant	Minor	Minor	Le-So
Dominant	Minor	Minor	Re-Me
Submediant	Major	Major	Le-So
Subtonic	Major	Dominant	Re-Me, Le-So*

Locrian

Scale Degree	Diatonic Triad	Diatonic Seventh Chord	Half Step Relationships
Tonic	Diminished	Half-diminished	None
Supertonic	Major	Major	Ra-Do, Fa-Se
Mediant	Minor	Minor	Ra-Do*
Subdominant	Minor	Minor	Fa-Se
Dominant	Major	Major	Ra-Do, Fa-Se*
Submediant	Major	Dominant	None
Subtonic	Minor	Minor	Ra-Do, Fa-Se

*Only applies to the seventh chord built on the given scale degree.

Listening to the Modes

Tracks 17 (disc 2) through 23 (disc 2) play a piano improvisation in each of the seven modes in order from Ionian to Locrian. Most of the tracks start and often end with a taste of the "essential" or most stereotypical flavor of each mode. The middle of the pieces often venture into some different harmonic territory, still staying within the mode, but not necessarily emphasizing the stereotypical expression of the mode as clearly or prominently. I do this so that you can get a taste of both the essential character of each mode as well a sampling of different things that might happen within the context of the given mode.

Take a moment to listen through each of these tracks, taking note of which track is in which mode. See what you notice about both the general expression of these modes as well as the way each of them resolves to pitch centers and what kind of sound that creates in each case.

- Analysis of Faure's "Pavane" -

In this section, we will embark on our first analysis of a well-known classical piece. I will hold up this piece and the other two works we will analyze from this tradition – Beethoven's Fifth and Pachelbel's Canon – as models of great art for us to study and learn from. The piece we will be looking at here is Gabriel Faure's "Pavane," one of my all-time favorites. For the sake of brevity, we will just be looking at the first sixteen measures of the piece. With a piece like this, that will give us more than enough to talk about. We are going to use this piece, primarily, as an example to talk about melodic writing.

Context

First, let's take note of some of the basic characteristics of the piece. This piece is in F# minor. It uses both Te and Ti for the seventh degree of the scale at different points. It is in 4/4 time and was written in the Romantic period[1] of classical music in the year 1887.

1. *The Romantic Period*, page 292

Pavane

Faure

Overview Analysis

Looking over the notation for Faure's "Pavane," we can see some remarkable similarities between each of the four lines. Each line has almost the same rhythm, with small variations at the end of each line. Lines one and three are exactly the same in both rhythm and notes. Line two uses the same general numeric intervals as line one while starting a perfect fifth higher.[1] It does, however, deviate from this pattern in the very last interval of the line. Line four also uses very similar intervals to other lines, though it starts on a different note and includes a few variations in the second half of the line.

1. As just another way of saying the same thing, we could describe lines one and two as being a *sequence*. See the box entitled *Sequence* on page 340.

Looking throughout these four lines, we can see there are two major musical ideas or motifs at work. I'll call the first of these the building motif, which is presented in the first measure. The first measure of each line plays some variation of this motif. I call it the building motif because this short phrase serves to increase the energy of the melody in several ways, while also increasing the anticipation for or gravity toward the later parts of each line. The building motif goes upward in pitch and uses sixteenth rhythms, both of which contribute to its sense of energy. The building motif starts on the downbeat and then creates a micro-approach to beat three with a sixteenth note on the "a" of 2. It then creates another micro-approach on the "a" of 4, which leads into the next musical idea. But before it does that, there is a pause starting on beat three, where the pitch has increased, rhythmic complexity is present, and a space is provided to translate that energy into a short moment of suspense. All these interactions are subtle. The general feeling of the melody is soft and on the lower energy side of things. So these building measures are far from a dramatic expression, but in the context of the piece these measures serve to create energy. And the subtlety of the musical elements generates a beautiful, delicate quality.

The second motif, which I'll call the wandering motif, takes the energy from the building motif and moves toward resolution, slowly, with twists and turns, never creating a complete release until the end of the fourth line. I describe this motif as wandering because it dances around the chord tones in a state of near constant approach that descends in both pitch and expressive energy. The result sounds something like wandering, a somewhat aimless journey that never quite seems to make it home, at least not until the resolution of the fourth line.

The wandering motif uses mostly eighth notes but also includes sixteenth note micro-approaches. We can see that in measures two and three, both the rhythm and the general numeric intervals are repeated (except for the last interval in the third bar), creating strong similarity between these measures. Something similar happens in the second and third measures of each line.

Overall then, each line builds up in pitch and expressive energy during the first measure and then meanders down in the following three measures. Each line lands on the root note of the sounding chord on the downbeat of its fourth measure and stays there for a full four beats, creating a strong sense of separation between each line.

The lines all have nearly the same rhythm and a lot of similarity in interval structure. The rhythm emphasizes the strong rhythmic positions of beats one and three with micro-approaches and uses very little syncopation. The rhythm is repetitive and relatively simple, with the sixteenth note micro-approaches serving to inject subtle increases in energy and complexity, while reinforcing the strong rhythmic positions.

This gives us a good overview of the four lines as a whole and the structures Faure is working within. Keeping these observations in mind as context, we can now move forward to look at some of the specific notes and harmonic relationships in this melody.

The First Line

The micro-approaches to the downbeats of bars two and three land on fairly high tension or high energy notes, both of which have a half step relationship to a sounding chord tone. The approaching note, which leads into the downbeat of the third bar, is also a fairly high tension note, with a half step relationship to a sounding chord tone. The note on the downbeat of the third bar is a G#. This note sounds reminiscent of the Lydian mode because it is a tritone away from the root note of the sounding chord, just as the characteristic note Li would be a tritone away from the tonal center in a Lydian mode. Now using the definitions that I've presented in this book, we would probably not think of this one measure as being in a D Lydian mode because there is not enough time or strong resolutions to qualify D as an actual tonal center. In other words, to consider D as a tonal center we would have to argue that the piece has changed scales from F# minor to a new scale centering on D and there is simply not enough time or emphasis on D to create this effect. The center of D is operating at the level of relationships to the harmony, rather than to the tonal center. That being said, we can still hear and feel a Lydian-*like* expression in this measure, which is certainly significant to the energy of this moment and to the emotions it conveys, especially because this note is emphasized by its placement on the downbeat of the measure.

The third beats of measures two and three both create small resolutions by pausing on chord tones. Both of these resolutions land on a minor chord after being proceeded by a major chord. This creates the feeling that we are moving away from harmonies with a more major or happier or brighter expression and then we are resolving to and, thus, emphasizing a sadder, darker, minor expression.

The first line ends with the use of Ti as a micro-approach to the fourth bar. This note is part of the harmonic and melodic minor scales. However, it does create some tension in the brief quarter of a beat in which it is sounding, as it is a half step away from the fifth of the chord being played in the accompaniment. This high energy approaching note resolves to a C#, accompanied by a C# chord on the downbeat of the fourth bar. The motion of the melody here creates a distinctive downward leap of a major third, which stands out in contrast to the mostly conjunct,[1] step-driven melody that has preceded it.

The resolution at the end of this line is very weak or incomplete, because we are ending on the dominant chord, which is the primary mover toward the tonal center. This would be an example of a half cadence.[2] It is also worth noting that this dominant chord does resolve to the tonic chord in the next line. However, the melody ends the phrase of the first line clearly on the downbeat of the fourth bar, only to pick up with a new phrase on the downbeat of the fifth bar. This means that while the harmony is creating a resolution from the dominant to the tonic, the melody is not following that resolution. Instead, the melody ends without full resolution and then picks up again in the next phrase with a new building motif. So, we have the parallel experience of the melody partially resolving followed by the harmony resolving and the melody launching off into new higher energy melodic territory at the same time. The result is that the energy of the piece shifts around in interesting ways, rebalancing, we could say, while never providing a complete resolution.

1. Meaning that the melody uses lots of steps rather than leaps, see *Conjunct and Disjunct* on page 155.
2. *The Half Cadence*, page 261

The Second Line

The second line serves to increase the energy of the piece. This is the micro-level climax of these four lines. After the second line, the remaining two lines will serve to slowly bring down the energy into a resolution, somewhat like the way the energy of each individual line increases quickly early on and then slowly falls down into a resolution.

The second line creates increases in energy in several ways. It brings the pitch of the melody up. The first three measures of this line all have a small resolution on beat three, and each of these resolutions features the seventh of the sounding chord, a somewhat less resolved chord tone than the resolutions we heard in the first line. In particular, the third beat of the third measure of the second line features a C# as the major seventh of a D chord. This moment creates a lot of energy, being only a half step away from the root of the sounding chord. It also creates a beautiful, major expression in contrast to the minor landscape of the piece.

Another thing that makes this moment high energy is that it uses a chromatic note, B# (equivalent to C natural), as an approach to the downbeat of the fourth measure. This chromatic note creates a half step resolution to the C# of the fourth measure but does so by going outside of the scale, creating additional tension. The resolution of this phrase goes from C# down to B# (or C natural) and then back up to C# again. This motion creates a few interesting relationships. First, the second line has matched the contour and rhythm of the first line very closely up to this point. And in the first line, this part of the phrase uses a distinctive downward leap of a major third. This creates the expectation that something similar will happen at the end of the second line. However, Faure defies this expectation, breaking the descending pattern of the wandering motif to resolve upward by a step. At the same time, he also deviates from the previous line's rhythm. Once again, there is a subtlety to all this. The unexpected upward motion at the end of the second line lands the melody on to a C# that is exactly one octave above the C# that the first line ended on. Like the end of the first line, we have ended on the dominant chord but this time with a higher pitched melodic note and a higher energy approach to it.

The Third and Fourth Lines

We'll go through the third and fourth lines comparatively quickly. The third line serves a simple function of bringing the energy down, while repeating the first line. In relation to the second line, the third line is heard as decreasing in pitch and probably volume as well. The repetition also creates a low energy expression.[1] So the energy is falling here in some significant ways, and, yet, we are presented with that same incomplete resolution on the dominant chord.

The fourth line starts with an A in the melody and an A chord. This line sounds particularly major, as it is reminiscent of the relative major scale[2] – A major. The resolutions in this line are probably the lowest energy out of all the lines, usually landing on strong chord tones like fifths and thirds. The approach into the third bar features a leap of a third, which increases the energy slightly. This is followed by a repeated note, something we have not heard in the melody up to this point. Both the leap and the repeated note create the sense that the motion of the melody is changing away from the step-dominated patterns that have been prevalent so far.

1. *The Spectrum of Change*, page 51
2. *Relative Minor Scales and Relative Major Scales*, 264

At the end of the fourth line, we finally get our complete resolution. The melody moves from Ti to Do while the harmony moves from dominant to tonic. The rhythm slows in comparison to endings of the previous lines, allowing us to savor the moment and increasing the sense of gravity. The piece resolves on both the level of the harmony and the tonal center. There is a sense of having experienced a brief period of more major expressions and then resolving into the contrasting minor tonic harmony.

Connecting Musical Elements to Musical Expressions

Now, pausing right there, we can inquire, "What do all these musical elements contribute to in the final expression of this music?" When I listen to these four lines, I feel the following expressions arising from the music (among others, of course): exquisiteness, flowing, wandering, awe, gentleness or maybe even kindness, a slow, longing feeling of sadness. What do you feel? Would you add any other descriptors or perhaps replace some of the ones I've given? Take a moment to answer this question for yourself. Your answers don't have to be perfect. After all, it seems there is always some degree of artistic expression that is difficult to encapsulate and so finds itself beyond words.

So far, we have analyzed the musical elements of these four lines, and we have just now described, as best we can, the musical expression of the same music. The great question then becomes, "How do the musical elements create the expression?" If we can answer this, we can connect our theories and abstract knowledge to the felt expression of the music, so that we may deepen our understanding and our ability to create similar or even opposing expressions in our own music.

Conclusions

With this perspective in mind, let's move ahead and take each of the expressions I listed and look at them one at a time.

Exquisiteness is, at least in part, the product of a low energy expressive state generally across the four lines in combination with small variations up and down in energy. The smallness or subtlety of the variations means that we are drawn in to pay even more attention to catch what is happening. It means that we reset our relative frame of reference to hear even minute variations in expression. At the same time, the pitch relationships presented in this piece contain surprising degrees of complexity underneath the surface of a soft, relatively repetitive, rhythmically simple melody. The presence of emphasized tritone, seventh, and half step relationships are common. And yet this complexity never strays too far into the land of dissonance. By the end, we do get a final resolution and a sense of completeness. Taken all together, we find an expression of completion within subtlety of motion and complexity of relationships – exquisiteness.

We'll consider the expression of flowing and wandering together because they are deeply related. They both refer to the movement of the melody. The "wandering motif" along with all its variations makes up the greatest portion of the sixteen bars. The wandering feeling comes about as a combination of continuously decreasing energy along with a lack of a complete resolution. What is left is a feeling of falling, without clear destination – wandering. The flowing aspect is similar though may have more to do with the micro-approaches, which move the melody continually onward in an almost hypnotizing, repetitive rhythmic structure.

The expression of awe we can trace back to this aspect of harmonic complexity as well as the genius way in which the harmonic complexity is subtly brought out and then reduced, bringing us just within arm's reach of resolution before turning away into higher energy again. There is a complexity and masterful artistry here that feels inspiring and awesome – as in full of awe.

The music also evokes sadness and longing in the way that it pulls us so close and so subtly within reach of the pitch centers without landing upon them. And while we do hear a complete resolution at the end of the sixteen bars, there is still a dominance of the minor quality throughout the piece.

The gentleness and kindness certainly come from this aspect of subtlety in energetic motion that we have been talking about. However, the more major focused moments like the D major seventh chord at the end of the second line or the A major chord at the beginning of the fourth line create the sense of a more positive expression in an atmosphere that is minor, dark, and moderate in its energetic movement. This moderately moving positivity in the face of a dark environment comes out sounding gentle and kind, though with a poignant sadness present as well.

At this point, we have really just started to uncover how the musical elements of Faure's "Pavane" translate into the *general* or *big-picture* expressions of the piece. We'll stop here for now, but in Chapter Twelve we will analyze two other pieces – Beethoven's Fifth Symphony and Pachelbel's Canon in D. There we will get a chance to dive into analysis again, going a bit deeper into the mysteries of music and progressing our understanding a bit further.

If there are any expressions you experienced from this piece that I didn't cover, I invite you to do some of your own analysis to explore their underlying causes in terms of musical elements.

You can also jump ahead to the box entitled *Analyzing a Piece of Music* on page 379 for an outline of my analysis process and perspective. You can use this box to do an analysis of one of your own favorite pieces of music.

- Lyrics -

In this section, we are going to briefly dive into some theory about lyric writing. Just so you know, the ideas we are going to cover here are not so much about relationships in pitch (the topic of this chapter) as they are about relationships in timbre. However, I thought it would be helpful to include this section in this chapter before we look at the subject of writing musical themes. That way if you want to include lyrics with your melodic themes you can draw upon the information below.

A sung melody invites the possibility of *lyrics* – words that accompany the pitches of the melody. The addition of lyrics creates two important avenues in which we can create musical expression, the learned meaning we associate with language and the timbre[1] of the words. The timbre of the voice is incredibly dynamic in comparison to most instruments. The difference between each of our words in every language is based on a changing timbre produced by our voices. Every letter, every syllable, and every word is a learned pattern of timbre.

In lyric writing, we will associate each syllable of a word with a musical note. A new syllable creates a sound much like the start of a new note on an instrument. Even if a series of syllables stays on the same pitch, it is best to think of and notate this as a pitch that is rearticulated (or played multiple times) with each syllable.

We have the choice as lyric writers to use more or less connected sounding words on the level of timbre. Many poetry techniques make use of a shared timbre between words. For example, words *rhyme* when the ending sounds of the words are shared. Words have *alliteration* when the words have the same beginning sound. *Assonance* is the term that describes words with a shared vowel sound, and *consonance* is the term for words that share a consonant. (Note that this type of poetic or literary consonance is a different concept than the notion of musical consonance in groups of pitches – although both describe a certain kind of commonality!)

1. *Timbre and Harmonic Composition*, page 34

There is a spectrum from low to high energy created by a natural vocal progression through the sounds "ooo-awww-aaaaa-eeeeee."

Low and High Energy Vocal Timbres

Keep in mind that the spectrum being used here is one from simple to complex timbre. Therefore all connection or disconnection between syllables aside, more complex timbres will produce more energetic expressions, while simpler timbres will produce less energetic ones.

So which vocal timbres fall on the low energy side of the spectrum and which fall on the high energy side? Well, the answer can be a bit complex. After all there is a considerable area of study devoted to the sounds used in speech – *phonetics*. However, a summary of the most important insights from this field can be helpful, I believe, to the lyric writer.

Vocal sounds are produced as air, moving out of the lungs, vibrates the *vocal folds* (also known as the *vocal cords*) inside of the throat. These vibrations travel up the throat, out of the mouth, and through the nasal cavity. As vibrations pass through the mouth and nasal cavity, different frequency ranges may be filtered out or amplified depending on the physical shape of the area the vibrations pass through.

There are two categories of speech sounds that we probably have all heard of – *consonants* and *vowels*. Vowels are sounds produced with a generally open vocal tract, so that air moves freely throughout the body, with no buildup of air pressure above the vocal folds. Whereas consonants are created through some form of constriction of airflow generally created by the tongue or lips. Consonants tend to create percussive, non-pitched sounds, automatically putting them at the high energy pole of the timbre spectrum.

For the moment, let's focus on vowel sounds. When singing, vowel sounds are generally held out during the sustained portion of notes, and, for this reason, they are emphasized in singing when compared to normal speech.

The study of phonetics tells us that there are three primary ways in which we are able to manipulate the timbre of vocal sounds. The first is the level of the tongue, from the *open* position, where the tongue rests on the bottom of the mouth, to the *closed* position, where the tongue is placed at the top of the mouth. Secondly, the position of the tongue from *back* to *front* is also influential – in other words, from the position toward the back of the throat to the position toward the opening of the mouth. Lastly, the shape of the lips also has an impact. We describe this on a spectrum from *unrounded*, meaning to have relaxed lips, to *rounded*, meaning to contract the lips as you would while saying "oo."

To summarize, the spectrum of vowels, as ranked in general complexity of timbre from low to high, progresses from closed and back to open and back to open and front to closed and front. And each of those can then be filtered by rounding the vowel, thus producing a lower energy expression, or may be produced unfiltered in the unrounded variation of the vowel.

To take a few examples, the "oo" sound mentioned earlier represents the lower energy end of the spectrum of possibilities we are describing here. "Oo" is a closed and back, rounded vowel. If we open and un-round the vowel while keeping it back, we can produce an "aw" sound. If we now move the vowel forward, keeping the rest the same, we create a sound like the vowel in the word "had." Closing the vowel again, results in a sound like the vowel in "hid" or if we close further like the vowel in "heed." Taken together, there seems to a spectrum from low to high energy created by a natural vocal progression through the sounds "ooo-awww-aaaaa-eeeeee."

> **Consonants**
>
> There are a wide variety of possible consonant sounds, the full extent of which we will not go into here. However, just briefly consider that some consonants produce sharp sounds and others are more mellow. For example, the sound of "m," "n," "r," "h," "v," "f," "s," and "l" tend to be more mellow, lower energy expressions; and the sound of the hard "k" or "t" is a little higher energy.

> **Examples of Low and High Energy Expressions in Words**
>
> Consider the difference in sound between these two poetic lines:
>
> *Mellow was the sound of the blue, hollowed willow.*
> *"Crack!" went the tree as the tight branches snapped against the breeze.*
>
> Notice how the first line uses lots of lower energy vowel sounds like "oo" and "o" as well as lower energy consonant sounds like "m," "w," and "l." In contrast, the second line features lots of "i" and "e" vowel sounds as well as higher energy "t" and "k" consonant sounds. Without even needing to understand the linguistic meaning of these sentences, the second line *sounds* more dramatic – higher energy.
>
> We can also consider that "mellow" and "willow" share a similar ending sound. Although they don't form a *perfect rhyme* – one where the final, stressed vowel and all the following sounds are the same – the repetition of the "low" sound in both words nevertheless creates a sense of similarity and, thus, produces a lower energy expression. As mentioned earlier, any way of creating similar sounds between words, whether with rhyme, alliteration, assonance, consonance, or another technique, will create connection and similarity between the timbres of words.

We won't go any further on the topics of lyrics or poetry here, but I hope this short section has given you an overview of how to think about the sounds of words within the low to high energy model of analysis we have been constructing throughout the book.

- Writing Themes -

This is an important moment in the book for us. One where we will integrate and apply much of the material we have covered so far. Our topic is writing themes or musical ideas – so melodies, chord progressions, and combinations of melodies with accompanying chords. These are the building blocks of musical compositions. After this point, we are going to start moving toward piecing different musical ideas together into sections of music and full-length compositions.

Holding Expression in Mind

We keep coming back to the concept of musical expression and the different mechanisms that are involved in its production. Understanding this translation from musical elements like notes and rhythms to the more subjective emotional or aesthetic perception of music is the essence of our goal as musical creators and theorists. If this concept of musical expression is so central to this art, it makes sense to develop a very clear grasp on what expression we are intending to create with our music. One approach is to decide on what you want to express through your music before even writing a single note. This can be a challenge to pull off successfully, but it is a wonderful exercise to develop your compositional skills and you may find that this works for you not just as an exercise but as a typical writing process too. I highly recommend trying this out for the experience if nothing else.

The other, and probably more common, approach is to experiment with different musical ideas until you find something that strikes you. From there you can develop other related ideas and start to mold your musical expression based off the inspiration you started with. Below, I walk through these two approaches in more detail. In either case, I advocate being aware, throughout the creative process, what expressions you *are* creating and what expressions you *want* to be creating, while also accepting that your desires and the nature of the work may shift over time like a moving target.

Starting With the Expression

If you are starting with the expression, that means you are not starting with the music. So put away all the instruments and allow your auditory imagination to rest. You can start by brainstorming words or phrases that represent the emotions and ideas you want to express in your music. I recommend not getting too complex intellectually if you go this route. You can definitely include multiple and even opposing emotions and experiences but stay away from detailed stories, dialogues, and conceptual chains of ideas. Instead focus on things that are emotional, sensory, or experiential. I recommend this because music excels at expressing these aspects of life. If you want to express something more intellectual than emotional, you are probably better off using conventional language.

You can also start with imaginations or memories of the direct experience of emotions or events. You can come up with words to represent these if you want, but you can also just hold them in mind.

Work with this process until you have something that you feel excited and inspired to express. It can be something very simple or it can have several different dimensions to it. In either case, you will want to have something specific by the end of this process – either a single specific expression or a few different expressions that have relationships to one another.

When you have an expression that you want to work with, you can begin to brainstorm ways to translate this expression into musical terms. For an extra challenge, you can try to do this while continuing not to play any music or use any instruments!

To begin with, we need to figure out how to describe your expression in the language of low and high energy elements. It is often easier to start general here. In the big picture, where does your expression fall on the spectrum from low energy, including ideas and emotions associated with resolution, calm, and connection, to high energy, including ideas and emotions associated with excitement, drama, and tension? Is it extreme on one end or the other? Or is it more moderate? After you answer these questions, you can start getting more detailed. Are there secondary aspects of the expression that move in different directions on the spectrum? And there even more subtle qualities beyond that?

To get more specific, we can start to include more complex types of musical expressions. Are there elements in your target expression that seem like a major quality or a minor quality? Perhaps one part of it reminds you of the 3/4 meter.

Once you have your map of different kinds of expressions, you start connecting together the expressions you want to create with specific musical elements. We could, for example, try representing that exciting aspect of our target expression with a particular dissonant interval, while representing the subtly of it with quiet dynamics, and the optimism with a major key.

I'll leave it open to you what you want your theme to be exactly. It could be just a melody, just a chord progression, or both.

If you are going for the extra challenge option, try writing a whole theme (or an entire song or composition for an even bigger challenge) just using this kind of thinking, writing down your musical ideas on notation without playing them. At the end, play back your composition and see how close you got to your target expression.

Otherwise, think of a way you can represent part of your expression in musical terms and then try it out and see what happens. Keep experimenting, doing new iterations with different strategies to represent your target expression, and editing until you arrive at a theme that you like.

Starting With an Inspiration

Writing a theme by starting with an inspiration is basically a process of experimentation guided by your auditory imagination and theoretical knowledge of musical elements like meters, scales, and chords. You will want to play with musical elements like these that you know beforehand will tend to build connective relationships and musical expressiveness into your work. Experiment with notes in a particular scale or chord. Experiment with rhythms in popular meters. And see what you hear. See what you like.

You can even go so far as to take someone else's musical work and begin altering and modifying it to create new expressions. Using this approach, you can explore the intelligent musical ground that other musicians have already cultivated. What we are describing here is essentially the creative activity of arranging.[1]

1. *Arranging*, page 59

Through the process of experimentation and observation, you will encounter different expressions that will both broaden your horizons and inspire you. When you find a musical idea that you like, take note of its expression, as best you can, and begin crafting other similar or complementary elements around the original inspiration until you feel that your theme is complete.

Concluding Thoughts

Both of these approaches will get you well on your way to writing excellent musical themes. You can certainly combine these two approaches, and you may well find some mixture of the two to be the most useful for your particular creative process. While doing these activities, keep in mind as much of the theory we have covered up to this point as you can. Feel free to review any concepts that you need to by going back and reading earlier sections. Also remember to take the experimenter's mindset in the beginning. Try things that may not work and be okay with whatever result might come about. Focus on the learning process itself more than the outcomes. When the time is right, you can make the conscious decision to switch over to a performer's mindset and focus on creating the highest quality piece of art possible.

Writing a Modal Theme

For a variation on these theme writing activities, try writing a *modal* theme – modal, in this context, meaning written in one of the modes other than the major and minor scale. Considering that the Locrian mode is rarely ever used, my invitation is really narrowed down to four possibilities: Dorian, Phrygian, Lydian, and Mixolydian. You can try writing a theme in one or all of these modes to further your understanding of the expressions of the modes and the inner workings of their melodic and harmonic landscapes. If you take on this activity, be sure to keep in mind where the half step relationships are in your mode. Consult the tables on page 265 and, for harmonic properties, the tables on pages 267 through 269 if needed.

Theme Library

You may want to start a library of themes and musical ideas that you like and might want to write a full composition based on some day. You can do this by recording audio samples of your themes, and these can be low quality. The idea is just to be able to remember the theme. Alternatively, you can write out the theme in notation.

Summary for Group Four
The Expression of Proportional Relationships

Undivided Measure	Beat 1															
Measure Divided into Two Parts								Beat 3								
Measure Divided into Four Parts					Beat 2							Beat 4				
Measure Divided into Eight Parts			and of 1								and of 3					
							and of 2								and of 4	
Measure Divided into Sixteen Parts		e of 1								e of 3						
					e of 2									e of 4		
				a of 1								a of 3				
								a of 2								a of 4

TPLC Group:
Strong Rhythmic Position – Louder Volume – Greater Change
Weak Rhythmic Position – Quieter Volume – Less Change

Low pitch sounds are more weighty and heavy sounding. Higher pitched sounds are more commonly used for rhythmically complex parts.

Groove – Accompaniment of a piece of music

Syncopation – Emphasis of weak rhythmic positions

Approaches – Music expressing the sense of leading up to or being pulled into a strong rhythmic position

Micro-Approaches – An approach taking place on a small scale, probably within a section of one measure

Swing Rhythm – Moves "ands" from halfway point between beats to the point two-thirds way through the beat

Two Levels of Pitch Relationships:
- ❖ Relationships to the Tonal Center
- ❖ Relationships to the Harmony

Root, third, and fifth are usually the only chord tones that can be resolved to.

Gravitational Positions (from low to high energy):
1. Pitch Centers
2. Notes With Whole Step Relationships
3. Notes With Half Step Relationships

Major Scale Resolutions:
- Fa to Mi
- Ti to Do

Minor Scale Resolutions:
- Re to Me
- Le to So

Sixth and Seventh Degrees of the Different Flavors of Minor:
- Natural Minor Scale – Le, Te
- Harmonic Minor Scale – Le, Ti
- Melodic Minor Scale – La, Ti on the way up and Le, Te on the way down
- Jazz Melodic Minor Scale – La, Ti

Differentiating Notes for Modes and Scales:
- Major Scale – Mi, La, Ti
- Natural Minor Scale – Me, Le, Te
- Dorian – La
- Phrygian – Ra
- Lydian – Fi
- Mixolydian – Te

Chord Progressions and the Circle of Fifths

It is common to write chord progressions where the roots move by fifths. The II-V-I progression in major and harmonic minor is an example of this.

Seven Modes for One Set of Notes

Different modes may share the same notes but will still produce different expressions because they have different tonal centers.

Musical Gravity Between Chords

When a chord becomes similar to a central chord, the expression of musical gravity is created. The more similar the approaching chord is to the central chord, the stronger the pull is to the central chord. The stronger the proportionality of the central chord to the tonal center, the stronger the pull is to the central chord.

Relationships Between Harmonic Centers

Consonant interval relationships between harmonic centers will create a greater sense of connection and similarity whereas dissonance interval relationships will create a greater sense of disconnection and unrelatedness, feeling as though the harmony is leaping from one place to another.

The Progression of Vowel Sounds

There is a spectrum from low to high energy created by a natural vocal progression through the sounds "ooo-awww-aaaaa-eeeeee."

Holding Expression in Mind

Writing a musical theme or idea is best done when holding a clear and well-defined musical expression in mind throughout the creative process.

Part Three

Creation and Exploration

Group Five

Putting It All Together

You have arrived at Part Three – *Creation and Exploration*! This is the part of the book where we get to focus on dabbling, experimenting, and creating. You can feel free to treat this part of the book more "buffet style," so to speak, reading only what you are interested in or you can read straight through. However, I recommend not skipping over Chapter Twelve when you get to it, as this is a culminating moment for the book.

In Group Five, we are going to begin looking at complete pieces of music and topics that relate to complete pieces of music, specifically styles (Chapter Ten), arranging and production (Chapter Eleven), and then development and structure (Chapter Twelve).

It should be noted that this book is not a comprehensive guide on styles, arranging, or production. However, Chapter Ten and Chapter Eleven will present an *introduction* to these topics. And I believe that basic knowledge of styles of music, arranging techniques, and music production technology serves any musical composer or musical artist of any kind well as a general foundation. After reading these sections, you may be inspired to learn more about a specific area. In this way, Part Three will help to set you up to continue your musical journey after completing this book. So, keep your eye out for topics of interest for further pursuit.

Chapter Ten
Musical Styles

- Introduction to Musical Styles -

Learning From History

Musicians have written music and studied the musical art for millennia all across the globe. Their endeavors have produced a plethora of knowledge, experiments, and experience waiting to be learned from. We can progress much faster on our musical journey if we are willing to learn from our predecessors throughout history. The study of musical history invites us to find out what we like and what we don't. It invites us to learn how different combinations of musical elements produce different expressions and how musical artists have evoked their own unique musical expressions through the ages. And finally, the study of musical history invites us to examine the works of master composers and challenges us to comprehend why their art embodies the highest reaches of excellence.

What Are Musical Styles?

A musical *style* is a conglomeration of various musical elements, artistic techniques, and expressive attitudes that a group of musicians learned from, used, and developed throughout time.

Our perception of musical expression is not just shaped by musical properties of sound but also by our cultural conditioning. When we hear a particular set of musical elements together again and again, we begin to associate certain sounds together into a pattern, a category – a style in fact. And the more we hear a particular pattern of sound, the more familiar it feels. The effect of this kind of long-term repetition is a low energy expressive influence on the particular pattern or musical element but, importantly, only in the subjective experience of those who have been exposed to the pattern or element repeatedly.

Once we become aware of different styles and patterns that have been used throughout history, new options will open up for us as musical creators. We may choose to write within a style in a very generic or traditional way or to play with the expectation of stylistic patterns, surprising the listener with interesting deviations from common patterns. Composers may also experiment with mixing different elements of different styles to create something new – this is how many new musical styles form. All of the above possibilities become available through the study of musical styles.

Embarking on an Overview of Western Music

An almost countless number of styles have emerged throughout history in different cultures and time periods of musical creation. What follows is an attempt to summarize, at a very broad level, the progression of musical styles in the Western tradition from ancient Greek and European medieval music up through the contemporary, popular music that is commonly heard throughout the digitally connected sound stage of the world today.

The study of musical styles is an enormous subject and truly could (and does) occupy the contents of many books. Unfortunately, many types of world music, styles that use different pitch systems, and many subgenres could not be included in this chapter. To do them justice is outside the scope of this book.

Despite the limitations of a short overview, I think it is of value to look at the big-picture development of music to further our understanding of how this art has progressed. In addition to illuminating a diverse array of musical possibilities that have thus far been explored, this summary will also put in context where the condition of the musical community stands in today's world. This hopefully may inform your place in continuing the story of music. What will be the next chapter in this musical story? It is up to us, and our contributions, whether they be big or small, to determine the answer.

Listening to Musical Styles

To fully appreciate the information in this chapter, you will need to listen to the music that is being discussed. Example artists are given for each musical style. I encourage you to take the time to listen (and listen well) to a lot of music while studying this chapter. The examples artists are meant to be good representative starting points, but please don't feel that you have to stop there! Take this chapter as an invitation to explore the breadth and diversity of musical creation throughout history.

Distilled Genres

Starting at least in the twentieth century with the advent of radio, every era is accompanied by a form of generic "pop" music that merges together elements of many styles. Additionally, both popular and "underground" artists, from all time periods, have blended together styles to create unique musical expressions. The effort was made in the following sections to focus the content on distilled musical styles and examples that capture the essence of these artistic movements. Please keep in mind that many forms of pop music, fusions, variations, and altogether difficult to categorize music exist in parallel to the stereotypical genres discussed here.

Three Stages of Stylistic Development

As a broad generality, musical styles tend to develop in three stages. For our purposes, I'll refer to these stages as the *formative stage*, the *popular stage*, and the *experimental stage*.

In the formative stage, different elements of preexisting musical trends are put together and combined in new and different ways. A diverse range of ideas is present and experimentation is prevalent. Original ideas and philosophies are often put forward that are referenced throughout the rest of the style's development. The inspiration for the birth of the style emerges here. What is the style about? What is the style not about? These questions are answered at this stage. What people think of as the authentic or original version of a style often comes out of this formative period.

In the popular stage, a set of norms are established that emerge out of the diversity of the formative stage. Simultaneously, this is generally the time period when a style progresses from being "underground" or only known to a small number of artists and appreciators to being popular and well-known throughout a broader audience. Sometimes, this means that the style is combined with other popular styles to form a synthesis originating from a variety of sources. Often, a style's most recognizable characteristics develop or at least are popularized in this stage.

In the experimental stage, musicians begin to feel that the style's patterns and traditions have been thoroughly explored and that novelty is needed to reinvigorate the creative spirit. Musicians begin breaking the standard "rules" set up in the popular stage and search for new ways to express themselves. In this stage, musicians take the style and turn it into a vehicle of creative experimentation. Experimentation occurs in a variety of ways. Fusions with other styles, intensifications of previous ideas, striving to elevate the music to the level of virtuosic performance, philosophical questioning, challenging expectations, and different manifestations of complexity are all ways that we have seen music progress into this stage. Often many of these trends may be happening at once, creating a diverse musical culture, which breaks apart the unity of the popular stage. The formation of subgenres is common at this point. Progressively throughout the experimental stage, the style will fall out of popularity and once again return to the domain of smaller groups of musicians and appreciators. This will make room for new styles to emerge on to the popular scene. Not uncommonly, there are movements to return to a style's roots at this point, in reaction to the feeling that some piece of a style's value has been lost along the way.

Outline

First, we will examine the European classical tradition of music. The height of classical music is known as the *common practice period* (approximately 1600 CE – 1910 CE). We will begin before the common practice period to get a brief sense of the origins of classical music, and we will end in the contemporary practice of classical music, extending well after the common practice period.

Next, we will examine the birth of blues and gospel, as African musical influences blend with European and folk traditions in the United States. From here we will examine the progression of jazz music. And finally we will look at a few examples of the diverse musical culture of contemporary times, including rock, R&B, country, reggae, Brazilian, hip-hop, and electronic as well as subgenres of each.

- Classical -

Prior to the Common Practice Period

The presence of music in human culture extends back a very long way indeed, well into ancient and prehistoric times. Greek philosophers, such as Pythagoras (570 BCE – 495 BCE) and Aristoxenus (4th century BCE), a student of Aristotle, seem to be among the first people to study the proportions and ratios present in musical pitch and time as well as the effect of strong or weak proportions on musical expression. The musicians of ancient Greece created some of the earliest Western musical scales and tuning systems. The musicians of ancient Greece also developed an early system of musical notation. However, the notation of ancient Greek music eventually was lost from memory, only to be reinterpreted in modern times. While we know of a few examples of ancient Greek music, little of what was created remains.

After the fall of Rome, music continued into the medieval era, in the West largely through the Catholic Church. The creation and performance of Christian hymns led to the beginnings of the modern notation system and theory we know today. *Gregorian chant* emerged in the 9th and 10th centuries, as one of the first Western European styles that we can easily access and study through written records of musical notation. Gregorian chant is a monophonic,[1] vocal style of music, sung by a choir in Latin. The music was used in religious ceremony and worship in the Catholic Church.

1. Meaning that the music contains a melody but no accompaniment. See *Three Textures* on page 58.

Three Periods of Common Practice

The common practice period is broken up into three parts – the *Baroque period*, the *Classical period* (not to be confused with classical music as a whole), and the *Romantic period*. These three periods at least vaguely correspond to the three stages of development mentioned previously – formative, popular, and experimental.

The Baroque Period

The Baroque period extends for a full one hundred fifty years from the birth of Italian opera in approximately 1600 to the death of Johann Sebastian Bach, one of the genre's most famous composers in 1750. Although polyphony has been used probably from the beginnings of music itself, counterpoint comes to a height of artistic excellence in this era, especially as exemplified by the work of Bach. Many instruments come out of this era, including much of the string family and early versions of the piano called the *piano-forte* because of its ability to play notes at a variety of volume levels unlike previous keyboard instruments like the harpsichord. Some of the most well-known composers from this period include Antonio Vivaldi, Claudio Giovanni Antonio Monteverdi, Johann Pachelbel, George Frideric Handel, and, of course, Johann Sebastian Bach.

The Classical Period

The Classical period extends from approximately 1750 to 1820 and brings with it the standardization and popularization of musical structural forms. The relatively detailed sonata form, which describes sections, subsections, and prescribed key changes, is used commonly. The rondo and the minuet and trio are a few other common forms of this period.[1] The use of larger orchestras becomes prevalent in this time period, in contrast to *chamber music*, which is music written for a small ensemble of instruments (an ensemble that might fit in a "chamber" or moderately large room). A more modern version of the piano comes into existence in the Classical period, featuring louder volume levels and a wider pitch range. Some of the most well-known and influential composers from this period include Wolfgang Amadeus Mozart and Joseph Haydn. Interestingly, Beethoven is generally seen as straddling the line between the Classical period and the Romantic period. Beethoven's early work may be more characteristic of the Classical period, while his later work may be more characteristic of the Romantic.

1. For more information about these various structures, see *Possibilities in Form* on page 346.

The Romantic Period

The Romantic period, lasting from approximately 1820 to 1910, represents the beginning of classical music's turn into the experimental phase. Structural norms for composition are broken. A higher level of *chromaticism* and complex *modulation* arises.[1] Romanticism as an artistic attitude includes a focus on introspection and subjectivity. The pull to musically create one's individual experience, feeling, and nature grows in the artistic culture. Expressively, Romantic classical music is eclectic, but includes some darker themes, an aspect of emotionality and gentleness at times, subtlety, and an intense striving toward capturing beauty and the indescribable.

1. Chromaticism meaning music that ventures outside a given scale. Modulation meaning to move from one scale to another. See *Modulation* and *Chapter Fourteen* as a whole on page 412.

Virtuoso performance is highly regarded and sought after in this period, though examples of amazing talent are present all throughout the previous two periods as well. Some of the prominent figures from the Romanatic period include Frederic Chopin, Felix Mendelssohn, Johannes Brahms, Franz Liszt, Pyotr Ilyich Tchaikovsky, Richard Wagner, and Gustav Mahler.

The Impressionist Period

Although common practice, classical music is often split into three periods, some would argue for the existence of a fourth distinct period – the Impressionist period, lasting from about 1875 to 1925. The Impressionist period of classical music parallels the Impressionist period of the visual arts, known for painters like Claude Monet and Pierre-Auguste Renoir. The works of each medium are thought to mirror each other in terms of philosophy and artistic expression. The Impressionist period continues many of the aspects of the Romantic period and in many senses encapsulates the same values. The Impressionist movement in music brings with it an expansion of the harmonic vocabulary. Composers begin to use more complex chords, not so different from the sophisticated harmonies that would later become integral to jazz. Music from the Impressionist movement might be described as less narrative and more focused on harmonic and textural sounds occurring in each moment of a composition. The Impressionist movement has a soft and spacious side to it. Somewhat more relaxed perhaps than some of the virtuosic music the Romantic era is known for. The interest in music from the Impressionist period comes from a play with subtlety, ambiguity, and explorations of "color" (here meant to describe expressive confluence of timbre, dynamics, harmonic relationships, and chord voicing). Maurice Ravel and Claude Debussy are two well-known composers from the Impressionist period.

The Modern Period

If the Romantic and Impressionist periods can be seen as the earlier phase of experimental classical music, the Modern and Post-Modern periods are the later half of this evolution. The Modernist period, which represents the time from around 1900 to 1975, intensifies the experimentalist attitude. This period is associated with an entire Modernist movement of art, aesthetics, philosophy, and culture in the nineteenth and twentieth centuries. In all walks of life, the old was being replaced by the new. Technological innovation formed the background for a paradigm of questioning traditions and radical development.

For music, the Modern period introduces new theories about how music operates and can be constructed. *Atonality* (or as Arnold Schoenberg, one of the concept's pioneers, preferred to called it, *pantonality*) arises as an alternative to the conventional paradigm of *tonality* or *tonal music*. Since the very beginning of our story, a tonal center featured prominently in musical composition. Atonality introduces the notion for the first time that music might be composed not just with ambiguity around the position of the tonal center but with no tonal center at all. *Serialism* comes into being as the result of a quest to create an atonal or pantonal musical framework. The serial paradigm relies on creating artistic variations of *tone rows,* which are sequences of pitches that contain exactly one instance of each of the twelve notes.

The experimentalism of the modern period escalates until music begins to blend with philosophy. Musicians begin to question what music really is and what it really means for something to be music. As an example, the modernist composer John Cage wrote a piece in 1952 entitled "4'33"" that consists only of a silence, lasting four minutes and thirty-three seconds.

The Post-Modern Period

It may seem confusing that the Modern period is now in the past and that there exists a currently unfolding Post-Modern period, which describes the style of classical music after 1975 or so and extending all the way to present day. However, what is meant by these terms is that the Modern period embodied the Modernist philosophy, which emphasized a radical evolution from the past and a questioning of even the most fundamental ideas about music. The Post-Modern period is characterized, partially, by a reaction against these ideals or at least a developmental departure from them. However, Post-Modernism is still, in many significant ways, a continuation of the Modern period and, thus, the two are somewhat similar. The Post-Modern period blends together experimental music with popular music. The Post-Modern period retains the experimental attitude of the Modern period but tempers it with a return to simplicity. The *minimalist* movement arises in this period, in which themes are repetitiously *looped* (meaning that the same short recording is made to play over and over) or reiterated in live performance unfolding in progressive stages of evolution throughout a piece. Music from the minimalist movement has been described as "pattern and process" music. Steve Reich, Terry Riley, and Philip Glass are some of the figures who pioneered this style of music. The Post-Modern period is ongoing and is still developing. For that reason, it is difficult to characterize. Its essence may be yet to fully form or it may represent the merger of classical music with other styles, implying the end of truly novel genres of classical music. The future of the classical tradition is, as of yet, undetermined.

- The Birth of Blues and Gospel -

The Beginnings of Popular Music in the United States

A fundamental change occurs in the course of music history when the musical traditions of Africa come in contact with musical traditions of European classical music through slavery in the United States. Inspired by their rich musical heritage, black slaves in America between the 17th and 19th centuries developed *work songs* that helped ease the strain of their labor and were used as a way of sending each other covert messages, escaping the notice of watchful slave owners. African-American slaves also sang *spirituals* – prayers of music that offered hope and communion with God. By the 1880s, the first forms of *gospel* music emerged as a combination of church hymns and African-American spirituals. Gospel music is an art form of spiritual purpose, fulfilling the needs and wants for elation, passion, and connection on both the divine and human levels. Gospel music is meant to be spirit lifting and, as such, is overwhelmingly positive in expression and message.

If gospel is the music of our elevated souls, the *blues*, which emerges out African-American work songs and spirituals, is the music of our downtrodden, rugged yet vulnerable selves seeking to heal through expression and connection. Gospel music and the blues form a bedrock foundation of African-American music upon which much of today's popular music is built.

Musical Characteristics of the Blues

The blues differs from the European classical tradition in several striking ways. The blues involves the use of its own special scale, chord progression, rhythmic pattern, and structure.

The *blues scale* can be described as a minor pentatonic scale with the addition of a note a diminished fifth or tritone above the root. This note is represented by the solfege syllable Se and gives the scale a distinctively bluesy sound.

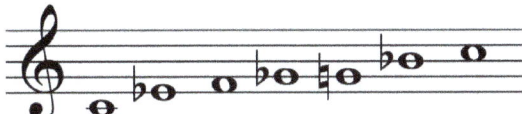

One major difference between the paradigm of blues and the European tradition is that the chord progressions used in the blues do not fall within the scale used to create the melody. In classical music, a scale is generally applied to all pitched sounds in the piece, but in the blues the melody and the accompaniment seem to play by independent rules.

The standard *12-bar blues progression* forms the basis of all blues harmony and has now accumulated countless variations. In European classical music, the dominant seventh chord had been predominantly used to set up a resolution to the tonal center or at the very least to set up the expectation of the resolution to the tonal center. In blues, however, the dominant seventh chord is generally used, not as a way to resolve the progression, but rather as a constant element that produces an overall texture and feel.

A basic form of the 12-bar blues is notated on the following page. Note that many variations of this basic chord progression and structure have been used in blues music and related genres over time.

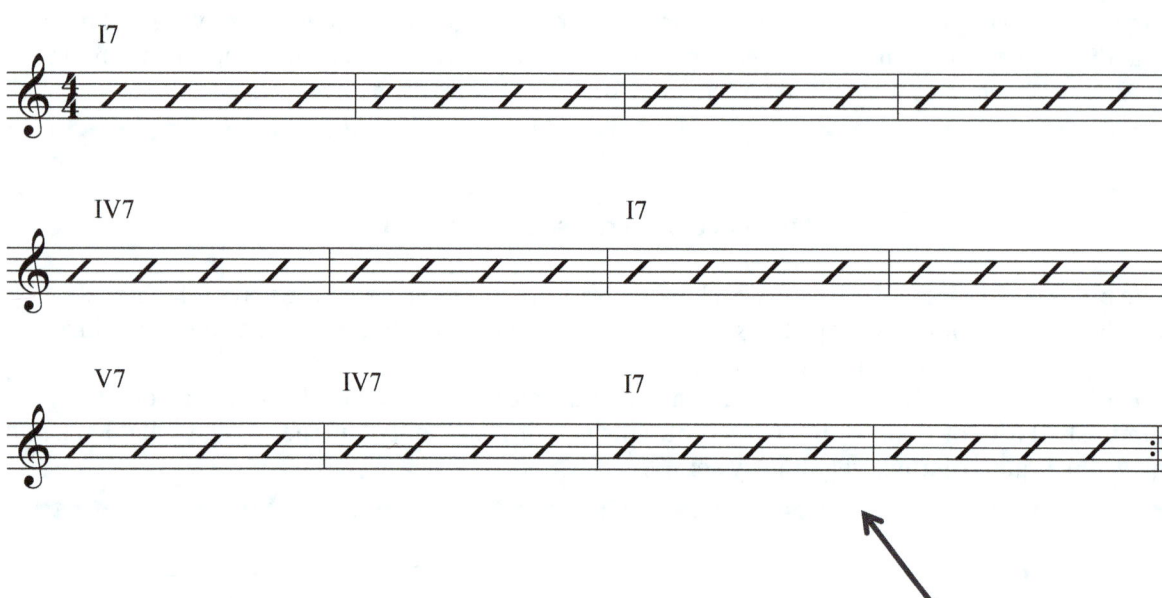

Blues also generally uses swing rhythms, making it rhythmically distinctive from European classical music as well.

The structure of blues music is dictated by the 12-bar blues progression, which is further divided into groups of four measures. The traditional blues structure can be described as an AAB pattern,[1] where a melodic idea is played in the first four measures, repeated in the second four measures, and then a different, concluding phrase is played in the last four measures. The twelve-measure structure of the blues is also unlike music of the classical tradition, where musical ideas were commonly grouped in multiples of eight and sixteen.

1. For more information about structural patterns like "AAB" see the section entitled *Structural Development* on page 344.

What Do These Slashes Mean?

Slash notation, shown above, indicates that the performer should provide some kind of accompaniment that follows the given chord symbols. Voicings and specific rhythms are left up to the performer.

Listen to a blues piece on track 55 (disc 1). Can you hear all the musical elements described above?

Track 24 (disc 2) plays just the accompaniment of track 55 (disc 1). Try improvising over this groove using the blues scale.

Ragtime, Stride, and Boogie-Woogie

An important collection of piano-based styles emerged from the later parts of the 19th century into the early parts of the 20th century. *Ragtime* is born in the 1890s out a fusion of European classical, brass band music, and various types of folk. Scott Joplin's popular works the "The Entertainer" and "Map Leaf Rag" are two of the most iconic pieces of ragtime music. By the 1920s, Ragtime would develop into *stride piano* based on the left hand accompanying pattern of a bass note alternated with a chord. Unlike Ragtime, which was fully notated in the European classical tradition, stride allowed some room for improvisation. Around the end of the 1920s, *boogie-woogie* emerges as a more heavily blues-based, upbeat piano style with distinctive left hand patterns that keep a steady swinging eighth note pulse. Over these patterns, the pianist's right hand played chords that often would emphasize beats two and four in a 4/4 meter. The combination was danceable, rhythmic, and full of energy. The emphasis of two and four would be a crucial moment in the development of music. A rhythmic pattern played on beats two and four is now known as the *backbeat* and is an integral component of many styles of music, very commonly being heard on the snare drum of a wide range of drum set grooves.

- Jazz -

Jazz was born in New Orleans out of a diverse melting pot of cultures and musical traditions. As a former French colony and a port city, New Orleans was exposed to musical influences from around the world. Jazz merges the idioms of the blues, ragtime, marching bands, Creole and Haitian folk music as well as Cuban and French music. The result is a rich blend of "high-class" European classical and "low-class" folk music from different cultures around the world. Jazz, as it would form in the coming decades, is at times sophisticated and reserved, yet always full of spirit, free, and highly improvisational.

New Orleans Jazz

The first forms of jazz, now referred to as *New Orleans jazz* or sometimes as *Dixieland jazz*, arose in the early parts of the 20th century. These styles were highly energetic, featuring busy sounding bands of musicians, all improvising in tandem with one another. The art form created a new form of improvisational polyphony where melodic instruments joined together to create a cacophony of fun, loose, moving, and grooving sounds. King Oliver's Creole Jazz Band and the Original Dixieland Jazz Band were two of the most influential pioneers of this style.

Swing and Big Band Jazz

The swing era, which lasted from the mid-1930s into the mid-1940s, represents the shift of jazz music from the formative period into the popular period. *Big band jazz* or *swing* music is associated with the classic names of Count Basie, Benny Goodman, and Duke Ellington. As the name implies, big band jazz saw the expansion of the jazz band instrumentation to include a standard seventeen musicians. The sound was danceable, big, and upbeat. The complex polyphonic sound of New Orleans jazz gave way to more orchestrated and arranged melodies. Improvisation now takes the form of *solos* where a single musician improvises over the predetermined chord progression of the piece, sometimes including predetermined background melody lines or *hits* – short, emphasized background harmonies. Swing was entertainment music. Dancing, choreography, and outfits were all part of the show. Swing music reached a level of popularity previous unseen in the musical world because of radio and recording technologies, which were now becoming commonplace and easily accessible. The technological advances of the big band era also produced the first electric guitars, which were initially introduced to balance the volume levels of a guitar with a large, brass-filled jazz band.

Vocal Jazz

In addition to the instrumental music of the time, the New Orleans and swing jazz styles also produced a great tradition of jazz vocalists. These jazz vocalists combined influences from New Orleans jazz, swing, blues, and pop. Billie Holiday was an important early pioneer in this style, producing influential music from the 1930s to the 1950s. Ella Fitzgerald and Nina Simone are two other great jazz vocalists. And before moving on to later forms of jazz, I would be remiss not to mention the monumental contributions of Louis Armstrong. His influence goes wide and far in jazz through his five-decade career spanning from the 1920s to the 1960s as both a singer and trumpet player.

Be-Bop

Be-bop, developing in the mid-1940s, is the first form of jazz in its experimental period. Be-bop takes jazz back to the instrumentation of a small group but now with a much different feel. Be-bop is characterized by fast-paced melodic lines and complexity in both rhythm and harmony. Jazz up to this point is uniformly performed with a swing rhythm, but in be-bop and later forms of jazz the swing rhythm is sometimes left behind. The solo shifts in significance from an addition that creates variety and an opportunity to feature a performer to the main event of the music. The *head* of the piece – the main melody and accompanying chords that are composed beforehand – is reduced to an introductory and closing statement that provides a harmonic and rhythmic structure for improvisation. Multiple solos often occur in sequence, though not simultaneously as they would in New Orleans jazz. The art and technique of soloing is the focus of this music. Charlie Parker and Dizzy Gillespie are two of the masters that represent the style of be-bop.

Cool Jazz, Hard Bop, Avant-Garde, and Fusion

From here, jazz diversifies into several subgenres that could be collectively classified as the later experimental jazz styles. *Cool jazz* emerges in the 1950s as a development of be-bop. Cool jazz retains much of the experimentalism and complexity of be-bop but with a more reserved, sometimes even mellow, expression. Chet Baker, Stan Getz, and Dave Brubeck all contributed to the cool jazz genre.

Also arising in the 1950s, *hard bop* takes the essence of be-bop and adds a more rhythmic feel, more coordinated textures, and a more free, energetic expressive range than cool jazz. Don't let the name deceive you here. There is actually nothing particularly "hard" about this style. Hard bop is cultivated by artists such as Wes Montgomery and Art Blakey. As the experimentalism of jazz intensified, we eventually arrive at the genre we describe as *avant-garde jazz* or *free jazz* at the end of the 1950s. Miles Davis and John Coltrane, two very important names in these later styles of jazz, were involved in a combination of be-bop, cool jazz, and hard bop throughout their musical careers. John Coltrane was also an early pioneer of free jazz.

Later still, jazz began to combine with other genres forming various jazz fusion styles. *Jazz-rock fusion* (sometimes simply called *fusion*) attained popularity in the 1970s because of artists like Chick Corea and Herbie Hancock.

Samba and Bossa Nova

Samba is an Afro-Brazilian style of music and dance that developed in the early part of the 20th century. Samba can be rhythmically complex and often uses several percussion parts but is rooted in a strong 2/4 or 2/2 groove (samba is sometimes written in 4/4 but is still felt and played with two strong emphasized beats per measure). Some sambas may use complex harmonies but tend to unambiguously revolve around a strong tonal center. Songwriters like Noel Rosa and Ary Barroso helped popularize this style in the 1930s and 1940s. For a few more modern variations of samba, listen to the music of Martinho da Vila or Alcione Nazareth.

In the late 1950s, Brazilian music combines with the jazz styles of the time to create a new genre – bossa nova. Pioneered by artists like Antonio Carlos Jobim and João Gilberto, bossa nova (meaning "new way") used instrumentation more similar to a small jazz group but with many of the same Brazilian musical elements that we can recognize from samba. The rhythmic energy of bossa nova is somewhat more subdued. The overall expression is generally smooth and sophisticated.

- Country -

Introducing Country Music

Celtic folk music and blues create the foundation for *country* music to be born in the United States in the early parts of the 20th century. Country uses largely simple harmony with steady, un-swung or straight, 4/4 grooves, commonly including an alteration between a bass note and a chord on each beat. Like the blues, country music tells stories and has a very personal feel to it. However, culturally and historically speaking, country music has been the music of white people, whereas blues has been the music of black people. These two styles were born in racially divided times and remain descents of white and black culture. In this regard, blues and country have set up an essential dichotomy in music. Early popular music was regarded as either "hillbilly music" (country) or "race music" (blues). These two genres remain the foundations for much of modern popular music today.

Early Country and Honky Tonk

Early country music came into being in the 1920s and 1930s, with names like Jimmie Rodgers and the Carter Family. These two artists were very influential in setting the stage for country music. So much so that much of later country music can be traced back to the traditions formed by one of these two artists. In the 1940s, country music solidifies into its formative period with the genre known as *honky tonk* or *hardcore country*. This period is known for some of the biggest names in country like Hank Williams Sr. (note that Hank Williams Jr. is also a well-known country musician) and later Johnny Cash.

Bluegrass

At the end of the 1940s, a new style of country music emerged called *bluegrass*. Bluegrass is up-tempo, lively, and highly improvisational with an emphasis on string instruments like the fiddle, banjo, and mandolin. The term bluegrass came from one of the pioneers of the style, Bill Monroe and the Bluegrass Boys. In turn, the name of this group was inspired by the nickname "the bluegrass country" given to the state of Kentucky.

The Nashville Sound

Starting in the late 1950s and moving into the 1960s, Nashville, Tennessee, became a central hub of country music production and a great commercial success. This period of country music represents its popular era and is defined by artists like Tammy Wynette (famous for the song "Stand By Your Man") and Charlie Rich. Chet Atkins was also instrumental in the creation of the Nashville genre as both a guitarist and producer.

The *Nashville sound* is characterized by a softer, more "pop" sound that makes use of strings and bigger instrumentation in comparison to older, traditional country styles.

Outlaw Country and Contemporary

Starting in the 1970s, the country scene began to backlash against the soft, pop sound that had taken over the genre. The new wave of country music was defined by more reflective lyrics and mergers with pop and rock influences. This marked the transition of country into its experimental period. Some of the music adopted an edgy side to it, earning it the name *outlaw country*. This period of country music is represented by artists like Willie Nelson and Waylon Jennings. Garth Brooks is one of the biggest country names moving forward into the 1980s, 1990s, and 2000s. Garth Brooks is also an example of an artist who has successfully merged pop and rock elements into the country sound.

- Blues, R&B, and Rock -

Jump Blues, Chicago Blues, and Beyond

After blues music helps to give birth to jazz, it continues on as an independent and rich style in its own right. As swing music comes into popularity in the 1930s and 1940s, some blues musicians borrow elements from the popular jazz music of the time and develop an upbeat danceable blues style known as *jump blues*. Jump blues is based on boogie-woogie grooves and strengthens the backbeat, now often carried by an enthusiastic audience clapping along to the music.

Perhaps the most iconic version of the blues solidifies in the 1940s in the northern cities of the United States with artists like Muddy Waters and Howlin' Wolf. This type of blues is sometimes referred to as *Chicago blues* or *urban blues*. In the late 1940s, *distortion* is introduced to electric guitars and reshapes the sound of the blues in a major way. City life, distorted guitar sounds, and a loud, expressive vocal style all served to differentiate this sound from the earlier *country blues* styles, which used only acoustic instruments and came from rural areas.

Looking forward into the 1950s, 1960s, and beyond, B.B. King and later Stevie Ray Vaughan are two of the most important blues artists.

Early R&B

By the 1940s, artists like Fats Domino and Little Richard were pioneering the first form of *rhythm and blues* or as it is often abbreviated *R&B*. R&B was inspired from jump blues but now the instrumentation was more sparse and the singer often came into the spotlight as the central focus. The backbeat was a constant element of the groove, now carried by a drum set.

Rock 'n' Roll

After jazz moves from its popular period in the swing era into its experimental phase, a void is left for a new type of popular music. *Rock 'n' roll* fills this void starting in the 1950s and eventually giving rise to rock music in all its later variations. Rock 'n' roll music is very similar to the early R&B music of artists like Fats Domino and Little Richard. The primary difference was that now R&B music was being played by white artists who were integrating a country influence into the music. This early form of rock has sometimes been called *rockabilly* – alluding to the influence of "hillbilly" country music in the style. Rock 'n' roll music has a strong, catchy groove, still closely reminiscent of boogie-woogie patterns, with simple harmonic progressions. The electric guitar, which had been introduced in earlier forms of jazz and blues for the practical purposes of increasing the instrument's volume, is now transformed into the iconic *distorted* electric guitar sound that we all associate with rock styles. Elvis Presley achieved unprecedented success in this new genre, alongside other rock 'n' roll artists like Chuck Berry and Buddy Holly.

Rock Rises Into New Heights of Popularity

The formative period of rock can be seen as a combination of early R&B and rock 'n' roll. Rock 'n' roll, however, was already achieving incredible, unprecedented success, perhaps best exemplified by Elvis Presley, and had undoubtedly taken over for jazz as the most popular form of music. However, as we move into the 1960s and 1970s, rock's popularity skyrockets to new heights.

The British Invasion

During the 1960s, the Beatles redefine not only rock music but also what it means to be a celebrity on the music scene. "Beatlemania" is the term given to the manic zeal with which fans supported, lusted over, and idolized the Beatles. The Beatles were part of a larger movement known as the *British invasion* in which many rock bands from the United Kingdom rose to popularity both in their own country and in the United States. The Animals, the Kinks, and the Rolling Stones were a few of the bands that created the movement known as the British invasion. The uniform upbeat, swinging, boogie grooves of the rock 'n' roll music relax their hold on this new style of rock music.

Sometimes softer, soul-inspired[1] grooves are used. Other times more up-tempo grooves are formed out of fusions of R&B, soul, and rock 'n' roll influences. Straight rhythms are now more common than swinging ones.

1. *Soul, Funk, and Disco*, page 305

Folk Revival and Folk Rock

In the pure sense, *folk music* is less of a specific style and more of a broad category of music that is associated with the common people of a particular culture. However, in the 1950s and 1960s there was a *folk revival* movement that brought a new popularity to American and British folk music in tandem with the social revolutions of the time. Folk revival music was musically simple, often focused on just a guitar and a singer, and centered on political and social commentary. When I think of folk revival music, I think of Pete Seeger.

But there is also another very related category of music that we might call *folk rock* that came directly on the heels of the folk revival movement. Folk rock combined the lyrical themes and feel of folk with influences from the new musical ideas and timbres of rock. Important folk rock artists include Bob Dylan, The Byrds, Simon and Garfunkel, the group Crosby, Stills, & Nash (known as Crosby, Stills, Nash, and Young when joined by their fourth member Neil Young), and Joni Mitchell.

Note that in the later part of her career Joni Mitchell began infusing jazz influences into her music, deviating from what we might think of as a pure folk rock sound. Therefore, listen to Joni Mitchell's earlier work if your intent is hear conventional examples of this genre.

Hard Rock

In the late 1960s going into the 1970s, a new rougher, tougher, blues-infused variant of rock emerges – *hard rock*. This style is represented by artists like AC/DC, George Thorogood (famous for his song "Bad to the Bone"), and Aerosmith. The guitars in hard rock become more heavily distorted and play a prominent role. Hard rock popularizes the concept of a *guitar riff* – a recognizable, short, often repetitive melodic phrase.

Progressive (Prog) Rock

Around the same time hard rock emerges (late 1960s moving into the 1970s), a movement begins known as *progressive rock* or *prog rock*. Prog rock took the structure of rock and added classical and jazz influences, more technical performances, and a bit of experimentalism. This genre is contributed to by artists such as the Moody Blues, Yes, and Pink Floyd. An offshoot of this genre is *symphonic prog rock*, where classical orchestrations were combined with the concept of a rock band.

Glam Rock and Stadium Rock

In the 1970s, some "rock stars" like Bruce Springsteen and Tom Petty become so popular that their concerts fill entire stadiums, leading to the term *stadium rock*. Around the same time, many rock musicians began to take on eccentric personas, often accompanied by bizarre or outrageous fashion. David Bowie and Elton John are two examples of this movement, which is described as *glam rock* or sometimes *shock rock* for the shocking aesthetics, showmanship, and fashion the musicians employed.

Metal

The first forms of *metal* emerge in the 1970s and are initially created out of an extension of hard rock. Metal adds yet more distortion to the guitars and darker artistic expressions. Early metal or *classic metal*, as it is now known, is represented by artists like Black Sabbath, Deep Purple, and Led Zeppelin.

Moving into the 1980s, metal becomes faster and more aggressive as it transitions into what is known as *thrash metal*. It is sometimes said that the "big four" bands of thrash metal are Metallica, Megadeth, Slayer, and Anthrax. Later on, thrash metal turns into *death metal*, an even more extreme, dark, and brutal form of expression. Among others, death metal is represented by the music of Death and Morbid Angel.

Musically speaking, metal as a whole is characterized by complexity and speed. Metal often uses unusual and inconsistent time signatures and features technically complex, fast-paced guitar work and drumming patterns. These features in many ways make metal a natural match for prog rock. The progressive influences of experimentalism and genre-fusions meet metal in the 1970s going forward forming the genre of *progressive metal* or *prog metal*, represented by bands like Dream Theater and Queensrÿche.

Punk Rock

In the 1970s, punk rock emerges as a reaction against the idolization of celebrity seen in stadium rock and the complexity of prog rock and metal. Arising initially in the United Kingdom, punk rock takes us back to the basics. The music is stripped down, raw, rebellious rock. This style is exemplified by artists like the Sex Pistols, the Ramones, and Patti Smith. If metal goes in the direction of complexity, punk opposes it by pursuing simplicity. Punk eliminates extravagance and is anything but glamorous. The attitude of punk rock is brutally honest, unrestrained but also, interestingly, inclusive. Punk culture is welcoming in the sense that it does not put a high value on technical prowess or elaborate showmanship, which creates a space for everyone to participate. Punk reacts against elitism and fills the need for a common person's music.

Post-Punk

Post-punk, emerging in the late 1970s, adds a little experimentalism to punk while also smoothing out its edges. Post-punk is less aggressive. The music morphs into a mellower, dark expression. There is a little more complexity in post-punk and the sound is more filled out. Post-punk is an eclectic mix of sounds and produces many subgenres. One of the most iconic post-punk bands is Joy Division.

- Later R&B Styles and Jamaican Music -

Soul, Funk, and Disco

After R&B grew into rock 'n' roll in the 1950s, R&B music continued to develop in a more African-American dominated culture, independent from the rock scene. *Soul* music develops in the 1960s out of the R&B and gospel traditions. Soul music is heartfelt, sincere, and often warm and hopeful. Soul music was the voice of the civil rights movement, expressing an idealistic yearning for peace and unity. Motown becomes one of the most popular record labels in this genre and is sometimes referred to as a style in its own right. Aretha Franklin, Otis Redding, Sam Cooke, and Stevie Wonder all represent the style of soul music.

Soul music undergoes a radical transformation in the 1970s with the advent of *funk* – a more rhythmic, danceable, and upbeat variation of R&B music with rock influences. Funk music pioneers introduce new rhythmic patterns that emphasize the downbeat of each measure while exploring complex syncopations in between. The rhythms of funk music are sometimes referred to as *sixteenth note rhythms*, for their use and emphasis of the "e" and "a" positions of a measure. James Brown and Parliament are two of the most well-known artists in this style of music.

Based on funk rhythms but softened with pop elements, *disco* rises to popularity in the late 1970s and, significantly, brings with it the first continuous dance mixes, which were played at "disc-o-theques," a new brand of nightlife dance clubs. This set the stage for house music and later electronic genres, which would be based on continuous mixes, DJs, and the club scene. The Bee Gees and Gloria Gaynor are two popular disco artists.

Reggae

In the 1960s, *reggae* develops from a mixture of Jamaican styles with influences from R&B. Reggae is centered on a unique groove. The downbeat is often omitted by the bass and the guitar characteristically plays an "off-beat" (beats two and four) pulse. Reggae can be played either with swing or straight eighths. Reggae music is happy, rhythmic, peaceful, and yet also revolutionary music.

Reggae was inspired by political issues in Jamaica, a struggling, newly independent country, and the movements of social change in the 1960s. Bob Marley and Jimmy Cliff are two well-known reggae artists.

Hip-Hop

The first stages of *hip-hop* occur in the 1970s in the party scene of poor, African-American dominated communities in the South Bronx of New York City. Hip-hop combined influences from funk, disco, and Jamaican music and pioneered the concept of a *disc jockey* or *DJ*. A DJ is an artist who selects music for an event and mixes the music while it is being played. While this idea was not entirely novel, hip-hop introduces the idea that the DJ could affect, alter, or add to the music being played. A whole art form of techniques emerged around manipulating vinyl records to produce musical effects, creating smooth and artistic transitions between songs, and combining songs together (often in transitions) to create new musical expressions.

Another crucial component of hip-hop is introduced with the advent of *rap*, which can be described as a form of spoken-word poetry that is articulated in rhythm with a musical accompaniment. Hip-hop comes into popularity in the 1980s and 1990s with artists like N.W.A., 2Pac, and Notorious B.I.G. Getting started in the 1980s, both Dr. Dre (a member of N.W.A.) and Jay-Z both have hip-hop careers extending into the 2000s and 2010s. In the 1990s and 2000s, hip-hop is popularized among white audiences because of the success of white hip-hop artists such as Vanilla Ice, TobyMac, Macklemore, and Eminem. In the 2000s and 2010s, hip-hop merges with pop to produce the genre of *pop-rap* where pop songs include rap verses as a juxtaposition to sung choruses.

- Electronic Music (EDM) -

House and the Birth of EDM

In the 1980s, *house* music emerges as an evolution of disco. House music got its name from "The Warehouse," a popular club in Chicago where the style was born. The first house music artists, such as Frankie Knuckles, Larry Levan, and Ron Hardy, begin to deemphasize the role of vocals that was common to previous styles of dance music while experimenting with new electronic sounds in their place. Just a few years later, artists like Larry Heard (a.k.a. Mr. Fingers), Marshall Jefferson known for the song "Move Your Body," and Steve "Silk" Hurley solidify the essential early or classic house sound. Based on developing yet repetitive grooves, the resulting dance style is somewhat slower and more mellow than the later versions of house that would come to follow it.

This marks the beginning of a significant change in the history of music. House ushers in a new category of music genres – *EDM*, which stands for *electronic dance music*. EDM is constructed entirely or at least largely out of electronically synthesized[1] and sampled[2] sounds. The computer had now become not only a tool for recording and production but an instrument, in fact an entire band and orchestra of sounds. Unintuitively, EDM is now used as an umbrella term for all music produced through computer production and synthesis, even if it is not particularly dance oriented.

The *four-on-the-floor beat*, which was pioneered by disco, was brought into prominence by house music. The four-on-the-floor beat is an even 4/4 pulse played by the kick drum. An added off-beat (playing on the "ands") hi-hat completes the quintessential house groove popularized by the sound of *Euro-pop house* music.

In the 1990s moving into the 21st century, house takes on two new intertwined forms – *progressive house* and later *electro house*. Progressive house infused house music with more complexity but within an evolving, four-on-the-floor dominated structure. An earlier incarnation of this genre is represented by the artist Leftfield while a later incarnation, marked by the use of more modern production techniques and a continuation of progressive house's experimentalism, is exemplified by the artist Deadmau5. Electro house emerges in the 2000s and brings a bigger sound, sung choruses, and a more energetic spirit to the house groove. This style is represented by artists like Calvin Harris and Swedish House Mafia. The group Daft Punk, who combined several forms of house and EDM, is another important artist in the house music of the 1990s, 2000s, and beyond.

1. *Additive and Subtractive Synthesis*, page 325
2. *Sampling*, page 324

Techno

Techno arises in the 1980s inspired by and in parallel to house music. Techno is characterized by a stripped down, groove centric style, often venturing into minimalist realms. Like house, techno makes use of four-on-the-floor beats, though often incorporating a steady eighth note pulse on the hi-hat. There is a striking absence of sustained textures in this style, contributing to its barren, frequently minimal feel. Techno is repetitive, rhythmic, and often spotted with quirky electronic timbres. Examples of techno artists include Spiral Tribe, Robert Hood, and Derrick May.

Ambient, Downtempo, and Chill-Out

For an electronic style, *ambient* or *downtempo* music has long roots going back into the 1970s and was inspired by the Post-Modern movement of classical music. Simply put, ambient electronic music is relaxed, low energy expression, electronically created music that takes the focus away from rhythm, in sharp contrast to other electronic styles, and instead directs the listener's attention to elements of pitch, timbre, and locational space.

Early ambient music is represented in the work of Tangerine Dream. Coming into the 1980s, ambient music is influenced by house and regains some of its rhythmic energy. The new form of ambient music is often referred to as *chill-out*. This genre can be heard from artists such as The Orb, Air, and Moby in songs like "Porcelain."

Trance

Characterized by somewhat faster tempos (around 140 bpm) as well as ambient and classical influences, *trance* music emerges in the 1990s somewhat after house and techno. Trance features big sounds, uplifting energy, and long buildups. Trance has perhaps a somewhat more varied structural landscape when compared with house and techno, taking advantage of high energy expressions as well as low ones. DJ Tiesto and Armin Van Buuren are two well-known trance artists.

Drum 'n' Bass

Coming on the scene for the first time in the 1990s, *drum 'n' bass* music is different than house and techno in that it does not utilize a four-on-the-floor beat. Instead, drum 'n' bass grew out of R&B and funk drum *breaks* – short sections of the music where all the instruments drop out except for the drums playing a fill – which were sampled electronically and used as the basis for new, complex rhythmic grooves. Drum 'n' bass is characteristically fast, using tempos upwards of 150 bpm. To balance out and complement the complexity of the percussion parts, drum 'n' bass uses prominent, sustained "sub-bass" (meaning low bass) synths that glue the whole sound together. These two elements form the core of the style, as the name implies. Drum 'n' bass is infused with influences from Jamaican music, which as far back as the 1970s had begun incorporating electronic sounds and effects in their music, namely in the influential genre of *dub*. Sometimes variations of drum 'n' bass are more experimental, featuring complex, evolving electronic timbres. Other variations are closer to pop music and place a greater emphasis on vocals. Earlier examples of drum 'n' bass can heard from artists such as Evol Intent and High Contrast. Later, more mainstream examples are represented by artists like Rudimental and Sigma.

Dubstep

In the 2000s, a radical development of electronic music occurs. Based on drum 'n' bass music as well as dub, *dubstep* emerges with more mellow, experimental roots but quickly morphs into a high energy style of great complexity. Dubstep features intricate, evolving sounds and a characteristic "wobble bass," which is a bass synthesizer with a modulating filter rapidly fluctuating the presence of upper partials in the synthesizer's timbre. Dubstep is based on a half-time (in other words, half-tempo), triplet feel that is frequently contrasted to other rhythmic grooves within a musical piece. Examples of dubstep artists include Feint and Skrillex.

Additional Resources

If you are interested in learning more about musical styles, I highly recommend checking out the website www.musicmap.info. This web project features a massive visual representation of different musical styles and links to specific musical examples. I have drawn upon the excellent information on this website in my own research for this chapter, and it includes many more subgenres, details, and examples than I was able to include here.

The book *Essential Grooves for Writing, Performing and Producing Contemporary Music* by Dan Moretti, Matthew Nicholl, and Oscar Stagnaro is another great resource and one that I've also drawn upon. This book will help you go deeper into analyzing the musical elements of different styles, complete with audio examples (a few of which were used in Chapter Eight[1]) and accompanying notation.

For readers interested in going into more depth with the history of the jazz tradition, the documentary TV series *Jazz* directed by Ken Burns is fantastic and quite comprehensive. I highly recommended it.

1. See page 430 in the acknowledgments section for more details on this source.
❖ See the bibliography on page 431 for additional details about all of these resources.

Chapter Eleven
Arranging and Production

- Principles of Arranging and Production -

The big-picture basis for arranging and production consists largely of concepts that have already been discussed but need to be applied specifically to the new territory we will be covering. Here are five main ideas to hold in mind during this discussion of arranging and production and going forward into your own creative endeavors.

Separation

One central aim of arranging and production is to create the experience of multiple connected, interlocking, yet easily distinguishable parts. One can intentionally opt to move in the opposite direction to create the expressions of chaos or confusion. However, for general purposes we want to be able to listen to any individual part and clearly separate that part from the rest of the ensemble.

One of the primary ways that separation is created between musical parts is by clearly choosing to either combine multiple parts in a *unison rhythm* – meaning that all the parts are playing the same rhythm – or, alternatively, by ensuring that there is adequate time between the entrance of one part's sounds and the entrance of another part's sounds. It is when parts contain rhythms that are similar yet not the same that we begin to feel a sense of heightened complexity, eventually turning into chaos. One way to think about this is that parts should emphasize different rhythmic positions so we can hear them as separate, unless you wish to combine parts to create a unison timbre, which is then perceived like a single part in the listener's mind.

Separation can also be created through pitch range. When instruments are close together in pitch, they become harder for the listener to separate. When instruments are far apart in pitch, they are easier to separate.

Balance

If we place expressive energy in one area of a composition, we will generally balance this out by subtracting energy from others areas. The progression of a composition then can unfold as a redistribution of energy, which occurs over a narrative shape of introductions, buildups, climaxes, and conclusions.

Balance can occur between parts; for example, one instrument plays a highly energetic part while another instrument balances it out with a lower energy part. Or balance can occur between different aspects of the composition; for example, the harmony grows in complexity while the rhythm simplifies, or the rhythm grows in complexity while the harmony simplifies.

Once again, we can intentionally choose to go against this principle. If we are aiming to create an extreme expression of high or low energy, then we will want to avoid balancing the different expressive spectra or musical parts.

Focus

Arranging and production can be a lot about directing a listener's focus. Is there a clear central focus on one element while the others meld together to form a sonic background? Does the listener's focus encompass multiple parts? How is the listener's attention distributed? Focus is created by louder volume levels, closer, more central spatial positions, and use of the clarity-enhancing upper-mid pitch range. We can also create focus by using "big" timbres, meaning combinations of multiple instruments or parts coming together in one unison rhythm, like a chorus of singers or large ensemble of instruments all playing a single melody. Alternatively, timbres can become attention grabbing if they are higher energy or, in other words, richer or more complex, regardless of their perceived "size," from a single instrument to a large ensemble.

Pitch Range

As just mentioned, pitch range influences focus but it also influences the energy level of musical expressions. Lower pitch sounds form a kind of foundation for a musical piece that is comparatively sensitive to high energy or complex musical elements. As a general rule, we keep parts in the lower pitch range lower in energetic expression as well.

Also recall that when lower pitches are placed too close together, they create the muddiness effect, which is usually not desired.[1]

1. *Muddiness*, page 149

Structural Gravity

Musical gravity becomes important in arranging and production not just in creating parts but as a structural element. Commonly, we may want to create the sense of musical gravity leading into the entrances of new sections, but there are also many other related possibilities that involve playing with our sense of musical gravity on the structural level. For example, we may want to create the effect of anticipation, surprise, or entrancing repetitiveness in the way our compositions progress in terms of their structure. Does one section prominently announce the coming of the next? Does a section hint at the coming of the next section but keep us guessing? Does a new section arrive unannounced? These are all considerations to think about in terms of structural gravity.

- ❖ For more details see *Structural Development* on page 344 and especially *Structural Gravity Revisited* on page 345.

- Applications for Each Role in the Ensemble -

In this section, we will look at how to write parts for each of the four roles in the ensemble – percussion, bass, harmony, and melody. We will use the principles of arranging and production discussed in the previous section to inform our view of how to create these parts. If you are not familiar with the concept of the four roles or if you want a refresher on this topic, you may want to study the section *The Four Roles in the Ensemble* on page 56.

Percussion

When writing percussion parts, first we should consider the impact of pitch range. Although percussion instruments do not have defined pitches, the general pitch range of a percussive sound carries with it some important implications. Low percussive sounds will feel "weightier" and will be more sensitive to expressive energy and complexity. Generally, low percussive sounds are heard on strong rhythmic positions. Higher percussive sounds, however, have more freedom to explore rhythmic complexity, variety, and higher energy expressions. The lower sounds form the foundation while the high ones play on top of it.

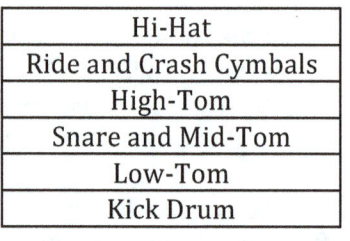

Though pitch considerations apply to all percussion instruments, let us take a moment to look at the pitch range of the sounds in a standard drum set. Note that these are only the basic components of the drum set, often additional percussion instruments are added.

A second consideration here is the backbeat. The backbeat is a prominent element in many, many styles. When writing drum beats, you may want to consider using the backbeat as a kind of foundation around which you can write in higher levels of complexity.

Percussion parts are often responsible for outlining the structure of a musical composition. Percussion parts let the listeners know where the music is in a larger structure. This is done primarily through fills[1] that are used as approaches to new sections. However, it is also common to see the percussion parts change to a new groove or drum beat upon the entrance of a section. This is another way that the percussion parts can signal the structure of the piece.

1. *The Drum Fill*, page 229

Bass

The primary role of the bass is to indicate what the rhythmic and harmonic foundation of the music is. The bass tells us more than any other part what the harmonic center is and where the downbeat of each measure is. The bass commonly plays the root of the chord any time the chord changes. If a chord is in an inversion rather than in root position, we will probably hear the bass part play whatever note is supposed to be on the bottom of the chord on the rhythmic position where the chord changes. In either case, whatever note the bass is playing when the chord changes is heard as the harmonic center and foundation of the chord. In between the chord changes, the bass may play low energy chord tones and may create micro-approaches to strong rhythmic positions. The bass frequently uses longer, sustained tones but, particularly in certain styles of jazz and funk, may also become more active.

The bass is intrinsically linked to the percussion parts. In particular, the kick drum and the bass can easily run into separation issues as prominent, low-pitched sounds. We will want to take extra care to deconflict the bass with the kick by either having the parts play the same rhythm or by playing rhythms that are clearly separated, avoiding any sense of being crowded.

Harmony Parts

If the bass line establishes the harmonic and rhythmic foundation, the role of the harmony parts is to fill in the tones of the chords and higher pitched rhythms of the groove.

Frequently, there will be multiple harmony parts and in these cases there arises the issue of separating the various harmony parts. This can be accomplished through a few different strategies. One strategy is to simply have the harmony parts play in different measures or different parts of the measure so that they deconflict.

Another strategy is to designate one part or a group of parts as sustaining harmony parts. These parts will play simple rhythms on strong rhythmic positions and will hold out or sustain their chords for extended durations. Then establish a second part or group of parts that will play more active rhythms, utilizing weaker rhythmic positions, and providing an added degree of complexity.

One can also alternate which harmony parts get to play the more active parts. This can create nice variety both for the listeners and for the performers.

Melody Parts

The melody is the primary center of focus. The music will need to be arranged so that the melody is the centerpiece. The percussion, bass, and harmony parts should surround the melody and support it, but should not distract from it. The melody is often played by multiple performers. This creates the effect of adding many *layers* of music all contributing to a big, prominent melodic part. We will look at some techniques for doing this in the coming sections.

Some music may also make use of background or secondary melodies. Background melodies can be played by monophonic instruments, like a saxophone or vocals, or may be played by polyphonic instruments, perhaps the instruments that are providing the harmony part of the groove most of the time.

- Harmonized Melodies -

A *harmonized melody* is a melody that is complemented by one or more secondary, harmonizing melodies. Each of these melodies can be referred to as a *melodic line* or simply a *line*. We can think of each line as a series of single notes progressing from left to right in the horizontal dimension of music notation.

Harmonizing melodic lines play different notes than the primary melody but the same rhythm. Most often, the primary melody is higher in pitch than all of the secondary, harmonizing melody lines. However, sometimes, especially in vocal harmonies, the primary melody can be below the harmonizing melodies.

There are two primary methods of creating harmonized melodies, which I call the *constant numeric interval method* and the *chord tone method*.

The Constant Numeric Interval Method

To use the constant numeric interval method, we will place the notes of a harmonizing melody line a given numeric interval above or below the notes of the primary melody, adjusting the quality of the interval so that the harmonizing line remains in the scale of the musical piece.

Below is an example of a melody that is harmonized by a secondary line that is placed one third below the primary melody. The interval becomes a major or minor third depending on what fits within the scale. Listen to this example played by a flute and an oboe on track 25 (disc 2).

The Chord Tone Method

The second approach to writing harmonized melodies is to have the harmonizing melody line or lines play chord tones that support the primary melody. Generally, when the primary melody moves up or down, it is desirable to have some sense of motion in the other harmonizing parts. In the constant numeric interval approach, this happens automatically. However, with the chord tone approach, we have to give this some thought. The standard approach in this technique is that if the primary melody stays on the same pitch, all the harmonizing melodies stay on the same pitch. If the primary melody moves either up or down, all the harmonizing melodies move as well though not necessarily in the same direction. This means that new chords tones must be available for the harmonizing melodies to move to every time the primary melody goes up or down. This is not always possible. For this reason, sometimes this technique is combined with the constant interval technique.

Examine an example of the chord tone method below and listen to the notation, played by a string quartet, on track 26 (disc 2).

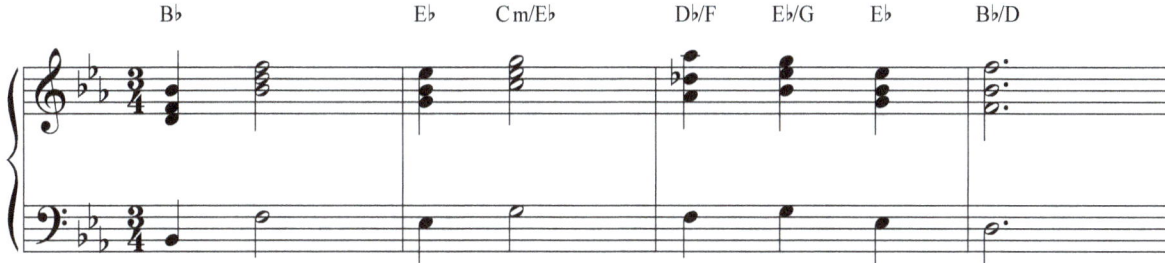

Slashes in Chord Symbols

Note that when a chord symbol is followed by a slash and a note name, this indicates that the note following the slash is meant to be the lowest note in the chord. See *Slash Chords* on page 400 for a complete explanation.

Implying Centers With Harmonized Melodies

Any given perfect fifth or fourth is found in exactly one major triad and one minor triad, both sharing the same root note. In contrast, thirds and sixths are found in one major triad and one minor triad of differing roots. This means that perfect fifths and fourths, with no help from any other notes, signify a clear harmonic center, whereas the thirds and sixths do not. A given unison or octave may appear in three separate major triads as well as three minor ones. Meaning that unisons and octaves are more harmonically ambiguous than even thirds and sixths. The seconds, sevenths, and tritones do not appear in major or minor triads at all.

When writing harmonized melodies, we will want to keep in mind that perfect fifths and fourths will imply a specific harmonic center – the lower note of a perfect fifth and the upper note of a perfect fourth.[1] If this center is not the center being implied by the harmony of our composition, we will create a clashing expression. This makes perfect fifths and fourths difficult to use in the constant numeric interval method. Every time the melody note changes, we will hear the harmonized melody implying a new harmonic center, which may or may not correspond with the center of the harmony part of the piece. For this reason, thirds, sixths, octaves, and unisons are the most common intervals used in the constant numeric interval method. These intervals are consonant and yet do not clearly imply a specific harmonic center on their own.

In the chord tone method, it may be easier to use perfect fifths and fourths in the harmonization of some melody notes. Though, you should check to make sure that these intervals are implying a center that is in alignment with the harmonic expression you are trying to create.

1. From a related series analysis perspective, we will find that the interval of a perfect fifth has a related fundamental an octave below the lower note of the interval, and a perfect fourth has a related fundamental two octaves below the upper note of the interval. Therefore, we can say that the perfect fifth has a related fundamental with the note name of the lower note in the interval, and the perfect fourth has a related fundamental with the note name of the upper note in the interval. See page 163 for a table of related fundamentals associated with the various intervals.

Try Harmonizing a Melody

This one is pretty straightforward, so I won't bother outlining a multistep process. The invitation is to apply this idea of harmonizing a melody. You can use a melody you have already written, someone else's melody, or something entirely new. Try both the constant numeric method and the chord tone method. Remember to pay attention to how your harmonized melody is interacting with the harmony of the music.

- *Counterpoint* -

The Vertical and Horizontal Dimensions

Counterpoint is the use of multiple, simultaneous melodies or melodic lines. To write counterpoint, one must think in terms of both the relationships from one line to another at a given moment in time as well as in terms of the relationships within a line over time. Borrowing from the visual appearance of music notation, we can refer to the relationships between the notes of each line in a given moment of time as *vertical relationships* and those relationships within a line over time as *horizontal relationships*. Choosing effective and artistic intervals in both the vertical and horizontal dimensions is central to the creation of counterpoint.

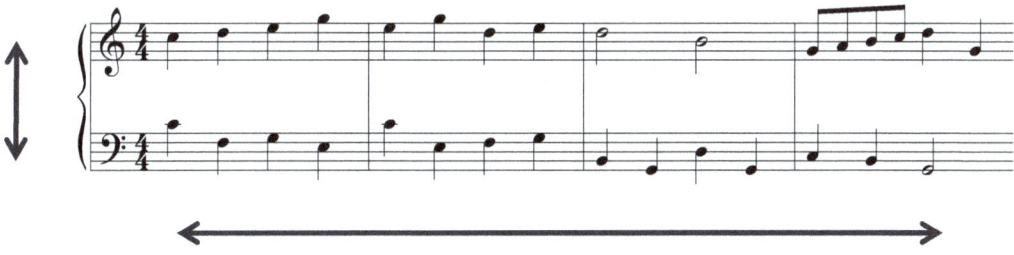

Contrapuntal Motion

Contrapuntal motion refers to the motion in pitch of the different melodic lines relative to one another. There are four types of contrapuntal motion:

1. *Parallel motion* refers to a situation where two lines move in the same direction (up or down in pitch) and by the same interval, both in terms of the number and quality of the interval.

2. *Similar motion* describes melodic lines that move in the same direction but not by the same interval.

3. *Contrary motion* occurs when melodic lines move in opposing directions.

4. *Oblique motion* is a kind of motion where one melodic line stays on a given pitch, while another melodic line changes.

Parallel Fifths and Octaves

Parallel fifths is a term we use to describe a situation where two melodic lines move in parallel motion with a vertical interval of a perfect fifth between the two lines. *Parallel octaves* describe a similar situation where the vertical interval is an octave. These scenarios are of special interest in contrapuntal writing and are traditionally avoided. The intervals of an octave and a perfect fifth are so consonant that we naturally group notes in these intervals together, as if they were one entity. If either of these highly consonant intervals occurs in serial, the sense of counterpoint – of multiple melodic lines – is lost. Instead the melodic lines blend together into the sense of a single, homogenized melodic line. With parallel fifths, there is the additional potential issue of implying an unintended harmonic center. Note that parallel fifths and octaves can indeed be used effectively in situations where a single, harmonized melodic voice is desired rather than a sense of counterpoint.

Listen to an example of parallel fifths on track 27 (disc 2). For contrast, an alternative version of the example, which eliminates the parallel fifths, is played afterward, separated by a brief pause.

Parallel Fifths

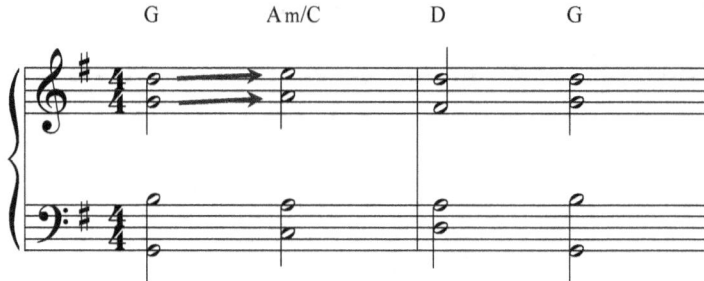

Without Parallel Fifths

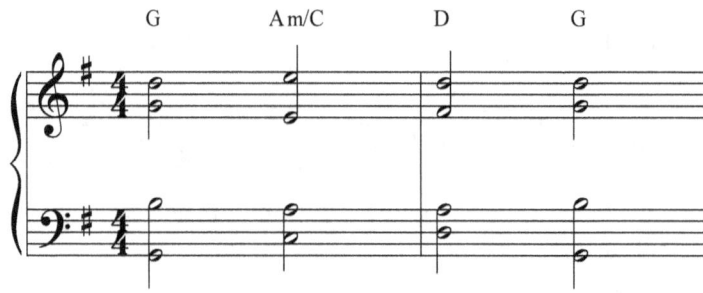

Analyze Bach, Write Counterpoint

Try writing some counterpoint. I recommend starting with two melodic lines and then working your way up to three or four.

There are two basic approaches here. You can write one melody in its entirety. Then, go back and write another line that harmonizes with the first. Depending on the piece, you could then write a third line that harmonizes with the other two and then write a fourth line and so on. Or you can write the all the melodic lines at the same time. Both approaches can work well, so feel free to experiment.

I find that counterpoint is manageable if you just slow down and take the time to consider all the relationships in the both the vertical and horizontal dimensions. It also will become important to focus on the harmonies that are being created or implied when writing counterpoint. Perfect fifths, especially, can have the effect of implying a chord based on the lower note of the perfect fifth. Perfect fourths can act in the same way with the upper note of the interval. Thirds and sixths may not be as clear as the perfect fifth or fourth, but they can imply a harmonic center as well in the context of a piece of music.[1] All of these relationships will create a rich harmonic environment even if only two notes are involved at any one time.

For some inspiration, listen to and study some music by Johann Sebastian Bach, who is widely regarded as the king of counterpoint. Bach's *Well Tempered Clavier* (which comprises two "books" or collections) is a very famous series of pieces that use counterpoint extensively. *The Goldberg Variations* are also wonderful examples of counterpoint.

1. For a detailed understanding of how intervals imply different harmonic centers, see *Related Series Analysis* on page 157 and especially the table on page 163.

- Transposing Instruments -

For many types of instruments, musicians can perform a piece of music on different versions of their instrument and produce transposed renditions of the piece. In other words, a musician can learn a piece, and using the same movements, produce the piece in a new scale just by switching to a different version of his or her instrument.

However, this creates an issue. What do you call the notes you are playing on each version of these instruments? For example, let's say a musician learns to play a piece on a trumpet. He or she could now perform the same movements on a different type of trumpet and produce the notes of the piece down a whole step, thereby transposing the piece into a new scale one whole step lower than the original. But now what sheet music shall we give this trumpet player? It makes sense to give the musician the original sheet music, the version he or she was using on the first trumpet. After all, the musician is performing the same movements. But now the sheet music does not match the actual notes that are being heard from the instrument.

This situation created what we now refer to as *concert* and *transposed pitch.* Concert pitch refers to the note names that are heard from an instrument, in a sense, the original pitch system. Transposed pitch, in the example above, would refer to the notes on the trumpet player's sheet music when he or she is playing the second trumpet and the notes the musician is reading do *not* match the sound coming from the instrument. So transposed pitch implies a modified or *transposed* system of pitches.

Transposing instruments are instruments that operate within a modified system of pitch like the second trumpet in our example. There are many transposing instruments in use today, and this is important to be aware of because if we do not take this transposition into account it can generate a lot of confusion.

Transposing instruments are named after the concert note that is produced when the performer plays a transposed C on the given instrument. For example, let's take the example we used above. A transposing trumpet produces pitches a whole step lower than the concert trumpet when the same mechanics or movements are performed on both trumpets. This means that when the movement to produce a C is executed on the transposing trumpet, the sound of a Bb will be produced. Therefore, we call this particular kind of transposing trumpet a *Bb trumpet.* There are also many other kinds of trumpets. For example, A, D, Eb, E, F, and G trumpets are all different kinds of transposing trumpets. There is also a commonly used concert or C trumpet.

Working With Transposing Instruments

The music notation that a musician reads when playing a transposing instrument is in *transposed pitch* not concert. This means we could give the same music notation to eight different trumpet players, with eight different kinds of trumpets, and get eight different corresponding notes.

So how can we write music notation for an ensemble of instruments all of which might have different transpositions? The answer, and this is important to keep in mind, is that we must transpose our notation to *compensate* for the transposition that will be applied by the transposing instruments so that the whole ensemble is in the correct key. This means, for example, that a Bb trumpet part will have to be written a whole step *up* so that when the trumpet transposes the music down a whole step it will match the rest of the ensemble. And then finally consider that if we are looking at a trumpet part and need to know what is being played in concert, then we will have to transpose the music on the trumpet part back *down* a whole step.

These scenarios describe the two basic operations that we need to be able to do: to move music from concert to transposed and to move music from transposed to concert. To do this correctly, we can remember and apply the following rules:

To convert from concert to transposed:

Find the interval and the direction of the interval (up or down) from the note in the name of the transposed instrument (for example Bb for the Bb trumpet) to C. Transpose the music by this interval and in this direction.

To convert from transposed to concert:

Find the interval and the direction of the interval from C to the note in the name of the transposed instrument. Transpose the music by this interval and in this direction.

- Creating and Capturing Sounds -

Digital Audio Workstations (DAWs) and Your Production Setup

A *digital audio workstation (DAW)* is a computer program designed for music production. DAWs are the tools we use as musicians to record, mix, and master our music (all of which will be defined in greater detail below). DAWs may be augmented by *plug-ins*, which are additional pieces of software that work in conjunction with a DAW.

To begin doing production work, you will need to select which DAW or DAWs (many producers use more than one, each for a different specialized purpose), plug-ins, and associated hardware like microphones and mixers you will be using. Taken all together, these different pieces of hardware and software form your *production setup*. Depending on what variety and level of music production you are interested in, requirements for your setup may vary dramatically. A production setup can range from a free DAW and nothing else all the way up to a professional-level studio of specially designed rooms, mixer boards the size of dinning room tables, and the whole works.

Creating the Base Sounds of Your Piece

The first stage of production is the creation of the base sounds that will be used in a musical piece. This is done through a combination of *recording*, *sampling*, and *synthesis*.

Recording

Recording is the process of using microphones to capture sounds in the external world. Recording always creates a reproducible form of the captured sound. In modern times, this generally means creating an audio file on a computer, but it could also mean creating a CD, tape, vinyl, or some other means of reproducing a single performance of a composition.

Types of Microphones

There are three primary categories of microphones that are used in music recording – *dynamic microphones*, *condenser microphones*, and *ribbon microphones*. Each of these types of microphones has some kind of a moving *diaphragm* that reacts to the sound waves in the air. The movement of the diaphragm is then translated into an electrical signal. How this general process occurs varies depending on the type of microphone.

In dynamic microphones, the diaphragm is attached to a coil that moves in and out of a magnetic field produced by a permanent magnet inside the microphone. The movement of the coil in and out of the magnetic field creates an electrical current that is used to record the movement of the sound waves in the microphone's environment. This is the same process that speakers use to produce sound from an electrical signal, only reversed. Dynamic microphones have relatively thick diaphragms and are considered fairly tough, physically durable microphones, in comparison to the other types of microphones. Dynamic microphones are good for recording loud, big sounds as well as percussive sounds that sharply increase in volume. Drums and distorted guitar amps are commonly recorded with dynamic microphones. Dynamic microphones are also common for live performances.

Condenser microphones use two parallel, electrically charged plates. The first plate moves in response to sound waves and acts as the diaphragm while the second is fixed. To charge the plates, an external power source must be provided for a condenser microphone. This often comes in the form of a *phantom power* feature, which can be activated on mixer boards or other hardware interfaces, though some condensers may use a battery. Be sure not to add phantom power to a microphone that does not use it, as this may damage your equipment. Once the plates of a condenser microphone are charged, an electrical field is created that stores electrical energy. A device that stores electrical energy in this manner is called a *capacitor*. As the distance between the moving and fixed plate changes, the amount of energy in the capacitor changes, and this changing electrical energy is used as the basis for recording the audio signal. Condenser microphones are more sensitive than dynamics and are generally better at capturing detail. Condenser microphones are known for a bright, crisp, full sound.

Ribbon microphones are somewhat less common. Ribbon microphones can be considered a type of dynamic microphone because they make use of a permanent magnet. However, in place of the coil design used in standard dynamic microphones, ribbon microphones use a very thin diaphragm that passes between two poles of the magnet. Ribbon microphones are the most sensitive of all microphones and are known for a warm sound. Ribbon microphones are said to capture somewhat less high frequency content, especially in comparison to condenser microphones.

Used in the right application, this can produce a very nice, natural sounding recording, minimizing some of the harshness that might be present in the recording made by a condenser.

Microphone Positioning

Once you have your hardware and software set up, you are ready to begin your recording session. There are two general ways in which we will purpose our microphones – as *spot microphones* and as *room microphones*. Spot microphones are placed close to a single sound source, a single instrument or vocalist, with the intention of recording just that sound source in relative isolation. Room microphone are positioned to capture the sounds in a more general area or space and as such are placed farther away from any one sound source. The distance between the sound source and the microphone affects the volume level of the recording in an exponential way – meaning that microphones that are far away from their sound sources produce increasingly quieter recordings.

In conjunction with this, we must also take into account something called *proximity effect*, which is a phenomenon where the presence of bass frequencies in a recording is amplified if the microphone is placed very close to the sound source. Considering these two factors, spot microphones will need to be positioned far enough away from the sound source to avoid proximity effect, while being close enough to produce a recording that isolates the sound source at a descent volume level. I recommend that you experiment with your own setup and equipment to find the ideal positions for your microphones. However, a good starting place for a spot microphone might be half a foot to a foot away from the sound source.

Setting Gain Levels

A *gain level* is a volume level that controls the level of a signal that is an input into a device. When recording, you will need to adjust the gain levels for each of your microphones. If the gain is set too high, a microphone will distort the sound. If the gain is set too low, the recording will be quieter and worse quality because any unwanted noise will be louder in comparison to the sound you are intending to capture. The basic technique for setting a gain level is to approximate the loudest sound you expect to record with a given microphone and set the gain so that this sound does not distort but reaches an otherwise high volume level on your system – ideally the highest possible without distorting, but leave yourself a little breathing room. Gain levels are generally set with mixing boards or whatever hardware interface you are using that connects to your microphone or microphones.

Editing

Recordings can be manipulated in DAWs in a process known as *editing*. Editing involves selecting preferred performances of various parts for various sections and merging all the desired recordings together. It also may involve removing, copying, looping (repeating a recording), or even reversing recordings (playing the end of a recording first and the beginning last).

Sampling

Sampling is the technique of using short recordings as the basis of constructing more complex musical parts. An example of sampling might be recording every drum and cymbal on a drum set and then sequencing the recordings together in a DAW to create a drum beat. Samplers are available that reproduce the sounds of all the instruments in the orchestra, the rock band, and more. These samplers call upon and manipulate very large numbers of recordings of different pitches, dynamic levels, and other performance parameters for each instrument to create realistic imitations.

MIDI Data and MIDI Controllers

MIDI data is a format of information that can store all the basic attributes of a musical performance, including notes, rhythms, and dynamic levels, on a computer or electronic device. Both samplers and synthesizers can record and play back MIDI data. *MIDI controllers* are electronic, hardware instruments, like electronic keyboards and drum pads, that allow you to connect to a computer and play a sampler or synthesizer in your DAW. MIDI controllers enable you to perform a musical part on the MIDI controller and record the MIDI data of what you are playing, if desired. MIDI controllers are very helpful additions to your production setup. The alternative is to manually select which notes, rhythms, and dynamic levels you want a sampler or synthesizer to play. This can be time consuming and usually cannot match the quality of using a MIDI controller, which allows you to capture a more nuanced performance.

Additive and Subtractive Synthesis

Synthesis is the creation of new timbres in the electronic medium. Synthesizers can be either hardware devices or can be software programs on a computer. There are two general schools of synthesis – *additive synthesis* and *subtractive synthesis.* Additive synthesis involves combining sine waves together at different volume levels to create an original timbre. Subtractive synthesis is the process of taking one or more complex timbres and *filtering* out spectrums of frequency so that the remaining frequencies produce the desired timbre. Subtractive synthesis has become the standard method of synthesis, but addictive synthesis is not uncommon.

Envelopes

Both additive and subtractive synthesizers will generally allow you to manipulate the *envelope* of the timbre or sound that you are creating. An envelope describes how a sound evolves from the start to the end of a single note. Commonly, envelopes are broken up into four stages – the *attack* (the beginning of the sound that increases in volume), the *sustain* (the portion of the sound that maintains in volume), the *decay* (the portion of the sound that declines in volume), and the *release* (the portion of the sound that occurs after the performer has stopped playing the note). These four phases are often abbreviated ADSR. Synthesizers will generally allow you to change the duration and volume levels of each of these stages.

Effects

Synthesizers also may offer various *effects* that can be used to further manipulate a sound. These generally overlap with the effects that can be applied during mixing and so will be covered in the next section.

Creating Musical Ideas in a DAW

The DAW can be a very powerful creative workspace. I invite you to try the following variation of the *Writing Themes* activity we did at the end of Chapter Nine.[1] Here, try creating a chord progression, melody, or both but this time using a DAW. You can use recording, sampling, or synthesis to create your music. With these various methods of creating sound, you will have a large array of timbres at your disposal. So take some extra time to explore the timbre of the sounds you are creating and how you can vary them in your production setup.

1. *Writing Themes*, page 278

- Mixing and Mastering -

After all of the sounds of a musical piece are created, either through recording, sampling, or synthesis, we are ready for the next step – *mixing*. All recorded or synthesized sounds are placed in *tracks* in a DAW. Each track represents a stream of audio. Each independent part of a composition will need its own track. Mixing consists of digitally modifying the audio of each track to produce a culmination of the sound in all the tracks, which we call the *mix*. After mixing a piece, we will modify the audio of the entire mix as a whole. This is referred to as *mastering* as it involves working with the *master track*, which is a track that contains the audio of all the other tracks in the mix. After mixing and mastering a musical piece, the tracks will be combined together into a single audio file, which can be distributed and shared.

In this section, we will examine the tools available to us in the mixing and mastering process. We will go through them in order of how one might generally approach mixing and mastering a track from start to finish, but, as with many other creative endeavors we talk about in this book, you'll have to find the process that works best for you.

Balancing Levels

Balancing the volume levels of the tracks relative to one another is one of the primary tasks of the mixing process. A useful strategy for balancing volume levels is to mute all the tracks except for a small group and work on balancing the levels for just that group. You can then progressively add in more tracks balancing each one at a time or, if necessary, work on other small groups of tracks until you are ready to progress to larger groups.

My general approach is to start with any percussion or drum tracks first (sometimes there may be many drum tracks for different drum and cymbal sounds). I'll then add in the bass and find a good balance between the drums and the bass. Next are the harmony parts. If there are a lot of harmonic or accompanying instruments, I may chose to mute the bass and drums and balance these separately before proceeding. Otherwise, I'll add in each harmony part one at a time and find a good volume level for each. Lastly, I will mix in the foreground and background melodic parts. Once again, balancing these separately if there are a lot of them or adding them in one at a time.

As a general rule, it is best to decrease the volume levels of tracks below the level of their original recording to achieve the relative balance that is desired rather than adding volume beyond the original level. Adding volume beyond the level of the original recording may decrease the sound quality of your music. Considering this, you may want to set all your tracks at an initial average volume level somewhat below the level of the original recording. This way you will have room to add volume to tracks without going above their original level.

Panning

Panning controls whether a track sounds as if it is coming from the left or right. I will generally do panning while I'm balancing the levels of the tracks. The general principle to remember with panning is that sounds on the periphery are less in focus while sounds in the center are more in focus. Kick drums, bass parts, and the primary melody are almost always in the center. Harmonic parts and secondary melodic parts are commonly panned to one side or another.

Ensuring a Good Foundation

Sometimes over-relying on fancy effects and the later steps of the mixing process can be an easy trap to fall into. Make sure the basics form a solid foundation. With no other processing, a mix that has well balanced volume and pan levels should already produce good results in terms of the separation of the parts and the control of the musical focus. At this stage, take the time to get a base mix that you are happy with. This will make the rest of the process much easier.

Automation

Automation is the term we use to describe how a setting or *parameter* in our DAW changes over time. Volume automation is commonly a crucial component of a good mix. Tracks may need to have different volume levels in different sections. They may need to *fade in* or *fade out*, requiring an increase or decrease in volume. You may decide to work with volume levels in two separate phases: first, setting good general volume levels and, second, adding in automation.

I almost always start the mixing process by getting good volume levels for the tracks, but I often end the mixing process by doing the volume automation. I do this because it is often harder to work with the general volume levels of the tracks after adding automation. Waiting on the automation helps keep the mixing process more flexible in case I want to go back and change the general volume level of a track in one of the later steps of the mixing process.

Keep in mind, as we go along through different mixing tools that most settings in DAWs can be automated and that this may be an added consideration for each step.

Reverb and Delay

Reverb and *delay* are two related types of sound processing that create the sense that an instrument or voice is in a certain type of space or environment, like a small or large room or a room with hard reflective surfaces or soft, sound-absorbing ones. These processors accomplish this by adding sound to your mix that imitates how real sounds reflect off of surfaces in different environments. An instrument played in a room, for example, will generate sound that travels directly to your ears but it will also generate sound that reflects off walls and objects in the room, which then is subsequently detected by your ears.

This reflected sound will reach your ears slightly later than the sound that traveled directly to you. Larger rooms will create a bigger difference between the original sound and the reflected sound because the reflected sound has a farther distance to travel before reaching your ears.

Delay generates individual, perceptible echoes of your original sound. Reverb is similar, except that it generates a diffuse blur of sound that follows the original sound. Both of these effects can occur in natural environments, although in music they are sometimes made more extreme than anything found in nature.

Reverb parameters will vary somewhat between processors but will generally involve controls that affect the length of the reverb, the timing and entrance of the reverb, the volume level of the reverb, and sometimes the frequency ranges that are emphasized in the reverb. Delay processors will include parameters that change the volume level of the echoes and their timing. Most delays include the option to either time the echoes to a note duration in the tempo of the music or otherwise time the echoes to a given amount of time unrelated to the rhythm of the piece.

Reverb and Delay Considerations for Recording

The general paradigm in today's music is to record in such a way that the least reverb and delay possible is captured. By creating a sound without any natural reverb or delay, the addition of simulated reverb can be done more easily and more cleanly. However, it is also possible to make recordings that intentionally capture the natural reverb and delay acoustics of a space. If you choose this approach, you will probably forgo adding any simulated reverb in the mixing stage.

In the traditional recording paradigm of adding reverb in the mixing process, you may want to consider the space you are recording in and the effect that this will have on the recording. The ideal for the traditional approach is to minimize the presence of hard, reflective surfaces and maximize soft, sound-absorbing materials.

Another consideration is the natural frequencies[1] of the room you are recording in. Each dimension of a room will have a corresponding natural frequency that vibrates evenly in that space as well as at harmonics of that frequency. We could also call these frequencies *resonant frequencies* or *resonances*. These resonances may result in unwanted frequencies being emphasized in your recording. These issues may be reduced by recording in a room where the dimensions of the room are not evenly divisible by each other. Irregular shapes and angles may also help to prevent waves from reflecting back and forth between surfaces, thus creating resonances.

1. *Natural Frequencies*, page 34

Dry and Wet Signal

In some of these mixing processors, you may hear the terms *dry* and *wet* signal. The dry signal is the sound prior to being altered by a processor. The wet signal is the sound after being altered by a processor.

Applications of Reverb

Recall that sounds that are close to us and centered within a mix are the most in focus, while sounds that are far away and on the periphery merge into the background. One way of bringing sounds into focus is to reduce their reverb, thereby creating the sense that they are closer to us. And in reverse, sounds can be placed into the background by adding more reverb.

Lower pitched sounds, such as kick drums and bass parts, are often left without reverb because they become muddy otherwise.

Auxiliary Tracks

Auxiliary tracks or *aux tracks* are tracks that receive a signal from another track and process it before outputting its signal to the mix. Generally, other tracks will have an *aux send* parameter that designates how much (what volume level of) signal is sent from that track to a given aux track. Reverb and delay are almost always added with aux tracks. The reason being that aux tracks allow you to create one reverb or delay setting and apply this processing to different tracks, at different volume levels. This is ideal for reverb and delay processing, which is intended to create the sense of the ensemble being in one space or environment. Aux tracks give us the ability to easily adjust all the reverb and delay settings to create the sense of the same environment while maintaining the freedom to reduce or amplify the volume level of the reverb or delay on a track-by-track basis. Aux tracks are set up differently in different DAWs, and you will need to consult your own resources on your specific DAW to see how this is accomplished in your setup.

Note that some mixes use multiple reverb or delay processors with different settings. Nevertheless, use aux tracks – one for each type – as you may want to use a given setting on multiple tracks.

Equalization (EQ)

Equalization (EQ) can be defined as a frequency-dependent volume control. In other words, EQ emphasizes or de-emphasizes different frequency ranges in volume. This type of processing is used for a variety of purposes. To start with, EQ can be used to make tracks sound either brighter or duller.

As with volume levels, it is best to subtract volume rather than add volume when possible. A sound can be made brighter by decreasing the level of the low frequencies so that the high frequencies are relatively louder. A sound can be made duller by decreasing the level of the high frequencies so that the low frequencies are relatively louder.

Every range of frequency has certain expressive characteristics and these may be important to know to achieve the ideal EQ for a given track or sound. For example, the lower-mid frequencies are often responsible for a muddy, overly dull sound when they are overemphasized. Mid-highs can create clarity but are harsh if they are out of balance. The highest frequencies are mostly heard in un-pitched, percussive sounds.

Lastly, EQ can be used to reduce the level of unwanted, extraneous noise that may have gotten picked up in a recording – the breath of a singer or a microphone that a musician accidentally bumped into are two possible culprits.

In all of the above applications, it can be helpful to find a way in your setup to isolate frequency ranges so that you can listen to just a certain band of frequencies within a certain track. This will allow you find exactly where that noise is residing or where exactly that irksome aspect of a timbre is coming from or where a desired expression can be brought out and enhanced.

Dynamics Processors

There are four common types of processing devices that affect the *dynamic range* of your music – the spectrum of volume from your quietest to loudest sounds. These are the *compressor*, the *expander*, the *limiter*, and the *gate*. There are both hardware and software versions of these devices. A compressor reduces the dynamic range of music, while an expander creates a larger dynamic range. Another way of saying this is that compression will make softer sounds louder, while making louder sounds softer. Whereas expansion will make softer sounds softer, while making louder sounds louder. A limiter is a more extreme form of a compressor. A gate is a more extreme form of an expander.

Interestingly, by condensing the range of soft to loud sounds while keeping the loudest sounds at the same level, compressors and limiters have the effect of increasing the average volume level of a track of music. This will make the music sound louder overall but with less variation. If you feel inclined to change the volume level of your track as you are listening to it because you can't hear the quiet parts or the loud parts are uncomfortably loud, this is an indication that you need more compression. If your track feels like it has lost some of its life and depth because there is so little room for sounds to express changes in volume, this may be an indication that you need less compression. Compression can also help to add more of a powerful presence to a sound. Music in need of more compression can sometimes sound weak or small.

Expanders and gates are less commonly used. The primary use for these devices is to eliminate unwanted noise from the mix. Often, unwanted noises are recorded at low volume levels. By applying an expander or gate, these quiet noises can be reduced in volume to make them inaudible while the sounds that were intentionally recorded will be maintained due to their relatively high volume levels.

Threshold and Ratio

Dynamics processors share a few common parameters or settings. Each will have a *threshold* setting and a *ratio*. The threshold defines the volume level at which the device will begin to affect the sound. For compressors and limiters, this is the minimum volume level *required* to activate the device. For expanders and gates, this is the maximum volume *allowed* for the device to active.

The ratio dictates how much the volume will be changed once the threshold is crossed. A compressor with a 3:1 ratio will reduce the volume of a sound that is 3 *decibels* (a unit of measurement for the volume or amplitude of sound) over the threshold to a level that is only 1 decibel over the threshold. An expander with a 3:1 ratio will reduce the volume of a sound that is 1 decibel below the threshold to a level that is 3 decibels below the threshold.

Strong and Light Compression Ratios

Although standards change depending on style, a 2:1 compression ratio is generally considered mild compression. A 3:1 compression ratio is a moderate level of compression. Ratios in the 4:1 to 5:1 range are common, somewhat stronger levels of compression. A 10:1 ratio or higher is limiter-level compression. This kind of compression is generally used in the mastering phase and, generally, uses a high threshold, meaning that it will not be activated as often.

I defined a limiter as an extreme form of a compressor and a gate as an extreme form of a expander. We can now be a bit more specific. Limiters are compressors with high ratios, and gates are expanders with high ratios. In either case, the threshold may be less extreme for limiters and gates. This means that the overall effect of a limiter or gate may not necessarily be any more extreme than a compressor or expander. It does, however, mean that these devices will alter the sound more dramatically when the given threshold volume level is crossed.

Classical or orchestral music is generally mixed without compression. A wide spectrum of dynamics is an essential aspect of much classical music. We will want to preserve this in the mixing process. Pop and electronic styles frequently use the strongest compression, with styles like R&B and rock coming in not far behind. Generally more acoustic music, including many jazz styles, will use lighter compression or no compression.

Envelope Settings

Similar to a synthesizer, many dynamics processors will also feature envelope settings. These settings will control how quickly the processor activates once a sound crosses the threshold and how long it takes for the processor to stop activating once the sound goes below the threshold.

Other Secondary Effects

Volume level, pan, reverb, delay, EQ, and dynamics processing make up the primary mixing tools or effects that you will encounter and use on a reoccurring basis. In addition to these, there other effects that may be used in special cases. Presented below are two of the more common types – *distortion* and *chorus*.

Note that you may end up using these in the "creation of your base sounds," as I described it earlier, before you even get into the mixing process. You also may end up adding them or adjusting them toward the end of the mixing process.

Distortion

Commonly used in guitar amplifiers, *distortion* boosts the volume level of a sound's upper partials (in other words, frequencies) creating a richer texture. This effect may be useful if you are looking to add energy into your music through timbre.

Chorus

A *chorus* simulates the effect that is produced by multiple performers playing a given part. When multiple performers play a part in unison, there will be very minor variations in how each musician performs the part, even among very skilled players. A chorus effect will add in small variations to give us the impression that many instances of a given sound are being performed. This effect can be used realistically or used with more extreme settings to produce an electronic sounding effect in our music.

Layering

Layering is a common recording technique where the exact same musical part is recorded multiple times by a single performer. This creates, in a natural way, the same effect that chorus digitally imitates. Layering creates a bigger, fuller sound, but without the electronic sound that will often arise from using a chorus effect. Layering is very common in vocals and can be an extremely useful recording technique.

Mixing and Mastering a Track

For your reference, the mixing and mastering process consists of the following basic steps either in this exact order or something close to it:

Mixing
1. Balance Levels
2. Panning
3. Reverb
4. EQ
5. Dynamics Processing
6. Automate Volume Levels

Mastering (applied to master track only after mixing)
1. EQ (if needed)
2. Compression and Limiting

You can try out this process on any of the music you created in the *Creating Musical Ideas in a DAW* activity.[1] However, you also may consider coming back to the mixing and mastering process at the end of the next chapter where we will be walking through the process of creating a full-length piece of music.[2]

You may consider applying reverb after EQ and dynamics processing if you feel that the reverb will inhibit your ability to listen to your music with detail as you are working through the mixing process. However, personally I often have a hard time getting into the music and seeing how it all comes together without adding reverb early on. You can add reverb before or after EQ and dynamics processing depending on the situation and what you find works for your process.

As you go through these steps, listen to your music on multiple sound systems. Try headphones, as well as low quality and high quality speaker systems. You want your music to sound as good as possible in as many different systems as possible. In particular, make sure that your panning does not sound too extreme in headphones and make sure that bass sounds are not overpowering on systems with good quality bass response while also hopefully being at least audible in lower quality speakers or headphones.

1. *Creating Musical Ideas in a DAW*, page 325
2. *Creating a Complete Composition*, page 380

Chapter Twelve
Development and Structure

- Structural Elements of Notation -

Thin Double Bar Lines

A *thin double bar line*, as shown below, can be used to indicate the end of one section of music and the beginning of another.

Measure Numbers

Often measures are numbered from the first to last measure in the piece. These *measure numbers*, as we call them, can be written below each measure or at the beginning of each line. Often, measure numbers are written below each measure for scores and written at the beginning of each line for parts, but you can also use either approach, depending on what you prefer.

Score

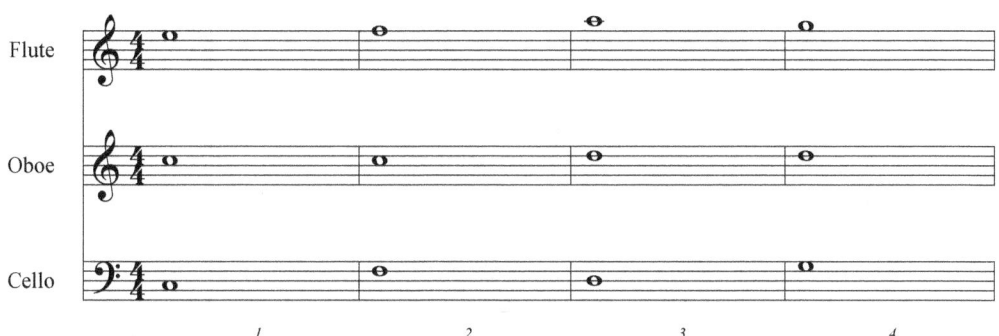

Part

Rehearsal Markings

New sections can be labeled with *rehearsal markings*. Rehearsal markings either use letters or measure numbers, which are placed above the staff, and are often outlined with a box. When rehearsal markings use letters, we call these markings *rehearsal letters*. Rehearsal markings are used to refer to a specific place in a piece of music and are commonly used in rehearsals to communicate to the musicians of an ensemble that they should begin playing at the given rehearsal marking. Please note that rehearsal markings are a different concept than the section names in structures discussed on page 344.

The first rehearsal marking should occur at the second section because rehearsing the first section of a piece is referred to as starting from the beginning, or as we musicians often say "from the top." Rehearsal letters start at the letter "A" and continue through the alphabet without repeating any letters (unlike section names). If more rehearsal markings are needed after reaching "Z," we use the markings "AA," "AB," "AC," and so on.

If rehearsal markings are using measure numbers, then we simply write the number of the measure the new section begins with.

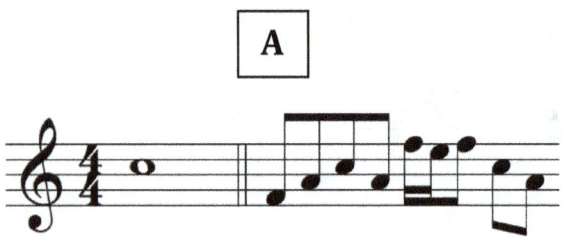

D.C. al Fine

In addition to the double bar line repeat symbols discussed on page 110, repeats may also be indicated with Italian phrases. "Da Capo al Fine" means "from the head (or beginning) to the end" in Italian. Upon reaching this instruction, the performer goes to the beginning and plays the piece until the word fine and a double bar line appear in the middle of the notation. Generally, in sheet music this phrase will be abbreviated as "D.C. al Fine."

As an example, the following notation…

…is equivalent to…

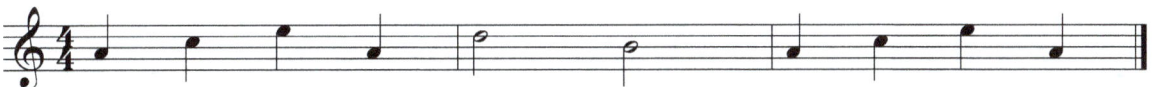

D.S. al Fine

"Dal Segno al Fine" means "from the sign to the end." This instruction, which is abbreviated as "D.S. al Fine," indicates that the performer should return to the symbol shown in the example below at the beginning of the second bar and play until reaching the fine instruction accompanied by a double bar line. For example, this…

…means…

D.C. al Coda and D.S. al Coda

A *coda* is an ending section of a piece of music. A coda is written beginning on a new line at the end of a piece's notation. The coda is marked by a coda sign that appears like this: ⊕.

The two previously described instructions can be modified by replacing the word "fine" with "coda." When this is done, it means that the performer should return to either the beginning (D.C. al Coda) or the sign (D.S. al Coda) depending on the instruction and continue until a coda sign is reached in the middle of the piece. Upon reaching the coda sign in the middle of the piece, the performer jumps straight to the coda section, found at the end of the notation and marked by a second coda sign, and finishes the piece from there.

For example, the notation of a D.S. al Coda below…

…is equivalent to…

- Thematic Development -

Motifs and Themes Revisited

Motifs and *themes* are musical ideas that reoccur, usually in different forms, throughout a musical piece. Motifs and themes form the basic building blocks or patterns around which the whole composition is constructed. Motifs tend to be shorter than themes, commonly lasting less than a measure. Themes usually last for several measures but generally occupy no more than a section of a piece.

- ❖ I originally presented this concept in Chapter Two. See *Motifs and Themes* on page 51. For a broader context, see *The Dance of Musical Elements* as a whole on page 50.

Introducing Development

In Chapter Two, we said that "meaning is derived from the fundamental dichotomy of commonality and difference."[1] We have explored this truth in many ways throughout the book so far. We have looked at how proportional relationships in both pitch and rhythm create a sense of either connection through simple relationships or disconnection through complex relationships. We have looked at how changes in the various gradated spectra affect musical expression through musical elements like tempo changes, crescendos and diminuendos, emphases, and so on. In every case, a few fundamental questions arise. Is this element staying the same or changing over time? Does this element express connection or disconnection? Is there a sense of commonality or a sense of difference?

Now we will explore how the principles of commonality and difference play out in the *development of our musical ideas* – in other words, the way that our themes or motifs change over time. The degree of commonality or difference between musical ideas can be thought of as another spectrum of musical expression. In Chapter Two, I introduced this spectrum as *the spectrum of change*.[2] The more commonality, the lower the energy and the more we feel a sense of resolution and stability. The more difference, the higher the energy and the more we feel a sense of excitement and exploration.

1. *What Is Meaning?*, page 46
2. *The Spectrum of Change*, page 51

Repetition creates a low energy expression.
Variation creates a high energy expression.

By examining the commonality or difference between musical ideas, we add a layer of complexity on top of the seven basic spectra. Throughout the book so far, we have been primarily looking at the characteristics of different musical elements or ideas on the seven spectra and the expressive implications of those characteristics. We have looked at chord progressions, melodies, rhythms, and so on. All of these were combinations of characteristics on the seven basic spectra, each with a different expressive result. Now, we will focus on the *relationships between* different musical elements or ideas. And of course, we will be uncovering what expressions arise from these relational characteristics as well. At this level of analysis, there will be more information to keep track of because we must consider both the expression of musical ideas on their own as well as in relationships to other ideas.

Less Is More

Very little material is needed in terms of musical themes or motifs to create a good composition. Often less is more in this realm. A single melodic fragment of just one measure or less is sufficient to create a long and elaborate piece of music.[1] My recommendation is to determine your central theme or motif for a composition early on in the creative process and then focus on creating variations and developments of this idea. You may work with a handful of different themes, especially if they are related, but even a single, simple idea works well.

1. Later in this chapter, we will see a clear example of this in our study of Beethoven's Fifth Symphony. See *Analysis of Beethoven's Fifth Symphony* on page 350.

The Basic Developmental Concept

The basic concept of development is to take a musical idea, change some aspects of it while keeping other aspects of it the same. The more aspects that are changed, the more sense of variation is created. Broadly speaking, all possible developmental processes can be contained in the notion of changing some aspects of the seven spectra in a musical idea while keeping others the same. In the following discussion, we will take a look at some specific techniques and processes that are commonly used to develop musical themes. However, extrapolating off the basic concept of changing some aspects of a theme while keeping others, you will be able to create your own developmental processes to suit your creative ventures.

Sequence

One of the most common developmental techniques is the *sequence*. To create a sequence, we take a musical idea and shift all the notes up or down by a given interval. Sequences can be performed by moving all the notes by a numeric interval, changing the quality of the interval so that the notes stay within a given scale, or it can be performed by moving all the notes by the exact same interval, in terms of both number and quality, regardless of the scale. The former version of this technique can be called a *diatonic sequence*, while the latter is called a *chromatic* or *exact sequence*. A chromatic or exact sequence is equivalent to transposing a musical idea.

Listen to the example of a sequence shown below on track 28 (disc 2).

Temporal Scaling

Temporal scaling is the term I give to a transformation where all the durations of sounds in a musical idea are uniformly multiplied or divided by a given number. For example, if we created a variation of an idea by doubling the length of all the notes, that would be an example of temporal scaling. In the example of temporal scaling below, a variation of a three-note motif is created by reducing the duration of each note by half.

Listen to this example of temporal scaling on track 29 (disc 2).

Changing Gradated Spectra While Maintaining Proportionality

The sequence maintains the same intervals between notes while changing the pitch of the musical idea. Phrased differently, we can say that a sequence changes the pitch of a musical idea while maintaining the pitch proportionality of the idea as well as all the other spectra. Temporal scaling changes the duration or time aspect of the musical idea on a gradated spectrum while maintaining the temporal proportionality and other spectra. These are both examples of changing a gradated spectrum while maintaining a corresponding form of proportionality – sequences in terms of pitch, temporal scaling in terms of time or rhythm.

Inversion

To *invert* a musical idea we will begin on the same pitch and then proceed to use the same intervals as the original idea but in the opposite direction. So if a melody begins by going up a whole step, then the inversion of that melody will begin by going down a whole step.

Listen to the following example of inversion on track 30 (disc 2).

Retrograde

A *retrograde* theme is a musical idea that is played backwards, so that the first note becomes the last note and last note becomes the first note.

Listen to the following example of a retrograde transformation on track 31 (disc 2).

Retrograde Inversion

Retrograde and inversion are often combined to create what we might visually imagine as upside down, backward variations of the original musical idea. These variations are referred to as *retrograde inversions*.

Listen to the example below on track 32 (disc 2).

Same Rhythm or Pitch

A simple, yet effective, form of variation is to keep the rhythm constant while changing the pitches of the notes in a theme or, alternatively, to keep the pitches of the notes the same while changing the rhythm.

Listen to an example of the same rhythm technique on track 33 (disc 2) and listen to an example of the same pitch technique on track 34 (disc 2).

Same Rhythm

Same Pitch

Common Section

Another frequently used technique is to keep one section of a musical idea the same while changing other surrounding sections. For example, you could keep the same beginning to a theme but vary the ending. Or you could keep the same ending and vary the beginning. Or you might find a specific motif in the middle of a melodic phrase that stays constant in the next phrase while the surrounding musical material changes.

As an example, the melody below, which you can listen to on track 35 (disc 2), uses a common beginning section between two phrases.

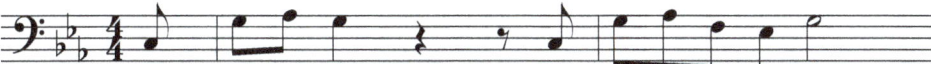

Combining Techniques

There are, of course, many more developmental transformations that we could use in our music. Also consider that just as we combined retrograde and inversion, all of these techniques could be combined. For example, what would it sound like to create a sequence with durations that are doubled in length? Or use a common beginning to a phrase but alter the second half of the phrase so that it is inverted?

- Structural Development -

Sections and Structures

We have already mentioned the concept of a musical *section*, and now we will address this notion more fully. A *section* is a segment of a musical composition that includes all the applicable melodic and accompaniment parts of the piece. A section is commonly 16 or 32 bars long, though it can be more or less. A given section can be represented and named with a letter of the alphabet. This letter refers to the general collection of musical ideas present in that section. A section can be repeated and even repeated with variations and still be referred to with the same letter. The series of section letters that describes a piece makes up the *form* or *structure* of the musical composition. For example, a common form, referred to as *song form*, can be represented as AABA. This means that a section is played, repeated, followed by a new section, and then the original section is repeated a final time. The three A sections of this structure do not have to be identical but merely contain the same essential melodic, harmonic, and rhythmic elements.

More complex structures can be created where each section has a certain purpose or has certain musical requirements such as being in a particular key or time signature. We'll look at some examples of common structures in the next section.

Macro Level Development

The concept of *structural development* is the macro equivalent of thematic development. Rather than looking at how one musical idea progresses to another, we are looking at how one section progresses to another. At this big-picture level perspective, we can see and deal with the overall shape and flow of a composition.

From Home, Out on a Journey, and Back

On the broadest level, most compositions follow a large-scale motion from low energy to high energy, and back to low energy. Put another way, the basic story of all stories is to start at home, to leave home on an adventure (which often builds into a climax), and to come back home. This motion occurs once in the big picture but occurs many times in smaller ways within sections and within sections of sections.

Distribution of Energy

In addition to the progression of the overall energy of the piece, the other primary concern of structural development is the distribution or balance of energy through different parts and different spectra. In some sections, the harmony parts may be more energetic, while in others the percussion parts or the melody may become more energetic. In some sections, one harmony part may be active while another rests and in the following section the parts might reverse their roles. Sections may create expressive energy mostly through rhythm while the pitch proportionality remains fairly simple. In contrasting sections, the composer may reverse the situation so that the rhythm becomes less energetic, while the pitch proportionality grows in complexity. Playing with these and other distributions of energy is the art of structuring and developing a composition. The goal is to create variety and interest in balance with continuity and connectivity, all in the service of the general narrative, story arc, or expressive motion of the piece.

Simple and Complex Structures

A simple structure contributes its own expression to a composition, as does a complex one. The effect of this expression unfurls slowly and in that way is subtle, but it has a very real effect. Structures with more parts and with more complex proportional relationships between the durations of sections produce more complex expressions.

Structural Gravity Revisited

Proportions in the durations of sections can set up expectations. Sections are commonly multiples of eight measures and create simple proportional relationships as a result. Failing this, we expect sections to be a multiple of four measures. Note that sometimes stylistic norms may influence our expectations here. For example, blues is traditionally structured in groups of twelve measures. When a new section arrives earlier than expected, there is a sense of surprise. When it comes later than expected, there is a sense of anticipation.

We can consider the EDM or electronic piece on track 71 (disc 1) as an example. This track starts out with a typical structure – first, a standard eight measure section and then another. The third section, however, sets up the expectation for a transition or resolution after eight bars but does not deliver it. Instead, many of the parts stop for two measures and a buildup is created to the new section, which is even more energetic than expected when it finally arrives. This delay of two measures past the expected eight measure section creates increased interest and anticipation. It also helps to signal that a bigger than average transition is coming.

- Possibilities in Form -

In this section, we will look at a few examples of common structures or forms from different stylistic traditions. Feel free to try these structures in your own work or to create variations of them.

Verse, Chorus, and Bridge

In many popular styles, songs are organized into *verses*, *choruses*, and *bridges*. These terms are generally used with pieces of music that have lyrics.

Each time the verse repeats, we hear the same melody and chords but a different set of lyrics.

The chorus is meant to be the most memorable part of the song and usually contains a catchy melody. The lyrics of the chorus never change. This means that people can often sing along, literally creating a chorus of singers.

The bridge is an entirely new section that is meant to provide some variety a little later in the song, most commonly after a chorus.

A typical pop song might use a structure that goes something like this:

Intro
Verse
Chorus
Verse
Chorus
Bridge
Verse
Chorus
Chorus
Ending

There are many variations of this concept and no definite standard organization of these parts. Next time you listen to a song that feels like it could be described in these terms, see if you can recognize where the verses, choruses, and bridges are and how long they last.

Pre-Chorus

Sometimes, another section is added to these structures right before the chorus. Known as the *pre-chorus*, this section, like the chorus, uses the same lyrics each time it is played. Its purpose is to set up the content of the main chorus section and provide another set of related musical ideas that repeat throughout the song.

The Jazz Tune

In the jazz tradition, there are two primary sections – the *head* and the *solos*. The structural norm in jazz styles is to play the head, followed by the solos, followed by a repetition of the head, creating an ABA form. The head of the *tune* (a common term for a jazz composition) contains a melody and chord progression that serve as the archer for the piece. The solos consist of repetitions of the same chord progression used in the head with a given musician improvising a solo. The chord progression may be repeated multiple times for one soloist, and many soloists may perform. When all the solos are finished, the head is repeated to end the piece.

The Classical Tradition: Movements, Forms, and Small Structures

In the classical tradition, musical compositions are often organized into *movements,* which are long sections of music equivalent in length to full jazz, rock, or pop songs. Movements are separated by a conclusion of the musical material and a silence. There are several types of multi-movement works. Among the most well-known is the *symphony*, which is a composition for full orchestra that generally consists of four movements. A multi-movement work like a symphony is perhaps comparable, in length, to an album in contemporary styles like jazz, rock, and pop.

Each movement of a classical work has its own structure, with its own sections. In turn, these sections have their own internal structures, which are sometimes described as *small structures*. We will examine three examples of small structures – *simple binary*, *ternary*, and *rounded binary*. We will then proceed to look at three common structures that apply to musical movements as a whole – *sonata form*, *minuet and trio*, and *rondo*.

Simple Binary, Ternary, and Rounded Binary

Simple binary equates to an AB form, while *ternary* describes an ABA form. Repeats are often added to binary creating an AABB form. In ternary, the B and second A are generally repeated together creating an AABABA form.

Rounded binary is a variation on binary where the second half of the B section comes back to the material in the A section. When repeats are added to rounded binary, we get an AABB where the second half of the Bs are like short A sections.

Structural Functions

Each section of these small structures has its own specific function. We will see these same functions mirrored in the larger structures of movements. In simple binary, the A presents a theme and the B provides a contrasting idea to complement the A. The sections of ternary form fulfill three specific functions – *exposition*, *contrasting middle*, and *recapitulation*. The exposition introduces the main thematic material. The contrasting middle creates variation and complementary material. The recapitulation serves to rearticulate the main thematic material and provide a sense of conclusion. Rounded binary follows the same pattern of functions as ternary.

Sonata Form

Sonata form is a type of large-scale ternary form often used for the first movement of a symphony. The three sections of the sonata form are closely aligned in function with the small ternary form. The first section fulfills the role of exposition, while the last section serves the function of recapitulation. However, the middle section is said to perform the role of *development*. This function is similar to that of the contrasting middle and, indeed, does provide a sense of contrast. However, the development section of the sonata is more concerned with creating variations of the work's thematic material rather than creating new contrasting themes. It is common practice to use the descriptions of these three functions – exposition, development, and recapitulation – to refer to the three sections of the sonata form. The recapitulation is sometimes followed by a coda section for additional ending material.

The exposition and recapitulation of the sonata form have their own specific, internal forms. The development is more loosely structured and does not adhere to any strict norms. The exposition and recapitulation follow a type of binary structure, working fundamentally with two themes. There are variations of these structures. However, the basic form consists of the following parts: *first theme*, *transition*, *second theme*, and *closing*.

In sonata form, the exposition and recapitulation follow specific harmonic guidelines. In the exposition, the first theme will establish the primary key of the whole movement. The transition will then lead us into second theme, which is played in a new key. Generally, if the first theme is played in a major key, the secondary theme will be played in the major key starting on the dominant or fifth scale degree of the primary key. If the first theme is played in a minor key, generally the second theme will be played in the relative major key (in other words, the major key starting on the mediant or third degree of the primary key). The second theme is followed by a closing statement in the key of the second theme.

The development will often explore several keys and does not have specific harmonic guidelines. However, it does serve the purpose of setting up the return to the primary key at the beginning of recapitulation. Often, this is accomplished by emphasizing the dominant harmony of the primary key at the end of the development section.

The recapitulation follows a similar structure to the exposition, except that this time the secondary theme is played in the primary key.

- ❖ If you are wondering about how pieces in sonata form are able to incorporate multiple scales, don't worry. We will cover this in more detail in *Chapter Fourteen* (page 412) and especially in the section entitled *Modulation* (also page 412).

Sonata Works vs. Sonata Form

Note that the term sonata may also be used to describe a multi-movement work, where at least one of the movements follows sonata form. Therefore, be sure to distinguish between sonata as a type of work and the sonata form.

Minuet and Trio

The *minuet and trio*, like sonata form, is, on a general level, a large-scale, ternary form. The minuet and trio is often in 3/4 time and is a standard choice for the third movement of a symphony. The functional layout of the minuet and trio is the same as the small ternary form – exposition, contrasting middle, and recapitulation.

Rondo

A *rondo form* contains a single *reprise* or repeated section alternated with new contrasting sections. Rondo form represents an endless pattern that can be conceptualized as ABACADAE and so on. Commonly, rondo form continues out to five sections creating an ABACA form.

- Analysis of Beethoven's Fifth Symphony -

In the next two sections, we will analyze two famous compositions from the common practice period of classical music – the first movement of Beethoven's Fifth Symphony and Pachelbel's Canon in D. These pieces are masterful examples of development as well as general composition and musical expression. However, as we will see, the two pieces approach the issue of development in dramatically different ways.

Beethoven's Fifth

Beethoven's Fifth is one of the most famous and, indeed, one of the most superb examples of the development of a theme. Beethoven builds an entire symphony off of a mere four notes – G, G, G, Eb. Just those four notes are now something of a cliché in modern culture. But behind the cliché is a work of great art. Let's take a look.

Context

To provide some context, consider that Beethoven is a central figure in the *transition* between the Classical and Romantic periods. Beethoven does not fall neatly into either category. Further more, Beethoven's Fifth was written between 1804 and 1808 in the so-called "middle period" of Beethoven's career. While Beethoven's earlier work was more representative of the classical traditions of Mozart and Haydn, in the middle period of Beethoven's career we begin to see some early examples of breaking away from the traditions of the classical period.

We will only be looking at the first movement of Beethoven's symphony. However, it is worth noting that the complete symphony consists of four movements, all of which, with the exception of the second movement, build on the same famous motif, presented in the first movement.

And now before we delve into the analysis of this piece, let's take inventory of a few basic characteristics of this musical environment. Beethoven's Fifth is written in C minor. It will move to other secondary scales through the piece, as is common for a work in this style, but the primary scale is C minor, with, of course, a primary tonal center of C. The piece is written in 2/4 time, and the tempo is described as "Allegro con brio" which means "Fast with spirit." And finally, the piece is written in sonata form. These attributes set up the structure in which Beethoven's work will unfold.

What We Will Look At

Endless volumes could be written about a piece like Beethoven's Fifth. For the purposes of this book, I have selected a few key points to look at, the culmination of which should give us a reasonable picture of the overall expression and technique of the first movement.

To begin with, we will analyze in detail the first theme of the exposition. Next, we will more briefly look at how things develop in the second theme. I'll bring everything together in the climactic moment of the development and then say a few, final words about the rest of the piece to wrap up.

- ❖ See *Sonata Form* on page 348 for a description of the terms *exposition*, *development*, *recapitulation* as well as *first theme* and *second theme*.

A Few Notes on Reading Scores

Before we begin analyzing Beethoven's Fifth, I'd like to go over a few notes about reading musical scores to help you follow along with the notation examples below.

First of all, scores are organized into *systems*, which consist of one staff per part for a single line of music from the left edge of the page to the right edge of the page. In the score we will be looking at, there is one system or a line a of music for every part on each page. It is common to leave out staves for parts that do not play in a given system. For example, on page five of this score, the trumpet and timpani parts have been omitted because they do not play in that system. However, the first system of a score will always list all of the parts as a reference so that we may easily see what instruments are involved in a piece.

Note that the excerpts from this score are of a *transposed score* rather than a *concert score*. In a concert score, all parts are written in concert pitch or as they sound. In a transposed score, transposing instruments are written as they would appear in the parts for those musicians, maintaining their transpositions. For this score, the clarinet is a Bb instrument and therefore sounds a major second below where it is written. The horn is an Eb instrument and sounds a major sixth below where it is written. All the other instruments are concert instruments and therefore sound as they are written.

I'd also like to acknowledge that the key signature has been left out for the brass and timpani parts. It is traditional to leave out key signatures for these parts in favor of notating with accidentals, though you may see these parts notated with key signatures in other places.

A Few Unfamiliar Symbols

The score we will be using includes a few symbols that we haven't covered yet.

One of the important ones is the *C clef*. You can see this symbol at the beginning of the viola part on the first page. Like the F clef and the G clef, the C clef is a heavily stylized letter, in this case the letter "C." The "C" can be seen in the small curve in the very center of the clef. In the viola part, this curve is placed on the middle line of the staff. Whatever position the center of the C clef is placed on in the staff is designated middle C. This clef shows up later on in the bassoon part as well, only placed on the fourth line of the staff from the bottom, which is then designated as middle C.

I'll also take this opportunity to mention the *fermata*, which is the ⌒ symbol. The fermata indicates that the duration of the given note should be extended for an undetermined length of time at the performer's discretion or in the case of an orchestral piece like this, at the conductor's discretion.

There may be a few remaining symbols in this score that you are still unfamiliar with but none should affect your ability to follow along with the analysis. If you have any further questions, you may consult a resource like *The Essential Dictionary of Notation* by Tom Gerou and Linda Lusk.[1]

1. See the bibliography on page 431 for additional details.

The following excerpts of the scores for Beethoven's Fifth and Pachelbel's Canon in D are adapted from work by Brede Sørøy. Thanks, Brede!

As a supplement, you can also visit the website www.imslp.org to find several public domain, free versions of the scores for both of these pieces. You may find this helpful so that you have a copy of the full score from start to finish in addition to excerpts printed here along with the analysis.

Analysis of the First Theme

Beethoven begins with no leadup or introduction. Instead, he gives us a double forte statement of his motif in unison orchestration (in other words, the melody is played alone with only octave and unison harmonizations). And what are the contents of this famous motif? Interestingly, in the first four notes of the movement there are only two pitches, G and Eb. G is repeated three times in eighth notes and lands on the downbeat with Eb. Then, the Eb is sustained for the entire next measure. These inconspicuous details will become important to remember as we follow Beethoven's development of his theme.

In the third and fourth measures, the same rhythm is repeated with the notes shifted down one step in the scale. This is a diatonic sequence. Next, we are presented with a dramatic shift in both dynamics and in musical expression. In piano dynamics, the rhythm of the motif is repeated in many parts throughout the orchestra sequentially. Interestingly, Beethoven overlaps the parts such that new iterations of the rhythm begin when the previous iteration reaches the sustained note. This approach creates sustaining notes that serve as harmony for the eighth note portion of new phrases. Another effect of this is a sense of continuity that was previously absent. The beginning of the movement has a prominent expression of starting and stopping. Now a steady stream of eighth notes is allowed to produce continuous motion.

And what of the harmony at this point? There is a change here, too. In the sixth and seventh bars, we find a restatement of the initial motif, now only in the second violins. The next phrase, provided by the violas, has a critical impact on the expression of the music at this point. Here, we have an Ab repeated, in the now familiar rhythm of the motif, leading down to G. The half step connection of Ab to G creates a higher energy expression harmonically, but this is balanced by the quieter dynamics. The result is a wonderful redistribution of energy. But there is more to come. The next phrase uses the notes Eb and C. Over the course of these three phrases, all the notes of an Ab major seventh chord are present. Yet we find a light, sustaining middle C in the cello part serving as the lowest note or bass note. But middle C is far too high to create any sense of foundational security around this note. Thus, an ambiguity is created as to whether the harmony at work is C minor with Ab as a simple melodic note or if the harmony has shifted to an Ab center and the cellos merely create an inversion of the Ab chord.

These interactions serve to create tension while also introducing a possible major quality – an interesting mix of expressions, which the quieter dynamics make room for in our attention. It is also important to remember that the *change* of the louder volumes to the quieter ones is a dramatic shift and adds it own high energy contribution to this moment on an expressive spectrum of change or variation.

Next, Beethoven lets the Eb to C phrase complete its sustaining note uninterrupted and then continues on with the concept of overlap for three more phrases. This time with different notes, creating the harmonic implication of a G dominant seventh in first inversion. Interestingly, he keeps the Ab to G phrase as the second phrase of this grouping. The Ab is now producing significant tension, but this is mitigated by the fact that the Ab is allowed to resolve naturally to the G. In addition, we have already heard this phrase once, making it somewhat familiar – thus lower energy on the spectrum of change or variation. The last phrase of this grouping contains the notes F and D. The F of this phrase is the highest note of the entire G dominant seventh grouping and surpasses the highest note of the first grouping by one step. This elevation in contour creates a subtle sense of building and progression.

The original motif of this movement presents two notes, a third apart. The interval of the third is then used in many of the variations on this motif. In the next phrase, Beethoven will "fill in" the third, meaning that he will put a note between the top and bottom notes of the third. Beethoven begins using this idea with the first violins, starting on G just like the beginning of the movement. Following this, the second violins play a similar phrase, only this time inverted. The exchange is repeated creating a "call and response" or "question and answer" expression.

The volume increases and Beethoven's pauses on the dominant chord of the scale, setting up a return the original motif. The motif does return but not in a way that implies the tonic harmony as we might expect. Instead, the motif now starts on Ab and lands on F, implying an F minor harmony – the subdominant or IV chord. At this moment, our somewhat longer-term memory recalls the very beginning of the piece where the motif is presented a step lower in the scale. Like the sense of rising contour created in the quiet section, this serves to create the expression of building and increasing energy.

The music becomes quiet again, returning to the overlapping idea with a new selection of pitches, and an interesting selection they are. The first phrase uses the notes Ab and F, reinforcing the F minor harmony set up by the double forte unison phrase preceding it. Then the notes D and B are used creating the sense of a whole diminished seventh chord,[1] when combined with our memory of Ab and the sustaining F in the first violins. Next, we find the Ab to G phrase coming back once again.

With D and B in our memory we feel that we have now traveled to a G chord. But then another new element presents itself. The rhythm of the motif is played again for the first time in an ascending motion. The cellos and basses play the motif from G upward to C, implying a movement from the dominant chord to the tonic. But the phrase is not allowed to sustain and only half a beat later the whole cascade repeats itself. The expressive result of all this is the feeling that the center of the harmony is moving more quickly than before. This serves to continue to move the energy of the piece forward in a new way.

But it does more than just increase the sense of pace between harmonies. Amazingly, Beethoven manages to transition between harmonies in an ambiguous, gradated kind of way. In other words, it is hard to say where one harmony ends and another begins. We start out with an F minor chord. Then, what was an F minor chord becomes retrospectively part of a whole diminished seventh, perhaps based on B. But then the notes of the whole diminished chord are used to imply a G dominant seventh chord! The result of these retrospective implications is that one chord seems only to form in context of the last, blurring the harmony together, as it were.

1. This type of chord is covered in the box *The Whole Diminished Seventh Chord* on page 398.

Notice that in the first quiet section the phrases create an ascending contour but now in the second quiet section we have a descending contour, creating a falling gesture. The only phrase that goes against this downward motion is the last phrase of the group, which brings the harmonic motion back to C. After the two falling gestures, the piece begins to gradually transition to an ascending, building section. First, the upper strings play an upward phrase arriving on C. C is played three times. The first two act as an approach. The last C lands on the downbeat. In the original motif, there are three approaching notes followed by a landing note. So this seems to be a truncated version of this idea. The sense of this connection is strengthened in the next phrase, which continues the pattern. In this phrase, also played by the upper strings, the arrival note is D, a step higher than the previous phrase. Here, the D is preceded by only one approaching note. These phrases seem to be creating a pattern of taking away or truncating approaching notes. But while the upper strings have been acting out that pattern, the lower strings, the cello and bass parts, have been providing answering phrases on C, playing three approaching notes followed by an arrival note on the downbeat, just like the original motif. This seems to create a context in which the phrases of the upper strings are heard in comparison to the rhythm of the original motif.

There is another attribute of the most recent phrase, the one that lands on D, that should be discussed. The phrase begins with three notes on the pitch of C before proceeding to play a single approaching D and an arrival D. The three eighths on C mimic the rhythm and interval structure used in the first three notes of the original motif. Only here, the rhythm of this phrase starts on the downbeat rather than the "and" of 1, as in the original motif. This phrase has both a similarity to the original motif in the beginning as well as a continuation of the pattern of decreasing approaching notes at the end of the phrase.

The next phrase starts again with three notes of the same pitch, this time one step higher in the scale compared to the previous phrase. And once again the phrase is finished with a single approaching note and a landing note, now on Eb. But then something new happens. The phrase is extended. Two notes are played down a second and then two notes are played up a third, with the last note landing on the next downbeat and the second to last note serving an approaching role – the single approaching note, just as it occurred at the end of the previous sequence of phrases. The music continues to repeat this pattern of two notes down a second, two notes up a third in a rising, building contour. While the upper strings do this, the lower strings and woodwinds play harmonies on the downbeat. This serves the important function of keeping us anchored in the rhythm of the piece and thus allowing us to hear the approaching function of the notes that come on the "and" of 2, leading back to the downbeat. Without these chords on the downbeat, we would likely start to feel the pattern as groups of two without much sense of approach or arrival.

The rising motion eventually crescendos into a falling gesture, accompanied by sustained chords in the woodwinds and lower strings. The falling gesture is repeated, with variations in pitch, once, and then again landing on an unsustained chord played by the whole orchestra. There are three beats of space, a sense of stopping. With another short chord, the first theme is over, and we have the sense of starting again moving into the second theme.

358

Expression of the First Theme

We have now taken an account of the details – the techniques, relationships, and movements through different musical elements – present in the first theme. Now we are in a position to ask, "What does this theme express overall?" and perhaps even more importantly "Why?" The beginning of this movement is certainly dramatic. The large changes in dynamics and expressive qualities stand out as key factors in that capacity. But the quiet sections, in particular, bring a surprising quality of gentleness and beauty into the mix. And beauty seems to infuse the whole work as a result of the connectedness between the loud and soft sections.

In fact, the connectedness between all the elements of the first theme seems to be central. The rhythm of the original motif, in particular, is repeated many times in this theme. When we stand back and think about it, it becomes apparent that this level of repetition would become boring if not for the very dramatic variations in dynamics, pitch, and arrangement. So we see a divergent, extreme level of both connection and disconnection present in the musical elements of the piece. And the overall resulting expression seems to be a mixture of drama and beauty.

I'll leave it there for now but as we move forward through the next three sections, we will continually revisit how this expression progresses and unfolds through this movement.

Analysis of the Second Theme and Closing Section

The second theme of the movement has a much different feel than the first – more flowing, less edges and more curve, lighter overall, and much less dramatic. In fact, the second theme itself seems to provide an opposite expression to the first theme, drama contrasted against ease and peace. Though as the second theme goes on and progresses into the closing section of the exposition, more elements of the first theme come back and some measure of drama returns, although this time colored by a major flavor.

But there are several notable elements of the first theme that carry over to the second theme. First, we could examine the introductory phrase of the theme played by the horns with no accompaniment. There isn't much of a transition section between the first and second themes in this piece; though if you wanted to argue that there is a transition, this phrase is essentially it. Here three approaching notes are used, just as in the motif of the first theme. However, rather than resolving down a third, here the phrase goes down a fourth, expanding the interval.

The strings then enter with what would probably be considered the main idea of the second theme. The melody is continuous and flowing, very much in contrast to the first theme. It does, however, end with a repeated note that then resolves downward like the first theme, providing a modest degree of connection. The lower strings play ascending phrases following the rhythm of the original motif in the background. One last connection to the first theme worth mentioning is the repetition of the second theme's melodic idea three times in different instrumental groups, first in the violins, then the clarinets, then the violins and flutes. This triple repetition among different instruments is something Beethoven used in the quiet sections of the first theme in a very similar way, though entirely within the string section.

Moving forward, the second theme transitions into a continuous alternation of notes going up and back down through the range of a third. This is reminiscent of the filled-in third concept we saw in the first theme. But now, the alternation is continuous and long-lasting generating a suspenseful expression in combination with the harmonic properties of the section.

The suspense culminates into a closing section featuring falling gestures much like the first theme, though in a major key now. And also like the first theme, the closing section ends with a feeling of starting and stopping, though now featuring the rhythm of the original motif.

Page 8

Expression of the Second Theme

The second theme creates a new form of contrast. It represents a dramatic change in the overall expression and feel of the piece. This contrast is arguably more severe than the juxtapositions of quiet and loud sections in the first theme. Though it is held together by some thematic similarities, the piece moves in a foundationally different direction here. The whole summation of the music seems to create an opposing expression and that is a bigger difference than anything on the scale of themes, motifs, or individual musical elements. The interesting thing is that while this level of contrast creates a high energy expression, the expression of the music in the second theme, in and of itself, is lower energy, more gentle and flowing, less dramatic and abrupt. So the high energy of the dramatic change is somewhat balanced by the low energy of what we are changing to. Nevertheless, the second theme can seem a bit surprising as it invites a new energy and emotional spectrum into the work.

A Key Moment in the Development

For me, all the details of Beethoven's intricate work come together into a single idea during the climax of the development and its transition into the recapitulation. Here, a conversation starts between the woodwinds and the strings. At first, two chords for one and then two for the other. Then, the alternation speeds up, moving to one chord for the woodwinds, one for the strings. And back and forth they go, developing harmonic movement that takes us far away from the land of C minor. The development settles on a pair of chords and goes back and forth, becoming quieter. The harmony at this point seems to center on F# minor, a very distant and disconnected chord in relationship to the primary key of the piece, C minor.[1] In the analogy of a story where our protagonist starts at home, leaves on an adventure, and returns home, this moment represents our traveler going to the most distant land, the furthest place from home.

Suddenly, the strings and woodwinds come together for a momentary loud section and then the alternation resumes. Now, on a whole diminished seventh chord centering on B. Though, Beethoven makes good use of the ambiguity a diminished chord can provide to rapidly shift the harmonic center back in the direction of C minor.[2] A loud section comes in with a phrase in the rhythm of the original motif using the notes Ab and F. Ab and F are chord tones of the B diminished seventh but also have been used in the exposition in context of the F minor chord, which is the subdominant or IV chord of C minor. The phrase on Ab repeats. It then comes back again, but this time the long note is not allowed to sustain. Instead, the next phrase begins on the very next "and" of 1, producing a continuous stream of eighth notes. The phrase repeats in this form four times, dramatically building up to a sustained chord on F minor.

This is one of my favorite moments in the whole movement. It is, in many ways, the quintessential climax. Next, the orchestra plays another phrase in the rhythm of the motif with the melodic motion of F to D. At this point, we are essentially at the recapitulation. F to D, is the very first variation of the motif and second phrase overall that we hear in the movement. And so Beethoven has connected us back to the beginning. From here we go to the quiet section of the first theme and go through the rest of recapitulation.

1. In the section *Modulation* (page 412) and especially in the box entitled *The Circle of Fifths* (page 413), we will discuss how harmonies or scales that are close together on the circle of fifths are heard as related, and harmonies or scales that are far away from each other on the circle of fifths sound unrelated. So, here in the climax of the piece, the harmony has actually traveled as far away as possible on the circle of fifths – going from a center on C to a center on F#. See more details on this concept in the aforementioned sections of Chapter Fourteen.
2. See *The Whole Diminished Seventh Chord* and *Inversion-less Chords* on page 398.

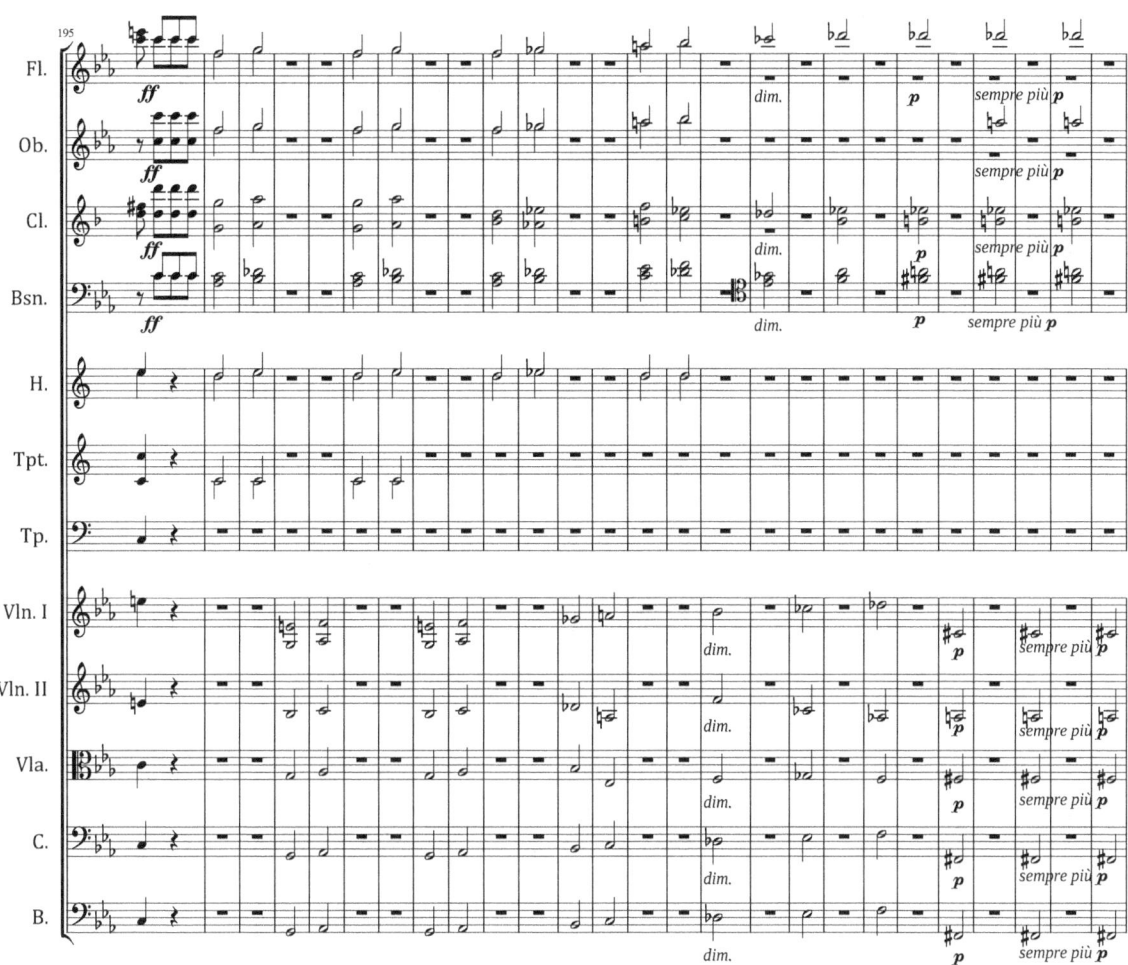

Jumping ahead to page 13

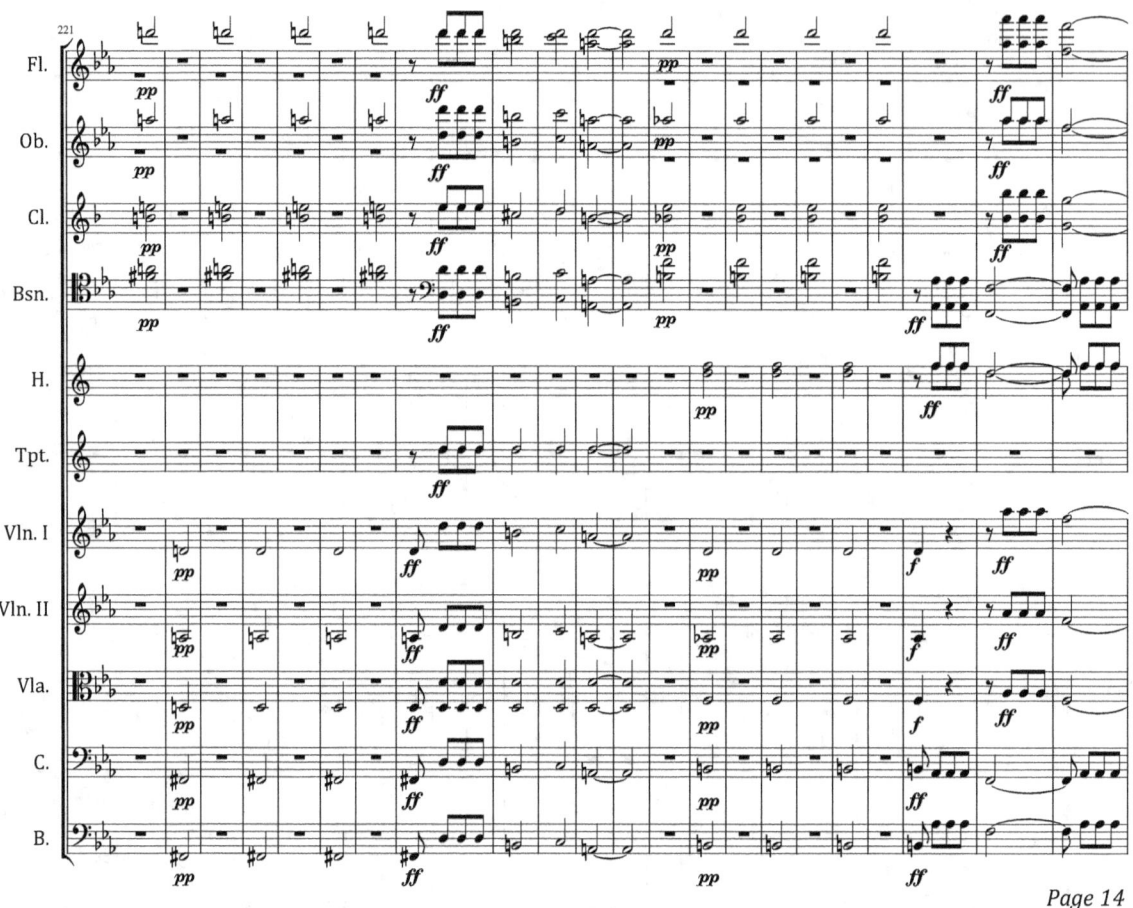

Page 15

The Central Expression

Though hinted at and built upon from the very beginning, the central expression of Beethoven's movement now becomes clear in this climactic moment and in the music that leads up to it. The back-and-forth conversation between the strings and woodwinds is a representation of contrast in a smaller form. Back and forth, this and that, here and there... it seems to say. On the larger level, the music alternates between quiet and loud. Contrast and connection are the ideas at play here.

But all music relies on contrast and connection to some degree. More specifically, Beethoven's Fifth is the expressive result of using dramatic, intense contrast with a single motif that is constantly used to connect the entire work into a whole. Beethoven also transforms the notion of contrast into alternation and, in turn, extends alternation into suspense and grand motions of building energy.

So the story here is one of not just contrast, but sharp contrast, tied together by a single idea. An idea that itself encapsulates duality and a sense building: two pitches, repetition building into a landing note. Amazing how those four notes seem to say it all.

Emotionally, we have the components of a suspenseful story. A story with a wide breadth of feeling and experience. A story of drama and contrasting forces. But also a story about beauty and the relationship between things that are, on one level, very different and yet are also connected.

The Oboe Solo and the Ending

Beethoven's Fifth is often commented on for the unexpected, strange yet beautiful oboe solo in the recapitulation as well as the much longer, more prominent than usual coda. Although we have now arrived at the primary destination of our analytical adventure, from details to central expression, I think it is worth mentioning, at least briefly, these two notable aspects of Beethoven's Fifth and how they relate to the larger picture.

The oboe solo, unexpected though it might be, is directly in line with the notion of sharp and striking contrast. The whole orchestra stops for a moment to let the oboe sing for just a couple of measures. This dramatic shift from orchestra to solo instrument is yet another manifestation of the central expression.

The unusual oboe solo and the long coda are perhaps signs of a shift into more of a Romantic era mindset, a breaking away from the Classical period traditions. And both divergences from the norm work well in my opinion. The oboe solo is a well-executed, unexpected direction that has not been explored yet, nor did we necessarily think it would be explored as listeners. But when we hear it, the expression falls into the central concept while also showing us a new way in which that concept could be used.

The coda contains some spectacular variations on earlier themes as dramatic building blocks to the final conclusion. Though we won't look at them in detail here, I encourage you to try analyzing them yourself. The coda ends with an alternation between two chords, somewhat like the alternation in the development. However, the alternation is faster, played at quarter note speed, rather than half note, and it is played by the whole orchestra at fortissimo volume. It is altogether more dramatic but serves to reinforce and conclude the central ideas of contrast, alternation, extension, and suspense.

- Analysis of Pachelbel's Canon -

Pachelbel's Canon in D

Pachelbel's Canon is an example of musical excellence, just as Beethoven's Fifth is. It is a worthy endeavor to study the piece for this reason alone. However, there is another reason why Pachelbel's Canon is useful for us at this juncture. This piece approaches development in an opposing fashion to the method that Beethoven offers us in his Fifth Symphony. Looking at both examples side by side will outline a broad spectrum of developmental approaches. And hopefully, by the end you will have a wide range of possibilities at your disposal for artistic creation.

Beethoven's Fifth uses a high degree of contrast while tying the composition together with a singular, ubiquitous motif. Pachelbel's Canon changes very, very gradually. The degree of contrast is very low. But to balance things out, the thematic variation is highly active. There is no central motif here like you find in Beethoven's Fifth. Rather Pachelbel presents a wide range of melodic ideas that are interwoven and connected together.

The means of this connection largely come from the *canon* structure of the piece. A *canon* is a type of polyphonic or contrapuntal (involving counterpoint) work where each part or melodic line plays the same music, only offset by a certain number of measures or beats. "Row Row Your Boat" is a commonplace example of a canon.

In Pachelbel's Canon, there are three violins all playing according to the rules of the canon. One violin begins, and two measures later the next violin plays what the first violin played at the beginning. Meanwhile, the first violin plays something new. Two measures later, the third violin comes in playing what the first violin played at the beginning. And so all three parts continue for the whole piece, with the second violin always two measures behind the first and the third violin two measures behind the second.

Underneath the violins, there is a simple quarter note bass line outlining an eight chord progression that repeats exactly, with no variation, for the whole piece.

How Does the Canon Structure Affect the Spectrum of Change?

Whenever the first violin does something, that thing will be repeated by the second violin two measures later and then repeated by the third violin four measures later. This means that no abrupt changes are possible. Everything is repeated with new elements, once and then again with still new elements. For the music to change entirely, in other words, to change in all parts, at least six measures must go by. This sets a kind of speed limit on the piece's ability to change.

Between the repeating eight measure chord progression of this piece and the very gradual pace of change overall, we have a setup for a very low energy piece of music. Melodic variation and the *lack* of a central motif then comes in to balance the equation. Pachelbel masterfully shapes the expressive result of these interactions so that we continuously hear new, interesting melodies that feel inexplicably connected and beautiful in their evolution.

Though the melodic variation brings a measure of relative balance to this piece, the overall expression certainly is a lower energy expression when compared to Beethoven's Fifth. Pachelbel's Canon is less of a dramatic story and more of a beautifully unfolding flower. It seems to point to connectivity, flow, and reverence.

Context

Once again, a general orientation is in order. Pachelbel is a composer from the Baroque period. The exact date of creation for Pachelbel's Canon is not known. The piece is in 4/4 time and in D major. The piece has been performed with a wide range of tempos from adagio to more moderate speed.

Canon in D

Johannes Pachelbel
(1653-1706)

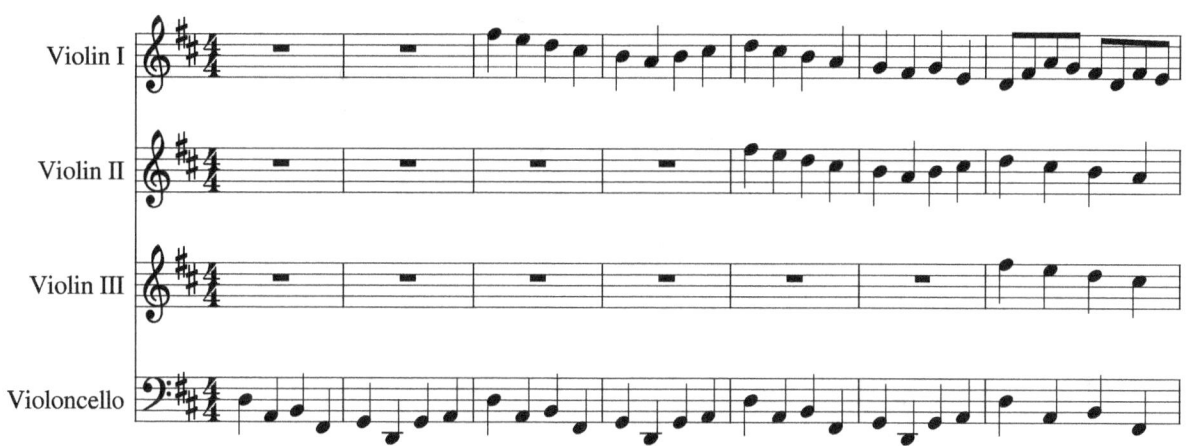

Analysis

The piece starts with just the bass line for two measures. Then, the first violin comes in with a very simple melody. We have clearly the diatonic progression: D, A, Bm, F#m, G, D, G, A.

The second violin comes in with the same simple melody two measures later, of course, following the rules of the canon. The first violin now plays a melody a third above what it played two measures earlier and what the second violin is playing currently. The effect is a harmonized melody[1] in which the first violin seems to have the primary melody because it is higher in pitch, while the second violin seems to have the secondary or harmonizing line. Now, the third violin comes in. The second and third violins do what the first and second violins did two measures earlier. And underneath that, the first violin plays an eighth note melody.

In the next two measures, the second violin plays the eighth note melody from the previous two bars and the first violin plays a new eighth note melody. Something interesting happens here. The first violin starts out with the higher pitch for a single note but then is overtaken by the second violin. But then the first violin overtakes the second again. The effect is that what is heard as the primary melody goes back and forth between the first and second violins. This technique is used throughout the piece to create a kind of texture where melodies flow in and around each other with some melodies coming on the top of the others but then diving back down into the layers of harmony while another line takes its place as the primary melody. The effect is dazzling, complex, and beautiful.

Next, a sixteenth note melody comes in, starting as the top line, overtaken by the second violins, and then re-emerging as the primary melody. The progression from quarter note, to eighth note, to sixteenth note melodies creates a clear building of energy in terms of rhythmic pace and complexity.

Another sixteenth note line is added next. After that, a high part is added with sustaining notes. In the first measure of this high part, there is an interesting pause that allows some of the other parts to come through a little more. In the second measure, notes B, A, B, C# are used as quarter notes over top of the other parts. At this point, we are at the sixteenth measure. Both the structure and pitches of the piece are creating a sense of gravity toward the seventeenth measure, which is expected to complete an even sixteen bars of music with the resolution of C# to D, the half step, Ti-Do, resolution of this scale.[2]

Pachelbel indeed delivers the resolution. However, that bar with the interesting pause comes back in with the second violin and the first violin then harmonizes with it, playing the same rhythm. So now there is a pause in two of the lines. This creates the sense of space, where we might have expected something more climactic. But now that second measure with the building line comes back and the first violin builds with it, creating an even greater sense of escalation.

This time Pachelbel doesn't hold back. A new, intricate melody emerges in the first violin part, using sixteenth and thirty-second notes. The fast-paced rhythms and variation between sixteenth and thirty-second notes helps to introduce some energy into the piece.

1. This would be an example of the constant numeric interval method of harmonizing a melody. See *Harmonized Melodies* on page 314.
2. *Structural Gravity Revisited*, page 345

After this, the melody is harmonized by the second violin and then the piece begins a gradual shift toward the minimalistic. The energy of the whole piece is brought down. And then a slow build begins back up to the final climactic conclusion.

I want to jump ahead to the ending now and examine Pachelbel's use of dissonance at the end of his piece. In bar 49, there is a C natural in the first violins, above all the other melodic lines. C is generally sharp in the D major scale so this is a chromatic note. At this point, the effect isn't too dramatic. But two measures later when the second violins play this C natural, the real magic happens. While the second violins play the C natural, the first violins play an F# underneath it, creating a tritone, a strong dissonance and prominently positioned in the high register of the violin, too. However, the dissonance is short lived because just a quarter of a beat later the first violins shift to an E, creating a major sixth with the C and thus resolving the dissonance. The harmonic tension is further resolved on the downbeat on the next measure when the sixth collectively moves down a step harmonizing well into a G major chord. Though, for the complete resolution we must wait another half of a beat until the third violin moves down from A to G.

And so, the resolution from this tritone is progressive. Flowing and completed gradually, like the character of the piece in general. And while the tritone only forms for a moment, it is long enough to feel it and what a heart-aching beauty it creates. It is the climax of the piece. The strings are high in their registers, and the harmonic tension is high. The pace of the notes slows for the most part to give the sense of greater longing, anticipation, and weight.

The dissonance of the tritone and the events that follow it repeat two measures later, according to the rules of the canon. Meanwhile, the first violin has started an eighth note figure that restores harmonic stability and gradually brings us back to resolution. The piece ends on a simple D major voicing landing on the downbeat, a complete resolution.

376

*Skipping ahead to measure 42

The Expression of Big-Picture Development

If we look at the various melodic themes throughout this canon, we will undoubtedly find some amount of connection between them. If nothing else they share the same harmonic environment. However, these melodic ideas have quite distinct elements. This piece is not focused on the motif or the theme but rather on the larger picture of development. And so we must analyze the piece in this way, on its own level.

The piece creates smoothly flowing developments that feel connected because of the repeated phrases that echo through the canon structure. Different melodic lines appear as the top note of any given moment, drawing our attention away from any particular line as the melodic centerpiece. The music takes our focus outward to the big picture, rather than in toward the details. And perhaps this speaks to something of the piece's expression, its feeling of connection, of wisdom and peace, perhaps even divinity.

If we take these attributes as getting at least close to the central expression of the piece, we can see how Pachelbel takes these basic ideas and varies them throughout the big-picture development of the piece. The whole piece creates two primary building motions. The first culminates in the introduction of a fast-paced melody; the second in a sustaining, beautiful harmonic tension. Both builds are gradual in their rise and in their fall.

Especially toward the beginning of the piece, there is an expression of a slow, measured, and graceful unfolding. In addition to the structure of the canon, this is largely created through the even and predictable way in which the piece introduces rhythmic complexity (or other variations in the later parts of the piece). The fast-paced melodic lines in the climax of the first build create an expression of joy, revealing a more energetic side to wisdom and peace. The second build moves the expression into a slightly different territory. There is more harmonic complexity, and this creates a beauty that is strained, almost painful. But when the piece resolves back into harmonic simplicity the expression of peace is renewed and in fact deepened, seeming to encompass all the more and be all the richer.

Analyzing a Piece of Music

I invite you to do your own analysis of a piece of music you like. Following, at least generally, these steps:

1. **Expression:** Consider what the expression of your piece of music is. What emotions or ideas does this music convey?

2. **Musical Elements:** Make a list of different notable musical characteristics or musical elements in the piece. Consider relationships in both pitch and rhythm as well as dynamics, timbre, and anything else you think might be important. Consult the seven spectra if needed.[1]

3. **Connection:** Mentally connect and compare the musical elements to the expression. Would you have predicted this expression from these elements? Are you missing some piece of the picture? Keep working at understanding the translation from musical elements to musical expression. Go back and forth between this step and step two if necessary.

As you go through the process of listing musical elements in step two, start with specific details and then work your way to the broader patterns and tendencies of the piece as a whole. Then, when you reach step three, go back the other direction, first making connections to musical expression on a general level and then becoming more specific. Start with questions like: Can you say why this piece might be generally higher energy or lower energy? Are there elements that seem to explain it being generally uplifting or generally sad or sorrowful? And then progress to more detailed aspects of the piece's expression.

Don't expect perfection in this process. Do not expect to explain everything there is to explain. Get as detailed and specific as you can but no more. There is no need to grasp at straws to explain what may be unexplainable, at least unexplainable for now. Simply *increasing* our understanding to a level that is deeper and more complete than before is enough.

Analyzing a wide variety of pieces can help give you a sense of contrast, which can be very useful for cultivating your musical understanding. Try some pieces in different styles of music. Consult Chapter Ten for ideas.[2]

1. *Seven Basic Spectra of Musical Expression*, page 47
2. *Chapter Ten*, page 288

- Creating a Complete Composition -

The Creative Process

The time has come to write, to create! How do we take all of the knowledge and creative skills that we have been developing and put it all together into a musical composition?

A common question for music writers is what should one start with – the melody? the chords? both simultaneously? something else entirely? And where do we go from there? Ultimately, you'll have to find the creative style that works for you through experimentation and experience. However, to give you a starting place, here is an outline of my personal process of musical creation.

I start with an inspiration. For me, inspirations often come from improvisation. An inspiration could be any musical element – a melody, a sequence of chords, a rhythm, a single voicing, a timbre. It could be that I'm looking for a specific musical idea that captures a musical expression I know I want to create beforehand or it could be that I discover a musical idea and then begin to cultivate the musical expression based on that initial idea or element.

From whatever musical element I discover, I will then create other musical elements around the inspiration to create a complete section with chords, rhythms, timbres, and melodies. Next, I'll experiment with variations of my musical idea. I'll create juxtaposing and complementary ideas. As I refine and select the ideas I like, I begin to structure my piece in sections. As the full structure comes into view, I'll write any remaining material I need to connect the whole work together.

From here, I move on to the arranging step. Generally, I've already considered what instruments will be involved and what functions or roles they will be serving but at this stage, I'll fill in the details for the parts all the musicians will be playing. And finally, there comes the production stage. The music is performed and recorded, synthesized, edited together on the computer, mixed, and mastered.

Depending on the type of music I am creating, this process may change. For example, in a work for solo piano, there will be no need for a separate arranging step. For a jazz tune, instead of writing out exact parts, I may simple write out the melody and chords in a lead sheet[1] and let the musicians improvise the specifics of their parts. With an EDM track, I do my synthesis in combination with my writing and arranging. I'll also create a preliminary mix while writing, so I can hear how the track is sounding.

1. *Lead Sheets and Scores*, page 248

All variations aside, the general process can be summarized in the following steps:

1. Discover inspiration (often through improvisation)

2. Create a full idea or section by writing complementary musical elements to add to the inspiration

3. Experiment with variations of the musical idea, create juxtaposing and complementary material

4. Shape variations into a structure

5. Arrange the composition by creating specific parts, with filled out details as necessary

6. Record acoustic sounds, synthesize digital sounds (if this hasn't been done already)

7. Edit and mix sounds together

8. Apply mastering to the track as a whole

Composing a Piece of Music

When we discussed writing themes, we focused on the perspective of intending to create a specific expression with our music. This is a good perspective to hold for writing full-length compositions as well. However, I'd like to offer you a variation on this idea, which applies especially well for longer creative projects where structure and development come more into the forefront. What I have in mind is to consider the notion of telling a story as an analogy to writing a piece of music. After all, music and language are very connected. In music, we will not have all the conceptual details that language might provide, but the emotional arc of a story – the highs, the lows, the anticipation, the different places our protagonist might travel – this is what a musical work conveys.

What we want to hold in mind for a full-length composition is a *narrative of musical expressions* or perhaps a narrative with a single, unifying theme or idea. Each section of the composition is like a chapter in our story, and each section should have a function in the overall arc of the story. As mentioned earlier, these functions will fall under three basic categories: starting at home, leaving on an adventure (culminating in a climax), and coming back home again. Within this large structure, there may be many micro-story arcs that contain their own smaller homes, adventures, climaxes, and returns.

As a final word, there are two big ideas that I think are very important to the compositional process and to your own learning as a musician. The first idea is being intentional: Setting the intention of creating a certain expression. Setting the intention of telling a certain story. This is especially important at the beginning of the creative process but needs to remain an aspect of everything you do from start to finish. The second idea is take a moment to review your own work after completion. You may want to wait a bit after finishing a composition or song, to give you some distance and perspective. However, at some point, go back and learn from your past. What worked well? What didn't? What worked as intended? What was surprising? Ask these questions yourself and solicit feedback from others. It may be hard to receive criticism, even from yourself, but taking even a little bit of time to learn from your past creative endeavors can help you grow immensely.

With that, I invite you to write a piece of music or two (or more)! Feel free to review any old material you want in the process. And once again, embrace the experimenter's mindset until it is time to embrace the performer's mindset.

Summary for Group Five
Putting It All Together

Classical	Jazz	Blues, R&B, and Rock	Country
Baroque Period (1600-1750) Classical Period (1750-1820) Romantic Period (1820-1910) Impressionist Period (1875-1925)		Work Songs (17th-19th Centuries) Gospel (1880s)	
		Country Blues (1910s)	
	New Orleans (1910s/20s)		
			Early Country (1920s/30s)
Modern Period (1900-1975)	Swing (1930s/40s) Be-Bop (1940s)	Jump Blues (1930s/40s) Early R&B (1940s) Chicago Blues (1940s/50s)	Honky Tonk (1940s) Bluegrass (1940s/50s)
	Cool Jazz Hard-Bop Avant-Garde (1950s/60s)	Rock 'n' Roll (1950s) British Invasion Folk Revival (1960s)	Nashville Sound (1950s/60s)
Post-Modern Period (1975-present)	Fusion (1970s)	Hard Rock, Prog Rock, Glam Rock, Early Metal, Punk Rock (1970s) Post Punk (late 1970s)	Outlaw (1970s)
		Trash Metal (1980s) Death Metal (late 1980s)	Contemporary (1980s onward)

Later R&B	Brazilian	Jamaican	Electronic (EDM)
	Samba (1920s/30s) Bossa Nova (late 1950s)		
Soul (1960s)		Reggae (1960s)	
Funk (1970s) Disco (late 1970s)			Ambient (1970s)
			Early House Techno (1980s)
Hi-Hop (late 1980s and beyond)			Prog/Electro-House Trance Drum 'n' Bass (1990s onward) Dubstep (2000s onward)

Principles of Arranging and Production
- ❖ Separation
- ❖ Balance
- ❖ Focus
- ❖ Pitch Range
- ❖ Structural Gravity

Roles in the Ensemble
- ❖ Bass Line – *Outlines foundation of rhythm and harmony*
- ❖ Percussion – *Fills in rhythmic groove and outlines structure*
- ❖ Harmony Parts – *Fills in harmony, provides quality of the chords*
- ❖ Melody – *Primary focus*

Harmonized Melodies
- ❖ Constant Numeric Interval Method
- ❖ Chord Tone Method

Counterpoint – *Multiple melodies or lines of music at the same time*
- ❖ Consider vertical and horizontal dimensions
- ❖ Parallel fifths and octaves reduce the sense of motion between lines

> **To convert from concert to transposed:**
>
> *Find the interval and the direction of the interval (up or down) from the note in the name of the transposed instrument (for example Bb for the Bb trumpet) to C. Transpose the music by this interval and in this direction.*
>
> **To convert from transposed to concert:**
>
> *Find the interval and the direction of the interval from C to the note in the name of the transposed instrument. Transpose the music by this interval and in this direction.*

> *Repetition creates a low energy expression.*
> *Variation creates a high energy expression.*

Themes or Motifs – Simple musical ideas that reoccur, usually in different forms, through a musical piece

- ❖ *The basic concept of development is to take a musical idea, change some aspects of it while keeping other aspects of it the same.*

- ❖ *The basic story of all stories is to start at home, leave home on an adventure (which often builds into a climax), and come back home.*

Musical Analysis
1. What musical expression do you feel or experience from the music?
2. What are the notable elements of the music?
3. How do the musical elements connect to the expression?
4. Repeat as necessary

Ideas to Hold in Mind for Creating Music:
1. Be Intentional – *Think in terms of creating a narrative of musical expressions*
2. Learn From the Past – *Review past successes, failures, and surprises*

Creation Process
1. Discover inspiration (often through improvisation)
2. Create a full idea or section by writing complementary musical elements to add to the inspiration
3. Experiment with variations of the musical idea, create juxtaposing and complementary material
4. Shape variations into a structure
5. Arrange the composition by creating specific parts, with filled out details as necessary
6. Record acoustic sounds, synthesize digital sounds (if this hasn't been done already)
7. Edit and mix sounds together
8. Apply mastering to the track as a whole

Mixing Process
1. Balance levels
2. Panning
3. Reverb
4. EQ
5. Dynamics Processing
    - Compressor – Reduces dynamic range
    - Expander – Increases dynamic range
    - Limiter – Compressor with high ratio
    - Gate – Expander with high ratio
6. Automate Volume Levels

Mastering Process
1. EQ (if needed)
2. Compression and Limiting

Group Six

Advanced Harmony

Chapter Thirteen
Additional Chord and Scale Types

In this chapter, we will go through many different chord and scale types. There are a lot of different possibilities presented here so you might want to work through it in chunks. There are some examples and activities along the way, but I also recommend taking some additional time to experiment with each of the chords and scales as they are presented. In particular, you may want to experiment with some different voicings of each of the chord types presented in this chapter. Do this with each new chord type individually or perhaps with small groups of chords at one time.

- Ninth, Eleventh, and Thirteenth Chords -

Chords are traditionally constructed in thirds in their root position,[1] close voicings,[2] or their "original voicings" as I described it with my own phrase in Chapter Six.[3] The triad is constructed with a pair of thirds. We can create a seventh chord by adding a note a third above the fifth of a triad. Now, we will learn how this pattern continues to form larger chords.

A *ninth chord* is created by adding a note a third above the last note of a seventh chord. An *eleventh chord* is created by adding a note a third above the last note of a ninth chord. And finally, a *thirteenth chord* is created by adding a note a third above the last note of an eleventh chord. Thirteenth chords are generally considered the largest chords because they use all seven letters in the musical system. Adding a note a third above the last note of a thirteenth chord will give you the same letter as the root of the chord.

1. Meaning the root is the lowest note of the chord, see *Inversions* on page 148.
2. Meaning that the notes of the chord are as close together as possible rather than spread out in different octaves, see *Open or Close* on page 150.
3. *Original Voicings*, page 139

Extensions or Tensions

Notes placed at ninth, eleventh, or thirteenth intervals above the root of a chord are sometimes called *extensions* or *tensions*.

Re, Fa, and La

Examine the ninth, eleventh, and thirteenth chords built off the major, minor, and dominant sevenths below.

Unless otherwise indicated tensions follow the notes of a major scale built on the root of the chord. The ninth corresponds to the solfege syllable Re; the eleventh corresponds to the solfege syllable Fa; and the thirteenth corresponds to the solfege syllable La. This is true regardless if the chord is major, minor, or dominant.

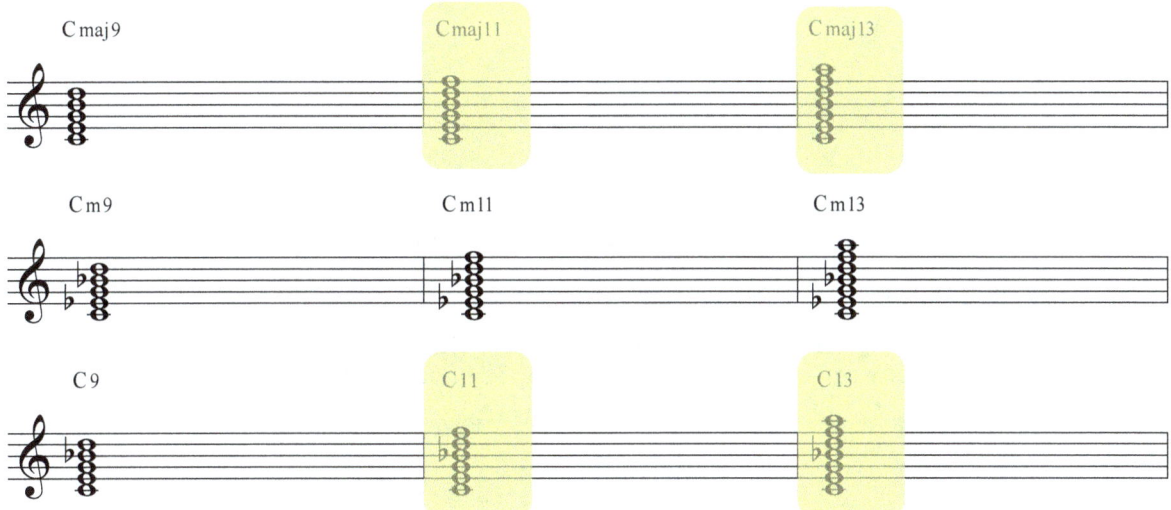

The Highlighted Chords

The highlighted chords above are not commonly used but are written here to illustrate the interval pattern used in the construction of larger chords. We will discuss this point in more detail in just a moment.

❖ *Common Tensions Used in Major, Minor, and Dominant Chords*, page 390

Alterations

Tensions can be *altered* by raising or lowering their pitch by a half step. To write a chord symbol for an *alteration*, write the seventh chord that is being used as the base for the chord and then write the tensions of the chord in parenthesis. Include a flat symbol before tensions that are lowered a half step and a sharp symbol before tensions that are raised by a half step. For example, the chord below can be written with the chord symbol: C7(b9).

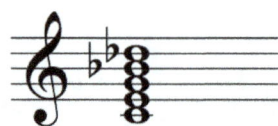

Pick and Choose Your Tensions

You can also use parenthesis to pick and choose the tensions you want. To do this, list the tensions you want to be included in the chord in parenthesis, separated by commas. For example, the chord below can be written with the chord symbol: C7(9,13)

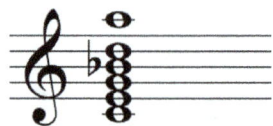

Common Tensions Used in Major, Minor, and Dominant Chords

Different types of chords are commonly used with different tensions and tension alterations based on the interval relationships that form in each scenario.

The major seventh chord is usually not combined with an unaltered eleventh, as this creates the interval of a minor ninth between the third of the chord and the eleventh, which stands out as a prominent dissonance. Instead, composers often use a sharp eleventh in conjunction with the major seventh chord. This seems to produce a softer, considerably less harsh effect. The ninth and thirteenth added to a major seventh chord usually remain unaltered. When the sharp eleven is added to a major seventh chord, Lydian-like expressions are created as the sharp eleven, equivalent to the solfege syllable Fi in the context of scales or modes, is the differentiating note of a Lydian mode.

The minor seventh chord works well with unaltered tensions. The harsh interval between the third and the unaltered eleventh is eliminated in a minor chord because the third is lowered a half step in comparison to the third of a major chord. This creates a less dissonant major ninth relationship instead.

Most altered tensions appear with a dominant seventh chord base. Similar to the major seventh chord, the unaltered eleventh is usually avoided to prevent a clash with the third. A sharp eleventh can be used instead. The ninth and thirteenth can remain unaltered or can be altered in several ways. The flat ninth and the sharp ninth are both commonly used with the dominant seventh chord. The flat thirteenth is also commonly used. A sharp thirteenth has the same note name as the seventh of a dominant chord and, therefore, is not really an addition to the chord. Similarly, a flat eleventh is the same as the third of a dominant seventh or major seventh.

Chord Quality	Common Tensions
Major	9, #11, 13
Minor	9, 11, 13
Dominant	9, b9, #9, #11, 13, b13

Dissonant Intervals and the Expression of Complexity in Larger Chords

The more notes that are added to a harmony the more relationships are created and generally the more complexity and dissonance as well. Where small chords have very direct and simple sounding expressions, larger chords have an increasing degree of complexity and sophistication to them. If used skillfully, ninth, eleventh, and thirteenth chords have the potential to generate some very rich expressions, full of subtlety and meaning. However, they are not always the best choice. You must consider if you want to create a sense of simplicity or complexity.

Style also enters into the equation. Ninth, eleventh, and thirteenth chords are most commonly used in jazz. Blues and funk as well as Impressionistic, Modern, and Post-Modern classical music also may incorporate some of these sounds. Pop, rock, and most classical music from the common practice period will probably use largely triad-based harmonies, perhaps with some seventh chords as well. In contrast, many jazz styles use seventh chords as their basic harmonic framework adding in tensions to achieve various musical effects.

You may notice that in larger chords the dissonance of any one interval stands out less. The sounds all blur together into a complex element, and we perceive the total effect, which becomes further and further removed from the level of a single interval. This can be an interesting opportunity to explore the expression of more dissonant intervals in a musical context that minimizes their harshness. However, as a composer it is also important to remain aware of what is happening on every level of your chords. Listen to these larger chords carefully and make sure that you are consciously choosing to create a dissonant relationship if one exists. You may find it helpful to play a portion of your chord in isolation to hear what is going on in just that portion of the chord. If needed, you can even alternate between listening to the whole chord and different subgroups within it.

Getting Acquainted With the Expression of Ninth, Eleventh, and Thirteenth Chords

Combining different seventh chords with different tension notes produces a great variety of different possible chords. Below are just three examples of chord voicings that include tensions: a C major ninth, a C minor seventh with the ninth and thirteenth, and finally a C dominant seventh with the ninth and sharp eleventh. Listen to these chord voicings on tracks 36 (disc 2), 37 (disc 2), and 38 (disc 2), respectively.

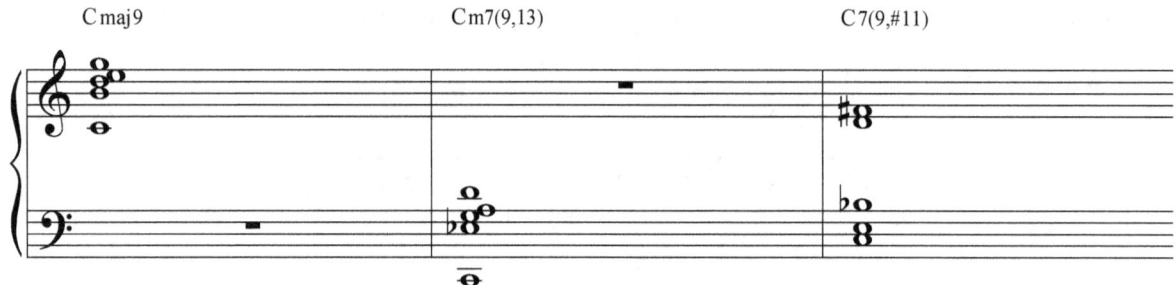

- Polychords -

With five, six, or seven notes in a chord, complex centrality[1] becomes common and intensified in its degree. It is even possible to perceive multiple chords in one moment of harmony. Collections of notes that inspire such experiences are known as *polychords*. In contrast to more subtle forms of complex centrality and expressive subgroups within a harmony, polychords generally create a sense of multiple (usually two) clearly separated chords occurring at the same time. Polychords usually have all of the notes of one chord in the lower pitch range of the harmony and all the notes of another chord in the upper pitch range.

To write a chord symbol for a polychord, write the chord symbol for the upper chord and then underneath it separated by a line write the chord symbol for the lower chord. To the right is an example of a polychord that combines the C and D major triads. Listen to this chord on track 39 (disc 2).

1. *Simple and Complex Centrality*, page 56

- Constant Interval Voicings -

With larger chords, it becomes possible to create voicings that use a single interval many times or even ubiquitously throughout an entire voicing. I call these kinds of voicings *constant interval voicings*. Constant interval voicings can create a repetition of an exact interval or of a general numeric interval.

The constant interval technique, especially when done with exact intervals, can have the interesting effect of emphasizing the expression of a certain interval while creating a larger harmony while doing so. Using a constant interval of a fourth or a fifth can also be a good way to "open up" your voicings by spreading the notes of the chord out over a large range of pitch, in an even and patterned way.

Below is a C minor ninth chord in a constant interval voicing. This voicing creates four perfect fifths. It is not perfectly constant because the ninth and the third of the chord create a minor second. However, the repetition of the perfect fifth is perceptible and contributes to the beautiful sound of this voicing. Listen to this voicing on track 40 (disc 2).

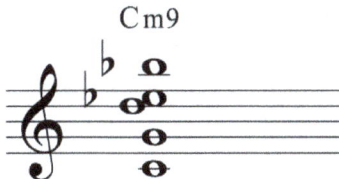

We can also extend this voicing by adding an eleventh a perfect fifth above the seventh of the chord. Listen to this voicing on track 41 (disc 2).

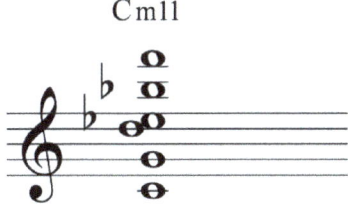

Below is a constant interval voicing of a C7 (9, 13). This voicing emphasizes the general numeric interval of a fourth. It creates to two perfect fourths and one augmented fourth for a total of three fourths. You can listen to this example on track 42 (disc 2).

Leaving Out the Fifth

You may notice that the fifth of the chord is omitted in the example above. This is quite common in larger chords or even in seventh chords. The fifth of the chord does not characterize a major, minor, or dominant quality nor is it often necessary to establish the harmonic center of a larger chord. Taking out the fifth can thin out the sound of the chord while maintaining a similar sound. Note that when dealing with any kind of diminished or augmented chord, the fifth will become much more important to the character of the chord and, therefore, probably should be included.

- More Chord Types -

Sus4 Triad

The *suspended triad* or *sus4* triad is defined by the interval of a perfect fourth between the first and second notes of the chord, the interval of a major second between the second and third notes of the chord, and the interval of a perfect fifth between the first and third notes of the chord. The major second stands out as a dissonance in this chord. The perfect fourth and perfect fifth have different related fundamentals,[1] meaning that the two consonant intervals of the chord are not aligned in centrality. As a result, there can be a gravitational pull for the suspended triad to resolve to a major triad of the same root.

You can listen to a sus4 triad on track 43 (disc 2).

1. *Related Series Analysis*, page 157

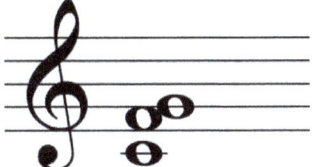

C suspended 4
Chord Symbol:
Csus4 or Csus

Sus2 Triad

The *sus2 triad* is defined by the interval of a major second between the first and second notes, the interval of a perfect fourth between the second and third notes, and the interval of a perfect fifth between the first and third notes of the chord. Note that the sus2 chord is equivalent to the first inversion of a sus4 chord.

You can listen to a sus2 triad on track 44 (disc 2).

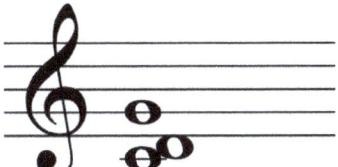

C suspended 2
Chord Symbol:
Csus2

More Seventh Chords

We have now studied six types of triads – major, minor, augmented, diminished, sus4, and sus2. Each of these triads can be made into a seventh chord by adding a note a major or minor seventh away from the root. These six triads and two possible sevenths will give us a total of twelve possible chord types. Of these, the diminished triad with the major seventh, the sus4 triad with the major seventh, and the sus2 triad with either seventh are rarely used or likely to be written a different way. Excluding these rarely used chords and the major, minor, and dominant seventh, which have already been covered, the remaining seventh chords are the *minor-major seventh*, the *major seventh sharp-five*, the *augmented seventh*, the *half-diminished seventh* otherwise known as the *minor seven flat-five*, and the *suspended seventh*.

You can listen to each of these chords on tracks 45 (disc 2) through 49 (disc 2). For your reference:

Track 45 (disc 2) – Minor-Major Seventh
Track 46 (disc 2) – Major Seventh Sharp-Five
Track 47 (disc 2) – Augmented Seventh
Track 48 (disc 2) – Half-Diminished Seventh (Minor Seventh Flat-Five)
Track 49 (disc 2) – Suspended Seventh

| C Major Seventh
Chord Symbol:
Cmaj7 | C Dominant Seventh
Chord Symbol:
C7 | C Minor-Major Seventh
Chord Symbol:
C-(maj7) | C Minor Seventh
Chord Symbol:
C-7 |

| C Major Seventh Sharp-Five
Chord Symbol:
Cmaj7(#5) | C Augmented Seventh
Chord Symbol:
C+7 | C Diminished Major Seventh
Chord Symbol:
Cº(maj7) | C Half-Diminished Seventh or C Minor Seventh Flat-Five
Chord Symbol:
Cø7 or
C-7(b5) |

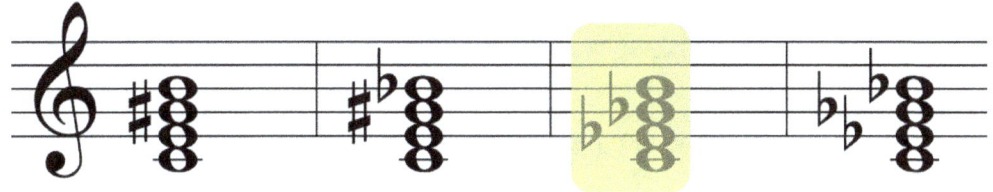

| C Suspended Major Seventh
Chord Symbol:
Csus(maj7) or Csus4(maj7) | C Suspended Seventh
Chord Symbol:
Csus7 | C Suspended Two Major Seventh
Chord Symbol:
Csus2(maj7) | C Suspended Two Seventh
Chord Symbol:
Csus2(-7) |

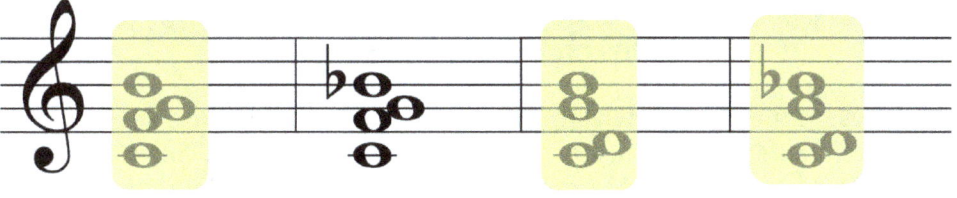

*Highlighted chords are not commonly used.

"maj" can be replaced with "M" or "Ma"
"-" can be replaced with "m" or "min"
"+" can be replaced with "aug" or "(#5)"
"o" can be replaced with "dim"

The Whole Diminished Seventh Chord

There is one more commonly used seventh chord. This one does not quite follow the pattern. It is the *diminished seventh chord.* We may also call this chord the *whole diminished seventh chord* or *fully diminished seventh chord* to differentiate it from the half-diminished seventh chord.

As the name implies, the diminished seventh chord creates the interval of a diminished seventh[1] between the root and the top note of the chord in its original voicing. In the C whole diminished seventh chord below, the top note is spelled or named as a B *double* flat. This is done to maintain this diminished seventh interval between the top and bottom notes of the chord. Generally, the notes of other whole diminished seventh chords will be named in a similar way, using whatever spelling creates a diminished seventh interval between the top and bottom notes of the chord and a minor third interval between each adjacent pair of notes in the chord's original voicing.

You can listen to a whole diminished seventh chord on track 50 (disc 2).

1. The diminished seventh interval is equivalent, in terms of sound, to a major sixth or nine half steps. See *Why an Augmented Fifth? (Diminished and Augmented Intervals)* on page 144 for more information.
❖ See *Enharmonic Spellings* and *Getting a Bit More Advanced...* on page 68 for background information on double flats and the concept of spelling.

C Whole Diminished Seventh or C Diminished Seventh
Chord Symbol:
C°7

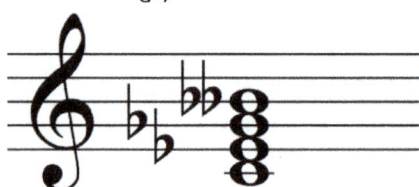

Inversion-less Chords

The diminished seventh chord creates the interesting effect of dividing the octave into even quarters. The adjacent notes of a diminished seventh chord in its original voicing are always a minor third apart. This means the chord can be put into any inversion while keeping the interval structure exactly the same. For example, a first inversion C whole diminished seventh is equivalent to a root position Eb whole diminished seventh. A second inversion C whole diminished seventh is the same as a root position Gb whole diminished seventh, and the third inversion is the same as the root position A whole diminished seventh. In practice, we simply use the names of the root position chords, as the concept of an inversion in this situation is basically meaningless.

A similar situation arises with the augmented triad, which divides the octave into even thirds. Chords like these are essentially "inversion-less" if you will. These chords tend to be heard as ambiguous in their centrality and can produce floating, weightless, wandering, or sometimes even magical sounding expressions.

Sixth Chords

Sixth chords are triads with an additional note a major sixth above the root. Take a look at the notation and construction of the *major* and *minor sixth chords*. Note that the major sixth chord is equivalent to the first inversion minor seventh and that the minor sixth chord is equivalent to the first inversion half-diminished seventh chord.

Listen to a major and minor sixth chord on tracks 51 (disc 2) and 52 (disc 2), respectively.

C Major Sixth
Chord Symbol:
C6

C Minor Sixth
Chord Symbol:
Cm6 or Cmin6 or C-6

Power Chords

Commonly played on distorted guitars in rock styles, the *power chord* is a chord of just two notes separated by a fifth. Often power chords are played with the root doubled an octave above the lower root of the chord.

Listen to a power chord played on a distorted guitar on track 53 (disc 2). For this track, you will first hear a sustained power chord and then afterward a brief example of how the guitar part of a song might use power chords.

C Power Chord
Chord Symbol:
C5

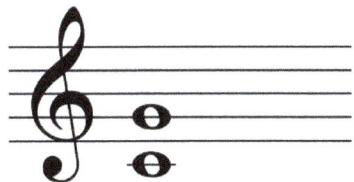

Adds and Omits

Adds and *omits* are used to add notes that are not normally part of the chord or leave out notes that are normally part of the chord. You will see adds and omits written in parenthesis after the main part of the chord symbol. For example:

C Add Nine
Chord Symbol:
C(add9)

C Major Seven Omit Five
Chord Symbol:
Cmaj7(omit5)

You can listen to a C(add9) chord on track 54 (disc 2) and a C major seventh omit 5 on track 55 (disc 2).

Slash Chords

You may indicate a specific note to be the lowest note of a chord by writing a slash after the chord symbol followed by the name of the *bass note* or the note you want to be the lowest pitch in the voicing of the chord. Slashes may be used to indicate an inversion or they may be used to place a note not normally in the chord in the bass part of the harmony. The first chord below is an example of the former, while the second is an example of the latter.

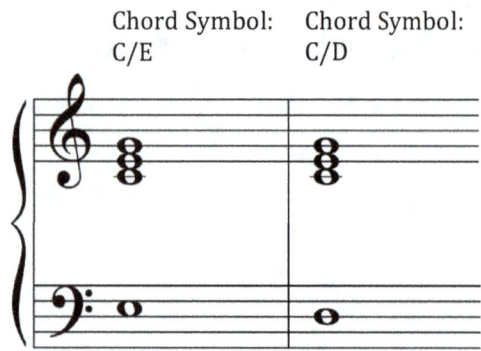

C Over E
Chord Symbol:
C/E

C Over D
Chord Symbol:
C/D

You can listen to a C over E chord on track 56 (disc 2) and a C over D chord on track 57 (disc 2).

Inventing Your Own Chords

At this point, we have now covered all the commonly used chord types but the possibilities are really endless. Any combination of notes can be a chord. I invite you to try inventing your own chord types. Maybe the chords you invent will unwittingly already exist in the commonly used structures we have covered. That's okay. Or maybe they exist as particular voicings where notes are rearranged in a particular way or certain notes are omitted or added. That's okay, too. The idea with this exercise is simply to let go of the prescribed structures and infuse some creativity in your harmonic writing, learning, and exploration.

You may consider the following factors when inventing your chord type:

1. **Intervals** – First and foremost, what are the intervals between the notes? What is the sonance of the intervals like? Are intervals repeated or emphasized?

2. **Centrality** – Look at the related fundamentals in your harmony.[1] Do they have consonant relationships or dissonant ones? Is there a clear overtone series that is referenced or is it ambiguous? Do you hear and feel a clear center in your chord? Do you hear multiple centers?

3. **Size** – Does your chord have a lot of different notes or only a few?

4. **Range** – Are your notes spread out over a large range or condensed into a small range?

5. **Auditory Imagination** – As you are putting together your chord, what do you hear? Do you hear the need for a certain pitch or for a certain expressive quality? When you discover the desire for something to happen to your chord, use your ear to find that something on your instrument.

Once you put together a new harmony, take note of the expressive effects of that harmony. Notice especially how the various factors you are manipulating, like the ones listed above, are correlated with the expression that you perceive or feel from the sound of your harmony. Another question to ask is "Do you like this chord?" Was your attempt successful or unsuccessful? In either case, learn from the experience of seeing musical elements translate into an expressive result.

1. *Related Series Analysis*, page 157

Listening to Advanced Harmonies in a Composition

To pull everything together, we will listen to and examine a short musical example that uses several of the new chord types we have studied in this chapter. You can listen to this piece on track 58 (disc 2).

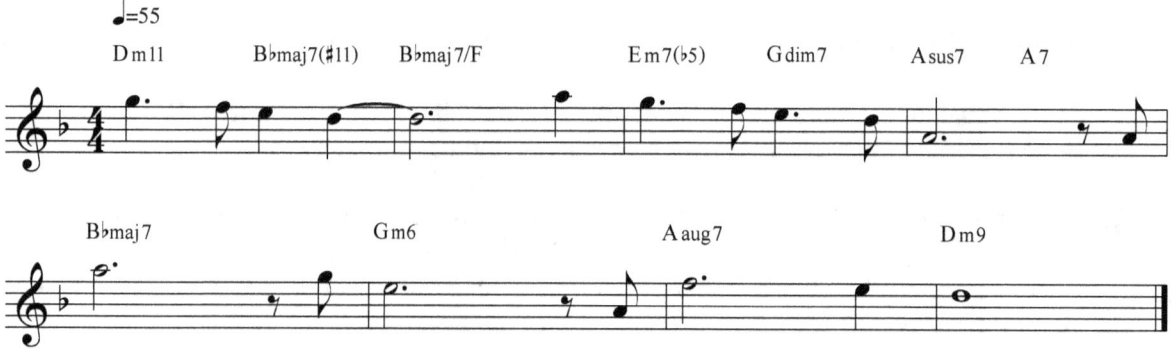

In general, this piece evokes an expression of sophistication and complexity that is typical of larger and more complex chords. The music is completely diatonic, which connects all the harmonies together strongly and provides a clear tonal center. Being in D minor and at a slow tempo, the piece is somewhat somber. The complexity of this story seems to be a deep and saddening one.

I recommend going through and noticing the expression of each chord in context, while following along with the notation. I'm going to leave that kind of exploration up to you here. I will, however, mention two interesting moments in this piece. Both concern the movement of harmony and specifically the harmonic resolution that takes place at these points.

The first is in measure four, at the end of the first line. Here, the dominant chord is played first as a suspended seventh and then as a dominant seventh. This is a common pair of chords, and it acts like a micro-resolution, which anticipates the larger resolution returning back to the I chord or tonic. However, in this piece the chords do not return to I but instead move to VI. This is a deceptive cadence. With the energy increased once again, the music sets up for the resolution of the second line, which now delivers the expectation of coming home to I. This second resolution uses an interesting variation on the standard V to I, which we are already familiar with. Here, the V is an augmented seventh chord. This variation works quite well in many situations and, in fact, may increase the gravity to the I chord by substituting a half step relationship for a common tone relationship between the two chords.[1]

1. See *Musical Gravity Between Chords* on page 253 and *Relationships Between Chords* also on page 253.

Though this is somewhat tangential to the primary topic of harmony we are exploring here, I'll also make a few comments about the melody in this piece, which has a few noteworthy examples of developmental strategies. The first phrase of this melody, played in measure one and held over into measure two, is quite similar to the second phrase, which starts at the end of measure two and lasts into measure four. To illustrate this point, notice that the notes and rhythms of measures one and three are exactly the same, except that the last note of measure three comes a half of a beat later than the corresponding note in measure one. The second phrase differs in its starting note, played on beat four of measure two, and its ending note, played on the downbeat of measure four. The harmonic accompaniment also differs between the two phrases. We could say that this is a form of a common section technique, as we discussed in Chapter Twelve,[1] combined with a new accompanying harmony part.

The melody in the first line sets up the rhythmic motif of using eighth note micro-approaches to lead into beats one and three. This rhythmic motif is extended in line two, but with the variation that only beat one is approached and played. This has the effect of spreading out the melody notes and creating more space, while also referencing the previous rhythmic pattern.

1. *Common Section*, page 343

Writing a Chord Progression With Advanced Harmonies

Let's try using some of these new chords in your own musical writing. For this activity, you may write a chord progression or a full musical piece or a section of one. We have already covered the basic process for writing chord progressions as well as full pieces at this point.[1] However, I'll make a couple of specific points about writing with the more advanced chord types we have covered in this chapter here.

First of all, let's discuss the use of tensions – the various ninths, elevenths, and thirteenths. We can essentially approach this as adding new elements to a progression of seventh chords. When selecting tensions, consider the table of common tensions on page 391. Also consider what tensions will be diatonic to the scale you are writing in. You may notice, for example, that the ninth of a dominant chord in a minor scale is a chromatic note. However, the flat ninth fits into the scale well and also works with the dominant seventh chord type.

Using chromatic tensions is certainly a valid possibility and if you would like, you can experiment with this or perhaps try it as a follow-on activity to writing with diatonic tensions and some of the other chord types presented in this chapter. The key is to be aware of what you are doing and how the various attributes you are creating will affect the expression of your composition. Chromatic tensions may create additional complexity and may move away from the sense of cohesion that a scale can provide.

Consider different inversions and voicings for all the chords you experiment with. Voicings can be especially important when using tensions, perhaps because there are simply more possibilities with voicings of larger chords. Refer to the material presented on polychords and constant interval voicings to give you some ideas on creating voicings for larger chords.[2] You also may consider revisiting the section *Voicing Considerations* in Chapter Six.[3]

To experiment with some of the new seventh sevenths chord we discussed, you might consider writing in a harmonic or melodic minor scale (or mixture of the two), as this provides several good opportunities to use these kinds of chords. For example, augmented sevenths can be used as a dominant chord in both the harmonic and melodic minor scales. The half-diminished seventh can be built off of the second degree of any minor scale – natural, harmonic, or melodic. In the harmonic or melodic versions, a whole diminished seventh can also be built off of the second degree. These are just a few ideas to get you started.

There are obviously a lot of possibilities here, so you may want to break things up a bit. You can take just one or two of the new chord types presented in this chapter and find scales that these chords fit into. You can then write a short chord progression just to test out the one or two chords you chose and gain experience in using them. Repeat the process with other chord types and slowly build up to a more diverse harmonic vocabulary that you can draw upon in your musical writing.

1. See *Writing Chord Progressions* on page 156, *Writing Themes* on page 278, and *Creating a Complete Composition* on page 380.
2. See *Polychords* on page 392 and *Constant Interval Voicings* on page 393.
3. *Voicing Considerations*, page 148

- More Scale Types -

Shorter Lived Scales

In this section, we will discuss some scales that form more dissonant relationships and may have a limited capacity for strong resolutions. These scales are often used for a shorter period of time to generate a certain musical effect, after which a return to a more common scale will occur. For these scales, think less in terms of writing an entire composition with these groups of notes and more in terms of palettes that can be used at certain times or in certain circumstances.

Whole Tone Scales

As the name implies, the whole tone scale is a scale built entirely on whole step intervals. Proceeding in whole steps, we divide the octave into six equal parts. The whole tone scale creates a perfectly ambiguous centrality like the augmented triad and the whole diminished seventh chord. The expression of this scale has a sense of being ungrounded or floating, an element of mystery, or a magical quality as well as an inability to strongly resolve to any one particular place. The whole scale is a cliché sound for the musical accompaniment to magical effects in movies or TV shows. However, it can be used effectively in a wide variety of circumstances.

To get a feel for the expression of this scale, you can listen to a short musical piece in the whole tone scale on track 59 (disc 2).

Whole Tone Scale

Symmetric Dominant and Diminished Scales

Both the *symmetric dominant scale* and the *symmetric diminished scale* are constructed out of an alternating series of half and whole steps. The symmetric dominant scale begins with a half step while the symmetric diminished scale begins with a whole step. They are called symmetric scales because they are symmetrical across the halfway point, meaning that the first half of the scale is constructed out of the same interval pattern as the second half of the scale. These scales are also sometimes referred to as *octatonic scales* because they contain eight notes.

Both the symmetric dominant and the symmetric diminished scales contain whole diminished seventh chords, which can be built off of the first and second degrees of the scale. And because of the "inversion-less" structure of the whole diminished seventh,[1] it is possible to build a diminished seventh chord off any degree of a symmetric dominant or diminished scale, though all of these chords will share the same notes as either the whole diminished seventh built on the first scale degree or the whole diminished seventh built on the second scale degree.

Unlike the symmetric diminished scale, the symmetry dominant scale can also construct a dominant seventh chord off of the tonic note of the scale. Though the symmetric dominant scale can be used in a diminished context, it is often used over a dominant harmony. In this context, the symmetric dominant scale may feel similar to a dominant seventh chord with possible tensions at the scale degrees b9, #9, #11, and 13. In contrast, the symmetric diminished scale will create an unambiguously diminished tonic harmony.

You can listen to an example musical piece in the C symmetric dominant scale on track 60 (disc 2) and another in the C symmetric diminished scale on track 61 (disc 2).

1. *Inversion-less Chords*, page 398

Symmetric Dominant Scale

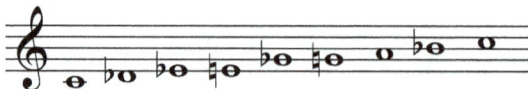

Symmetric Diminished Scale

The Altered Scale and Lydian Flat-Seven

I remember the notes of the *altered scale* as the three most important notes of a dominant seventh chord – Do (root), Mi (third), and Te (seventh)[1] – along with all the possible altered tensions that we can add to a dominant seventh chord – Ra (b9), Ri (#9), Fi (#11), and Le (b13).

The Lydian flat-seven scale, as you might guess, is a Lydian mode with seventh degree lowered by one half step. The reason I group these two scales together is that building a scale off of the fifth degree of an altered scale (which, relative to the tonic of the altered scale, is represented by the syllable Se) will result in a Lydian flat-seven scale. Therefore, the Lydian flat-seven scale is equivalent to using the fifth degree of an altered scale as a tonal center and, likewise, the altered scale is equivalent to using the fourth degree of a Lydian flat-seven scale as the tonal center. These scales are like "modes of each other."

There is an example of a piece in the altered scale on track 62 (disc 2) and another for the Lydian flat-seven scale on track 63 (disc 2).

1. I say that these notes – Do, Mi, and Te or root, third, and seventh – are the most important chord tones for a dominant seventh chord because the fifth does not significantly alter the centrality or quality of the harmony. For this reason, the fifth is often omitted from major, minor, and dominant sevenths as well as larger harmonies that use these sevenths chords as a base. See *Leaving Out the Fifth* on page 394.

Altered Scale

Lydian Flat-Seven

Inventing Your Own Scales

After seeing many examples of different types of scales, I invite you to try your hand at inventing your own scales. To test out your scale, I recommend that you improvise in your scale as well as write melodies, chord progressions, or other music in the scale, and then you can make modifications in response to your experience.

Here are some factors to keep in mind while designing your scale:

1. **Intervals** – Look at the intervals in your scale and particularly at the intervals between adjacent notes in the scale. Scales are often used in conjunct melodic situations where the music moves from one scale degree to the next. It is, therefore, very important to see how your scale sounds being played up and down. Are there any big leaps? Is the pattern of intervals varied? Symmetrical? Alternating? Uniform?

2. **Half Step Resolutions** – Where are there opportunities for half step resolutions in your scale? What scale degrees can act as pitch centers? What notes can act as points of tension?

3. **Intensity of Gravitation** – Do you want a high degree of musical gravity in this scale or a low degree of musical gravity? The potential for musical gravity can be increased by creating more half step relationships to notes of strong centrality or, in other words, notes that form consonant relationships with the tonal center. More musical gravity will create more opportunities for narrative-like expressions to unfold over time. Less musical gravity will create an expression more like a static picture painted in sound and less like an evolving movie or story. Intense musical gravity will also tend to create more diversity in the level of tension each note evokes. Some will seem very resolved while others will seem very tense. In contrast, less musical gravity will create a more uniform sound. You may even create a floating, undirected kind of feeling by reducing the expression of musical gravity.

4. **Chords** – What chords will be possible in this scale? Do you imagine that there will be a lot of harmonic movement or will the scale function mostly as the note group that accompanies one static harmonic center? What are the qualities and types of chords that will be available to you in this scale? What opportunities are there to create progressions and resolutions between chords?

5. **Larger Intervals** – Are there any particular larger intervals that you would like to be available in this scale? Is there an interval you want to use in melodic leaps or in harmony perhaps? If this is a desire of yours, how are these important intervals situated in the scale? Do they occupy scale degrees that are likely to be used while leaving a pitch center or resolving to one?

- Chord and Scale Structure Reference Charts -

Chord Type	Chord Symbol (Using C as an example)	Interval Between 1st and 2nd Notes	Interval Between 2nd and 3rd Notes	Interval Between 3rd and 4th Notes	Interval Between 4th and 5th Notes	Interval Between 5th and 6th Notes	Interval Between 6th and 7th Notes
Major Triad	C	M3	m3				
Minor Triad	C-	m3	M3				
Diminished Triad	C°	m3	m3				
Augmented Triad	C+	M3	M3				
Suspended Four Triad	Csus	P4	M2				
Suspended Two Triad	Csus2	M2	P4				
Major Seventh	Cmaj7	M3	m3	M3			
Minor Seventh	C-7	m3	M3	m3			
Dominant Seventh	C7	M3	m3	m3			
Minor-Major Seventh	C-(maj7)	m3	M3	M3			
Augmented Seventh	C+7	M3	M3	M2			
Major Seventh Sharp-Five	Cmaj7(#5)	M3	M3	m3			
Half-Diminished Seventh	C⌀7	m3	m3	M3			
Whole (Fully) Diminished Seventh	C°7	m3	m3	m3			
Suspended Seventh	Csus7	P4	M2	M2			
Major Sixth	C6	M3	m3	M2			
Minor Sixth	C-6	m3	M3	M2			
Major Ninth	Cmaj9	M3	m3	M3	m3		
Major Ninth Sharp-Eleven	Cmaj9(#11)	M3	m3	M3	m3	M3	
Major Thirteenth Sharp-Eleven	Cmaj13(#11)	M3	m3	M3	m3	M3	m3
Minor Ninth	C-9	m3	M3	m3	M3		
Minor Eleventh	C-11	m3	M3	m3	M3	m3	
Minor Thirteenth	C-13	m3	M3	m3	M3	m3	M3
Dominant Ninth	C9	M3	m3	m3	M3		
Dominant Ninth Sharp-Eleven	C7(9, #11)	M3	m3	m3	M3	M3	
Dominant Thirteenth Sharp-Eleven	C13 (#11)	M3	m3	m3	M3	M3	m3

Scale Type	Interval Between 1st and 2nd Notes	Interval Between 2nd and 3rd Notes	Interval Between 3rd and 4th Notes	Interval Between 4th and 5th Notes	Interval Between 5th and (1st) 6th Notes	Interval Between 6th and (1st) 7th Notes	Interval Between 7th and (1st) 8th Notes	Interval Between 8th and 1st Notes
Major Scale	W	W	H	W	W	W	H	
(Natural) Minor Scale	W	H	W	W	H	W	W	
Harmonic Minor Scale	W	H	W	W	H	m3	H	
Melodic Minor Scale	W	H	W	W	W	W	H	
Major Pentatonic	M2	M2	m3	M2	m3			
Minor Pentatonic	m3	M2	M2	m3	M2			
Blues Scale	m3	M2	m2	m2	m3	M2		
Whole Tone Scale	W	W	W	W	W	W		
Symmetric Dominant	H	W	H	W	H	W	H	W
Symmetric Diminished	W	H	W	H	W	H	W	H
Altered	H	W	H	W	W	W	W	
Lydian Flat-Seven	W	W	W	H	W	H	W	
Ionian (Major Scale)	W	W	H	W	W	W	H	
Dorian	W	H	W	W	W	H	W	
Phrygian	H	W	W	W	H	W	W	
Lydian	W	W	W	H	W	W	H	
Mixolydian	W	W	H	W	W	H	W	
Aeolian (Minor Scale)	W	H	W	W	H	W	W	
Locrian	H	W	W	H	W	W	W	

These charts are not meant to be totally comprehensive but should be a good reference guide as you build your vocabulary of chords and scales. Remember that tensions can be altered by moving the ninth, eleventh, or thirteenth of a chord up or down a half step. More variations are possible with these alterations than the chord types listed on page 409.

In addition, remember that there are different ways of writing the same chord symbol. See the chord symbol chart below for information on equivalent chord symbols.

Key

M – major
m – minor
A – augmented
H – half step
W – whole step

"maj" can be replaced with "M" or "Ma"
"-" can be replaced with "m" or "mi" or "min"
"+" can be replaced with "aug"
"o" can be replaced with "dim"

Chapter Fourteen
Chromaticism

- Modulation -

In a composition that stays within one key for its whole duration, the tonal center of that key is clearly the primary center of pitch for that piece. But what if a piece moves from one key to another?

The event of changing from one key or scale to another in a piece of music is called a *modulation.* Using multiple keys throughout a piece creates another layer of expressive relationships to the interactions of a musical composition. When multiple scales are used in a piece of music, generally one key in particular arises as the *primary key*, while the other scales fall into some varying degree of a secondary role. And along with primary and secondary keys, we may also describe primary and secondary tonal centers that are associated with those keys.

Although there is no definite method of determining the primary key and tonal center of a piece, the scale the piece begins in and the scale the piece ends in are good starting places.

Notating Modulations

Sometimes, in music notation the key signature will change when the piece shifts into a new key; but other times, especially if the scale of the piece is changing quickly, the music notation will simply use accidentals when the key changes. See the notation below for an example of how a key signature looks in music notation when it is introduced in the middle of a piece. Notice the thin double bar line and the natural signs used to negate the accidentals of the previous key signature.

Telling a Story in Scales

The scales we use in our pieces help to shape the large-scale structure, development, and ultimately expressive story that our music creates. As the keys we venture into become less related to our primary key and tonal center, we evoke the sense of traveling farther away from home. When we shift back to keys that are more similar to the primary scale, with tonal centers that have stronger relationships to the primary tonal center, there is the sense of returning back to home. While melodies, chords, and rhythms craft an immediate short-term narrative, the structure and the movement from tonal center to tonal center shape the long-term, big-picture narrative of the piece.

The Circle of Fifths

Scales are more related when they are closer together on the circle of fifths. For example, notice that the C major scale and the G major scale are only different by one note and in addition their tonal centers form a highly consonant interval of a perfect fifth.

Using this circle of fifth paradigm will help us to evaluate and understand the progression a piece goes through from one scale to the next. It also reveals a particular technique for modulation. If you desire to travel from one key to another, find the shortest path to go from the first key to the second key on the circle of fifths and progressively modulate along the circle of fifths until you arrive at your destination. This technique ensures that the music will move in gradual small steps. This is often desirable. However, it is also possible to create expressions of sudden change by modulating directly to less related scales.

Pivot Chords

One technique for modulating is to use a chord that is shared by the current scale and the new scale you wish to go to, as a point of transition. A chord that is shared by two scales in this manner is called a *pivot chord*.

Parallel Scales

Parallel scales are scales that share the same tonal center but differ in scale type. For example, the D minor scale and the D major scale are parallel scales. Because parallel scales share the same tonal center, they are relatively easy to modulate to. There is no sense of shift in the centrality of the music. However, the mood of the music will change and the music will need to naturally follow this change for the modulation to work well.

Listening to a Modulation

Listen to track 64 (disc 2) to hear an example of a piece of music that modulates from one key to another. In this case, our example is a piano piece that moves from the key of C major to the key of Ab major. To do this, the piece gradually moves the harmony along the circle of fifths until it reaches the target key of Ab major on bar 7. The rest of the piece establishes the key of Ab by playing diatonic chord progressions that resolve to Ab as a tonal center.

The rhythm of this piece varies quite a lot in terms of meter and tempo. Starting around bar 10, however, a meter of 4/4 becomes relatively consistent though still varies somewhat. The shift toward relative rhythmic consistency helps emphasize the narrative of going out on a journey during the section where the harmony is shifting to a new key and the rhythm is changing frequently, and then arriving to a new destination when the harmony settles on Ab as a tonal center and the rhythm more consistently starts to revolve around a 4/4 meter.

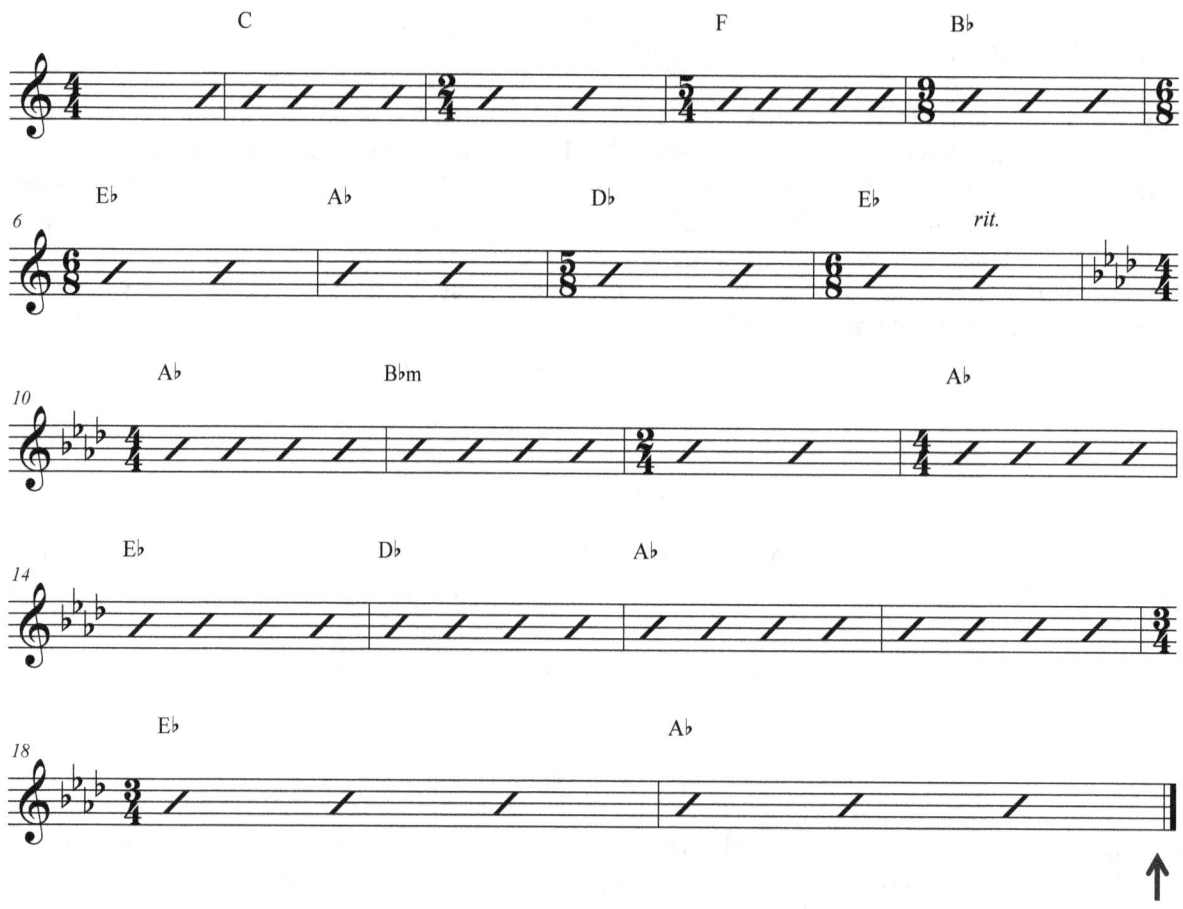

Why Place Time Signatures and Key Signatures at the End of Lines?

When the time signature or key signature changes at the beginning of a new line of music, we notate the time signature or key signature change at the end of the previous line to give the performer a warning that the time signature or key signature is about to change.

- Chromatic Harmony Techniques -

Relatedness in Chromatic Harmony

When using chords that fall outside of the scale, we are faced with the question "How can we create a sense of continuity, connection, and relatedness while exploring the realms beyond the boundaries of the scale?" The following three techniques – *modal interchange*, *secondary dominants*, and *tritone substitution* – are a few ways in which this can be accomplished. Each ensures a certain element of continuity, while venturing outside of the scale.

Modal Interchange

Modal interchange is the use of chromatic chords that are borrowed from parallel scales or modes. Most commonly, modal interchange occurs when a piece in a major scale uses chords from the parallel minor scale or when a piece in a minor scale uses chords from the parallel major scale. However, it is also possible to borrow from other modes or scales that begin with the same tonal center as the current key of a given piece.

Modal interchange functions on a principle similar to modulation via parallel scales. Parallel scales are related because they have the same tonal center. Their difference lies solely in the character and mood of the scale. So, modal interchange allows us to have access to a wider array of expressions while staying connected to the same center.

Listen to track 65 (disc 2) to hear a short example of modal interchange. Here a Bb minor chord is used as a chromatic chord in the scale of F major. This chord is borrowed from the parallel F minor scale.

What Is the Difference Between Modal Interchange and Modulation to a Parallel Key?

It is possible for the difference to become ambiguous. However, modal interchange generally borrows a single chord or a small number of chords from a parallel scale without establishing the parallel key as a constant element. In contrast, modulation is a transition that sets up a whole section of music in the parallel key.

Secondary Dominants

Secondary dominants are chords that are built a perfect fifth above the diatonic chords of the scale. The conventional dominant chord of a scale is the chord that is built on the fifth degree of the scale. This chord is built a fifth above the tonic chord of the scale and can be considered the *primary dominant chord* of a scale. In contrast, secondary dominant chords are built a fifth above other diatonic chords in the scale. We can name secondary dominants by describing them as the "five of" the scale degree they are built a fifth above. For example, the five of two (V of II) is the secondary dominant chord that is built a fifth above the diatonic chord built on the second degree of the scale. Secondary dominant chords can be major triads, dominant seventh chords, or larger chords that use a dominant seventh chord as a base.

The secondary dominant technique works on the tendency for harmony to resolve and connect by a fifth. The perfect fifth is a highly consonant and, thus, connecting interval. In addition, major triads and dominant seventh chords form useful half step relationships with chords built a fifth below them. As a result, secondary dominants sound connected to the scale and can produce a sense of musical gravity that leads into a diatonic chord in the scale.

Listen to track 66 (disc 2) to hear an example of a secondary dominant chord. In this example, a D7 is used as a chromatic chord in a Bb major scale. The D7 is a five of six (V of VI), which resolves as expected to a G minor chord, in this case a G minor eleven.

Tritone Substitution

A *tritone substitution* is a technique where a dominant seventh chord resolving down a fifth is replaced by a different dominant seventh chord built on a root a tritone away from the original chord. The result is a dominant seventh chord, which resolves to a chord built on a root a half step lower than the dominant seventh chord. Part of the reason why tritone substitution works is that a given dominant seventh shares two notes, the third and seventh of the chord, with the dominant seventh a tritone away. For example, the third and seventh of the C7 chord are E and Bb. The third and seventh of the Gb7 are Bb and E. So while dominant seventh chords separated by a tritone have very unrelated roots, the notes of the chords are actually similar.

Tritone Substitution With the II Chord

The very common II-V-I progression can be transformed into a II-bII-I progression by using a tritone substitution on the V chord. This progression has the added element of creating a pattern of descending half steps in the roots of the chords.

On track 67 (disc 2), you can hear an example of this kind of progression. In this example, the music starts on the tonic or I chord to give you a reference point and then proceeds to play a II-bII-I progression, giving us a combined I-II-bII-I progression.

Creating Other Chromatic Harmony

How else can you create a sense of relatedness and connection while venturing out into the realms of chromaticism? I invite you to explore some other possibilities of your own invention. Look for ways to connect harmonies together through shared notes and strong proportional relationships. Also keep in mind what effect you want to generate. Set up your music so that it naturally develops in the expressive direction your chromaticism creates. What expressive function does your chromaticism serve? Does it evoke complexity, drama, magical qualities, or something else? Whatever the answer may be, shape your composition around the expression so that the addition of chromaticism can enhance and cooperate with that expression and the other elements that serve it.

- Melodic Chromaticism -

While this last group of chapters is mostly focused on the harmonic aspect of music, I want to take a brief detour to talk about the melody and its own relationship with chromaticism.

We are only going to talk about melodic chromaticism briefly because, in essence, this topic is a minor extension of the principles of melodic analysis that were covered in Chapter Nine.[1] In Chapter Nine, we said that melodic notes became progressively higher energy as they moved through three primary categories – pitch centers, notes with whole step relationships to pitch centers, and notes with half step relationships to pitch centers. With the introduction of chromaticism, we will consider notes outside of the scale as falling into an additional category of high energy melodic notes built on top of or in conjunct with this paradigm we laid out in Chapter Nine. Chromatic notes may also have half or whole step relationships to pitch centers and this will create musical gravity just as before, particularly with half step relationships. However, chromatic melody notes will likely create more dissonant relationships in general to the harmony of a piece.

If a more moderate expression is desired, we will balance chromatic notes with musical elements like low energy positions on the TPLC group[2] or shorter durations. We will also likely set up chromatic melody notes as an expression of tension, which then resolves shortly after.

Let's examine the example below for a reference to what chromaticism in the melody can look and sound like. You can listen to this short segment of a melody on track 68 (disc 2).

1. See *Gravitational Positions* on page 242 and also, for a broader perspective, *Melodic Analysis* on page 245.
2. *The TPLC Group*, page 222

In this example, the piece is in the key of G major and C# is used as a chromatic note. Here, the chromatic note is balanced by a low energy position on the TPLC group. It lasts for only an eighth note and resolves immediately afterward to a strong chord tone. All in all, these balancing elements create a very moderate expression.

- Music Without a Scale -

With the use of increasingly frequent modulation and chromaticism, you may find yourself in a world where the scale is really only a reference point rather than a strict set of possibilities you must stick to. In fact, you may forget about the scale entirely and instead focus purely on pitches and relationships. This is an interesting paradigm to adopt and I encourage you to try it on. Though, thinking in scales does have a place, and I would not recommend forgetting about them either. However, when we explore musical territory beyond the scale, many new doors open for us as music creators and the vastness of musical expression increases still more in its dazzling diversity.

As an example, let's consider the piano composition below. You can listen to this piece on track 69 (disc 2).

Analysis

This piece starts out on a Bb major seventh chord, but it ends with the harmonic center a tritone away on E. This represents the largest possible movement on the circle of fifths, meaning that these harmonic centers are the least related in our musical system. While moving from Bb to E, the harmony and sense of centrality changes around in several interesting ways and never stays in any one place for very long. By the fourth bar, all twelve notes have been used at least once. This is truly music without a scale.

However, if we go through the piece measure by measure, we will find that scales are used and implied, just not in the ordinary way. Here, scales are not used as a constant aspect of the composition or as a palette of possibilities. Instead, the scales are groups of notes that are traveled to, one after another, measure by measure – more like the function we would normally associate with a chord.

The first measure seems to be in a Bb Lydian mode, the second in a Db Lydian mode. Notice how in these opening measures, the melody is harmonized with chord tones. The melody will continue to be harmonized in the third measure but after that it is only periodically joined by chord tones.

The jump from Bb Lydian to Db Lydian is a rather dramatic leap, as these scales differ in three out of seven notes. There is some modest connection in the fact that these scales are both Lydian scales and the Db major seventh could be considered a modal interchange chord from Bb Dorian. However, these connections are rather weak and the expressive result does feel like a bit of jump. The melody is ascending by steps when the chord changes and so this high energy harmonic movement seems to meaningfully emphasize the melodic motion at this point. The progression from Bb to Db Lydian also serves to create expectations from the very beginning that this work will not be a simple and diatonic one. This is helpful because later harmonic movements that travel beyond one particular scale are heard as less surprising with this expectation created up front.

In the third measure, the melody continues to be harmonized, first by an E augmented triad, then by an E major triad. At this point, a subtle pattern has been created in that the harmonic center is moving up by minor thirds. This is only the second time it has done so and yet it does still seem to serve as a point of connection, relating all of these otherwise relatively unrelated chords. The pattern of moving up in thirds is emphasized when the melody mimics this motion traveling from G# up a minor third to B and from B up a minor third to D on the downbeat of measure number four.

Looking at the harmony of the first four measures as a whole, we will find that in measures one and two, the movement between chords was high energy but the actual harmonies at each moment were fairly consonant, which helps to generate a relatively relaxed mood. In contrast, the augmented triad in bar three creates some dissonance and a corresponding increase in expressive energy. However, it resolves quickly into a major chord. Next, comes the movement from E major to B minor. These chords are a bit more related than what has come before. The progression here sounds perhaps like a IV to I movement in a B Dorian mode. But while the harmonic progression is becoming more related and, thus, lower energy, the melody is balancing that expression by reaching a climactic height in pitch and volume.

Taken together, this rebalancing of energy sets up the next two measures where the harmony settles into a B minor scale. In context of what we have heard before, these two measures feel like a considerable sense of arrival or coming home. In bar six, the harmony moves to a B dominant seventh chord. This chord shares the same harmonic center as the B minor scale that was being used in the last two bars but moves outside the minor quality of the scale. The B dominant seventh chord is then used to resolve down by a perfect fifth to an E minor, taking advantage of the strong resolving function of the authentic cadence. Measure six also creates a sense of connectivity by repeating the melodic rhythm of the previous two measures. Bar seven sets up a new melodic phrase and makes use of the note D# in the melody, implying a harmonic (or melodic) minor scale based on E.

The harmony now jumps to F#7 in bar eight, which is heard as fairly unrelated though there is a connection. In measures leading up to this point, we have set up E as a new harmonic center. The F#7 chord can be a considered a borrowed chord from E Lydian around this same harmonic center. This connection seems to be confirmed, when in the next measure – measure nine – the harmony returns to an E major seventh chord, the tonic chord of the E Lydian mode.

The rhythm of the melody has slowed to dotted quarters at this point but continues to rise higher and higher in pitch, creating a drawn out climax. The harmony next moves to a C major seventh harmony. This is felt to be another borrowed or modal interchange chord, now from the E minor scale.

The harmony moves one last time back to an E major seventh chord. A sharp eleventh is included here, creating an E Lydian sound (as the sharp-eleven or Fi is the differentiating note of the Lydian mode). We feel a sense of resolution, as we have been dancing around E for a few measures and now feel that we have landed in E Lydian. And so we have moved a full tritone away from Bb Lydian, where we started.

The Blurring of Chords and Scales

Due to this relatively strong resolution in E Lydian and the focus this scale was given in the second half the piece, one could make the argument that the primary scale of this piece should be considered E Lydian. However, I think this example serves the purpose of bringing to our attention the use and conception of scales in highly chromatic works or works with lots of harmonic motion from scale to scale. At this point the function of chord and scale is blurring and, in fact, some schools of thought in music have used the term *chord-scale* to define this very concept.

In any case, what we are fundamentally dealing with are groups of notes and different layers of harmonic centers, creating relationships over different durations in time. Some harmonic centers are related to the groups of notes in a measure, others to a section, others to a whole composition.

Analysis of Expression

This piece is a good example of what expressions are possible when chromaticism is balanced by low energy elements like soft dynamics, slow tempos, repeated rhythmic motifs, and consonance within single moments of harmony. Chromaticism, without balancing elements like these, can sound much more jarring or dramatic. But in this example, the expressions take on more of a floating character. To me, the expression also feels mysterious, deep, sad at times, but also subtly magical or wondrous. All of these are possibilities when we introduce complexities in harmonies and pitch centrality while also balancing that complexity with other low energy elements.

Complexity in harmonic movement introduces expressions that fall under the general categories of surprising, unexpected, or interesting motion. When that surprising movement is contextualized by lower energy expressions, we create subtly, mystery, intricacy, sophistication, and so on. The sense of floating can be created when we are uncertain of where the harmonic center is. The magical qualities can arise from unexpected events that are interpreted in more of a positive light.

Writing Chromatic Harmonies

For this activity, I invite you to try writing a chord progression or musical composition that uses chromaticism. Whether that means just a little bit of chromaticism, perhaps using a modal interchange chord here and there or maybe a single modulation, or using a lot of chromaticism, to the point where the concept of a traditional scale begins to break down, is up to you.

In the following boxes, I will outline some ideas to help you in this activity and then we will proceed to describe the process of writing with harmonic chromaticism in more detail.

Using Chromaticism With Intention and Purpose

In my own experience of learning to write music, I started to really understand how to use chromaticism for the first time when I internalized the ideas of being intentional and keeping expression in mind. These are concepts we have talked about before in other contexts. When I started experimenting with chromaticism, I would try using a chord or note outside of the scale just to see what happened. And this perspective was useful for learning about what kinds of expressions were created in what situations. However, I found that I did not start truly enjoying the results of chromaticism in my own compositions until I begin writing the chromaticism into the piece *for a purpose*. When I began using chromaticism because I was going for an expression of higher energy or drama or mystery or uncertainty or a quality of floating, that's when I got really effective musical results. Although this is an internal mindset, the result is that I was using different contextual elements on the seven spectra in conjunction with the chromaticism. I was increasing the volume or the tempo perhaps to signal a sense of drama. I was creating preceding material that anticipated and set up the expressions of chromaticism. Changes like these made the chromaticism *meaningful* and *purposeful*. It connected the musical elements with an intentional expression.

Balance

Another key principle to keep in mind with this activity is balance. When we use chromaticism we are introducing a high energy element into the music. This means that, unless we want a higher energy expression, we will have to balance chromaticism with low energy elements. Repeated interval structures, repeated rhythms, slower rhythms, or softer dynamics are all common approaches to this. And, of course, all the harmonic techniques we covered – pivot chords, parallel scales, moving by circle of fifths, modal interchange, secondary dominants, and tritone substitution – are all ways of creating harmonic connection to counterbalance otherwise less connected, less related chromatic harmonies.

However, if it sounds appealing, you can always take on the endeavor of creating dramatic music, which will fail to balance the energy of chromaticism and, in fact, will probably emphasize it with other high energy elements. Chromatic motion and complex centrality over the course of a chord progression are especially useful for surprising or unexpected expressions in a dramatic context. In contrast, anticipation, dread, and suspense are more often generated with dissonance combined with a more simple, clear harmonic center.

Summary

To review, we have two big ideas to hold in mind while writing chromatic harmony:

1. Writing in chromaticism for a specific, expressive purpose
2. Balancing the high energy expression of chromaticism with low energy elements

We have mentioned three specific techniques for modulation:

1. Pivot Chords
2. Parallel Scales
3. Moving by Circle of Fifths

And three specific techniques for chromatic harmony:

1. Modal Interchange
2. Secondary Dominants
3. Tritone Substitution

And further possibilities can be created by following the general principle of creating connection between chromatic elements.

Steps for Writing Chromatic Harmony

With this paradigm in mind, we are ready to take on the challenge of writing chromatic music. I'll briefly outline some steps to keep in mind as you go through the process:

1. Consider what expression you intend to create. We have a few options here. Combining chromaticism with simple centrality, we can create suspense at the high energy end of the spectrum or a more mild engaging complexity at the lower end. Combining chromaticism with complex centrality, we can create expressions of surprise at the high energy end of the spectrum or a sense of wandering or floating at the lower end. And, of course, all kinds of different possibilities exist in between these options or in combination with other musical elements.

2. With your target expression in mind, you can begin working on your piece. As you go, track the centers that you are creating. Are there perhaps multiple layers of centrality? An overall center and other layers of centers for sections, subsections, individual measures, and so on?

3. As you experiment with chromaticism, notice when the expression might be too jarring, in which case you will need to balance the expression out with more connection, or not dramatic enough, in which case you will to balance the expression in the other direction.

4. Take notice of the expressive depth you are able to create with all the possibilities that chromaticism opens up for us as musical creators. Expressions that work on different levels or expressions that contain a complex set of distinct expressive qualities can be created when venturing into this new musical territory.

5. As always, I recommend reviewing your work after completion and learning from the successes, failures, and surprises.

Summary for Group Six
Advanced Harmony

Tensions – Ninths, elevenths, and thirteenths
Tensions can be altered up or down a half step.

Chord Quality	Common Tensions
Major	9, #11, 13
Minor	9, 11, 13
Dominant	9, b9, #9, #11, 13, b13

Common Seventh Chords

Major Seventh
Minor Seventh
Dominant Seventh
Minor-Major Seventh
Half-Diminished Seventh or Minor Seventh Flat-Five
Whole Diminished Seventh
Major Seventh Sharp-Five
Augmented Seventh
Suspended Seventh

Scales Introduced in Chapter Thirteen

Whole Tone Scale
Symmetric Dominant
Symmetric Diminished
Altered
Lydian Flat-Seven

See the tables on pages 409-410 for a review of the interval structures of the chord and scale types we have covered in this book.

Polychords – Collections of notes that create the impression of multiple (most often two) distinct chords

Constant Interval Voicings – Voicings that emphasize a particular interval between the chord tones

Steps for Writing Chromatic Harmony

With this paradigm in mind, we are ready to take on the challenge of writing chromatic music. I'll briefly outline some steps to keep in mind as you go through the process:

1. Consider what expression you intend to create. We have a few options here. Combining chromaticism with simple centrality, we can create suspense at the high energy end of the spectrum or a more mild engaging complexity at the lower end. Combining chromaticism with complex centrality, we can create expressions of surprise at the high energy end of the spectrum or a sense of wandering or floating at the lower end. And, of course, all kinds of different possibilities exist in between these options or in combination with other musical elements.

2. With your target expression in mind, you can begin working on your piece. As you go, track the centers that you are creating. Are there perhaps multiple layers of centrality? An overall center and other layers of centers for sections, subsections, individual measures, and so on?

3. As you experiment with chromaticism, notice when the expression might be too jarring, in which case you will need to balance the expression out with more connection, or not dramatic enough, in which case you will to balance the expression in the other direction.

4. Take notice of the expressive depth you are able to create with all the possibilities that chromaticism opens up for us as musical creators. Expressions that work on different levels or expressions that contain a complex set of distinct expressive qualities can be created when venturing into this new musical territory.

5. As always, I recommend reviewing your work after completion and learning from the successes, failures, and surprises.

Summary for Group Six
Advanced Harmony

Tensions – Ninths, elevenths, and thirteenths
Tensions can be altered up or down a half step.

Chord Quality	Common Tensions
Major	9, #11, 13
Minor	9, 11, 13
Dominant	9, b9, #9, #11, 13, b13

Common Seventh Chords

Major Seventh
Minor Seventh
Dominant Seventh
Minor-Major Seventh
Half-Diminished Seventh or Minor Seventh Flat-Five
Whole Diminished Seventh
Major Seventh Sharp-Five
Augmented Seventh
Suspended Seventh

Scales Introduced in Chapter Thirteen

Whole Tone Scale
Symmetric Dominant
Symmetric Diminished
Altered
Lydian Flat-Seven

See the tables on pages 409-410 for a review of the interval structures of the chord and scale types we have covered in this book.

Polychords – Collections of notes that create the impression of multiple (most often two) distinct chords

Constant Interval Voicings – Voicings that emphasize a particular interval between the chord tones

Two big ideas to hold in mind while writing chromatic harmony:

1. Write in chromaticism for a specific, expressive purpose
2. Balance the high energy expression of chromaticism with low energy elements

Three techniques for modulation:

1. Pivot Chords – Shared chords between the current scale and the new scale
2. Parallel Scales – Scales that share the same tonal center
3. Moving by Circle of Fifths – Scales are most connected when close together on the circle of fifths

Three techniques for chromatic harmony:

1. Modal Interchange – Borrowing chords from parallel scales
2. Secondary Dominants – Major triads or dominant seventh chords a perfect fifth above a diatonic chord
3. Tritone Substitution – Replace a dominant V chord with a dominant bII chord

Further possibilities can be creating by following the general principle of creating connection between chromatic elements.

Conclusion

- Acknowledgments -

Creating *The Theory and Creation of Music* was an immense undertaking, which drew upon the knowledge, insights, and support of many people. I would like to take a moment to recognize and appreciate all of the people who were involved in this project.

Content Editor
Jeffrey Chappell

Jeffrey Chappell was and continues to be one of my most important teachers, in music and in life. He served as a technical advisor for this project, and also helped to inspire many of the ideas presented in this book. Specifically, I learned the improvisation techniques of closing your eyes while playing and singing while playing from Jeffrey, and have presented them in Chapter Nine in my own words. The section entitled *Five Musical Activities* in Chapter Two and the concept of the three stages of a style's development presented in Chapter Ten are both inspired by Jeffrey's teachings, as well.

I owe Jeffrey a lot, and I am honored by his participation in the creation of this book. His accomplishments are too many to enumerate here, but, nevertheless, here is a brief summary:

Jeffrey is a faculty member at Goucher College of Music, in Baltimore, Maryland. As a pianist, he has performed throughout the United States and abroad, with performances at venues like Carnegie Hall and Wolf Trap Park. Jeffrey once substituted for Claudio Arrau playing Brahms Second Concerto with the Baltimore Symphony Orchestra on four hours' notice and with no rehearsal. Even considering the circumstances, he went on to receive critical acclaim for the performance. Jeffrey is also a recording artist and award-winning composer. He holds degrees from both Curtis Institute and Peabody Conservatory.

Last but not least, he is a kind soul and a source of profound wisdom.

For more information about Jeffrey, visit: http://jeffreychappell.com/pianist/.

Copy Editor
Kris Patenaude

Kris is my loving aunt, and, luckily for me, an editor by profession. She helped me to refine my writing and correct the many mistakes that found their way into the later stages of the project. Truly, Kris's careful and perceptive editing made this a higher quality book. Furthermore, I became a better writer in the process of responding to her suggestions.

I want to express my immense gratitude for your help, Kris. Thanks so much for all the time you put into this project.

Cover Art and Illustrations
An Kelley

An created the cover art for this book and a couple of the more complex illustrations: specifically, the image of a person playing a guitar in Chapter One and the image of a drum set in Chapter Eight. I love An's work and am very grateful to have it included as part of the project. It took a lot of time and patient discussion to complete these illustrations. Your sacrifice and contribution are deeply appreciated. Thanks, An.

My Parents
Lynn Haas and John Taylor

From day one of my musical journey, my parents have supported my education and encouraged me on my path. Some of the content in this book is fairly original, but, as is always the case in the developments of any field, my work is based on the instruction of others. It is only through my education that I could have produced the work you are reading today.

I also want to especially thank my mother for engineering the web components of this book.

Thank you, my very special mom and dad.

Guitarist and Content Advisor
Marcos Mayo

Marcos played guitar (beautifully I should add) on several of the example audio tracks that accompany this book. He also gave me feedback and suggestions on my writing about musical styles. Thanks a lot for your contributions, Marcos. Your advice about the musical styles chapter was very useful and improved the quality of this work.

Content Advisor
Scott Welker

Scott gave me feedback on the book as a whole. In addition to some very important suggestions, Scott also advised me on the publishing aspect of book writing. Thank you so much for your support, Scott!

Content Advisor
Dan Haas

Dan Haas is my wise and passionate uncle. He also generously gave me feedback on this book and his suggestions made a difference. Thank you, Dan. You improved the quality of this book. I really appreciate your interest and thoughtful engagement.

Musicians for Additional Audio Tracks

The authors of the book *Essential Grooves for Writing, Performing, and Producing Contemporary Music* generously allowed me to use a few of their audio tracks in this book. Specifically, the examples taken from their work are tracks 72 (Funk Groove), 73 (Soul Ballad Groove), and 78 (Swing Groove). Please check out their book! It is highly recommended, especially if you are interested in exploring different contemporary styles. Thanks so much to Sher Music Co. (www.shermusic.com) and the following musicians who created these superb musical examples:

Author, Recording, and Mixing
Dan Moretti

Guitar
Kevin Barry and Gustavo Assis-Brasil

Author, Keyboards
Matthew Nicholl

Author, Bass
Oscar Stagnaro

Drums
Eric Doob

Percussion
Paulo Stagnaro

Notator for Beethoven's Fifth and Pachelbel's Canon
Brede Sørøy

Brede generously allowed me to use his scores for my analysis of Beethoven's Fifth and Pachelbel's Canon. Note that I have altered his work for the purposes of the book. Thank you so much for your generosity and contribution.

Berklee College of Music

I attended Berklee College of Music and received my undergraduate degree from this great institution. I learned a lot from Berklee's faculty, students, facilities, and books. Much of what I learned there made its way into this book in one way or another. I appreciate and thank you all, members of the Berklee community.

Sources

I also want to thank the authors of all the sources I consulted during my research for this project. All of you have also made this project possible. Please see the bibliography on the following page for specific details.

- Bibliography -

Campbell, Murray, and Clive Greated. *The Musician's Guide to Acoustics*. New York: Schirmer, 1988.

"Chicago House." *University of Vienna*, www.univie.ac.at/Anglistik/webprojects/LiveMiss/Chicago-House/house-text.htm. Accessed 3 Aug. 2016.

Cormier, Stephen M. *Modal Music Composition*. Expanded ed. Arlington, VA: Inman & Artz Publishers, 2006.

Feezell, Mark. *Music Theory Fundamentals*. LearnMusicTheory.net, 2016.

"Frequencies of Equal Tempered Scale." *Michigan Tech*, www.phy.mtu.edu/~suits/notefreqs.html. Accessed 15 Sept. 2016.

Gerou, Tom, and Linda Lusk. *Essential Dictionary of Music Notation*. Los Angeles: Alfred Music, 1996.

"IPA Chart with Sounds." *International Phonetic Alphabet*, www.internationalphoneticalphabet.org/ipa-sounds/ipa-chart-with-sounds/. Accessed 9 Dec. 2016.

Jazz. Directed by Ken Burns, PBS, 2001.

"Ludwig van Beethoven: Symphony No. 5, Analysis by Gerard Schwarz." *Kahn Academy*, www.khanacademy.org/humanities/music/music-masterpieces-old-new/ludwig-van-beethoven-music/v/ludwig-van-beethoven-part-1. Accessed 15 Sept. 2016.

Miller, Michael. *The Complete Idiot's Guide to Music Composition*. New York: Penguin Group, 2005.

Moretti, Dan, et al. *Essential Grooves for Writing, Performing, and Producing Contemporary Music*. Petaluma, CA: Sher Music, 2010.

Music Map. musicmap.info/#. Accessed 1 Aug. 2016.

New World Encyclopedia contributors. "Country Music." *New World Encyclopedia*, 26 June 2013, www.newworldencyclopedia.org/p/index.php?title=Country_music&oldid=970331. Accessed 17 Mar. 2017.

New World Encyclopedia contributors. "Swing." *New World Encyclopedia*, 9 Nov. 2015, www.newworldencyclopedia.org/p/index.php?title=Swing&oldid=991828. Accessed 1 Aug. 2016.

Ohala, Diane, Dr. "Introduction to Phonetics." 28 Oct. 2004. *The University of Arizona*, www.u.arizona.edu/~ohalad/Phonetics/. Accessed 1 Oct. 2016.

Parncutt, Richard. *Harmony: A Psychoacoustical Approach*. Berlin: Springer-Verlag, 1989.

Pirsig, Robert M. *Zen and the Art of Motorcycle Maintenance*. New York: Quill, 1979.

Roederer, Jaun G. *Introduction to the Physics and Psychophysics of Music*. New York: Springer-Verlag, 1973.

Seashore, Carl E. *Psychology of Music*. Mineola, NY: Dover, 1967.

Shaffer, Kris, et al. *Open Music Theory*. Edited by Kris Shaffer, and Robin Wharton. Hybrid Pedagogy Publishing, openmusictheory.com/. Accessed 1 Sept. 2016.

Strain, George M. "Frequency Hearing Ranges in Dogs and Other Species." *Louisiana State University*. Accessed 11 Mar. 2016.

Taruskin, Richard, and Christopher H. Gibbs. *The Oxford History of Western Music*. New York: Oxford UP, 2013.

"World Music." *University of Western Michigan*, www.wmich.edu/mus-gened/mus150/WorldMusic.htm. Accessed 11 Jan. 2017.

- Track List -

Disc One

Chapter One
1. Pulses to Pitch
2. Six Frequencies
3. Timbres

Chapter Two
4. Expected Resolution
5. Unexpected Resolution
6. Four Roles in the Ensemble
7. Melody
8. Accompaniment
9. Bass Line
10. Harmony
11. Percussion
12. Flute part

Chapter Three
13. C Major Triad
14. C Major Triad E up an Octave
15. C Major Triad Doubled C
16. C Major Triad Arpeggio
17. C Major Triad Pattern
18. Seven Triads of C Major

Chapter Four
19. Composition at 110 bpm
20. Composition at 220 bpm
21. Whole, Half, and Quarter Notes
22. Piece in 4/4
23. Piece in 3/4
24. Sixteenths Rhythm
25. Use of Space 1
26. Use of Space 2
27. Pick Up
28. Crescendo and Diminuendo
29. Accelerando
30. Ritardando
31. A Tempo

Chapter Five
32. Unison
33. Minor Second
34. Major Second
35. Minor Third

36. Major Third
37. Perfect Fourth
38. Tritone
39. Perfect Fifth
40. Minor Sixth
41. Major Sixth
42. Minor Seventh
43. Major Seventh
44. Octave
45. Sonance of the Intervals
46. Dissonance in and out of Context
47. Sonance of the Intervals in Just Intonation
48. Alternate Tuning System

Chapter Six
49. Major Triad and Example
50. Minor Triad and Example
51. Diminished Triad and Example
52. Augmented Triad and Example
53. Major Seventh and Example
54. Minor Seventh and Example
55. 12-Bar Blues
56. Inversions of C Major
57. Inversions of C7
58. Muddiness
59. I-IV-V-I Progression
60. Voice-Led Progression

Chapter Seven
61. Twinkle Twinkle Little Star
62. Gb Major Pentatonic Solo
63. Eb Minor Pentatonic Solo
64. Gb Major Accompaniment
65. Eb Minor Accompaniment

Chapter Eight
66. Slur
67. Staccato
68. Temporal Proportionality Balanced With Loudness
69. Starting on Different Rhythmic Positions
70. Starting on Different Rhythmic Positions Accompaniment
71. House Beat
72. Funk Groove
73. Soul Ballad Groove
74. Playing Behind or Ahead of the Beat
75. Triplets
76. Polyrhythms
77. Swing Eighths
78. Swing Groove

79. The Rhythms of Many Travels

Chapter Nine
80. Character of the Scale Degrees (Major)
81. Character of the Scale Degrees (Minor)
82. Ti-Do Resolution
83. Fa-Mi Resolution
84. Re-Me Resolution
85. Le-So Resolution
86. Relationships to Chord Tones
87. Relationships to Chord Tones Accompaniment

Disc Two

1. Musical Gravity Between Chords 1
2. Musical Gravity Between Chords 2
3. III-I in Major
4. Harmonic Minor Melody
5. Melodic Minor Melody
6. Jazz Melodic Minor Melody
7. Perfect Authentic Cadence
8. Imperfect Authentic Cadence
9. Dominant Seventh Cadence
10. Plagal Cadence
11. Half Cadence
12. Deceptive Cadence
13. II-V-I Major Triads
14. II-V-I Major Sevenths
15. II-V-I Minor Triads
16. II-V-I Minor Sevenths
17. Ionian
18. Dorian
19. Phrygian
20. Lydian
21. Mixolydian
22. Aeolian
23. Locrian

Chapter Ten
24. 12-Bar Blues Accompaniment

Chapter Eleven
25. Constant Numeric Interval Method
26. Chord Tone Method
27. Parallel Fifths

Chapter Twelve
28. Sequence
29. Temporal Scaling

30. Inversion
31. Retrograde
32. Retrograde Inversion
33. Same Rhythm
34. Same Pitch
35. Common Section

Chapter Thirteen
36. Major Seventh With Tensions
37. Minor Seventh With Tensions
38. Dominant Seventh With Tensions
39. Polychord
40. Constant Fifths
41. Constant Fifths Plus the Eleventh
42. Constant Fourths
43. Sus4
44. Sus2
45. Minor-Major Seventh
46. Major Seventh Sharp-Five
47. Augment Seventh
48. Half-Diminished Seventh (Minor Seventh Flat-Five)
49. Suspended Seventh
50. Whole Diminished Seventh
51. Major Sixth Chord
52. Minor Sixth Chord
53. Power Chord
54. Adds
55. Omits
56. Slash Chord Over E
57. Slash Chord Over D
58. Advanced Harmony Combinations
59. Whole Tone Scale
60. Symmetric Dominant Scale
61. Symmetric Diminished Scale
62. Altered Scale
63. Lydian Flat-Seven Scale

Chapter Fourteen
64. Modulation
65. Modal Interchange
66. Secondary Dominants
67. Tritone Substitution
68. Melodic Chromaticism
69. Music Without a Scale

- Glossadex -

12-Bar Blues – A chord progression and structure of twelve measures used, in many forms and with many variations, in blues music. See page 295.

"A" – The rhythmic position halfway between an "and" and the following beat. "A" positions come after an "and" but before the next beat. See page 98.

A Tempo – A direction that indicates that the music should return to its original tempo after either speeding up or slowing down. See page 110.

Accelerando – A direction that indicates that the music should become faster or, in other words, increase in tempo. See page 109.

Accent – A symbol that indicates that the performer should emphasize a given note in terms of volume. See page 215.

Accidental – A sharp, flat, or natural sign that appears outside of the key signature in music notation. See page 179.

Accompaniment – The background of a composition, including the harmony parts, percussion parts, and the bass line. See page 57. Further information is provided about the function of the accompaniment and its relationship to the melody in the section entitled *Applications for Each Role in the Ensemble* on page 312.

Acoustics – The study of sound, as it occurs in the physical, external world. See page 30.

Action Learning Process – The process of learning through doing. This type of learning includes practicing one's craft and learning from one's own successes, failures, and surprises. It is one of the three aspects of learning, namely concept, expression, and action learning. See page 10.

Additive Synthesis – A type of synthesis that involves combining sine waves together at different volume levels to create a new timbre. See page 325.

Additive Time Signature – A time signatures that expresses groupings of the divisions of the beat in place of the top number. For example, 3+2+2/8 is an additive time signature. See page 106.

Aeolian – A type of scale defined by the following interval pattern: whole step, half step, whole step, whole step, half step, whole step, whole step. Aeolian is one of the seven modes and is also equivalent to the minor scale or natural minor scale. See page 263.

Ahead of the Beat – Occurring earlier in time than the established rhythm would otherwise dictate. See page 231.

Alberti Bass – A chord pattern that repeats the following sequence: lowest note, highest note, middle note, highest note. See page 81.

Alliteration – A description of words that share a beginning sound. See page 276.

Alteration (for Chords With Tensions) – A tension other than the notes Re, Fa, or La. See page 390.

Altered Scale – A scale defined by the following interval pattern: half step, whole step, half step, whole step, whole step, whole step, whole step. See page 407.

Ambient – A spacious and mellow form of electronic music that emerged initially around the 1970s. See page 307.

Anacrusis – See entry for pick up. See page 107.

"And" – The rhythmic position halfway between the beats in a measure. See page 98.

Anti-Node – A point on a wave or vibrating object that moves the most. See page 37.

Approach – The sense that music is leading up to or being pulled into a strong rhythmic position. This term is in contrast to arrival. See page 229.

Arpeggio – A chord played one note at a time from bottom to top or from top to bottom. See page 80.

Arrival – The expression of having arrived at a strong rhythmic position. See page 229.

Articulation – A category of directions used in music notation that provides details about how the performer should play a note in terms of length and emphasis in volume. See page 214.

Assonance – A description of words that share a vowel sound. See page 276.

Asymmetric Time Signature – See entry for complex time signature. See page 100.

Atonality – The characteristic of not have a tonal center or pitch center of any kind. This term is in contrast to the term "tonality." See page 293.

Attack – The sound at the beginning of a note. See page 325.

Augmented Fourth – An interval equivalent to six half steps. See page 123.

Augmented Seventh Chord – A chord defined by the following interval pattern: major third, major third, major second. See page 396.

Authentic Cadence – The progression of V to I, used as an ending to a piece or section. See page 260.

Automation – The data that describes how a setting or parameter changes in a DAW over time. See page 327.

Auxiliary Track – A track that receives a signal from another track and process it before outputting its signal to the mix. See page 329.

Avant-Garde Jazz – A later style of jazz, initially arising in the late 1950s, featuring an experimental attitude. See page 299.

Backbeat – Beats two and four, in 4/4 time. See page 226. Historical information about the backbeat is presented in the box entitled *Ragtime, Stride, and Boogie-Woogie* on page 297 and other sections of Chapter Ten.

Background Melody – A melody that is part of the accompaniment or background of the piece. See page 58.

Balance – One of the three tools of musical analysis, namely common expression, balance, and context. The principle of balance says that extremely low or high energy musical elements can be combined with other elements on opposing ends of the expressive spectrum to form overall moderate musical expressions. See page 52.

Bar – See entry for measure. See page 89.

Bar Line – The vertical lines used to separate each measure in music notation. See page 89.

Baroque Period – The period of classical music from approximately 1600 CE to 1750 CE. See page 292.

Bass Clef – A clef is a symbol used in music notation to signify what set of notes or pitches a given staff covers. The bass clef indicates that the fourth line from the bottom on the given staff represents the note F3 or the first F below middle C. See page 75.

Bass Line – Part of the accompaniment that consists of the lowest single note in a composition at any given moment. Like the melody, the bass line is a series of single notes in a specific rhythm. See page 57.

Be-Bop – A style of jazz that first emerged in the mid-1940s. See page 298.

Beat – A recurring increase in volume or loudness, the pulse or emphasis that you might tap your foot to while listening to a piece of music. See page 86.

Behind the Beat – Occurring later in time than the established rhythm would otherwise dictate. See page 231.

Big Band Jazz – See entry for swing. See page 298.

Bluegrass – An upbeat style of country that emerged in the late 1940s. See page 300.

Blues – A style of music that arose out of the merger of African-American work songs and spirituals. Blues comes into being in the late 19th century and continues in many different forms through the 20th century and all the way up to present day. See page 294.

Blues Scale – A scale defined by the following interval pattern: minor third, major second, minor second, minor second, minor third, major second. See page 295.

Boogie-Woogie – A piano-based style that first arose in the late 1920s. See page 297.

Bossa Nova – A style that emerged in the late 1950s onward through a combination of Brazilian and jazz styles. See page 299.

BPM – Stands for "beats per minute" and is used to measure the tempo of a piece of music. See page 87.

Bridge – A section of a song used to create variety or create contrast from the verse and chorus. See page 346.

British Invasion – A movement of rock music during the 1960s in which many bands from the United Kingdom rose to popularity both in their own country and in the United States. See page 302.

C Clef – A type of clef that designates a given position on the staff as being middle C. See page 351.

Cadence – A sequence of two chords that is used at the end of a progression. See page 260.

Canon – A type of polyphonic or contrapuntal (involving counterpoint) work where each part or melodic line plays the same music, only offset by a certain number of measures or beats. See page 369.

Cent – A unit of measurement for pitch or frequency equivalent to a hundreth of a half step. See page 161.

Center – A position of low energy in a system of proportional relationships. See page 54. See page 240 for information specifically about centers in the domain of pitch.

Chamber Music – Music written for a small ensemble of instruments. This term is generally used in the classical tradition. See page 292.

Chicago Blues – A style that emerged in 1940s as blues music moved from the rural country into urban settings. See page 301.

Chill-Out – A form of electronic music that emerged in the 1980s, inspired by ambient and downtempo music. See page 307.

Chord Pattern – An arrangement of the notes of a chord into specific octaves and into specific sequences and rhythms over time. See page 80.

Chord Progressions – Sequences of chords. See page 151.

Chord Symbols – Abreviated ways to write chords, including the root of the given chord and additional letters or symbols that specify the given chord type. See page 139.

Chord Tone – A note that is part of a chord. See page 139.

Chord Tone Method – A method of creating harmonized melodies by using chord tones that support the primary melody. See page 314.

Chord Type – A group of chords that shares a specific pattern of intervals. See page 137.

Chords – Groups of notes that sound good together or, at least, groups of notes that produce a certain useful effect from a composer's point of view. See page 78. Intermediate and advanced information about chords can be found in Chapter Six (page 137) and Chapter Thirteen (page 388).

Chorus – A section of a song that repeats in terms of both melody and lyrics. The chorus is often meant to be memorable, catchy, and easy to sing along to. See page 346. In the context of music production, a chorus can refer to an effect that simulates the sound that is produced by multiple performers playing a given part. For information about this definition, see page 332.

Chromatic – Outside of a scale. See page 82.

Chromatic Sequence – A type of developmental technique where the pitch of a musical idea is changed while maintaining the same intervals in terms of both number and quality. See page 340.

Circle of Fifths – An arrangement of the twelve notes or note names where each note is placed a perfect fifth away from the last. See page 181.

Classic Metal – An early style of metal that developed in the 1970s. See page 304.

Classical – The style and tradition of music that first arose in Europe around the beginning of the 17th century. The primary period of classical music – known as the common practice period – ended around the beginning of the 20th century, but forms of classical music continue to evolve up to the present day. See pages 291-294.

Classical Period – The period of classical music from approximately 1750 CE to 1820 CE. See page 292.

Clef – A symbol used in music notation to signify what set of notes or pitches a given staff covers. See page 75.

Close Voicing – A voicing where the notes are as close together as possible in terms of pitch. This term is in contrast to open voicings. See page 150.

Closing (in Sonata Form) – The last section of the exposition and recapitulation of a piece in sonata form. The closing is part of the internal structure of both the exposition and recapitulation, which generally progresses from first theme to transition to second theme to closing. See page 348.

Common Expression – One of the three tools of musical analysis, namely common expression, balance, and context. The principle of common expression says that musical elements with similar positions on the seven basic spectra will have similar musical expressions. See page 52. One example of the principle of common expression, in this case concerning intervals, is presented on page 119.

Common Practice Period – The primary era of classical music extending from approximately 1600 to 1910 CE. See page 290.

Common Time – Another name for the time signature 4/4. See page 91.

Common Tone – A note that is shared between two chords. See page 154.

Complex Centrality – The characteristic of an unclear or ambiguous center or, alternatively, a collection of competing centers. This term is in contrast to simple centrality. See page 56. More advanced information about complex centrality is presented in the section entitled *Related Series Analysis* on page 157.

Complex Time Signature – A time signature that is not a simple or compound time signature. In other words, a time signature where the beats do not consistently and uniformly divide into either two or three parts. Often in complex time signatures, some beats are divided into two while other beats are divided into three. See page 100.

Composition – A complete musical work. A composition is synonymous with a piece of music. See page 51.

Compound Duple Meter – A time signature or meter with two beats per measure, where the beats divide into groups of three. For example, 6/8 is a compound duple meter. See page 105.

Compound Intervals – Intervals larger than an octave. See page 128.

Compound Quadruple Meter – A time signature or meter with four beats per measure, where the beats divide into groups of three. For example, 12/8 is a compound quadruple meter. See page 105.

Compound Time Signature – A time signature where the beats are divided into three parts. See page 100.

Compound Triple Meter – A time signature or meter with three beats per measure, where the beats divide into groups of three. For example, 9/8 is a compound triple meter. See page 105.

Compressor – A type of sound processor that reduces the dynamic range of a given sound. See page 330.

Concept Learning Process – A type of learning that deals with ideas, systems, labels, naming, abstractions, patterns, and principles. This is one of the three aspects of learning, namely concept, expression, and action learning. See page 10.

Concert Pitch – The unmodified and original system of pitches. This term is in contrast to transposed pitch. See page 320.

Condenser Microphone – A type of microphone that uses two parallel, electrically charged plates. See page 322.

Conjunct – A description of music that has little movement or, in other words, uses mostly small intervals between notes over time. This term is in contrast to disjunct. See page 155.

Consonance – Strong pitch proportionality, forming simple ratio relationships in terms of frequency or pitch. See page 129. For the poetic or lyric-writing device, see entry for literary consonance. See page 276.

Consonant – A discriptor of sounds that are characterized by strong pitch proportionality. See page 130. In the context of speech and language, consonants are sounds produced through some form of constriction of airflow, generally created by the tongue or lips. This term is in contrast to the term "vowel." See page 277.

Constant Interval Voicing – A voicing that creates a repetition (either ubiquitously or partially) of a given interval (either a general numeric interval or an exact numeric-quality interval). See page 393.

Constant Numeric Interval Method – A method of creating harmonized melodies by placing harmonizing lines a given numeric interval above or below the primary melody. See page 314.

Context – One of the three tools of musical analysis, namely common expression, balance, and context. The principle of context emphasizes the importance of considering what impact surrounding musical elements might have on the expression of one particular aspect of a composition. See page 53. One example of this principle is presented in the box entitled *The Application of Dissonance in Context* on page 131.

Contour – The general shape of a melody in terms of pitch. See page 247.

Contrapuntal Motion – The motion in pitch of the different melodic lines relative to one another. See page 317.

Contrary Motion – A type of contrapuntal motion where the melodic lines move in opposing directions. See page 317.

Contrasting Middle – The structural function of providing variation or contrast. See page 348.

Cool Jazz – A later style of jazz music that emerged as a continuation and reaction to be-bop. Cool jazz comes into being in the 1950s going forward. See page 299.

Count Off – Beats or rhythmic positions that are said aloud to set the tempo for a piece. See page 91.

Counterpoint – Music that uses multiple, simultaneous melodies. The term "counterpoint" is interchangeable with the term "polyphony." See page 58 for the original presentation of this term and page 317 for additional information.

Country – A style of music that emerged in the early 20th century in the United States and continues in many forms all the way up to present day. See page 300.

Country Blues – Early styles of blues that emerged in rural areas during the early parts of the 20th century. See page 301.

Crescendo – Music that grows louder or increases in volume. See page 108.

Cut Time – Another name for the time signature 2/2. See page 102.

DAW – Digital audio workstation. DAWs are computer programs designed for music production. See page 321.

Death Metal – A dark variation of metal music that emerged in the late 1980s and 1990s. See page 304.

Deceptive Cadence – A cadence that progresses from the dominant chord or the V chord to any other chord except for the tonic. See page 262.

Decibel – A unit of measurement for amplitude. See page 331.

Delay – An echo effect. See page 327.

Derivative Center – A position of relatively low energy in a system of proportional relationships, which is not the position of lowest energy or the position known as an original center. See page 54.

Descriptive Non-Linear Format – A presentation format where the material can be referenced in a variety of sequential orders and additional information is provided that describes the characteristics of the primary content and helps the reader or learner navigate his or her own learning process. See page 11.

Development – The concept of musical ideas that change and grow in patterned ways over time. See Chapter Twelve (page 334) as a whole for information about this concept. The term "development" can also refer to the second section of a composition in sonata form. For information about this definition, see page 348.

Diatonic – In a scale. See page 82.

Diatonic Sequence – A type of developmental technique where the pitch of a musical idea is changed while maintaining the same general numeric intervals. See page 340.

Differentiating Note – A note that characterizes a given type of chord or scale. See page 242.

Diminished Fifth – An interval equivalent to six half steps. See page 123.

Diminuendo – Music that becomes quieter or decreases in volume. See page 108.

Disco – A style of music that became popular in the late 1970s, fusing pop and funk elements together. See page 305.

Disjunct – A description of music that has a lot of movement or, in other words, uses mostly large intervals between notes over time. This term is contrast to conjunct. See page 155.

Dissonance – Weak pitch proportionality, forming complex ratio relationships in terms of frequency or pitch. See page 129.

Dissonant – A discriptor of sounds that are characterized by weak pitch proportionality. See page 130.

Distortion – An effect that alters a sound by increasing its upper frequencies or upper partials. See page 332.

Divisi Notation – Notation that places two musical parts on one staff. One part has the stems going up and the other has stems going down. See page 212.

Division of the Beat – The fraction of a beat that is produced when the beat is first divided in a given time signature. Generally, divisions are either half or one third of a beat. See page 104.

Dixieland Jazz – See entry for New Orleans jazz. See page 297.

Dominant – The fifth note of a scale. See page 184.

Dominant Seventh Chord – A chord type defined by the interval of a major third between the root and third, the interval of a minor third between the third and fifth, and the interval of a minor third between the fifth and seventh. See pages 145-146.

Dorian – A type of scale defined by the following interval pattern: whole step, half step, whole step, whole step, whole step, half step, whole step. Dorian is one of the seven modes. See page 263.

Dots – Dots increase the duration of a note or rest by half its original value. See page 99.

Double Bar Line – A set of two, thicker than normal, bar lines indicating the end of a piece of music. See page 110.

Downbeat – The first beat of a measure. See page 89.

Downtempo – A mellow form of electronic music that emerged initially around the 1970s, similar to ambient. See page 307.

Drum 'n' Bass – A form of EDM music that emerged initially in the 1990s. See page 308.

Drum Fill – A short section of a drum part used to set up a new section of music and create the expression of moving from high to low energy or, in other words, moving from the sense of approach to arrival. See page 229.

Dry Signal – Sound prior to being altered by some kind of processor. See page 329.

Dub – A form of Jamaican electronic music that emerged initially in the 1970s. See page 308.

Dubstep – A form of electronic music or EDM that emerged in the 2000s. See page 308.

Dynamic Marking – An indication in music notation that the music should be played at specific loudness or volume level. See pages 88-89.

Dynamic Microphone – A type of microphone where the diaphragm is attached to a coil that moves in and out of a magnetic field produced by a permanent magnet. See page 322.

Dynamics – The volume or loudness of a section of music. See page 88.

"E" – The rhythmic position halfway between a beat and an "and." "E" positions come after a beat but before the next "and." See page 98.

Ear Training – The skill of being able to imagine sounds and translate those sounds into useful musical terms like specific pitches and rhythms. See page 61.

Editing (in Music Production) – The music production process of selecting preferred performances of various parts for various sections and merging all the desired recordings together. It also may involve removing, copying, looping, or even reversing recordings. See page 324.

EDM – Electronic dance music. EDM is now used an umbrella term for all music produced entirely or largely through electronic production. See page 306.

Eighth Note – A type of note value. In 4/4, an eighth note lasts for a half of a beat. See page 92.

Electro House – A subgenre of house music that emerged in the 2000s. See page 307.

Eleventh Chord – A chord that consists of six notes. See page 388.

Emphasis – A brief moment in a piece of music where the loudness or volume is temporarily increased. See page 86.

Enharmonic – A description of notes that sound the same but are named or spelled differently. See page 68.

Ensemble – A group of musicians who play music together. See page 56.

Envelope – A description of how a sound evolves from the start to the end of a single note. See page 325.

EQ (Equalization) – A frequency dependent volume control. See page 329.

Equal Temperament – The modern standard tuning system. See page 132.

Exact Sequence – See entry for chromatic sequence. See page 340.

Expander – A type of sound processor that increases the dynamic range of a given sound. See page 330.

Exposition – The structural function that introduces the thematic material of a piece. The exposition can also refer to the first section of a composition in sonata form. See page 348.

Expression – The emotions, ideas, and general experience that are evoked or conveyed through music. See page 47.

Expression Learning Process – A type of learning that deals with observing, analyzing, and generally learning from different examples or expressions of an idea. This is one of the three aspects of learning, namely concept, expression, and action learning. See page 10.

Extension – See entry for tension. See page 388.

Fermata – A symbol indicating that the duration of a given note or given notes should be extended by an undetermined length of time at the discretion of the performer or conductor. See page 352.

Fifth of a Chord – The third note of a chord. This is also the note a fifth above the root in a chord's original, root position voicing. See page 139.

First Inversion – A voicing where the third of the chord is the lowest note. See page 148.

First Theme (in Sonata Form) – The first of two themes that are presented in the exposition and recapitulation sections of a piece in sonata form. The first theme is part of the internal structure of both the exposition and recapitulation, which generally progresses from first theme to transition to second theme to closing. See page 348.

Fixed-Do System – A system of naming notes that makes use of solfege syllables. In the fixed-do system, the note C is called Do. See page 189.

Flags – The part of a note that extends off of the stem signifying a note value of an eighth note or faster. See page 92.

Flat – To be lower in pitch. See page 67.

Folk Revival – A movement in the 1950s and 1960s where folk music gained popularity in the United States and the United Kingdom. See page 303.

Folk Rock – A style that emerged in the 1960s through a fusion of folk and rock elements. See page 303.

Form – See entry for structure. See page 344.

Four-on-the-Floor Beat – A type of drum beat where the kick or bass drum is played on every beat of the measure in 4/4. See page 227.

Free Jazz – See entry for avant-garde jazz. See page 299.

Frequency – The physical property of sound that describes the speed or rate of oscillation in a sound wave, often described in the unit of hertz, which represents oscillations per second. See page 30.

Fully Diminished Seventh Chord – See entry for whole diminished seventh chord. See page 398.

Fundamental Frequency – The first frequency in the harmonic series. The fundamental frequency is heard as the primary frequency of a sound and is usually the lowest and loudest frequency of a sound. See page 39.

Funk – A later form of R&B that developed in the 1970s. Funk is characterized by sixteenth note rhythms and upbeat rhythmic grooves. See page 305.

Fusion – A merger of jazz and rock styles that came into existence in the 1970s. See page 299.

Gain Level – A volume level that controls the level of a signal that is an input into a device. See page 323.

Gate – An expander with a high ratio. See pages 330-331.

General Numeric Interval Name – An interval name that includes a numeric component but not a quality. For example, second, third, and fourth are all examples of general numeric interval names. General numeric names can act as a broader category, including multiple numeric-quality names. For example, minor seconds and major seconds are both different types of seconds. See page 125.

Georgian Chant – A style of vocal music which initially developed in the Catholic Church in the 9th and 10th centuries. See page 291.

Glam Rock – A style of rock popular in the 1970s known for the eccentric personas of the performers and their bizarre or outrageous fashion. See page 304.

Glossadex – A combination of a glossary and index. A glossadex is a list of vocabulary terms with associated definitions and page numbers that connect the reader to the original presentation of the term and perhaps other important related sections of the book. See page 16.

Gospel – A style of music, born out of combinations of church hymns and African-American spirituals. The first forms of gospel emerged around the 1880s. See page 294.

Gradated Spectrum – A spectrum that smoothly and continuously evolves from one end to the other. This term is in contrast to a graduated spectrum. See page 48.

Graduated Spectrum – A spectrum that changes in steps that are defined by a unit of measurement. This term is in contrast to a gradated spectrum. See page 48.

Grand Staff – A combination of two staves meant to be played by a single musician, often with one staff using a treble clef and the other using a bass clef. See page 77.

Gravitational Position (Pitch) – The position a pitch occupies within a scale in relation to the properties of proportionality and musical gravity of that pitch. Gravitational positions describe the relationship of a given pitch to the centers of a piece of music. See page 242.

Groove – The accompaniment of a piece of music, especially the percussion parts and bass line. Elements of the harmony parts may be included as well. See page 225.

Guitar Riff – A recognizable, short, often repetitive melodic phrase played in the guitar part of a (usually rock) song. See page 303.

Half Cadence – Any cadence that ends on the dominant chord or the V chord. See page 261.

Half Note – A type of note value. In 4/4, a half note lasts for two beats. See page 91.

Half Step – The distance or interval between one note and a note directly adjacent to it. See page 119.

Half-Diminished Seventh Chord – A chord defined by the following interval pattern: minor third, minor third, major third. See pages 396.

Hard Bop – A style of jazz music that arose in the 1950s going forward. See page 299.

Hard Rock – A style of rock that emerged in the late 1960s and 1970s. See page 303.

Hardcore Country – See entry for honky tonk. See page 300.

Harmonic – A vibration with a frequency at a whole number multiple of the fundamental. See page 37 for the original presentation of this term and page 41 for an explanation that differentiates the terms "harmonic," "overtone," and "partial." The term "harmonic" can also mean related to harmony or chords.

Harmonic Beating – A pulsing sound creating by two frequencies that are very close together. See page 134.

Harmonic Composition – The physical property of sound that describes a sound's harmonics or partials and their relative volume levels. See page 39 or, for a more general perspective, the section *Timbre and Harmonic Composition* on page 34.

Harmonic Minor Scale – A scale defined by the following solfege syllables: Do-Re-Me-Fa-So-Le-Ti. See page 257.

Harmonic Positions – Locations in a scale where a chord is constructed. See page 251.

Harmonic Rhythm – The rhythm in which a chord progession changes. See page 153.

Harmonic Series – The collection of harmonics that emanate from a single sound source. The harmonic series follows a pattern of frequencies at whole number multiples of the fundamental frequency (which is a term for the first frequency of the series). See page 39.

Harmonized Melody – A melody that is complemented by one or more secondary melodies. See page 314.

Harmony Part – Part of the accompaniment that outlines the chords of a composition. See page 57 for the original definition of this term. See the section entitled *Chords and Chord Voicings* on page 78 for an introductory presentation of constructing a harmony part. Intermediate and advanced information on harmony can be found in Chapter Six (page 137), the sections of Chapter Nine entitled *Harmonic Positions and Relationships* (page 251), *Cadences* (page 260), and *Progression by Fifths* (page 262) as well as Group Six (page 387).

Head – A section of a jazz tune that includes a composed melody. The head is generally played at the beginning and end of a tune with solos occurring in the middle. See page 347.

Hi-Hop – A style of music that first became popular in the 1980s and 1990s. Hi-hop combines elements from funk, disco, and Jamaican music. Hi-hop includes the art form of rap as a central component of the music. See page 306.

High Energy Expression – Musical expressions related to intensity, activity, excitement, complexity, power, interest, drama, or tension. See page 47.

Hit – An emphasized rhythm that is played together through a whole ensemble. See page 237.

Homophony – Music that comprises both a melody and an accompaniment. See page 58.

Honky Tonk – An early style of country music that developed around the 1940s. See page 300.

Horizontal Relationships – Relationships between notes within a single part or line over time. This term is in contrast to vertical relationships. See page 317.

House – A style of EDM music created in the 1980s and continuing into the 1990s and beyond. See page 306.

Imperfect Authentic Cadence – The progression of V to I, used as an ending to a piece or section. An imperfect authentic cadence does not meet the conditions of a perfect authentic cadence, meaning that one or both of the chords are not in root position or the top note of the I chord or tonic chord does not use the tonal center of the scale as the top note of its voicing. See page 260.

Implied Notes – Notes that may be relevant to various relationships in a group of notes but are not being heard and played. See page 164.

Impressionist Period – The period of classical music from approximately 1875 CE to 1925 CE. See page 293.

Inharmonic Partial – A frequency in a sound that does not follow the pattern of the harmonic series (and therefore is not a harmonic). See page 40. See the box entitled *Harmonics, Partials, and Overtones* on page 41 for additional information on related terms.

Interval – A group of two notes. Intervals also can be seen as the distance from one note to another note, like a musical measuring tape. See page 119.

Interval Structure – A specific pattern of intervals. See page 137.

Inversion – A voicing of a chord that specifies what the lowest note of the chord is. See pages 148. In the context of developmental techniques, an inversion can refer to a transformation of a musical idea where the intervals and starting pitch of an idea are maintained but the direction of the intervals is reversed. See page 342.

Ionian – A type of scale defined by the following interval pattern: whole step, whole step, half step, whole step, whole step, whole step, half step. Ionian is one of the seven modes and is also equivalent to the major scale. See page 263.

Irregular Time Signature – See entry for complex time signature. See page 100.

Jazz – The style and tradition of music that first arose in the United States around the beginning of the 20th century. Jazz was born out of a fusion of many styles, including blues, ragtime, marching bands, Creole and Haitian folk music as well as Cuban and French music. See page 297.

Jazz Melodic Minor Scale – A scale defined by the following solfege syllables: Do-Re-Me-Fa-So-La-Ti. See page 259.

Jump Blues – A style that developed in the 1930s and 1940s through combinations of blues and swing music elements. See page 301.

Just Intonation – A type of tuning system where the tuning of notes is based on simple ratio relationships. See page 133.

Key – The physical part of a piano or keyboard that the performer presses down on to produce a note. The term "key" can also mean scale. See entry for scale. See page 82.

Key Signature – A group of sharps or flats placed at the beginning of a staff to indicate what scale a piece is being played in. The sharps or flats in a key signature indicate that every note played in a given line or space (or even notes in different octaves with the same note names as those lines or spaces) should be played as a sharp or flat, repsectively. See page 178.

Layering – A recording technique where a single part is recorded multiple times. See page 332.

Lead Sheet – A piece of music notation that outlines the most essential aspects of a piece of music while leaving certain details up to the performer's interpretation. A lead sheet includes notation for the melody with chord symbols that describe the harmony of the piece. See page 248.

Leading Tone – The seventh note of a scale where the given note is a half step away from the tonic or tonal center. See page 184.

Leaps – The category of intervals containing all intervals larger than a whole step. See page 122.

Ledger Lines – Short lines that can be added above the top line of a staff or below the bottom line of a staff. Ledger lines act as an extension of the regular five-line staff. See page 77.

Legato – A style of playing where notes slightly overlap with one another. This term is in contrast to staccato. See page 214.

Limiter – A compressor with a high ratio. See pages 330-331.

Line (Melodic Line) – A series of sequential notes played one at a time. A line is similar to a melody, except that lines are not necessarily the primary center of focus like melodies are. See page 314.

Literary Consonance – A description of words that share a consonant sound. See page 276.

Location (Perceptual Elements of Sound) – The sense of what physical area a sound is coming from. This is one of the four perceptual elements of sound, namely pitch, loudness, timbre, and location. See page 44.

Locrian – A type of scale defined by the following interval pattern: half step, whole step, whole step, half step, whole step, whole step, whole step. Locrian is one of the seven modes. See page 263.

Loop – To play a recording multiple times. See page 324.

Loudness – The perceptual property of sound that can be defined on a spectrum from soft to loud. Loudness is correlated with the physical property of amplitude. This is one of the four perceptual elements of sound, namely pitch, loudness, timbre, and location. See page 33.

Low Energy Expression – Musical expressions related to release, rest, simplicity, beauty, or connectivity. See page 47.

Lydian – A type of scale defined by the following interval pattern: whole step, whole step, whole step, half step, whole step, whole step, half step. Lydian is one of the seven modes. See page 263.

Lydian Flat-Seven Scale – A Lydian mode with the seventh degree lowered by one half step. See page 407.

Lyrics – Words that are sung to the pitches of a melody. See page 276.

Major Pentatonic Scale – A scale defined by the following intervals between each of the adjacent notes in the scale: major second, major second, minor third, major second, minor third. See page 199.

Major Scale – A scale defined by the following interval structure: whole step, whole step, half step, whole step, whole step, whole step, half step. See page 174.

Major Second – An interval equivalent to two half steps or a whole step. See page 123.

Major Seventh – An interval equivalent to eleven half steps. See page 123.

Major Seventh Chord – A chord type defined by the interval of a major third between the root and third, the interval of a minor third between the third and fifth, and the interval of a major third between the fifth and seventh. See page 145.

Major Seventh Sharp-Five Chord – A chord defined by the following interval pattern: major third, major third, minor third. See page 396.

Major Sixth – An interval equivalent to nine half steps. See page 123.

Major Sixth Chord – A chord defined by the following interval pattern: major third, minor third, major second. See page 399.

Major Third – An interval equivalent to four half steps. See page 123.

Major Triad – A chord type defined by an interval of a major third between the root and third of the chord and an interval of a minor third between the third and fifth of the chord. See pages 137.

Marcato – A strong accent. This symbol indicates that the performer should strongly emphasize a given note in terms of volume. See page 215.

Master Track – A track that contains the audio of all the other tracks in a mix. See page 326.

Mastering – The process of modifying all of the audio for a piece of music as a whole. See page 326.

Measure Numbers – In music notation, the measures are often numbered from first to last. These numbers are referred to as measure numbers. See page 95 for the original presentation of this term and see page 334 for a more complete explanation.

Measures – Short sections of music made up of a set number of beats. See page 89.

Mediant – The third note of a scale. See page 184.

Melodic Minor Scale – A scale defined by the solfege syllables – Do-Re-Me-Fa-So-La-Ti – in the ascending direction and defined by the solfege syllables – Te-Le-So-Fa-Me-Re-Do – in the descending direction. See page 258.

Melody – A series of single notes in specific rhythms that is used as the centerpiece, focus, and foreground of a composition. See page 57.

Mensural Notation – An old system of notation used in the Medieval and Renaissance time periods. See page 103.

Metal – A style of music that emerged in the 1970s and 1980s inspired by hard rock. See page 304.

Meter – See entry for time signature. See pages 90 and 100 for additional information.

Micro-Approaches – Short approaches. Micro-approaches lead up to and create a sense of arrival on strong rhythmic positions within a measure or perhaps going from one measure to another. In contrast, regular approaches, generally, lead up to and create a sense of arrival on the downbeat of the measure of a new section. See page 230.

Microtonal Music – Music that uses finer gradations of pitch than the standard twelve-note system of pitches. Music that uses intervals smaller than a half step could be described as microtonal. See page 68.

Middle C – The fourth C to appear on a full-sized, 88-key piano. See page 71.

MIDI Controller – An electronic hardware instrument, like an electronic keyboard or drum pad, that allows you to connect to a computer and play a sampler or synthesizer in your DAW. See page 324.

MIDI Data – A format of digital information that stores all the basic attributes of a musical performance, including notes, rhythms, and dynamic levels. See page 324.

Minor-Major Seventh Chord – A chord defined by the following interval pattern: minor third, major third, major third. See page 396.

Minor Pentatonic Scale – A scale defined by the following pattern of intervals: minor third, major second, major second, minor third, major second. See page 200.

Minor Scale – See entry for natural minor scale. See pages 174-175.

Minor Second – An interval represents notes that are adjacent to each other. The minor second is equivalent to a half step. See page 123.

Minor Seventh – An interval equivalent to ten half steps. See page 123.

Minor Seventh Chord – A chord type defined by the interval of a minor third between the root and third, the interval of a major third between the third and fifth, and the interval of a minor third between the fifth and seventh. See pages 145-146.

Minor Seventh Flat-Five Chord – See entry for half-diminished seventh chord. See page 396.

Minor Sixth – An interval equivalent to eight half steps. See page 123.

Minor Sixth Chord – A chord defined by the following interval pattern: minor third, major third, major second. See page 399.

Minor Third – An interval equivalent to three half steps. See page 123.

Minor Triad – A chord type defined by an interval of a minor third between the root and third of the chord and an interval of a major third between the third and fifth of the chord. See page 137.

Minuet and Trio – A type of large-scale ternary form or ABA structure. The minuet and trio is written in 3/4 time and consists of an exposition, contrasting middle, and recapitulation. See page 349.

Mixing – The process of modifying and combining together different tracks of audio together. See page 326.

Mixolydian – A type of scale defined by the following interval pattern: whole step, whole step, half step, whole step, whole step, half step, whole step. Mixolydian is one of the seven modes. See page 263.

Modal Interchange – The use of chromatic chords that are borrowed from parallel scales or modes (in other words, scales or modes with the same tonal center as the key of the given piece). See page 415.

Mode – A type of scale belonging to a collection of seven different interval patterns. These seven interval patterns are represented by the names: Ionian, Dorian, Phrygian, Lydian, Mixolydian, Aeolian, and Locrian. See page 263.

Modern Period – The period of classical music from approximately 1900 CE to 1975 CE. See page 293.

Modulation – The event of changing from one scale to another. See page 412.

Monophony – Music that comprises only a single melody with no accompaniment. See page 58.

Motif – A short musical element (or idea) that is repeated throughout a musical piece, often in different forms or with variations. Motifs are often less than a measure long. See page 51.

Movable-Do System – A system of naming notes that makes use of solfege syllables. In the movable-do system, the first note of the given scale is called Do. See page 187.

Movement – A large section of a classical piece. Movements have their own internal structures and are separated by a conclusion of the musical material and silence. See page 347.

Muddy – A description of the sound that occurs when low notes are close together in pitch. See page 149.

Music – An expression of meaning in the domain of sound that relies heavily, though not exclusively, on the physical properties of sound and their basic perception by the sensory systems of the body. See page 27.

Music Notation – The set of symbols we use to write down music on paper or on a computer. See page 74.

Music Theory – The intellectual or conceptual study of music.

Musical Element – Any position on one of the seven basic spectra of musical expression or any combination of positions on one or more of the seven spectra. Chords, scales, intervals, rhythms, dynamics, melodies, and musical structures are all examples of musical elements. See page 50.

Musical Gravity – The sense of "pull," "wanting," or "gravity" that is experienced as a position of high energy approaches a musical center. See page 54.

Musical Idea – See entry for musical element. See page 50.

Nashville Sound – A style of country popular in the late 1950s and 1960s. See page 300.

Natural Frequency – The primary frequency an object tends to vibrate at. See page 34.

Natural Minor Scale – A scale defined by the following interval structure: whole step, half step, whole step, whole step, half step, whole step, whole step. See pages 174-175.

Natural Note – A note that is neither sharp nor flat. The natural notes are played on the white keys of a piano. See page 66.

Natural Sign – A sign that indicates that the effect of a key signature should be negated. See page 180.

Neutral Clef – See entry for percussion clef. See page 211.

New Orleans Jazz – The first style of jazz, emerging in the early parts of the 20th century. See page 297.

Ninth Chord – A chord that consists of five notes. See page 388.

Node – An unmoving point on a wave or vibrating object. See page 37.

Non-Pitched Sound – A sound that does not evoke a clear sense of pitch. See page 40.

Note Head – The circle or oval shape on a written note in music notation. See page 74.

Note Name – The name of a note or pitch. For example, C or F#. See page 66.

Note Value – The duration of a note in time. See page 90.

Numeric-Quality Interval Name – An interval name that includes both a numeric component – such as second, third, or fourth – and a quality descriptor – such as major, minor, or perfect. This term is in contrast to general numeric interval names. See page 122, and see page 125 for the differentiation from general numeric interval names.

Numeric-Quality Interval Naming System – A naming system for an interval that includes both a numeric name such as second, third, or fourth and a quality description such as major, minor, or perfect. See page 122.

Oblique Motion – A type of contrapuntal motion where one melodic line stays on a given pitch, while another melodic line changes. See page 317.

Octatonic Scale – A scale consisting of eight notes. See entries for the symmetric dominant scale and symmetric diminished scale. See page 406.

Octave – A single cycle through all twelve note names. An octave can be considered an interval equivalent to twelve half steps or the group of notes that includes two notes of the same name (spaced twelve half steps apart) and all the notes in between. See page 70. Also see page 122 for an explanation of the octave in context of the other intervals.

Open Voicing – A voicing where the notes of the chord are spread out in terms of pitch. This term is in contrast to close voicings. See page 150.

Original Center – The position of lowest energy in a system of proportional relationships. See page 54. A tonal center and the duration of one beat are two possible examples of original centers.

Original Voicing – The voicing of a chord where the root is the lowest note in the chord and all the chord tones are spaced out in thirds. See page 139.

Oscillation – One cycle through a repeating pattern in a sound wave. See page 30.

Out of Time – Not adhering to any strict, set rhythm. See page 156.

Outlaw Country – A later style of country that developed in the 1970s. See page 301.

Overtone – A frequency in a sound, which is above the fundamental. See page 41.

Overtone Series – See entry for harmonic series. See page 39.

Panning – A control that affects whether a track sounds as if it is coming from the left or right. See page 327.

Pantonality – See entry for atonality. See page 293.

Parallel Fifths – A situation where two melodic lines move in parallel motion with a vertical interval of a perfect fifth between the two lines. See page 318.

Parallel Motion – A type of contrapuntal motion where two lines move in the same direction (up or down in pitch) and by the same interval, both in terms of the number and quality of the interval. See page 317.

Parallel Octaves – A situation where two melodic lines move in parallel motion with a vertical interval of an octave between the two lines. See page 318.

Parallel Scale – A scale that shares the same tonal center as another scale but is of a different scale type. See page 413.

Parameter – A setting in a DAW. See page 327.

Part – The music that one musician plays within an ensemble. See page 56.

Partial – Any frequency present in a sound. See page 41.

Pentatonic Scales – A scale consisting of five notes. See page 199.

Percussion Clef – A clef indicating that a staff uses percussion notation and is notating non-pitched sounds. See page 211.

Percussion Notation – Notation used for writing non-pitched sounds. See page 211.

Percussion Part – Part of the accompaniment that uses only non-pitched or percussion sounds. See page 57. Information on notating percussion parts can be found on page 211. Information on writing percussion parts can be found on page 312.

Perfect Authentic Cadence – The progression of V to I, used as an ending to a piece or section. Both chords of a perfect authentic cadence are in root position, and the I chord or tonic chord also uses the tonal center of the scale as the top note of its voicing. See page 260.

Perfect Fifth – An interval equivalent to seven half steps. See page 123.

Perfect Fourth – An interval equivalent to five half steps. See page 123.

Perfect Rhyme – A pair of words where the final, stressed vowel and all the following sounds are the same. See page 278.

Phantom Power – A power source that can be turned on from mixing boards and other hardware interfaces that powers some condenser microphones. See page 322.

Phonetics – The study of sounds used in speech. See page 277.

Phrase – A short section of a melody. See page 204.

Phrygian – A type of scale defined by the following interval pattern: half step, whole step, whole step, whole step, half step, whole step, whole step. Phrygian is one of the seven modes. See page 263.

Pick Up – A partial measure used at the beginning of a piece when the music starts on a rhythmic position other than the downbeat. See page 107.

Piece of Music – A complete musical work. A piece of music is synonymous with a composition. See page 51.

Pitch – The perceptual property of sound that can be defined on a spectrum from low to high. Pitch is correlated with physical property of frequency. This is one of the four perceptual elements of sound, namely pitch, loudness, timbre, and location. See page 30.

Pitch Center – A musical center in the domain of pitch. Both tonal centers and chord tones can be considered pitch centers. These are positions of strong pitch proportionality, resolution, and low energy expressions. See page 240.

Pitch Proportionality – The concept of being related through proportional relationships in terms of pitch or frequency. This term represents the spectrum from strong pitch proportionality, where pitches or frequencies are related through simple ratios, to weak pitch proportionality, where pitches or frequencies are related through complex ratios. See page 50. The musical community often talks about pitch proportionality in terms of a concept called sonance. Additional information related to pitch proportionality is presented in the section entitled *The Sonance of Intervals* on page 129.

Pivot Chord – A chord that is shared by the two scales a piece is moving between in a modulation. See page 413.

Pizzicato – A string part that is plucked rather than bowed. See page 236.

Plagal Cadence – The progression of IV to I, used as an ending to piece or section. See page 261.

Plug-In – A piece of software that works in conjunction with a DAW. See page 321.

Polychord – A group of notes that is perceived as multiple (usually two) chords. See page 392.

Polyphony – Music that uses multiple, simultaneous melodies. The term "polyphony" is interchangeable with the term "counterpoint." See page 58 for the original presentation of this term and page 317 for additional information.

Polyrhythm – A rhythm where a unit of time is divided in two or more ways in which the divisors are not even multiples of each other. See page 231.

Post-Modern Period – The period of classical music from approximately 1975 CE to present day. See page 294.

Post-Punk – A follow-on style to punk rock that emerged in the late 1970s. See page 305.

Power Chord – A chord of just two notes where the interval between the two notes is a perfect fifth in its original voicing. See page 399.

Pre-Chorus – A section of a song used to lead up to the chorus. See page 347.

Production Setup – A combination of software and hardware that is used for music production. See page 321.

Progressive House – A subgenre of house music that emerged in the 1990s. See page 307.

Progressive Metal – A fusion of metal and progressive influences of experimentalism as well as classical and jazz elements initially emerging in the 1970s. See page 304.

Progressive Rock – A style of rock that developed in the late 1960s and 1970s that infused experimentalism as well as classical and jazz elements into the rock styles. See page 303.

Pulse – See entry for beat. See page 86.

Punk Rock – A style that emerged in the 1970s as a reaction against the idolization of celebrity seen in stadium rock and the complexity of prog rock and metal. See page 304.

Pure Sine Wave – The sound of a pure sine wave can be thought of as a timbre consisting of only a fundamental frequency and no other harmonics or partials. See page 40.

Quality-Expression – The expression that is characteristic of a certain type of chord, scale, or mode. The expression associated with major chords and scales and the expression associated with minor chords and scales are two general and common examples of this concept. See page 246 (see especially the second item in the notes section). The box entitled *Differentiation* on page 241 also contains some relevant background information for this concept.

Quarter Note – A type of note value. In 4/4, a quarter note lasts for one beat. See page 91.

R&B – Rhythm 'n' blues. A style, inspired from jump blues, that developed around the 1940s. See page 302.

Ragtime – A piano-based style that emerged out of a combination of European classical music, brass bands, and the blues in the 1890s. See page 297.

Rallentando – See entry for ritardando. See page 109.

Rap – A form of spoken-word poetry that is articulated in rhythm with a musical accompaniment. See page 306.

Recapitulation – The structural function of restating or rearticulating the thematic material of a piece, sometimes with certain elements of variation. The recapitulation can also refer to the third section of a composition in sonata form. See page 348.

Recording – Capturing sounds in the external world with microphones into a reproducible form such as a computer file. See page 322.

Reggae – A style that developed in the 1960s from a mixture of Jamaican styles with influences from R&B. See page 305.

Related Fundamental – The fundamental of a related series. See page 161.

Related Series – A harmonic series (or overtone series) where the ratio that defines a given note group corresponds with the numbered positions where we find the notes of the group in the harmonic series. See page 161.

Related Series Analysis – A system of analysis that uses related series to better understand the properties and expressions of note groups. See page 164 or, more generally, the entire section beginning on page 157.

Reprise – A repeated section. See page 349.

Resolution – The movement from high to low energy in pitch proportionality. See page 55.

Resonant Frequency – See entry for natural frequency. See page 34.

Rest – A period of silence in music. See page 94.

Retrograde – A type of developmental technique where a musical idea is played backwards, so that the first note becomes the last note and last note becomes the first note. See page 342.

Retrograde Inversion – A type of developmental technique where a musical idea is played both backward and with intervals that move in the opposite direction of the original idea. See page 342.

Reverb – A type of sound processing that imitates the sound of being in a certain environment or space. See page 327.

Rhyme – A description of words that share an ending sound. See page 276. Also, see entry for perfect rhyme.

Rhythm – The dimension of music that deals with the characteristics of time, and secondarily, though still significantly, loudness or volume. See page 86 for the original presentation of this term. See Chapter Eight (page 211) for more intermediate and advanced information on rhythm.

Rhythmic Position – A specific place or point in a measure. See page 97.

Ribbon Microphone – A type of microphone that uses a permanent magnet and a very thin diaphragm that passes between two poles of the magnet. See page 322.

Ritardando – A direction that indicates that the music should slow down or, in other words, decrease in tempo. See page 109.

Rock 'n' Roll – An early style of rock music which developed in the 1950s. See page 302.

Rockabilly – See entry for rock 'n' roll. See page 302.

Romantic Period – The period of classical music from approximately 1820 CE to 1910 CE. See page 292.

Rondo – A type of structure that consists of a repeated reprise section alternated with new contrasting sections. See page 349.

Room Microphone – A microphone that is positioned to capture sounds in a more general area or space. This term is in contrast to spot microphones. See page 323.

Root – The first note of a chord. See page 139.

Root Position – A voicing where the root of the chord is the lowest note. See page 148.

Rounded Binary Form – A variation on simple binary form where the second half of the B section or sections comes back to the material in the A section. See page 348.

Rubato – A direction indicating that the performer has liberal freedom to alter the tempo by speeding up or slowing down at his or her own discretion. See page 258.

Samba – A style of Brazilian music that developed in the early parts of the 20th century. See page 299.

Sampling – The music production technique of using short recordings as the basis of constructing more complex musical parts. See page 324.

Scale – A group of notes that sound good together or produce a certain useful effect. Unlike chords, composers generally commit to being "in" a scale or, in other words, using only the notes of a scale for a period of time in a composition. See page 82 for the original presentation of this term. See Chapter Seven (page 174) for more information on scales, and see the section entitled *More Scale Types* (page 405) for information on more advanced or unusual types of scales.

Scale Degrees – A position within a scale. See page 184.

Scale Type – A group of scales that shares a specific pattern of intervals. See page 174.

Scientific Pitch Notation – A system of naming pitches that combines note names – such as C or F# – with numbers that signify which octave the note appears in. The first C to appear on a full-sized, 88-key piano is named C1. The second C is called C2 and so on. See page 71.

Score – A type of music notation that includes a staff for every part of a piece of music. Scores are used to notate works for ensembles of instruments rather than solo works. See page 248. See an example of the first page of a score on page 352.

Second Inversion – A voicing where the fifth of the chord is the lowest note. See page 148.

Second Theme (in Sonata Form) – The second of two themes that are presented in the exposition and recapitulation sections of a piece in sonata form. The second theme is part of the internal structure of both the exposition and recapitulation, which generally progresses from first theme to transition to second theme to closing. See page 348.

Secondary Dominant – A chord that is built a perfect fifth above a diatonic chord of the scale. Secondary dominant chords can be major triads, dominant seventh chords, or larger chords that use a dominant seventh chord as a base. See page 416.

Secondary Melody – See entry for background melody. See page 58.

Section – A segment of a musical composition that includes all the applicable melodic and accompaniment parts of the piece, commonly 16 or 32 measures in length. See page 344.

Sequence – A type of developmental technique where the pitch of a musical idea is changed while maintaining the same intervals (either the general numeric intervals or the exact numeric-quality intervals). See page 340.

Serialism – A style of working with music based on sequences of pitches called tone rows. See page 293.

Seven Basic Spectra of Musical Expression – The seven basic spectra of musical expression are a group of fundamental musical qualities. These are: pitch, loudness, timbre, location, time, pitch proportionality, and temporal proportionality. See page 47.

Seventh Chord – A chord that consists of four notes. See page 145.

Seventh of a Chord – The fourth note of a chord. This is also the note a seventh above the root in a chord's original, root position voicing. See page 139.

Sforzando – A strong accent or local increase in volume indicated by the abbreviation sfz or sf. See page 216.

Sharp – To be higher in pitch. See page 67.

Shock Rock – See entry for glam rock. See page 304.

Similar Motion – A type of contrapuntal motion where the melodic lines move in the same direction but not by the same interval. See page 317.

Simple Binary Form – A small structure defined by the arrangement of sections AB with potential for repeats to be added forming an AABB structure. See page 348.

Simple Centrality – The characteristic of a clear, unambiguous, primary center. This term is in contrast to complex centrality. See page 56.

Simple Duple Meter – A time signature or meter with two beats per measure, where the beats divide into groups of two. For example, 2/4 and 2/2 are simple duple meters. See page 105.

Simple Intervals – Intervals including an octave and all intervals smaller than an octave. See page 128.

Simple Quadruple Meter – A time signature or meter with four beats per measure, where the beats divide into groups of two. For example, 4/4 is a simple quadruple meter. See page 105.

Simple Time Signature – A time signature where the beats are divided into two parts. See page 100.

Simple Triple Meter – A time signature or meter with three beats per measure, where the beats divide into groups of two. For example, 3/4 is a simple triple meter. See page 105.

Sixteenth Note – A type of note value. In 4/4, a sixteenth note lasts for a quarter of a beat. See page 92.

Sixth Chord – A chord equivalent to a triad with an additional note a major sixth above the root. See page 399.

Slash Chords – A chord that specifies a certain note (and this note can either be a normal part of the chord or not) to be the lowest note of the chord. See page 400.

Slur – A symbol indicating that the performer should overlap the notes in the music slightly or, in other words, play legato. See page 214.

Small Structure – The structure of a section of a movement. See page 347.

Solfege Syllables – A collection of syllables that are used to name notes. See page 187.

Solo Work – A piece of music or composition meant to be played by only one musician. See page 56.

Solos – Melodic parts that are played by a single, featured performer. See page 203.

Sonance – The spectrum from consonance to dissonance. Sonance is equivalent to the concept of pitch proportionality. See page 129.

Sonata Form – A type of large-scale ternary form or ABA structure. The sonata form consists of three sections – the exposition, development, and recapitulation – with the potential for a fourth section – the coda. Each section has its own specific functions and requirements. See page 348.

Song – A piece of music with sung lyrics.

Song Form – A musical form or structure defined by the arrangement of sections AABA. See page 344.

Soul – A form of R&B that developed in the 1960s. See page 305.

Sound – A flux of pressure or density. See page 28.

Sounding Notes – Notes that are being heard and played. This term is in contrast to implied notes. See page 164.

Spectrum of Change – A kind of super-spectrum or overarching spectrum based on the relationships between the foundational seven spectra of musical expression. Greater change or variation creates a high energy expression, while greater adherence to stasis creates a low energy expression. See page 51. This concept is discussed in greater detail in Chapter Twelve on page 334.

Spelling – The way a note is named with letters, flats, and sharps. See page 68.

Spot Microphone – A microphone that is placed close to a single sound source, like a single instrument or vocalist, with the intention of recording just that sound source in relative isolation. This term is in contrast to room microphones. See page 323.

Staccato – A style of playing where small gaps, like short rests, are left between notes. This term is in contrast to legato. See page 214.

Stadium Rock – A style of rock popular in the 1970s. See page 304.

Staff – Set of five lines that are used to illustrate the pitch of the notes in music notation. See page 74.

Stem – The line portion of a written note in music notation. See page 74.

Steps – The category of intervals containing both half and whole steps. See page 122.

Straight Rhythm – A term used to specify that a rhythm is *not* a swing rhythm. See page 234.

Stride – A piano-based style that first arose in the 1920s. See page 297.

Strong Proportionality – The characteristic or quality of being related by a simple proportional relationship or, in other words, a proportional relationship that implies a small number of parts in the broader system at work. Strong proportionality arises in ratios where the largest number in the ratio is a relatively small number. See page 49.

Strong Resolution – A resolution that moves from a position of relatively extreme high energy to a position of relatively extreme low energy. This term is in contrast to a weak resolution. See page 195.

Strong Rhythmic Position – A rhythmic position that is characterized by strong temporal proportionality. See page 217.

Structure – The arrangement and characteristics of the sections of a composition. See page 344.

Style of Music – A conglomeration of various musical elements, artistic techniques, and expressive attitudes that a group of musicians learned from, used, and developed throughout time. See page 288.

Subdominant – The fourth note of a scale. See page 184.

Submediant – The sixth note of a scale. See page 184.

Subtonic – The seventh note of a scale where the given note is a whole step away from the tonic or tonal center. See page 184.

Subtractive Synthesis – The process of taking one or more complex timbres and filtering out spectrums of frequency so that the remaining frequencies produce the desired timbre. See page 325.

Supertonic – The second note of a scale. See page 184.

Suspended Four Triad – A triad defined by the following interval pattern: perfect fourth, major second. See page 395.

Suspended Seventh Chord – A chord defined by the following interval pattern: perfect fourth, major second, minor third. See page 396.

Suspended Two Triad – A triad defined by the following interval pattern: major second, perfect fourth. See page 395.

Sustain Pedal – The most commonly used pedal on the piano. The sustain pedal allows notes to sustain after being played and released. See page 81.

Swing (as a Style) – A form of jazz music popular in the 1930s and 1940s. See page 298.

Swing Rhythm – A type of rhythmic structure where the "ands" of the measure are moved from the halfway point between beats to the point two-thirds way through the beat. See page 234.

Symmetric Diminished Scale – A scale defined by the following interval pattern: whole step, half step, whole step, half step, whole step, half step, whole step, half step. See page 406.

Symmetric Dominant Scale – A scale defined by the following interval pattern: half step, whole step, half step, whole step, half step, whole step, half step, whole step. See page 406.

Symphony – A multi-movement work for orchestra. See page 347.

Syncopation – Emphasis of weak rhythmic positions in terms of volume or importance. See page 226.

Synthesis – The creation of timbres in the electronic medium. See page 325.

Systems (in Music Notation) – A group of staves in a score that contains the notation for all parts of a composition for one line of music. See page 351.

Techno – A style of EDM music that emerged in the 1980s and 1990s. See page 307.

Tempo – The speed or rate of the beat. See page 86.

Tempo Marking – An indication in music notation that the music should be played at a specific tempo. See page 87.

Temporal Gravity – Musical gravity that is created through relationships in time or rhythm. See page 229. For an example of how temporal gravity plays out over larger time scales, see the box entitled *Structural Gravity Revisited* on page 345.

Temporal Proportionality – The concept of being related through proportional relationships in terms of time or rhythm. This term represents the spectrum from strong temporal proportionality, where durations of time or rhythms are related through simple ratios, to weak temporal proportionality, where durations of time or rhythms are related through complex ratios. See page 50. This concept is discussed in detail in Chapter Eight on page 211.

Temporal Scaling – A type of developmental technique where all the durations of sounds in a musical idea are uniformly multiplied or divided by a given number. See page 341.

Tension – The experience of high energy pitch proportionality. See page 55. A tension can also refer to a chord tone that is a ninth, eleventh, or thirteenth interval above the root of a chord. For this definition, see page 388.

Tenuto – A multipurpose articulation. See page 216.

Ternary Form – A small structure defined by the arrangement of sections ABA with a potential variation including additional repeats forming an AABABA structure. See page 348.

Themes – A musical element (or idea) that is repeated throughout a musical piece, often in different forms or with variations. Themes can last for several measures and are generally considered to be somewhat longer than motifs. See page 51.

Thin Double Bar Line – A symbol used in music notation to indicate the end of one section of music and the beginning of another. See page 334.

Third Inversion – A voicing where the seventh of the chord is the lowest note. See page 148.

Third of a Chord – The second note of a chord. This is also the note a third above the root in a chord's original, root position voicing. See page 139.

Thirteenth Chord – A chord that consists of seven notes. See page 388.

Thirty-Second Note – A type of note value. In 4/4, a thirty-second note lasts for an eighth of a beat. See page 92.

Threshold – The volume level at which a dynamics processor – a compressor, expander, limiter, or gate – will begin to affect the input signal. See page 330.

Tie – A symbol used in music notation to connect two or more notes together into a single sustaining sound. See page 99.

Timbre – The quality of a sound at a given pitch and volume level. Timbre enables us to differentiate the sound of two instruments playing the same note. Timbre is associated with the physical property of harmonic composition. This is one of the four perceptual elements of sound, namely pitch, loudness, timbre, and location. See page 34.

Time Signature – A symbol that indicates how many beats are in each measure and what note value represents a single beat. See pages 90 and 100 for additional information.

Tonal Center – The first note of a scale, also the primary pitch center of a scale. See page 83.

Tonality – The characteristic of having a tonal center or pitch center. This term is in contrast to the term "atonality." See page 293.

Tone Rows – Sequences of pitches used in the stylistic movement known as serialism in the Modern classical period. See page 293.

Tonic – The first note of a scale. See page 184.

Track – A stream of audio. See page 326.

Trance – A form of EDM music that emerged in the 1990s. See page 308.

Transition (in Sonata Form) – The transitional section between the first and second themes in the exposition and recapitulation of a piece in sonata form. The transition is part of the internal structure of both the exposition and recapitulation, which generally progresses from first theme to transition to second theme to closing. See page 348.

Transpose – To move music into a different scale. See page 191.

Transposed Pitch – A modified system of pitches. This term is in contrast to concert pitch. See page 320.

Trash Metal – A style of metal music that emerged in the 1980s. See page 304.

Treble Clef – A clef is a symbol used in music notation to signify what set of notes or pitches a given staff covers. The treble clef indicates that the second line from the bottom on the given staff represents the note G4 or the first G above middle C. See page 75.

Triad – A chord that consists of three notes. See page 78.

Trill – A symbol indicating that the performer should alternate rapidly between the written note and the note a second or a step above it in the scale. See page 259.

Triplet – A type of tuplet where the duration of a division of a beat is defined as one third of a beat. See page 232.

Tritone – An interval equivalent to six half steps. The tritone is also equivalent to the augmented fourth and the diminished fifth. See page 123.

Tritone Substitution – A chromatic harmony technique where a dominant seventh chord resolving down a fifth is replaced by a different dominant seventh chord built on a root a tritone away from the original chord. See page 417.

Tune – A common term for a jazz composition. See page 347.

Tuning System – A standard that specifies the frequencies that each note represents. See page 132.

Tuplet – A category of rhythmic values that uses a given number to redefine the duration of a division of a beat. Tuplets are used to create rhythms that would otherwise not be possible to create in the structure of a given time signature. See page 231.

Unison – An interval that represents two instances of the same note, in the same octave. See page 123.

Unison Rhythm – The sound produced when all the parts in an ensemble play the same rhythm. See page 310.

Urban Blues – See entry for Chicago blues. See page 301.

Verse – A section of a song that uses a single melody and chord progression but different lyrics for each repetition of the section. See page 346.

Vertical Relationships – Relationships between notes in different parts or lines within a given moment of music. This term is in contrast to horizontal relationships. See page 317.

Vibration – A repeating motion that travels back and forth in opposing directions. See page 28.

Vibrato – A rapid fluctuation in pitch or frequency over the course of a single sound or musical note. See page 42.

Voice Lead – To create voicings for a chord progression that minimize the amount of movement between notes from chord to chord. See page 154.

Voicing – An arrangement of the notes of a chord into specific octaves. See page 79.

Volume – See entry for loudness. See page 33.

Vowel – Sounds in speech produced with a generally open vocal tract, so that air moves freely throughout the body, with no buildup of air pressure above the vocal folds. This term is in contrast to the term "consonant." See page 277.

Weak Proportionality – The characteristic or quality of being related by a complex proportional relationship or, in other words, a proportional relationship that implies a large number of parts in the broader system at work. Weak proportionality arises in ratios where the largest number in the ratio is a relatively large number. See page 49.

Weak Resolution – A resolution that moves from a position of relatively moderate high energy to a position of relatively moderate low energy. This term is in contrast to a strong resolution. See page 195.

Weak Rhythmic Position – A rhythmic position that is characterized by weak temporal proportionality. See page 217.

Wet Signal – Sound after being altered by some kind of processor. See page 329.

White Noise – A sound characterized by an even distribution in amplitude across all frequencies. See page 41.

Whole Diminished Seventh Chord – A chord defined by the following interval pattern: minor third, minor third, minor third. See page 398.

Whole Note – A type of note value. In 4/4, a whole note lasts for a full measure or four beats. See page 91.

Whole Step – The interval equivalent to two half steps or, in other words, the interval between notes that are one step more than adjacent apart from each other. See page 121.

Whole Tone Scale – A scale consisting entirely of whole step intervals. See page 405.

Work Songs – Songs created by African-American slaves to ease the strain of working and send covert messages in the 17th through 19th centuries. See page 294.

- About the Author -

Ryan Taylor teaches music lessons and classes in Maryland and around Washington D.C. He loved music from an early age and began learning piano at age seven. Though his primary instrument is piano, he also plays guitar and loves to experiment with different instruments whenever he can.

Ryan has performed at high level venues such as the Takoma Park Jazz Festival and won awards for his original compositions, such as his first place award for Best Original Film Score in the Montgomery County Film Festival in 2011. Ryan holds a Bachelor of Music degree from Berklee College of Music in Contemporary Writing and Production. He was accepted in 2013 with a scholarship and finished the four-year program in only two and a half years.

Ryan loves the diversity of music, and is constantly seeking to explore the different sounds, styles, and expressions that are possible. He is a philosopher at heart, and has a profound passion for deep thought, psychology, and self-development.

You can find out more about Ryan and his various endeavors at: http://projectado.com.

www.ingramcontent.com/pod-product-compliance
Lightning Source LLC
Chambersburg PA
CBHW051349070526
44584CB00025B/3698